To the Ends of the Earth

TO THE ENDS OF THE EARTH

The Age of the European Explorers

Peter O. Koch

McFarland & Company, Inc., Publishers

Jefferson, North Carolina, and London

All photographs were provided by the Library of Congress.

LIBRARY OF CONGRESS CATALOGUING-IN-PUBLICATION DATA

Koch, Peter O., 1953–
    To the ends of the earth : the age of the European explorers /
Peter O. Koch.
        p.   cm.
    Includes bibliographical references and index.
    ISBN 0-7864-1565-7 (softcover : 50# alkaline paper)

    1. Discoveries in geography—European.   I. Title.
G80.K57   2003
910'.92'24—dc21   2003007122

British Library cataloguing data are available

Cover art ©2003 PicturesNow.com

Manufactured in the United States of America

McFarland & Company, Inc., Publishers
  Box 611, Jefferson, North Carolina 28640
  www.mcfarlandpub.com

For Abelene, Eric, Alex and Sara

Contents

Preface   1

ONE • The Routes of Trade   5

TWO • In Search of Cathay   33

THREE • Following the Dream of Prince Henry   61

FOUR • The Spanish Crusade   80

FIVE • At the Edge of a New World   98

SIX • Visions of Cathay   118

SEVEN • The Spice Monopoly   135

EIGHT • Those Who Trespass Against Columbus   156

NINE • Same Planet, Different Worlds   174

TEN • The Grand Prize   203

ELEVEN • Colonization of the Caribbean   220

TWELVE • The Voyage of Magellan   242

THIRTEEN • When the World Became Whole   259

Bibliography   277

Index   279

Preface

I have tried in this book to dispel many of the old myths and modern prejudices that have succeeded in distorting the truth about the many European explorers who dared to go where others feared to tread. The story of these voyages of discovery has become, especially in recent times, a subject shrouded in controversy: no longer seen as heroes, except in their respective homelands, these bold explorers are now viewed as purposeful purveyors of disease, destruction, and slavery. As part of a concerted effort to discredit the documented accomplishments of the many seafarers who hailed from the shores of the Iberian Peninsula, a rash of revisionist writers, historians, and archaeologists have promoted a number of alternative theories about the true discoverers of routes to unknown lands and unfamiliar civilizations. We are now told that Egyptian sailors ventured far enough westward to lay claim to the lands opposite the known world long before the Europeans ever set sail, and they were followed by African mariners who rowed across a vast ocean to leave their own indelible imprint upon the ancient civilizations of Central America. Conjecture that Polynesian, Japanese, Chinese and Indian mariners sailed to either North, South, or Central America centuries before the epic voyage of Christopher Columbus has managed to become the basis of fact. With authors and publishers promoting such titillating interpretations of historical events that may or may not have occurred, the uninformed reader is denied access to what is the truth. History, as we discover, is far more compelling and often more interesting than fiction.

While there have certainly been many excellent biographies published about the individual discoverers of this era, there are few books that tell the collective story of the numerous explorers who ventured forth during this epic period. Most of these explorers were born to the same generation and a great many sailed together on these voyages of discovery. Within these pages lies the story within the story, for it was these joint ventures and shared experiences that ultimately led to the discovery of new lands and unknown civilizations.

Ever since his emergence on earth, man has endeavored to learn more about his immediate surroundings, and to this end he has continued to expand horizons for future generations. By various modes of transportation, he has ventured forth into the great unknown, and every step of the way he has discovered not only something new about the world around him but also learned a bit more about his own nature. In his eternal quest for answers, man has had to endure the harshest forces of nature, overcome seemingly insurmountable obstacles, and learn to confront his fears. For those fortunate enough to have reached the journey's end there were the earthly rewards of discovering a new land, crossing an unknown body of water, or encountering the wondrous marvels of another civilization.

Beginning with the worldly vision of Prince Henry the Navigator and concluding with the Homeric odyssey of Ferdinand Magellan, this book tells of the daring exploits, the great triumphs, and the terrible tragedies that befell the many bold explorers who sought to discover a route to the splendid treasures of the Far East. Motivated by a lust for wealth, a taste for spices, and a penchant for adventure, these intrepid sailors forever changed our perception of the world around us. This is a tale that started out as a religious crusade, a blind faith quest that led to the discovery of many earthly delights. It was Muslim merchants who first introduced the European palate to a vast assortment of rare spices and other unusual and exotic items that had their origins in a mysterious region of the world commonly referred to as the Indies. The spices that reached the many markets scattered throughout Europe came in a variety of forms and had a vast array of uses, but the spices that excited European senses the most were those that enhanced the flavor of food, produced a pleasing aroma, or possessed medicinal value. A burning desire to acquire that which did not come naturally to them evolved into a unique European trait, one which, besides sowing the seeds of capitalism, instilled the widely accepted concept that conquest and colonization could be justified as part of a grand scheme—a manifest destiny sanctioned in the name of Christianity.

This European race to become the first to reach the legendary lands of the Indies by way of the sea pitted the tiny nation of Portugal against its much larger neighbor Spain. While the emphasis of this book is on the many voyages of discovery launched from the shores of the Iberian Peninsula, the major contributions of another European peninsula have not been overlooked. Though they may have sailed under the flags of other nations, Christopher Columbus, Amerigo Vespucci, and John Cabot are explorers forever linked by a common heritage—they were all proud sons of Italy. These adventurous-minded foreigners had a great deal in common with visionary men such as Prince Henry the Navigator, Bartolomeu Dias, Vasco da Gama, and Ferdinand Magellan of Portugal as well as Alonso de Ojeda, Vicente and Martín Pinzón, Vasco Núñez de Balboa, and Juan Sebastián del Cano of Spain—in particular, a desire to discover a pathway to the treasures of the Far East.

My aim is to present this intriguing tale of discovery in as clear, concise and objective a manner as possible. This book offers a glimpse into the dreams, fears, disappointments, and triumphs of the many men who dared to face the perils of the great unknown. Together we shall stand beside Christopher Columbus at the shores of Hispaniola, sail along the virgin coast of South America with Amerigo Vespucci, march through the dense jungles of Panama with Vasco Núñez de Balboa, and bravely fight alongside Ferdinand Magellan at the Battle of Mactan. It is my hope that the reader will gain a better understanding of the major events and various circumstances, which, when combined, culminated in one of the most significant periods in all of history. These were the voyages of discovery that helped to tear down longstanding barriers, explode age-old myths and misconceptions, and broaden our horizons until finally, the world was made whole.

Those who have never seen themselves surrounded on all sides by the sea can never possess an idea of the world, and of their relation to it.

—Johann Wolfgang von Goethe

ONE

The Routes of Trade

Europe Awakens

The fatal depth to which the once mighty Roman Empire had fallen became clearly evident to the rest of the civilized world when Alaric, the king of the wandering Visigoths, conquered and ransacked the imperial city of Rome in A.D. 410. The Visigoths, along with the Lombards, Vandals, and Ostrogoths, had terrorized the borders of the vast Roman frontier for a number of decades prior to this invasion. These Germanic tribes, all of whom were being forced from their homelands by invading Hun armies, grew bolder with each victory over the faltering legions of Roman soldiers, and before long these barbarians had pushed their territorial claims to the very gates of the ancient city that had once lorded over much of the known world. Rome managed to survive the indignity of this brief occupation only to fall again in 455, this time to the hordes of migrating Vandals. The fall of the Western Empire became complete with the capture of the young Emperor Romulus Augustulus in 476 by Germanic warriors who had once pledged their allegiance to Rome.

Though a semblance of this once great empire survived in the East under the tutelage of the city of Constantinople, most of Europe quickly descended into a dark age. Gone were the laws that made for an orderly society, and the powerful armies that enforced those laws; gone were the rich patrons who supported both the arts and sciences; and gone were the many merchants who made Rome the epicenter of all the world's commerce. Once isolated from the strict rule of Rome, the remainder of Europe soon fragmented into numerous individual kingdoms.

The sole stabilizing force during the chaotic Middle Ages of Europe turned out to be the Roman Catholic Church. The Church strove to rebuild its Christian flock by converting as many of the barbarian settlers as possible; once they were converted, the clergy exerted its influence to make them a more civilized people. Much of mankind's accumulated knowledge had been carefully retained and preserved under papal control. It was, however, only to be doled out as the Church saw fit.

The fragmented kingdoms of the European continent were to soon encounter a new and even greater threat to their existing way of life. Across the Mediterranean Sea, in the ancient land of Arabia, a great number of people had begun to zealously unite under the common faith and flag of Islam. Anxious to spread the word of Allah and his devoted disciple Mohammed, vast armies of Berbers, Arabs, and Syrians swept across the coast of North Africa, forcing all in their path to submit to what they saw as the law of God. In the year 711, a massive force of Islamic crusaders boldly crossed the Strait of Gibraltar to begin their conquest of Europe's Iberian Peninsula. The armies of the Moors raced across the region then known as Hispania, vanquishing all enemy armies that dared to stand before them. Victory for the purveyors of the Islamic cause seemed assured following their crushing defeat of a large Christian army led by King Roderick, the last of the Visigoth rulers, at the Battle of Rio Barbate that same year.

The advance of the armies of Islam was eventually contained, but not until after they had crossed the rugged peaks of the Pyrenees mountains, where they were then struck down by a united and determined Frankish force. Settling for that which they already controlled, Mohammedan Moors focused their efforts on the complete subjugation of the peoples of Hispania. The religious conversion of the region was also accompanied by the welcome introduction of Arabic knowledge. Thanks to their occupation by the Moors, the citizens of Hispania were to benefit greatly from their conquerors' many advancements in mathematics, science, and navigation, and they were additionally rewarded with the cultural enrichment of art, architecture, and literature that derived from a more advanced and sophisticated Islamic society. Along with their teachings, the Moors brought with them a taste for the many exotic luxuries they obtained by way of commercial intercourse with merchants from the mysterious lands of the Far East.

While the strict discipline of Islam exerted a great deal of control over most of the people of the Iberian peninsula, a small following remained faithful to the tenets of Christianity. Finding sanctuary in the confines of the mountains, a devoted band of Christians bided their time until they were strong enough to wage a holy war for the reclamation of their homeland.

On the 800th anniversary of the birth of Jesus of Nazareth, the divine manifestation of the God of the Christians, Charlemagne, who was the supreme king of the Franks, strode up the steps of Saint Peter's Basilica in Rome and was ceremoniously crowned as Emperor of the Romans. The coronation of Charlemagne by Pope Leo III marked the beginning of the Holy Roman Empire—the Catholic Church's attempt to restore the power that once was Rome's. The papacy's scheme proved to be an extremely successful move. With other kings pledging their allegiance to Charlemagne and the emperor in turn pledging his devotion to Christ, ecclesiastical powers and wealth were to increase at a rapid rate.

The Catholic Church had willingly taken on the difficult task of reshaping ancient pagan beliefs into an acceptable form of Christian orthodoxy. By stressing blind obedience to the word of God, Christ, and the Church, Christianity had slowly, but firmly, become entrenched throughout the European continent. Through the preaching of moral lessons and the preservation of literature and art, the Church had succeeded in reviving the dwindling embers of civilization. But with the Church fulfilling so many of the basic functions essential to social order, many of the small kingdoms that dwelled within the realm of the Holy Roman Empire found themselves becoming overly dependent upon papal authority—a dependency which came at a steep price. Land grants allowed financially strapped rulers to overcome a monetary void in the fulfillment of their holy obligations, and over time the Church of Rome basked in the enormous wealth it derived from the many deeds it controlled. However, vast sums of money were needed to fuel the growing empire of the Church, and to gather these funds the papacy relied heavily on the power of the collection plate. Such were the tithes that inextricably bound together the people, the Church, the state, and the empire.

Political and military necessities of the Middle Ages precipitated the era of feudalism, which in turn perpetuated the social order known as seignorialism. The loosely aligned Holy Roman Empire constantly found itself under the threat of attack from heavily armed outside forces. From the south came the fanatical armies of the Moors, from the north came the terrible swift raids of the Vikings, and to the east lay the greatest threat of all, the advancing armies of the Mongols. The noblemen who resided along these threatened regions took it upon themselves to organize their own armies to fend off the constant advances of the enemy. Alliances were forged out of necessity, thereby forcing landowners of that time, including the Church, to cede titles to those who could provide them with protection. The lords, in turn, rewarded the loyalty of their vassals with the grant of a feudal estate, commonly referred to as a fiefdom. The feudal pyramid kept enlarging with the granting of each new fiefdom, as each recipient swore an oath of fealty to the grantor of the lands he now governed. At the base of the pyramid stood the peasant, who found himself subservient to many masters.

The social structure of the Middle Ages fostered a scattering of small self-supporting agrarian communities. While this was generally a stagnant economy, the system tended to work well within the confines of its own fiefdom. However, when lords needed financial aid, as was often the case, then the system usually found itself being taxed to death. The emerging cities of Europe placed ever greater burdens upon the peasants of the countryside, whom they increasingly relied upon to provide a steady flow of victuals for their daily sustenance.

Papal policy returned to the fore with a call to arms against the Islamic threat that was steadily massing along the borders of the Holy Roman Empire. In November of 1095, a concerned Pope Urban II called on faithful Christians from all over Europe to join in a sacred crusade to end once and for all the sacrilegious occupation of the Holy Land by Muslim infidels. An overwhelming number of nobles, knights, and humble peasants heeded the Pope's call and before long a massive army of Christian crusaders were assembled at the ports of Italy to sail to the Middle East. Once they had crossed the Mediterranean Sea, the valiant Christian soldiers marched onward, fully prepared to convert or kill infidels—either way made no difference to them or the leaders of the Church. Sweeping across the land, the crusaders managed to achieve their objective by conquering the sacred city of Jerusalem in July of 1099. This glorious victory was cause for great celebration in Rome. The liberation of Jerusalem not only reinforced the divine power and destiny of the Christian faith but also further strengthened the dominant position of Rome in political, intellectual, and cultural circles throughout Europe. Interestingly, instead of taxing the Church of Rome, the waging of this holy campaign had greatly increased her coffers. While these military operations were organized at the behest of the Pope, it was the noblemen who were ultimately responsible for the financing of these ventures. To cover the enormous expenses they incurred from having to raise and support their own armies, the nobles found themselves being forced to mortgage their lands to those who could supply them with money. It should be added that these faithful rulers fully expected to recoup their expenses and even to earn a substantial profit off the plunder they felt sure they would acquire on this crusade. Flush with funds, the Church gladly accepted the deeds to their property as collateral for the great Christian cause. When these land holdings were forfeited by default, either due to delinquency or the death of the borrower, the Church found itself in the enviable position of having become the largest landlord in all of Europe.

However, the Christian occupation of the Holy Land proved to be brief. The crusaders had defeated a number of Muslim forces that had stood individually against the unified armies of the European invaders. Shortly thereafter, the forces of Islam united with enough strength to dislodge the Christian forces that had remained behind at Jerusalem. Of course this led to the call for yet another Christian crusade. Between the years 1095 and 1270 there were five major crusades carried on against the Islamic infidels, but none were anywhere near as successful as the first.

While the crusades failed to deliver the Holy Land to Rome they did succeed in arousing European interest in lands which were entirely foreign to them. These were places that were shrouded in mystery and populated by civilizations that most of Europe had lost touch with following the collapse of the Roman Empire. All that they knew beforehand about the people of these lands was the preconceived notion that they were all heathens bent on the destruction of Christianity. Once there, the crusaders realized that these lands were comprised of a number of diverse and sophisticated cultures that seemed to know more about the Europeans than the Europeans knew about themselves. What certainly intrigued them the most while on their righteous path was the incredible amount of riches that sprang forth from these strange lands. While much of the region was but a barren wasteland, the soldiers soon discovered that these lands overflowed with items that were virtually unknown to the markets of Europe. The Christian knights sampled a variety of exotic spices that made food much more delectable; felt with their fingers the soft texture of finely woven silk garments; sniffed the alluring scents of various types of perfumes; held in their hands magnificent gems of enormous size and exquisite beauty; and beheld a spectacular treasure-trove of gold and silver shaped items.

These crusading knights returned to their respective homelands with numerous samples of their unique and splendid plunder, all of which further enhanced their spellbinding tales of adventure in a strange land. The spices and exotic items they introduced served to whet the appetites of the European communities and arouse a great demand for much more of the same. Italian ship-owners, who had been paid handsomely to transport the armies of the crusades across the span of the Mediterranean Sea, saw an additional opportunity to increase their profits from the ongoing war. Instead of returning to the ports of Italy with an empty hull they offered bargain cargo rates to any merchants interested in shipping their various wares back to Italy. Ironically, it was mostly Muslim merchants who took advantage of those low rates to transport their precious commodities to eager Christian merchants in Italy. Spices, fabrics, perfumes, jewelry, tapestries, fruits, herbs, and gold and silver wares were among the varied and valuable cargoes crammed on board vessels destined for the anxious markets of Europe. A fledgling traffic of merchandise soon blossomed into an extensive trade between Christian and Muslim merchants, with profitable benefits for all parties concerned.

Even from early on, the Europeans were cognizant of the fact that the Muslim merchants they dealt with were primarily middlemen of trade for items that originated elsewhere. They had heard vague tales about rich lands located further to the east, but the exact locations and names of these distant places remained a mystery to them. Normally boisterous Arab traders became uncharacteristically silent when curious Christian merchants took to questioning them regarding the source of their unusual commodities.

Arabian societies had long benefited from their unique position in the known world. Residing along the region known as the Levant, a synonym for the combined stretch of land east of Italy that bordered the coast of the Mediterranean Sea, Arab merchants earned their livelihood by bargaining and trading with anyone and everyone who possessed items that had any sort of redeemable value. However, Arab trade was not confined solely to this region. Their dealings extended deep into Asia, bringing them into contact with the equally shrewd and crafty merchants of India and China. It was at these busy markets that they obtained the exotic items that Europeans now craved so hungrily.

The cherished items of the Orient were transported to the Levant by way of two well-established trade routes: one by land, the second by sea. Trudging across land, Arab traders and their accompanying caravan of fully loaded camels followed the ancient Silk Road, a tortuous path clearly marked by the sun-bleached bones of the many men and beasts who never made it to the journey's end. Originating in China, the Silk Road crossed the towering snowcapped peaks of the Himalayas, cut through the bleak Taklamakan Desert, and following many months of arduous travel the path eventually emptied into various centers of trade located in the Middle East. Besides the Silk Road, there were other caravan routes, which were often traversed by a train of camels extending far beyond one's field of vision, that linked the Arab world to the riches buried deep within the continent of Africa.

By way of the high seas, Arab merchants maintained commercial ties at the busy trade centers of Goa and Calicut, both of which were ideally situated along the Malabar coast of India. Merchants from as far away as China and Java sailed to these bustling ports to carry on trade with the many merchants of India as well as the numerous Arab traders who had set up shop at these distant locations. The Arab merchants managed to extend their already vast network of trade even further with the establishment of permanent Muslim colonies in the major ports of Burma, China,

Sumatra, and Java. Arab vessels brimming over with the fine silks, spices, and jewels of the Orient found their way across the Indian Ocean on a regular and frequent basis. Some of these merchant ships sailed up through the Gulf of Oman and on into the Persian Gulf, while others cut across the Gulf of Aden and into the Red Sea to unload their valuable cargoes at various Arabian ports along the way. Goods that were destined for the markets of Europe still needed to be transported overland to the major trading ports positioned along the Mediterranean. These ports were as far as Christian merchants were permitted to travel for purposes of trade, and for several centuries the routes of trade that linked Europe, the Middle East, and Asia remained a mystery to most Europeans. Having grown rich off their foreign interests, the Arab nations utilized every available precaution to ensure that nothing would upset the delicate balance of trade that weighed so heavily in their favor.

Regardless of whether these imported items arrived by land or sea, European merchants could count on the fact that the cost of these greatly desired commodities was sure to rise at every point where they changed hands or wherever they happened to pass through the domain of another ruler. By the time the spices and products of the Far East reached the markets of Europe they were priced as much as a hundred times more than their original purchase price. Before the treasures of the East were allowed to flow to the various markets of the West they had to first filter through the meticulous ledgers of the merchants of Italy, who tacked on their own substantial markup, one which was large enough to guarantee them a handsome profit. Thanks to their carefully cultivated business connections with overseas Muslim merchants and traders, the merchants of Venice, Genoa, Pisa, and Florence helped their towns emerge as bustling centers of commercial activity and untold financial opportunity. The maritime republics of Venice and Genoa, both being ideally situated along the waters of the Mediterranean, succeeded at dominating the course of European commerce in a relatively short period of time. The merchants of both Venice and Genoa had initially garnered a small fortune selling supplies and armor to the numerous Christian knights preparing for the great crusade. Ship owners from these same ports were able to turn a tidy profit transporting the Christian armies across the Mediterranean to do battle with the forces of Islam. It did not take long for these same ship-owners to realize they could ply an even more lucrative trade by shipping back to the merchants of their homeland the many unusual and precious goods that flowed steadily throughout the markets of Africa and Asia.

Over time, the Italian merchants forged commercial alliances that granted them the right to establish trading posts at a number of major centers of trade within the well-guarded Arabian domain. Thanks to these restrictive trade arrangements, the Italians succeeded in establishing for themselves a near monopoly of the wholesale supply of Asian and Oriental spices that entered Europe, and this control allowed them to regulate and dictate prices as they saw fit. The steady upward shifts in supply and demand contributed greatly to the increasing wealth of these Italian states. The merchant vessels of Venice and Genoa, which increasingly grew in both size and numbers, had to ply the waters of the Mediterranean on a regular basis in order to accommodate the sudden surge in demand. After arriving at the ports of Italy, the precious commodities of the East were either carried overland to various commercial centers in Germany and France or transported by ship to European ports as far away as the island of England. Italian vessels were ferrying their precious commodities through the Strait of Gibraltar as early as 1277 for immediate delivery to the many desirous markets of northern Europe. Thus, in spite of their deep religious and cultural differences, an extensive and thriving commercial intercourse developed between the empires of the East and the kingdoms of the West. But the balance of trade continued to weigh heavily in favor of the East. Europe's finest linens and woolens, wood, and metals such as copper and lead were marketable items but those exports were not enough to offset the rapidly increasing flow of exotic imports. To continue satisfying their newfound sense of opulence, Europeans were forced to pay the difference in either gold or silver, but preferably gold; and neither metal was naturally abundant to Europe.

The Legend of Prester John

In the year 1145 a tale was spun regarding the extraordinary exploits of a man who would deeply inspire the imaginations of European Christians for several centuries to come. He was Prester John, a mighty Christian king who lorded over an exceedingly wealthy and powerful kingdom located somewhere to the East. It was during this year that Bishop Hugh of Gebel presented himself before the papal court, currently in session at the Italian town of Viterbo, to bring the glorious news of a priest king named John who faithfully carried on the great Christian cause against overwhelming numbers of Muslim infidels. He told of how this man, thought to be a direct descendant of one of the three Magi who paid homage to the baby Jesus, had led his multitude of Christian followers to glorious victories over the Persians and the Medes in an effort to free the city of Jerusalem; but, unfortunately, his army had been rebuffed at the banks of the Tigris. The bishop informed his holiness that this potential ally "...lives in the extreme Orient, beyond Persia and Armenia, and is a Christian although a Nestorian." Even though Bishop Hugh had never set eyes upon Prester John, his faithful reporting of all that he had heard while in Syria was taken as gospel. The account was recorded by Otto of Freising, a German bishop present at court on that day, and soon the legend of Prester John was known throughout Europe.

The story of how this Christian ruler came to be known as Prester John is probably best recorded by Sir John Mandeville, a 14th century knight who claimed to have come across this legendary potentate during his worldly travels.

> There was once an emperor in that land who was a noble and brave prince; he had many knights with him who were Christian, like he who is now Emperor. And one day this Emperor thought that he would like to see the manner of the services in the Christian churches. At that time Christian men occupied many countries towards those parts, that is to say, Turkey, Syria, Tartary, Palestine, Arabia, Aleppo and all Egypt. And so it fell that this Emperor and a Christian knight who was with him entered a church in Egypt and on the Saturday in Whit week, when the Bishop was holding an ordination service. The Emperor watched the service, and the way priests were made, and how solemnly and devoutly they were ordained. He then asked the knight what sort of people these were who were being ordained, and what they were called; the knight said they were priests. Then the Emperor said that no longer would he be called King or Emperor, but priest instead, and that he would take the name of the first priest to come out of the church. It happened that the first priest to come out of the church was called John; and so that Emperor and all the other Emperors since have been called Prester John, that is, Priest John.

Christian credence in the Prester John tale received universal European acceptance following the arrival in 1165 of a formal letter addressed directly to Manuel Comnenus, the Christian emperor of the Byzantine Empire. Claiming to be the written word of the mysterious Christian king, this letter told of the earthly paradise where he and his faithful followers dwelled. In the words of Prester John, "honey flows in our land, and milk abounds everywhere," and the commandments of God are obeyed without question. His letter further titillates the reader with the bold proclamation, "I Prester John, who reign supreme, exceed in riches, virtues and power all creatures who dwell under heaven. Seventy-two kings pay tribute to me. I am a devout Christian, and everywhere protect the Christians of our empire." He called upon the leaders of the West to join his great army in a united campaign against all enemies of God and Christ. Pope Alexander III and the Holy Roman Emperor Frederick Barbarossa were also recipients of the same ten page letter from Prester John. Pope Alexander responded favorably in a letter entrusted to his personal physician, Magister Philippus. Unfortunately, the good doctor never found either Prester John or his way back home. While the original letter was clearly a literary hoax, designed most likely to arouse support for yet another holy crusade, the copies that circulated freely throughout Europe simply further enhanced the legend of the mysterious and elusive Prester John.

Every legend carries with it a germ of truth, and with this in mind there has, over time, been much speculation as to the true identity of Prester John as well as the exact whereabouts of his kingdom. Eldad Ha Dani, also known as Ben Mahli, a Jewish wayfarer and writer from the 9th century, may have given rise to the legend with his often repeated tale of how one of the lost tribes of Israel, after much wandering, finally settled "beyond the rivers of Abyssinia." This account, as well as others, concerning the origin of the Prester John tale appears to have a common link to the many trials and tribulations of the devoted followers of a man by the name of Nestorius.

Nestorius, loyal citizen of Constantinople, had risen steadily through the ecclesiastical ranks and eventually, beginning in A.D. 428, reigned supreme as archbishop of the Church. However, this patriarch ignited a firestorm of controversy when he publicly acknowledged that Mary was the mother of Jesus Christ but, in the same breath, refused to endorse Mary as the "mother of God." A heated debate ensued between those who accepted Christ as a single man, both divine and human, and the supporters of Nestorius, who contended that the body of Christ was possessed of two independent entities, one godly and the other human, interacting within one soul.

Three years later, in 431, the Christian debate reached its climax when Nestorius was dragged before the Council of Ephesus and found guilty of heresy. The council stripped him of his religious ranking, and publicly condemned his doctrine, which later came to be known as Nestorianism, and all who refused to denounce it. Many continued in the faith, but when the wrath of religious persecution became absolutely unbearable the congregation took flight towards the East. They first immigrated to Persia around the year 489 but soon discovered that the Muslims were even less tolerant of their religious beliefs. Following the path of the established Arab trade routes, the Nestorians wandered throughout much of Asia, eventually establishing settlements in India, China, and even Siberia. These defenders of the faith carried on the Christian cause in lands that were inhabited entirely by "heathens, infidels, and idolators." These determined Nestorians succeeded in converting thousands of souls, and in the process they gained a small measure of political support and clout at the courts of a great number of powerful Asian rulers.

Europe lost touch with this banished branch of Christianity until sometime after 1141. It was during this year that Sanjar, the Seljuk prince of Khurasan, whose armies had swept through a number of European and Asian borders, suffered a devastating defeat at the hands of numerous Asian tribes momentarily united under the Khitan prince Yeh-lu Ta-Shioh for the common cause of defense. Participating in the heroic struggle against the forces of Persia was a small body of troops comprised of faithful Nestorians. As the tale of Sanjar's loss spread to Christian lands, the story began taking on an increasingly Christian tone. More than likely, this battle was the basis for the tale that Bishop Hugh heard while stationed in Syria, a land that bordered the homeland of Prince Sanjar.

Another name sometimes linked to the Prester John legend, even though it ignores the fact that he was a devout Muslim, is that of Mansa Musa, the exalted ruler of Mali who reigned during the fourteenth century. In 1324 Mansa Musa set out on a pilgrimage to Mecca, the most holy of Muslim cities, in the company of a large retinue of slaves, servants, soldiers, and mistresses. The prince had the great fortune to rule over a land naturally endowed with an abundance of gold, and he decided the time had come to share some of his wealth with the rest of the Islamic world. Every one of his five-hundred slaves carried staffs made of solid gold, each purported to weigh nearly a hundred pounds. Directly behind them was a train of camels numbering eighty in length with each beast of burden hauling a heavy load of pure gold. The prince ceremoniously presented a great many precious gifts at every city he visited on the way to Mecca. Mansa Musa died in 1332 but the legend of his enormous wealth and splendid generosity lived on in the tales of merchants and travelers along the Mediterranean basin. He also played a significant role in transforming the Malian cities of Timbuktu and Gao into important centers of trade between Africa and the Middle East. Mansa's name would adorn the face of a great many European maps, including the famous world map drawn by Martin Waldseemüller.

The fame of Prester John grew so great and his wealth and might became so magnificent in the minds of the Europeans of the Middle Ages that cartographers of this period took to charting his Christian empire on their maps of the world. Numerous missionary parties were sent out in hopes of locating and uniting with this powerful Christian monarch; but, to their great disappointment, his magnificent kingdom proved ever-elusive. The true believers, however, took comfort in the encouraging words that his divine province was close at hand. When they could not find him in Persia they simply expanded their search to Asia, only to learn later that he now dwelled somewhere in the heart of the mysterious continent of Africa. The first map depicting the Christian king's residence in Africa was drawn by the cartographer Angelino Dulcert in 1339. From this point on the learned men of Europe seemed to accept as fact that the exalted Christian kingdom of Prester John was located somewhere within the borders of Abyssinia, the ancient land now known as Ethiopia.

The Travels of Marco Polo

During the 13th century most of Eastern Europe and much of the Middle East fell before an invading horde of nomadic warriors led by the mighty Genghis Khan. The expanding Mongol empire eventually held sway over many of the Islamic regions that formed a continental divide between the lands of Europe and Asia. When the Mongols lifted the longstanding Muslim blockade to Asia, European traders suddenly had access to the mysterious trade route later known as the Silk Road, a direct overland link to the riches of China, an ambiguous and isolated region known to Medieval Europe as the land of Cathay.

The gateway to China was opened during the magnanimous rule of Kublai Khan, a grandson of the conqueror Genghis Khan. Following the warrior tradition of his grandfather, Kublai Khan led a mighty Mongol force that, in the span of just a few years, managed to conquer and consolidate the immense territory collectively known as China. As the king of kings, the "Great Khan" ruled over an empire thrice the size of the combined kingdoms of Europe. Possessed of an intelligent and inquisitive mind, Kublai Khan earnestly sought to learn as much as he could about the lands he lorded over as well as those that he did not. A devout Buddhist who made his beliefs the beliefs of his empire, he was, nevertheless, extremely tolerant towards the faith of others. By both land and sea, the Khan encouraged the advancement of China's already well established commercial intercourse with the known world. His regal court at Cambaluc, the future site of Beijing, extended an open invitation to all adventurous souls to make a journey that had now been rendered safe from marauding bands of Russians, Tatars, and Hungarians, thanks to the vigilant guard of the Mongols.

Among the many European travelers who took advantage of the newly opened trade route to Cathay were two enterprising Venetian merchants named Niccolò and Matteo Polo. The two brothers were partners in trade and, like many merchants of that era, had commercial interests at various ports in the Levant. Matters of business brought them to the city of Constantinople and from there they proceeded on to Sudak, a Venetian colony resting along the coast of the Crimea, to check on additional affairs of trade. In the year 1261, a time when Eastern routes of trade had become relatively safe, the Polos decided to venture further, eventually arriving by caravan at the city of Bukhara. Located in central Asia and conquered by Genghis Khan in 1220, Bukhara was a renowned center of trade situated along the fringe of the vast Mongol Empire. What was supposed to have been just a brief stopover ended up turning into a three year stay. During this time the brothers managed to ingratiate themselves with the exclusive circle of merchants and traders, as well as insinuate themselves into the closed ranks of Mongol rule. A chance meeting with an emissary in the service of Kublai Khan provided them with an unexpected opportunity. Impressed and intrigued by the manner of these two Venetian merchants, the envoy cordially invited them to travel as his guests to the distant court of the Great Khan.

Niccolò and Matteo Polo had the rare privilege of being among the first Europeans to visit the ancient land of China. The gracious Kublai Khan greeted them with a warm and royal reception and then attempted to learn as much as he possibly could about their distant homeland. The Great Khan was particularly interested in knowing more about the subject of Christianity, a religion he had first heard about from his mother, who was a baptized member of a Nestorian church in his native land of Mongolia. The Polos did their best to accommodate the request of their royal host by instructing him in the finer points of Christianity and the extensive role that the Church and Pope played in maintaining and spreading the chosen faith of their people. Held captive by the khan's curiosity, the Polos spent several years as honored guests at his royal court.

The khan did finally agree to let Niccolò and Matteo return home but only on the condition that they deliver to Pope Clement IV a request for other men of knowledge to be sent to his kingdom so that he could be instructed in greater detail about Christian doctrine and the intricacies of European society. The khan also decreed that a Mongol by the name of Cogotal was to accompany the Venetians on the their journey home. As he had grown quite fond of the Polo brothers, Kublai Khan provided them with his Tablet of Gold, a precious plaque that would guarantee them safe passage through his vast empire and which also commanded his loyal sub-

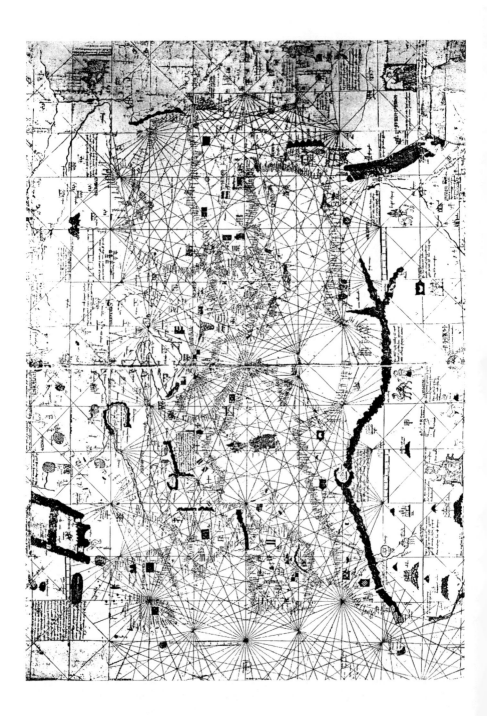

jects to provide these travelers with whatever comforts or necessities they might require along the way. Twenty days into the journey Cogotal contracted a mysterious illness, most likely an acute longing for home, that prevented his continuing on the long and arduous journey with the Polos. In April of 1269 Niccolò and Matteo arrived in Armenia where they received the sad news that Pope Clement IV had passed away the previous year. Learning that a new Pope had still not been elected by the high church officials, the weary travelers made their way back home to Venice.

No one was more excited over the return of these two merchants than fifteen year old Marco, the son of Niccolò. Marco was a popular name within the Polo family. Niccolò and Matteo were the sons of one Marco Polo and their oldest brother was baptized with the name of the father. Niccolò had embarked on his long journey while his young wife was still pregnant and she had given birth to their son shortly after his departure. Sometime thereafter, young Marco's mother had passed away and he had spent his formative years growing up in the household of his close relatives. Anxious to know more about the father and uncle he had never met, young Marco eagerly listened to their wondrous tales of adventure and their vivid description of the splendor they beheld at the court of Kublai Khan. Enthralled by these glorious accounts of Cathay, Marco begged his father to take him along on their next journey. Two years later, in 1271, Niccolò, Matteo, and the seventeen year old Marco set out on their historic journey.

Before heading out on their grand adventure, Niccolò and Matteo received Church permission to travel to Jerusalem in order that they might honor another of the khan's unique requests: to return with a small quantity of the holy oil that burned above the sepulcher of Jesus. Once they had obtained this oil sample, the father, son, and uncle returned to Acre where they hoped an accord had finally been reached as to who would reign supreme over the Holy See. Unfortunately, nothing had changed during their brief absence. The Polos obtained from Teobaldo of Piacenza, a good friend of theirs, official Church papers attesting to this current state of affairs and a pledge that once a new Pope had been elected the papacy would gladly comply with all the other requests of Kublai Khan.

The three bold adventurers had traveled only as far as the Syrian coast when word reached them that the Church had finally succeeded in electing a new Pope. Returning at once to Acre, they were granted an audience

Opposite: **1339 world map drawn by Angelino Dulcert: This Catalan map, besides giving a fairly accurate picture of the coastal region of the Mediterranean Sea and the Atlantic Ocean, charts the major trading centers of the known world.**

with the newly ordained Gregory X, who, much to their delight, turned out to be their faithful friend Teobaldo of Piacenza. The new Pope was very receptive to Kublai Khan's request to learn more about the Christian faith. He therefore appointed two Dominican friars, Brother Guglielmo di Tripoli and Brother Niccolò da Vicenza—both bearing numerous gifts for the Great Khan—to accompany the three merchants on their journey to the Far East. Unfortunately, these two missionaries displayed a weakness of both flesh and faith and turned back at the first sign of difficulty, leaving only the precious presents of the Pope in their wake.

The path that the three men traveled proved to be an extremely difficult course to follow. It was a route that took them overland to the city of Baghdad, through the rugged northern terrain of Persia, over the mountainous regions of the Pamirs, and across an ocean of sand known as the Gobi Desert. In Armenia, the travelers climbed Mount Ararat where, according to the Old Testament, the massive ark constructed by Noah came to rest after the great flood. During a brief stopover at Saba, Persia, Marco claims to have visited the tombs of the three Magi who had traveled to Bethlehem to pay tribute to the newborn baby Jesus. While crossing Persia the Polos barely escaped death when a band of bloodthirsty marauders swooped down and killed or captured a great many of the men who traveled in the company of their caravan. Eventually the trio found their way to the city of Hormuz, located at the tip of the Persian Gulf, and a major trade center for the merchants of Asia, the Orient, and Africa. The crossing of the Gobi Desert took them a full thirty days to complete, during which time they saw nothing but sand, sun, and sky. In the year 1275, following a journey that had taken three and a half years to complete and that covered a distance of nearly seven thousand miles, Niccolò, Matteo, and Marco finally arrived at Cambaluc.

Elated by the news that his Venetian friends had returned to China of their own free will, the khan immediately summoned them to his luxurious summer palace at Shung-tu. The moment they arrived at the royal residence the three adventurers presented the Great Khan with the letters and gifts sent from Pope Gregory X and the holy oil that they had obtained from the Church of the Holy Sepulcher. Years later, Marco would record his recollection of Kublai Khan's general appearance: "He is of good and fair size, neither too small nor too large, but is of middle size. He is covered with flesh in a beautiful manner, not too fat or lean; he is more than well formed in all parts. He has his face white and partly shining red like the color of a beautiful rose, which makes him appear very pleasing; and he has eyes black and beautiful; and the nose very beautiful, well made and well set on the face."

Marco Polo: After a grueling journey that lasted nearly three and a half years Marco Polo (with left hand across chest) arrives at the legendary kingdom of Cathay.

The now twenty-one year old Marco Polo had apparently created a favorable impression on the Emperor and before long he found himself in the diplomatic service of the khan. While his father and uncle served as advisers at the royal court, Marco became a student of Mongolian ways and means. For the next seventeen years Marco was employed by the khan as an official emissary and performed his duties so well that he quickly became one of the ruler's most trusted confidants. In his role as roving ambassador for the Great Khan it was Marco's duty to gather and record information about those regions of the Mongol Empire that were still a mystery to the emperor. These travels throughout the vast domain of the khan's allowed Marco to gaze upon the many wonders of an ancient and magnificent society, one which was entirely unknown to most Europeans. During his extensive travels he came across Christian churches at Quinsay that were attended by descendants of the banished Nestorians who had settled there long ago. It was a strange sight that convinced the young and impressionable Marco Polo, though only momentarily, that he had stumbled upon the legendary realm of Prester John.

During their lengthy stay in the service of Kublai Khan, Marco, Niccolò, and Matteo were exposed to a great number of Chinese innovations that were eventually incorporated into the European mainstream. The mariner's compass, block printing, and gunpowder are but a few of the extraordinary technological advancements of Eastern culture that went on to benefit Western society. Marco marveled at how the khan was able to convince the many citizens of China that small printed pieces of paper were worth far more than their weight in gold. Printed on mulberry bark paper and sealed in red dye, paper currency had been in use in China long before the Mongols ever ruled there, probably as far back as the 8th century A.D. Backed by the population's full faith in the emperor's wealth, Chinese merchants willingly accepted these pieces of paper as a medium of exchange for just about any kind of business transaction. Those monetary notes, which were certainly exceedingly lighter and easier to carry around than bulky precious metals, freed up the supply of gold for artistic and religious purposes. This peculiar transmutation of money confounded the nobles, merchants, alchemists, and scholars of Europe until (and not before the passage of several centuries) they were finally able to fully grasp the concept.

After seventeen years of faithful service to the Great Khan these merchants from Venice had grown extremely anxious to see their beloved homeland once again. While they may have been nostalgic for the sights and sounds of their native land they were much more concerned about their tenuous station at the royal court now that the emperor was getting on in years. Niccolò sought permission for the three of them to return home but the khan refused his request by stating, "On no condition in the world am I willing that you depart from my realm, but I am content that you go about it where you please." Time and time again the Polos pleaded with the Great Khan to let them leave but the ruler enjoyed their company and counsel far too greatly to grant them their request. Fate, however, interceded on their behalf with the sudden arrival of ambassadors from the faraway land of Persia.

In distant Persia, a vassal state of the Great Khan, King Argon mourned the loss of his beloved wife Bolgana, a woman of noble Mongol lineage who also happened to be his mother. In her will the queen stipulated that her replacement as Argon's wife must come from within her family line, a request Argon respectfully sought to honor. The king sent three envoys to the court of the khan at Cambaluc to relay the dying wish of the queen mother. Kublai Khan had every intention of granting this request; for not only was Argon the ruler of Persia, he was also a grandson of the emperor's brother. The Great Khan gave his royal blessing to their choice of a young and beautiful Tartar princess named Cocachin to become the bride of the widowed Argon. However, after traveling only a brief distance in the direction of Persia the seventeen-year-old princess and her entourage found the rugged overland route far too difficult and dangerous and returned to the court of the khan where they hoped to procure ships that could transport them safely back to Persia.

Sensing a golden opportunity for their long awaited return to the city of Venice, the Venetians offered their services to Argon's ambassadors. Their proposition was simple: if the Persian envoys could convince the Great Khan to let them join their group they would use their extensive navigational skills to guide them safely across the treacherous waters of the South China Sea. The Polos' reputation as experienced, worldly travelers preceded them, and the ambassadors gladly accepted their offer. They immediately submitted the Polos' names to the khan as personal escorts for the princess Cocachin. Though reluctant at first, Kublai Khan eventually agreed to allow Niccolò, Matteo, and Marco to go in order to assist Cocachin on her voyage to Persia and to avoid offending King Argon with any further delays.

Trusting to safety in numbers, Kublai Khan supplied Princess Cocachin and her extensive entourage with fourteen of his largest and sturdiest ships, vessels which are more commonly referred to as junks. These Chinese junks were manned by a crew numbering greater than six hundred and stored with enough supplies to last them for a voyage of two years in length. Bidding a fond farewell to the three men he had come to regard as friends, Kublai Khan gave them cordial messages to be distributed amongst the Pope and many of the Christian rulers of Europe. In addition to these notes, the khan provided them with two more golden tablets to aid and protect them on their long journey. Just before leaving Cathay, the Polos converted all the gold and money they had acquired during their extended stay into valuable rubies, emeralds, diamonds, and sapphires, all of which they wisely concealed inside the linings of their heavy garments.

Setting sail in the year 1292, the fleet slowly maneuvered its way through the South China Sea. It was on this voyage that Marco Polo got a firsthand look at the intricate and extensive network of routes which crisscrossed these waters to connect trade between the markets of Asia and the Middle East. From the deck of their ship, these three explorers were probably the first Europeans to cast their eyes upon the "land of the rising sun." After docking briefly at Sumatra, a large volcanic island blessed with an extremely fertile soil, Marco happened upon that which Europeans of sophisticated taste desired even more than gold itself, "all the precious spices that can be found in the world." Ideally positioned between the South China Sea and the Indian Ocean, Sumatra had been a principal supplier of spices to China and India for many centuries. Marco also took note of the spreading influence of Islam brought to the island by the many Arab traders eager to obtain ever greater quantities of spices for shipment to various markets in the Levant. He also claimed that during his stay at

Sumatra he encountered a barbaric people who dined on human flesh—
"...bad beastlike men who gladly catch and kill and eat men."

The fleet made additional stops at the bustling trading ports of Ceylon, India, and the Persian Gulf during its homeward bound journey. Most
of the voyage had proven to be a relatively smooth sail except for the last
leg of the voyage in 1294, which was interrupted suddenly by a devastating
tragedy that threatened the lives of nearly everyone aboard the fleet. At some
point between India and Persia a disease of unknown nature, probably Asi-
atic cholera, was contracted by the crew. The deadly malady ran rampant
throughout the fleet and by the time they reached their intended destination there were but a mere eighteen survivors. Fortunately, Marco, his father
Niccolò and his uncle Matteo, as well as the young Mongol princess and
one of the ambassadors from Persia, were to be counted among the few
survivors of this dreadful ordeal. The weary Venetians managed to muster
enough strength to fulfill their royal obligation and escorted Princess
Cocachin to the Persian court only to discover that Argon Khan had recently
passed away. After a lengthy stay at Tabriz, they left the princess in the care
of Argon's son and continued on their way to Venice. Grateful for this great
service that they had rendered, the heir to the throne of Persia supplied
the three travelers with a guard of two hundred royal horsemen to ensure
that their passage through his kingdom went without harm.

The tremendous joy that Marco, Niccolò, and Matteo must have felt
when they finally reached the Christian city of Constantinople was surely
dampened by the solemn news that their dear friend, the great and powerful Kublai Khan had passed away. In the winter of 1295, after an absence
of nearly twenty-four years, the three adventurers finally arrived at the city
of Venice. In addition to returning home with bountiful tales of adventure
to share with both family and friends, the three travelers had succeeded in
smuggling out enough precious jewels, particularly rubies and emeralds, to
enable them to enjoy the kind of life style and independence that only
wealth can provide.

The adventures of Marco Polo might very well have been relegated to
just a mere footnote in history had it not been for the misfortunes of war.
Shortly after the Polos' return, hostilities broke out between the city of
Venice and its commercial rival Genoa over control of the lucrative seafaring routes that crossed the Mediterranean Sea. As a loyal son of Venice,
Marco elected to serve his homeland by enlisting in the navy. By virtue of
his vast experience, as well as his elevated social station, he was appointed
captain of his own vessel. On September 6, 1298, the Venetian fleet in
which Marco sailed encountered an armada of Genoese vessels and a massive naval engagement soon ensued. After most of the shots had been fired

and the thick cloud of smoke that hovered over the battle had finally cleared, it was the Genoese navy that emerged as the clear victor. More than seven thousand Venetians were taken prisoner on that day, including Marco Polo.

Shipped back to Genoa in chains where he was to await his fate inside the walls of a prison at the Palazzo di San Giorgio, Marco struck up a close rapport with his assigned cell mate. Rustichello of Pisa, who had been taken prisoner in an earlier trade war, was a writer of some repute for having penned his own rendering of the King Arthur legend. Passing the time listening to Marco's intriguing tales of adventure, Rustichello persuaded his new friend to let him put the story of his amazing journey to paper. Marco, who probably had more freedom than most of the other prisoners, was allowed to send for his notes from Venice in order that he and Rustichello might put his remarkable adventure in book form. From that point on their incarceration became a close collaboration: Marco dictated to Rustichello all that he had seen and experienced during his many years in the service of the Great Khan while Rustichello put his own spin on the tale by embellishing upon those vivid remembrances.

A completed manuscript was secretly slipped out of the prison and it eventually found its way into the hands of readers of some prominence, who, in turn, showed their appreciation for Marco Polo's amazing adventure by managing to obtain his release. He returned to Venice in 1299 but little is known of his remaining years other than the fact that he died a very wealthy man on the 8th of January, 1324. The text of *The Book of Marco Polo, Citizen of Venice, Called Million, Wherein Is Recounted the Wonders of the World* found its way into the many different languages of Europe, with each translation taking on an altered, and often shorter, title. However, news of the Venetian's daring exploits spread slowly through Europe, as the copying of books by hand was a long and tedious process.

Marco Polo's marvelous tale of adventure provided the curious citizens of Europe with a vivid account of the vast wealth that freely circulated throughout the distant lands of the Far East. In telling his readers that "there are so many merchants and so rich and in such number that they cannot be counted," Marco inspired a countless number of future adventurers who dared to dream of following in his path. It was from the pages of Marco's book that Europeans first learned of the faraway lands that produced the many flavorful spices they had come to crave so greatly; were provided with a glimpse into the extensive power and splendor that was the kingdom of Kublai Khan; and, reading of his brief encounter with vigilant Christians living and worshiping in a strange land, were offered renewed hope in the existence of the legendary Prester John. Marco goes on to paint a particularly rich picture of a land he never even set foot in. "They have the greatest abundance of gold, for the sources of it are without end.... The entire roof of the palace is covered with plates of gold and the floors within are of gold tiles two fingers thick. The ceilings of the rooms are made of the same precious metal. Many of the rooms have tables of massive thick gold, and the windows are also decorated with gold. And great pearls of red and white colors abound so that the dead are buried each with a pearl in his mouth." This was his secondhand description of a place called Cipangu, a land we now know as the island of Japan. He also spoke of another region, one which would be of great interest to future explorers, a land that went by the name of either Mangi or Manzi. This land, which bordered Cathay to the south, was supposedly home to several hospitable harbors that were frequented by vast fleets of trading ships hauling rich and exotic cargoes from both nearby and distant lands.

The story of Marco Polo's extraordinary journey grew greater in grandeur with each subsequent telling. Before long it was accepted as fact that all the houses of Asia were adorned with roofs of gold; that pearls, rubies and emeralds were as plentiful as pebbles; and that the pleasant aroma of exotic spices permeated the entire region. Spurred on by these tales of incredible wealth, enterprising European merchants began to envision and entertain plans for establishing a direct trade link with the Orient, a commercial connection which would allow them to eliminate the enormous extra charges that were levied upon them by Arab traders. Suddenly, just at the very peak of European interest in these mysterious lands of Cathay, Cipangu, and Mangi, the seemingly invincible Mongol Empire crumbled. With the fear of the Great Khan now removed, Ottoman Turks swept through much of Asia Minor to reclaim these lands in the name of Islam. In the process of these conquests they inherited control of the heavily traveled overland spice routes. China would isolate itself once again from the rest of the world following a rebellion in 1368 that succeeded in wresting power from the Mongols and firmly establishing the Ming dynasty in its place. With the gateway to Asia once again sealed off, it now returned to business as usual between the Christian merchants of Europe and the Islamic merchants of the Levant.

However, visions of vast wealth waiting to be found at Cathay, Cipangu, and Mangi continued to linger in the minds of most Europeans. Before long the power of the press was unleashed upon the world with the invention of movable type by Johannes Gutenberg, and Marco Polo's tale of adventure was included among the many popular handwritten books that soon became available in print. His newly printed publication was first released in 1477 and soaring demand kept the presses churning out mass numbers of the book for the various separate states of Europe. Marco's almost incredible story could now reach and enthrall a new and even larger audience, and these recorded exploits would arouse the imaginations of countless future explorers, including those of Vasco da Gama and Christopher Columbus.

Another popular adventure book that caught the fancy of many a medieval reader was *The Voyages and Travels of Sir John Mandeville, Knight.* First published in 1370, this autobiography promotes its author as a Christian knight who set out on a grand adventure sometime around the year 1320. His quixotic, inspiring quest took him to the distant lands of Egypt, Jerusalem, Turkey, Persia, Ethiopia, India, Cathay, and even to the golden realm of Prester John.

Mandeville writes of islands off the coast of Asia that belonged to Prester John, and adds: "And there are further islands, and he who wishes to reach them must, with the help of God, travel around the earth in order to complete the journey. He might reach these countries whence he comes and where he belongs, round the earth. But since this takes so much time and there are so many dangers to be overcome, there are few who attempt to do this." He even goes on to tell of how one man boldly sailed around the world, not once but twice: one voyage ventured eastward while the other sailed westward. Mandeville's tale, just like Marco Polo's, was well known to a great many explorers of the coming age.

While taking much pleasure in describing the many wondrous sights he had seen during his incredible odyssey, Sir John Mandeville seemed to take even greater delight in playing on the superstitions and fears of his readers by recounting terrifying details of monsters and demons who lurked just beyond the known borders of Europe. Stricken with gout, Sir John Mandeville was eventually forced to return to England where he spent his remaining years putting to paper the account of his exciting and extensive travels across the world. This tale of strange lands inhabited by even stranger people and creatures became a bestseller that was translated, read, and studied throughout Europe. Sir John Mandeville's story exceeded even Marco Polo's book in popularity.

The Voyages and Travels of Sir John Mandeville, Knight, though an extremely entertaining and truly enlightening read for the medieval mind, was but an elaborate hoax, possibly the greatest in literary history. The true author was most likely Jehan à la Barbe, a renowned astronomer and physician from the Belgian city of Liège. His book was but a reworking of adventures in lands of intrigue recorded by other worldly travelers, and engagingly told as a first-person narrative. Nonetheless, this novel tale of Sir John Mandeville played a significant role in arousing the adventurous spirit inherent to the emerging era we have come to label as the Renaissance.

The Philosopher's Stone

The demand for more rare and exotic products from the Far East increased steadily throughout the numerous markets of Europe. The more Europeans sought to satisfy their newly acquired needs and desires, however, the more dependent they inevitably became upon the Arab traders who controlled the pipeline that transported those unique products. Items that once had been deemed to be mere extravagant luxuries were suddenly considered essential commodities for a changing European lifestyle. Spices and herbs made the taste of salted or rancid meat much more bearable and also helped to enhance the flavor of many other bland European dishes. Some of these same spices and herbs possessed great healing powers and were used to produce drugs of enormous medicinal value. With an eye for beauty, many Europeans sought out rare and unusual items from the Orient with an aesthetic value that would endow them with the trappings of wealth.

However, Europe's newfound taste for the finer things bore a burdensome price. Fine silks, peppers, cinnamon, and cloves were among the many items carted across both land and sea by adventurous Arab traders intent upon making a substantial profit either at home or in some foreign market. Aside from woolen products and timber, Europeans possessed few items that were of much interest to these savvy Arab merchants. Precious metals, particularly gold, provided an acceptable medium of exchange that helped to free buyers and sellers from the age old restrictions commonly associated with bartering. The precious gold that the Arab traders demanded for their expensive commodities also happened to be an ornamental metal that was greatly desired by their Asian trading partners.

As gold steadily drained from the West to the East, European rulers found that it was becoming increasingly difficult to replenish their rapidly diminishing supply of metal-based funds. Gold production in Europe was primarily confined to a small number of mines scattered in Spain, Saxony, and Austria, and this natural resource was quickly nearing exhaustion. Europe's monarchs were forced to face a difficult quandary: in addition to needing the commodities of the East they also needed gold, for without this precious metal they could not afford the many foreign items to which they had now become accustomed. Without ample resources of gold the fragile economies of the European kingdoms were destined to falter under the weight of their own demands, thereby setting the stage for a new state of poverty.

Knowing full well that the loss of material wealth was a potential prescription for anarchy and revolution, European rulers and merchants joined together in a desperate search for additional stores of gold. Since gold equaled wealth and wealth was equated with power, it was only natural for these rulers and merchants to seek the element which would enable them to preserve their elite positions in the current social order.

The search for gold followed a great number of paths—some were adventurous in nature, some were innovative in thought, and some were simply wild flights of fancy. There were those who strongly believed there was a magical formula just waiting to be discovered that could replicate the golden touch of King Midas, a belief which was supported by the teachings spewed forth from the influential and sagacious mind of the Greek philosopher Aristotle. Stating that since all elements of nature exhibited one of four qualities—heat, cold, moisture, or dryness—Aristotle concluded that it was possible to change the structure of a substance by simply altering the quality within that element.

The Greeks, as well as the Egyptians and the Chinese, firmly believed that gold was the purest form of metal, an evolutionary state that all other lesser metals sought to achieve. Chinese alchemists believed that gold, when consumed in liquid form, could heal all ailments and even offer immortality to the consumer.

The Islamic conquerors of Asia Minor and North Africa embraced many of the teachings of classical Greece, an acquired knowledge that they later passed on to Europe when they crossed the waters of the Mediterranean to conquer the Iberian Peninsula. Arabic alchemists practiced the arcane science of transmutation, searching endlessly for the illusory philosopher's stone, a pure substance that would enable them to transform ordinary base metals into a higher state of precious metals. Whoever could find the key that would unlock the process stood not only to enrich himself greatly but also the nation to which he claimed his allegiance. Intrigued by the prospects of producing untold wealth, a great number of European nobles of the Middle Ages financially supported the many trials and errors of their local alchemists.

While many of these professed alchemists were nothing more than charlatans seeking to squeeze money from the pockets of their noble benefactors, most of them worked diligently at their chosen craft. It was in the lonely confines of such workshops that the fumbling experiments and mystical speculations of the alchemist succeeded in laying the important groundwork for the more practical science of chemistry. While never succeeding in finding the mystical philosopher's stone, the alchemist nearly attained perfection by discovering reagents that would dissolve but, unfortunately, could not reproduce gold.

Fair Markets

This increased demand for items originating in foreign lands helped to ignite a commercial revolution, which, in turn, paved the way for the economic system known as capitalism. Merchants throughout Europe scurried to find their own profitable niche in a rapidly changing and expanding marketplace, and this creation of new commercial opportunities soon led to the destruction of many of the old ways of conducting business. The confining economic structure of feudalism and the rigid restrictions enforced under the guild systems were no longer economically viable. Trade, which had been primarily localized, now moved form town to town, crossed the borders of neighboring nations, and sailed across the high seas in constant search of new markets. Once the restrictions on trade had been removed an exponential growth in commerce occurred throughout much of the European continent. However, it was the opening of international trade that forever changed the internal structure of Europe.

Each independent European state pushed for the introduction of its natural resources and its finished products into the markets of neighboring states as well as those of distant lands. England profited greatly from its trade in garments, Italy from oil and wine, France from salt, the Dutch from fish, while the Baltic regions supplied much of the continent with valuable timber and fine furs. European trade to the north was dominated by the Hanseatic League, a federation of German and northern European cities allied to promote and protect their commercial concerns. To the south, the Italian republics of Genoa and Venice monopolized the lucrative spice trade emanating from Islamic lands while continuing to do battle with one another for control over the Mediterranean shipping lanes.

In the interest of promoting even greater international trade, large commercial fairs were organized, the most famous being in the French province of Champagne, which managed to attract merchants from all over Europe. It was at such fairs that buyers and sellers came together in large numbers to negotiate the sale of a vast and varied assortment of goods. Spices, furs, perfumes, and gems were among the many items transferred in bulk, the sales of which were tracked and recorded by an appointed fair banker. At the close of business, debits and credits were offset and the remaining difference was settled either through a payment of money or the issuance of a bill that could be used as credit at the next fair. Thus, these international fairs served as a clearinghouse for trade, a business function later performed more expediently and efficiently by independent banking institutions. The great fairs of trade, which usually occurred on either an annual or semiannual basis, tried, but failed, to keep up with the surge in consumer demand. They were eventually replaced by permanent market centers located directly within towns or cities. As these centers became regular fixtures of commerce, ambitious merchants discovered that they could penetrate distant markets by establishing a branch office wherever they desired to do business, a move that usually increased their profits at home.

From the ashes of feudalism arose a brand new economy, one that was predicated on the ebb and flow of money. European merchants, suddenly flush with unlimited commercial opportunities, discovered that it was now possible to alter their station within the previously closed ranks of society. For those willing to take the risk, success was measured in terms of financial gain and those pecuniary rewards grew even greater once those same merchants realized they could, with their newly acquired wealth, wield enormous power and influence over domestic affairs. The merchant class, an almost instantaneous by-product of capitalism, eventually became rich and powerful enough to manipulate the purse strings of their respective state economies. Instead of spending large sums on nonproductive structures, such as fortresses and holy shrines, most merchants chose to reinvest their hard-earned money back into their businesses. During this period of economic transformation there were more workers hired to handle the increased workload, inventories were enlarged to keep pace with the surge in demand, larger warehouses were constructed to store more goods, and bigger boats were built to carry more products. In the end, wealth was magnified, and a portion of it even managed to trickle down to the masses.

Empowered by his newfound wealth, the merchant prince, at the expense of the Church, became both noble lender and patron of the arts. Monarchs, who always seemed to be in desperate need of money to finance their numerous courtly affairs, slowly reduced their reliance on funds from the Church and instead began to borrow directly from the merchants. As a royal lender, the merchant banker found himself in a unique position to benefit greatly from royal favors, often receiving quid pro quo privileges in the form of charters that generally granted him an exclusive monopoly of a specified area of trade. In the wealthy merchant, the artist found a benefactor who no longer restricted his work within the rigid religious parameters of the Church. A new spirit of individualism suddenly emerged, the essence of which was at the very heart of the Renaissance movement.

The lending of money for the express purpose of profit, a practice commonly referred to as usury during the Middle Ages, was, according to the strict canon law of the Roman Catholic Church, an entirely forbidden practice. Was it not Jesus who uncharacteristically lost his temper over the sight of covetous moneylenders conducting their sordid business affairs in a "house of God"? While it may have been condemned as a practice unbecoming of a Christian, lending for profit was, for the sake of financial convenience, tolerated as a non-Christian business. The Jews, who, because of their religious beliefs, had been barred from many fields of business, were in a position to realize extraordinary profits from lending money to merchants in need of cash. With the coming trade expansion, there came a greater need for much larger infusions of working capital, which, in turn, led to an increased willingness on the part of Christian merchants to pay what was often a steep price for the temporary use of someone else's money. More and more, lenders and borrowers found creative ways to circumvent the religious prohibition on interest charges until finally acceptance became so widespread, the Church found it next to impossible to enforce its own ban on usury. Before the close of the 15th century, governing bodies began to assume the responsibility for regulating money-lending practices by implementing statutes that set a strict maximum interest rate a lender could charge a borrower on a loan. Any lender charging more than the legally defined rate was considered guilty of the crime of usury.

It was during the Renaissance period that a number of powerful financial dynasties arose from total obscurity to become the dominant figures in European trade and finance, both at home and abroad. The Bardis, Medicis, Lombards, and the Fuggers accumulated vast fortunes from their activities in trade and then skillfully managed to increase their own wealth and status by financing the various affairs of both Church and state. Of course lending to monarchs and nobles carried its own peculiar set of risks, the most notable being that a lender had little recourse in the likely event that a royal borrower decided to ignore or repudiate his outstanding debt. On more than one occasion, a noble's decision to forego his contracted financial obligation led to the bankruptcy of an unfortunate lender.

Merchants had always understood the basic business concept that it takes money to make money, but it was not until the Renaissance, an enlightened age when man began to view the world around him quite differently, that European men of business began to visualize the basic principles of banking. Moneylending evolved into the business of banking and the new banking houses managed to thrive wherever trade happened to flourish. At major cities such as Venice, Florence, and Augsburg, institutions of banking prospered due to their financing of international trade and their direct lending to both the Church and the state. The Bank of Deposit in Barcelona, established in 1401, and the Casa di San Giorgio in Genoa, founded in 1407, are two early examples of financial institutions that emerged during this transitional period to help facilitate the rapidly growing monetary demands brought on by the maturing of European trade.

TWO

In Search of Cathay

Prince Henry the Navigator

THE TAKING OF CEUTA

An uprising against Islamic rule, which first erupted in the late 10th century, gradually led to the reclamation of a large strip of land along the Atlantic Coast of the Iberian Peninsula that, by the mid-13th century, evolved into the independent Christian nation of Portugal. Suffering from a lack of natural resources and finding itself blocked off from the rest of Europe by Moorish borders, the tiny kingdom of Portugal turned to the sea for its livelihood. Finding its natural harbors ideally positioned for probing the waters of both the Atlantic Ocean and the Mediterranean Sea, bold Portuguese mariners ventured further and further out to sea.

As a means to open up new trade opportunities for his kingdom, as well as an excuse to launch another religious offensive against the much hated Moors, John I, king of Portugal, sanctioned the plans for a massive assault along the nearby northern coast of Africa. Their target was the city and seaport of Ceuta, an active Muslim trading center in Morocco located directly across the Strait of Gibraltar. Ceuta was also selected because of its symbolic significance, for this was where, in the year 711 , the armies of the Moors had gathered in preparation for their full-scale invasion of the Iberian Peninsula.

Since the element of surprise was to be their great weapon of advantage over the Moors, the plans for the invasion of Ceuta had to be completed in utmost secrecy. To conceal their true intentions from the rest of the world

33

King John let it be known that he was steadily building up his forces in preparation for war against the Dutch in retaliation for atrocities allegedly committed against Portuguese merchants in Holland. King John had sent advance word of his little ruse to Prince William of Holland, who willingly agreed to participate in his plot to capture the North African port city.

The opportunity to learn more about the city of Ceuta's strengths and weaknesses unexpectedly presented itself when the widowed queen of Sicily expressed an interest in forming a mutually rewarding marital alliance with Prince Duarte, the future heir to the throne of Portugal. In response to the queen's sudden romantic overture, King John sent two emissaries to her by ship with a counteroffer of marriage to the younger Prince Pedro, his second born son, knowing full well that such a union would be of no interest to this highly ambitious queen. On the way to Sicily the two Portuguese galleys put in at Ceuta's port, and while anchored there the two ambassadors took careful note of the city's design, with particular attention being paid to the defensive structure and the visible military might of this Moorish settlement by the sea. After having obtained as much information as they could without arousing the suspicion of the Moors, the king's emissaries continued on to Sicily, where, as expected, the queen promptly rejected their proposal of Pedro's hand in marriage. Her refusal allowed the two agents to return at once to Portugal. Once back home the two spies met in private with the king and members of his courtly counsel and, with the aid of some sand and a handful of beans, they constructed a remarkably accurate model of the peninsula where Ceuta stood as well as a detailed layout of the city which the king sought to conquer.

Assisting in the planning of this military campaign and actively participating in the subsequent invasion was young Prince Henry, the third son of King John I. Prince Henry, like most noble sons of that age, received extensive tutoring in both the classical arts and the strategies of military engagement, but it was the teaching of Christianity that proved to be the true passion of this immensely pious prince. Anxious to prove his worth as a crusader for the Christian cause and eager to earn the respect of his beloved father, the twenty-one-year old Henry ignored the privileges of noble birth and volunteered to lead the fleet that was anchored at Oporto. Prince Pedro was given command of the fleet docked at Lisbon. As for the eldest son, Prince Duarte, he was to remain behind to rule Portugal while his father, King John, personally led the gallant assault against the Moors of Ceuta.

Three years of intricate planning and careful organizing were to pass before King John decided that the time was right to launch his ambitious Enterprise of Ceuta. The Portuguese fleet was ready to set sail on July 10,

1415, but news of the queen's illness brought a sudden halt to the planned invasion. The dreaded plague had invaded the city with a devastating impact and counted among its many victims was Philippa of Lancaster, wife to King John I and mother of the six royal siblings. Queen Philippa's dying wish was that her husband and sons continue with the Enterprise of Ceuta. Ten days later, on July 25, Saint James' Day, an imposing Portuguese armada of four hundred ships with several thousand Christian soldiers aboard sailed down the Tagus River and passed a throng of patriotic citizens who had assembled along the docks to cheer their naval force on to victory against the Dutch. After sailing past the rocky promontory of Cape St. Vincent the fleet anchored at the nearby port of Lagos to take on additional provisions. It was during their brief stopover at Lagos that the Portuguese troops were finally made aware of the true purpose of their mission—to wage a holy war against the Moors of North Africa.

The Portuguese armada sailed from the port of Lagos on the 30th of July. While the bellies of their boats were loaded with essential supplies for waging war the thoughts of the men were filled with expectations of reaching the port of Ceuta within only a few days. Unfortunately for them, the wind refused to cooperate with their plans and the mighty Portuguese fleet drifted aimlessly atop calm waters for nearly a week before finally catching hold of a favorable blast of wind that put them back on course. The fleet was within striking distance of Ceuta by the second week of August but the strong currents of those waters broke up their formation so badly that the armada was forced to return to the Bay of Gibraltar in order to regroup. However, the sight of so many Portuguese vessels had not gone unnoticed by Sala-ben-Sala, the governor of Ceuta. Convinced that an invasion was under way, the governor immediately dispatched messengers to the rulers of neighboring towns and tribes with urgent pleas for their assistance against the Christian invaders. When he saw that the Portuguese ships were drifting back out to sea, Sala-ben-Sala, believing that Ceuta was no longer at risk, canceled his call for reinforcements.

Not until the next to last day of August, a day when the weather finally cooperated with their plans, could the Portuguese armada begin to maneuver into position for its assault against the fortress of Ceuta. While the main body of the fleet attacked from along the west side of the bay, Prince Henry's squadron of more than forty ships moved surreptitiously up the eastern side of the Moor's defenses. Having regained the essential element of surprise the Christian invaders were able to quickly rout the much smaller Islamic faction that guarded the city of Ceuta. When it became obvious that his city was about to fall into the hands of the enemy, Sala-ben-Sala and several of his officers escaped capture by sneaking out a secret back gate.

By that afternoon the Portuguese had succeeded in gaining control of much of the city and the victors took great delight in ransacking the vast storehouse of treasures that had been left behind. The victory at Ceuta was cause for much celebration for King John and his sons: Besides having granted them the strength to conquer so quickly what was long thought to have been an impregnable Moorish stronghold, God had graciously provided them with the great privilege of being able to slay a vast number of infidels in the process. Their conquest of Ceuta was so swift and complete that the Portuguese suffered the loss of only eight men during this military campaign. While he certainly took great delight in the spiritual rewards of such a glorious triumph, Prince Henry looked around him and saw the even greater material rewards that Ceuta had to offer his homeland.

The city of Ceuta had been an entrepot for Islamic merchants and traders for as long as anyone in that region could remember. Large caravans of camels, often extending for many miles in length, trudged across the hot "sea of sand" known as the Sahara, each carrying on their backs the fabulous cargoes of exotic items obtained from far off lands. Many of these commodities were unloaded at Ceuta where they then became part of the inventory for the estimated twenty thousand-plus trade shops that were crammed within the walls of the city. Pepper, cloves, and cinnamon were but a sampling of the many spices that arrived there on a regular basis. Fine silks, intricately designed tapestries, and beautifully woven carpets could be seen just about everywhere in the city. But it was Ceuta's magnificent stores of gold, silver, and precious gems that formed a lasting impression in the minds of most of the Portuguese soldiers and sailors. Unfortunately for the conquerors, once the Christian flag of Portugal wavered over their new city, the caravans of trade simply stopped coming to Ceuta. Instead of treasures streaming into the royal coffers of Portugal money steadily flowed out as the city of Ceuta required the constant protection of a garrison consisting of 3,000 troops. Three years after Ceuta had fallen into the hands of the Christians the Moors launched their own offensive to recapture the city that was presently under the command of Dom Pedro de Menezes. Though greatly outnumbered, his garrison managed to hold off their attackers until relief arrived from Portugal, and together they were able to send the forces of Islam into full retreat.

During his brief stay at Ceuta, Prince Henry learned a great deal about Arab commerce in North Africa. Through gathered intelligence from local traders and merchants, Henry was able to get a much clearer picture of just where these rare goods came from and how they actually got to their destinations. The prince heard intriguing tales of a marvelous city called Timbuktu, a center of great cultural and commercial importance located somewhere near the southern edge of the Sahara. He also learned of a place called Senegal, a vast West African coastal region that supplied most of North Africa with enormous quantities of gold, ivory, and slaves. As fascinating as these stories sounded to him, none succeeded in capturing Henry's attention more than the report of a mysterious land to the east purportedly ruled by a very wealthy Christian king. This clearly could be none other than the legendary Prester John, the powerful ruler who was waging a holy war to preserve the Christian faith in a land surrounded by a multitude of infidels. The young prince was tempted to lead his own expedition to find and join forces with him, but he was brought to his senses by the sobering realization that he did not know where such a journey might lead. Shortly thereafter, at his father's behest, Prince Henry reluctantly returned to Portugal.

THE SCHOOL OF SAGRES

Following the triumphant return home of his conquering son an elated and proud King John publicly rewarded Prince Henry's heroism with a knighthood, the governorship of the southern province of Algarve, and an appointment as grand master of the Order of Christ. The experience of the Ceuta expedition had matured young Prince Henry well beyond men of similar age. Proving himself to be a man of extraordinary vision, Henry abandoned, for a time, the ways of the noble warrior and set his sights instead on discovering a direct sea route to the lands that were home to the fine silk cloths and fragrant spices he had seen while stationed at Ceuta. He had the utmost faith that such an effort would also eventually uncover the whereabouts of the legendary Christian realm thought to exist somewhere to the east. Prince Henry was convinced that once his armies were joined with the armies of Prester John then the forces of Christianity would finally be strong enough to purge the Holy Land of its Muslim occupants.

Prince Henry also had a keen interest in locating any lands that might lie westward across the vast and unknown waters of the Atlantic. Such curiosity took root from the often repeated tale of seven devout Catholic bishops who had set out to sea in a desperate effort to escape the ongoing conquest of Hispania by the invading legions of zealous marauding Moors. The legend told of how each bishop brought along a substantial number of his most faithful and wealthy followers, and together they sailed across the vast uncharted breadth of the Atlantic Ocean until they finally came upon an idyllic land they christened Antilla. Here, it was said, each bishop founded his own city. Over time, those seven cities grew greater in stature and grandeur with each subsequent telling of the tale.

Sometime between the years 1418 and 1419, Prince Henry granted to two of his most faithful squires, João Gonçalves Zarco and Tristão Naz Teixeira, royal permission to search along the coast of Africa for the legendary land of gold known as Guinea, a name that Portuguese explorers commonly applied to the entire western coast of Africa. Thrown off course by contrary winds, their expedition happened upon a cluster of small islands near to the northwest coast of the African continent. Collectively, they became known as the Madeira Islands. The island they landed upon and christened as Porto Santo was chosen simply because it appeared to be the most suitable of the three for docking. After a brief bit of reconnoitering Zarco and Teixeira sailed back to Sagres to inform Prince Henry of their unexpected discovery. Envisioning these remote islands as a port of call for future Portuguese voyages along the coast of Africa, Henry encouraged both men to return to Porto Santo as quickly as possible. After receiving permission from the Crown, the two adventurers set sail once again, this time with three ships, a large group of eager settlers, and all the supplies necessary for establishing a permanent colony at Porto Santo. Also joining them on this major expedition was a gentlemen sailor by the name of Bartholomew Perestrello.

Upon their return to the Madeira Islands, Zarco and Teixeira formally laid claim to these remote lands in the name of Portugal and then founded a small settlement at Porto Santo. Unfortunately for these would-be settlers, a disaster came to pass that originated from a highly unusual and entirely unexpected circumstance. Included among the many animals brought aboard ship for the express purpose of stocking this barren island was a pregnant rabbit that Bartholomew Perestrello had received as a parting gift, and during the crossing she gave birth to a rather large litter. Once on land Perestrello's rabbits did what rabbits do best and before long the small island was overrun with these furry little creatures. Feasting on the vegetation of the island, the rapidly multiplying population of rabbits displayed a particular fondness for the carefully planted crops of the colonists. The settlers did everything they could to rid themselves of their initially invited guests, but the situation quickly grew out of control. After two years of constant struggle it became painfully clear to both Zarco, Teixeira, and even Perestrello that the rapidly expanding population of rabbits posed a very real threat to the colony's hopes for survival. The decision was then made to abandon the settlement at Porto Santo and to return at once to the safe haven of Portugal.

After conferring at great length with his two disillusioned captains, Prince Henry, who was still convinced of the strategic importance of these remote locations, persuaded them to make another attempt at settling the island of Porto Santo. They returned for a third time in June of 1424 but after having discerned that the rabbit situation had only worsened during their brief absence the captains decided to try their luck at the much larger neighboring island. They found this island to be entirely devoid of any animal life except for a large population of migratory birds. Many of the colonists thought it only appropriate that the island should be named in honor of its sole inhabitants, but after having noticed how "heavily wooded" the island was, the leaders of the expedition opted to christen their new colony Madeira. News of their decision to establish a colony at Madeira as opposed to Porto Santo was immediately dispatched to Prince Henry who, in turn, showed his appreciation and admiration for their perseverance by sending three more ships loaded with more colonists. Many of these settlers happened to be prisoners who were granted a royal pardon for their past crimes on the condition that they assist in the settlement of Madeira. Agricultural supplies such as seeds, plants, tools, and farm animals essential to the success of this colonial venture were also shipped to the colony.

Clearing the dense forest in order that the land might better suit their own purpose proved to be a more daunting task than they had envisioned. To expedite the process the decision was made to burn away the enormous mounds of fallen leaves that littered the ground as well as the multitude of trees from which they fell. But with the trees being bunched so close together the flames easily leapt from the limbs of one tree and on to the branches of another and before long their seemingly simple deforestation plan was burning out of control and threatening to undo all that they had achieved. It has been reported that the blaze burned with such intense brightness that it could be seen for many miles out to sea. Left unchallenged this conflagration continued to burn, though confined to certain pockets of the island, for several more years. While the immediate effect of this terrible and destructive fire was a vast trail of charred smoldering wasteland, the passage of time showed that the blaze was a wonderful blessing in disguise. Once the scorched land had cooled the colonists found the soil to be so rich and fertile that it would now grow just about anything they cared to plant. The introduction of sugar cane from Sicily enabled Madeira to become the leading supplier of sugar for the markets of Europe; the Malvoisie grape from Crete made it possible for the settlers to produce the sweet wine that the island is now famous for; the island's natural abundance of wood helped to serve the supply needs of the Portuguese ship building industry; and an indigenous red resin known as dragon's blood became a much sought-after dye for the garment trade.

Following the success of the Madeira expedition Prince Henry then turned his attention further to the west toward a group of islands that had appeared on Italian maps dating as far back as 1351. To satisfy his own curiosity, Henry sent forth Gonzalo Cabral, a veteran sailor and close friend, to locate what he suspected was either the Isles of St. Brendan or the islands where the legendary Seven Cities dwelt. Sailing due west Cabral happened upon islands at the very spot where they had expected to find land but these islands turned out to be nothing more than desolate rocks floating conspicuously atop the ocean's surface. The pounding surf prevented any possibility of their coming ashore, and even if they could have landed, the Formigas Rocks were too barren and inhospitable to support any sort of settlement. Returning at once to Portugal, Cabral informed Prince Henry of his disappointing discovery. Convinced that these legendary islands did in fact exist, and believing that Cabral had simply not sailed far enough, he exhorted his friend to sail once more in the same general direction. Cabral set sail once again in 1433 and after having ventured nearly eight hundred miles further out into the uncharted waters of the Atlantic the captain and his crew came upon the island of Santa Maria, one of the islands of the Azores. According to some historical accounts, a Portuguese pilot by the name of Diogo de Silves had discovered the Azores as early as 1427, but the fact remains that it was Gonzalo Cabral who charted, claimed, and colonized this small archipelago for Portugal. The Azores were similar to the Madeira Islands in the respect that no animal life could be found there other than for the large flocks of migratory birds that temporarily called the islands their home. Because these islands were so far out to sea, Henry decided to draw from the rabbit experience at Porto Santo and, for the time being, simply colonized them with a large variety of domesticated animals. Left free to multiply in the wild it was hoped that the livestock would become plentiful enough to serve as feast for famished sailors returning from their African expeditions as well as for a future planned colony there, a venture which Henry permitted Cabral to undertake in 1439. Disappointed that he could not find any sign of the fabled Seven Cities, Henry abandoned his western quest and instead focused all his time and energy on locating an eastern route to the Orient.

Desiring to establish a base nearer to the western coast of Africa, Prince Henry dispatched the sailor Fernando de Castro on an expedition to explore and settle a group of islands just to the south of the Madeira Islands. The Canaries had been known to the Romans as early as 40 B.C. and the island of Hierro, the farthest westward point of land then known to Europeans, was later depicted on the ancient maps of Ptolemy (a Greco-Roman scholar whose theories on world geography had a profound impact on medieval thought) as the earth's prime meridian. After the fall of the Roman Empire these remote islands were entirely forgotten until their accidental rediscovery in A.D. 1312 by Lanzaroto Malocello, a Genoan merchant en route to France to ply his trade. When Fernando de Castro reached the largest of the Canary Islands, aptly named the Grand Canary, he found the primitive inhabitants to be extremely hostile towards his efforts to come ashore. After taking into account their aggressive nature and the fact that they greatly outnumbered his crew the captain wisely chose to abandon any thoughts of establishing a settlement at this location. The king of Castile soon learned of Portugal's efforts to settle the islands that had been awarded to his province in 1344 by Pope Clement IV and he immediately registered a complaint with His Holiness. The ownership of the island continued to be a disputed topic for many years to come, but in the end the Canary Islands remained a prized possession of Spain while Portugal was granted a conciliatory right of passage along the sea lanes that bordered the Canaries. Portugal continued its colonization of Madeira and the Azores, and both island groups were to play an important role as part of an elaborate pipeline of supply bases for future expeditions along the coast of Africa.

After retiring to Algrave, the province which he henceforth presided over, Prince Henry immediately put into motion the founding of an observatory that would one day serve as a center for his ongoing navigational studies. At Sagres Point, a spot ideally situated at the Cape of Saint Vincent, a small promontory that juts a considerable distance out into the Atlantic Ocean, Henry began the construction of a chapel and observatory that eventually evolved into a makeshift school for navigational studies. The Villa de Infante was designed to Henry's precise specifications and paid for from both his personal fortune and the considerable resources of the Order of Christ. Once completed, Sagres Point became, along with the nearby town of Lagos, home to a great number of astronomers, cartographers, shipbuilders, sailors, mathematicians, and anyone else who could contribute to improvements in matters of maritime affairs. At Sagres, scientific purpose, commercial necessity, and religious faith combined to form a national enterprise intent upon reaching the Indies. History would later reward Prince Henry's contribution to this renewed interest in exploration and the subsequent discoveries it yielded by crowning him Henry the Navigator.

Henry and his assemblage of sea scholars found themselves confronted with a vast number of obstacles, all of which combined to make their Herculean task all the more difficult. Besides having to overcome age-old superstitions, which tended to cloud the minds of most sailors of that era, they were forced to rely on ancient teachings that shaped the present view of the world. A European's knowledge of the land was often restricted to his own borders, and the sea was an even larger mystery, with most sailors fearing to sail beyond the sight of the coastline. It was the nation of Italy, once the epicenter of civilization, that stood at the forefront of Europe's great

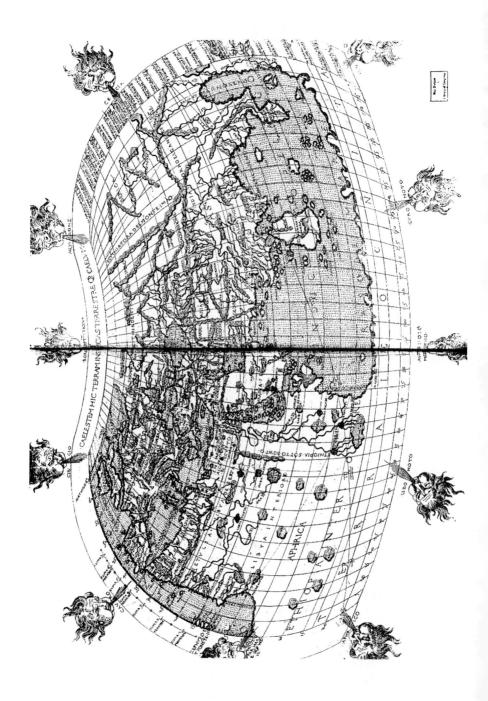

awakening—a period of intellectual rebirth we have come to know as the Renaissance. For quite some time, Italian scholars had been journeying to the city of Constantinople to study directly from the manuscripts that stored the classical writings of the ancient Greek and Roman civilizations. The knowledge they acquired at Constantinople and the books they brought back with them helped to revive European interest in the world that surrounded them.

The teachings of the Greek philosopher and scientist Aristotle had a profound impact upon the fertile minds of European scholars separated by an ocean of time. Geographers, sailors, rulers, merchants, along with any others who dreamed of the vast riches of the Indies, took great delight in Aristotle's statement: "Between the end of Spain and the beginning of India lies a narrow sea that can be sailed in a few days." Aristotle also proposed that the earth was a sphere, an idea believed to have been first advanced by the renowned Greek mathematician Pythagoras in the 6th century B.C.

It was, however, the rediscovery in 1406 of the various works of a noted Greek astronomer, mathematician, and geographer by Renaissance scholars that greatly stirred the imaginations of curious Europeans the most. Claudius Ptolemaeus, better known to his newly found students simply as Ptolemy, was born in Egypt during the 2nd century A.D. and spent most of his life as a resident of the great city of Alexandria. This cosmopolitan city founded by Alexander the Great, a former student of Aristotle, during his military campaign to conquer all of the known world, had become a vast storehouse for the accumulated knowledge of the ancient world, especially following the establishment of the famous Library of Alexandria. It was here that Ptolemy was provided access to the geographic treatise of Eratosthenes, the celestial studies of Hipparachus, and the voluminous recorded observations of the worldly traveler Strabo.

Drawing from the knowledge of those who had come before him, Ptolemy extrapolated conclusions that would become the basis for his lengthy eight volume *Geographia*. Within those tomes he theorized that the earth's surface was equally divided between land and water. In Ptolemy's world there were but three massive continents and one immense ocean extending to the west, which separated Europe from Asia. Since the Bible stipulated that there were but three continents on earth the existence of a fourth land

Opposite: **Francesco Berlingheri's 1482 rendition of Ptolemy's world map: Since none of Ptolemy's maps survived the ravages of time, European mapmakers had to reconstruct his maps from the vivid descriptions contained in his book.**

mass was an inconceivable concept to most scholars. His map showed the continent of Africa to be a land formation of enormous width and with no visible end to its length—a disconcerting prospect to a future generation of explorers. Though flawed by a lack of accurate cartographic data, his maps and their accompanying descriptions gave Europeans a first glimpse of a world that was completely foreign to them. His work was directly responsible for the launching of a great number of voyages of exploration, which, in the process of discovery, exposed the many errors of Ptolemy's concepts.

There was another ancient tale which lent credence to the idea that the riches of Asia could easily be reached by rounding the coast of Africa. The Greek historian Herodotus, who is generally regarded as the father of history, recounted the story of how a fleet of Phoenician ships had succeeded in finding a way around the extreme southern tip of the Dark Continent. Commissioned by the ambitious Egyptian King Neco, the Phoenician fleet set sail sometime between 616 and 600 B.C. These same ships returned three years later to tell of how they had managed to reach an unknown location along Africa's distant eastern shores. While Herodotus had his own doubts about whether such a voyage ever occurred he still felt it warranted inclusion in his massive work which he titled *History*.

These ancient teachings, which had only recently enlightened and propelled much of Europe into a new age of awareness, had long been available to the inhabitants of the Iberian Peninsula. Long before the works of the classical writers were translated into Latin these same writings had already been copied into Arabic and circulated freely among the scholars of the Islamic realms. Much of this knowledge accompanied the armies of the Moors when they crossed the Strait of Gibraltar to land upon the shores of Hispania. Following the subjugation of the Iberian Peninsula, the Moors passed onto the conquered barbarians their extensive knowledge of geography, mathematics, science, and the art of navigation. Thus, Portugal and Spain learned valuable lessons that were to provide them with a distinct advantage over their neighboring European nations.

Prince Henry's shipbuilders at Lagos experimented with a number of designs that drew from the very best features of European and Mediterranean craft currently in use. They sought to build a ship that could withstand the rigors commonly associated with a lengthy voyage at sea and their efforts were eventually rewarded with the construction of a new style of vessel expressly designed to meet the needs of the adventurous seafarer. Radical in design yet economical in features, the sleek caravel stood in stark contrast to the cumbersome cargo ships of that period. Lighter in weight, this ship was capable of traveling at greater speeds and its reduced tonnage allowed it to probe closer along an unfamiliar coast or sail further into an unknown estuary. An adjustable rigging design made the caravel a very versatile vessel, one capable of sailing directly into the wind while still maintaining some degree of control over its course. It was a handy design that proved essential for sailing against the prevailing winds of the African coast on their return voyages of discovery. Initially, this compact vessel could comfortably accommodate a small crew of between fourteen and sixteen and could hold enough supplies below its deck to sustain them on a voyage of considerable length. Over time, the caravel grew in size to accommodate even larger crews and bigger cargoes.

All pertinent geographical, astronomical, and navigational data was accumulated, compiled, and cataloged at Sagres. This knowledge was used by cartographers and ship captains to chart their planned routes of exploration. Techniques in celestial navigation were constantly being refined. The savants at Sagres came up with a great many devices that would aid the seaman on his long voyage, the most important of which was the quadrant, an instrument that helped sailors determine their present position in relation to the heavens above. The position of the stars and the designated names of their specific groupings enabled navigators to pinpoint their location in the water with a considerable degree of accuracy.

Sailors were able to determine their direction at sea with the aid of the trusty mariner's compass. A vessel's location at sea was calculated by determining both latitude and longitude—earthly degrees of measurement that had been previously established by the Greek astronomer Hipparchus. On a starry night sailors could fix their latitude with relative accuracy by the use of an astrolabe, a complex instrument that helped a skilled sailor to deduce his location by his relation to the current position of the celestial bodies, the pole star being the benchmark for the Portuguese navigators. By day, the sun's declination could reveal the present degree of latitude. Calculating longitude was, however, an entirely different matter, as navigators did their best to turn guesswork into a more exact science. Time was kept with the aid of a trustworthy sandglass, often referred to as the hourglass, though on most voyages the half-hour glass, also known as an ampoletta, was the instrument of choice. Speed and distance were estimated at a rate and measurement that drew upon the experience and skill of either the captain or the navigator.

Prince Henry required every one of his daring explorers to keep detailed and accurate records of all that they saw and experienced, including matters that may have seemed trivial at the time. Inching along Africa's foreboding shoreline, Portuguese sailors charted every nook and cranny until they finally formed a fairly accurate outline of the coast. In their logbooks they kept track of which way the winds blew and noted the general

Prince Henry the Navigator: The absolute determination of this pious prince to find a path to the wealth of the Indies and the legendary realm of Prester John set the course for the ensuing European age of exploration.

locations, times, and lengths of these gusts. This gathered information helped the cartographers at Sagres to map the trade winds, those streams of air that allowed captains to navigate their vessels to faraway places. Under Prince Henry's guidance navigation was elevated to an exact science and pilotage became a highly skilled and much respected profession.

TERRA INCOGNITA

Perhaps the greatest challenge faced by Prince Henry and his scholars at Sagres was finding a way to overcome the common man's fear of the great unknown. Educated men knew for a fact that the earth was round but very few men of this era benefited from any formal education. Sailors, an illiterate lot for the most part, believed in what they saw with their own eyes, what they heard with their own ears, and what they could touch with their own hands, and these observations often conflicted with the educated person's perception of the world.

The superstitious mind of this era was extremely susceptible to the conjured image of uncharted waters where terrifying sea monsters lurked or of unexplored lands where unsightly beasts freely roamed. Sailors heard tales of a "Green Sea of Darkness" just beyond the shores of Morocco. It was said that this inhospitable body of water was shrouded in a permanent fog and was home to numerous sea monsters who enjoyed feasting upon any ships that dared to enter their private domain. This sea supposedly contained fish large enough to swallow a ship whole, and even if sailors were lucky enough to avoid these horrible creatures they were sure to be at the mercy of the schools of roaming sea serpents. These giant beasts of the deep were said to measure hundreds of feet in length and to be capable of crushing even the mightiest vessel in just a matter of minutes. A great many of these sea fables were merely the clever imaginings of Arab merchants who desired to keep the curious Europeans at bay with tales tailored to instill fear. The less Europeans knew about the ocean the better it was for Arab traders who had already mastered much of the known sea.

All directions of travel contained their own unique forms of barriers; some were real, others were imagined. Europeans knew that the rich lands of Cathay and Cipangu lay somewhere to the east, and alongside them were the many islands that produced the aromatic and flavorful spices they craved so greatly. But ever since the collapse of the Mongol empire Christian merchants had no longer had direct access to these bountiful regions. To the west they had discovered the Azores but beyond that there was a vast ocean containing unknown lands that were believed to be inhabited by grotesque creatures. To the north lay a frozen wasteland where the betrayer Judas Iscariot guarded a gateway to hell. A voyage to the south became increasingly difficult as one came closer the equatorial line. It was generally accepted as fact that under the burning sun of the Torrid Zone, land turned to desert, a man's skin broiled until it faded to black, and the sea evaporated into an impassable swamp of tar. Even if one somehow succeeded in getting past the many dangers of the equator, what were the chances of surviving down under in lands populated by creatures who possessed the uncanny ability to walk upside down? To many this was simply a world without end and anyone foolish enough to venture too far out to sea might not be fortunate enough to find his way back home.

There did exist a basis of fact which made even the most learned men of medieval Europe believe that there were such strange lands inhabited by hordes of bizarre and terrifying creatures. The Roman scientist and historian Gaius Plinius Secundus, better known as Pliny the Elder, wrote the thirty-seven volume *Natural History* that was a well known source of study for many scholars. Pliny had recorded for posterity an encyclopedia of all known facts about the geography of the earth as well as the many myths that substituted as fact for that which remained unknown. Pliny wrote of a place called All-ears Islands, so named because its many inhabitants were endowed with ears so large they covered their entire bodies. He also wrote of a tribe that lived in the deserts, whose faces were freakishly embedded in their chests. In addition to the strange people that inhabited these far-away places, Gaius Pliny also described the even stranger animals that shared these lands. There was the griffin, a winged beast possessed of a head and wings similar to those of an eagle which were attached to a body resembling, in size and shape, that of a lion. In the distant Indian Ocean, the historian pointed out that a seafarer was sure to come across enormous turtles with shells so large they were commonly used as roofs for Indian homes or as sailing crafts for transporting goods and people.

The Catholic Church also played a prominent role in promulgating many of these fables, legends, and myths that freely circulated throughout Europe. During the so-called Dark Ages of Europe the Church expunged the teachings of civilizations that were ignorant of the God of the Christians. Ancient pagan knowledge of the known world was suddenly replaced by Catholic orthodoxy, but speculation and rumors still persisted. There was widespread belief in the existence of a mysterious region to the south of the equator known as the Antipodes. In these lands there lived the headless men whose faces were embedded in their chests; beasts with the body of a man and the head of a dog; and a bizarre creature known as a Uniped who hopped around on one enormous leg with a foot that was so large he could use it to shade himself while lying down. Unable to quell such superstitious beliefs, the Church simply incorporated those fears into their daily preachings. The Antipodes were alleged to be the Devil's den, a wicked realm inhabited by the abnormal offspring of Lucifer and well beyond the salvation of even God himself.

Such fears and superstitions made it extremely difficult for Prince Henry and his group of daring captains to recruit competent sailors for their voyages of discovery, the routes of which were planned to be along the unexplored western coast of Africa. Cloaked in mystery, Africa was an ominous land known to most men of the sea as the Dark Continent. Fearful sailors of this era did their best to arm themselves with protection against both the many real and imagined dangers of the sea. Many Portuguese sailors would not consider boarding a ship without wearing a talisman known to them as a *feitico* (Portuguese for fabricated), a carved image which was believed to possess magical powers that could ward off any danger; from this name we have formed our own word fetish. Saint Elmo, a Dominican priest who had provided spiritual guidance for the sailors of the Iberian Peninsula during the 12th century, was the anointed saint of those who ventured out to sea. The magical appearance of St. Elmo's fire, a glowing halo derived from the static electricity of a thunderstorm and often visible from the mast or yardarms of a ship, helped to reassure sailors that they had not been forsaken during their hour of need. Protection from harm also came from Saint Clare, Saint Nicholas, and the Virgins of the Conception of Fair Weather at Sea.

Prince Henry was determined to find a passage, either through or around Africa, that would deposit his ships on the other side of the world. His resolve became ever stronger after his brother Pedro, while on a visit to the city of Venice, obtained for him a copy of Marco Polo's engaging tale of adventure in Asia and the Far East, as well as a copy of the map that accurately plotted the course of the famed explorer. Rumors of a great river to the south of Africa, which supposedly emptied enormous quantities of gold into the Atlantic Ocean, encouraged Prince Henry to dispatch one ship after another to confirm the existence of such a golden depository. Fifteen expeditions ventured forth only to return with fifteen excuses as to why they could not round the ominous Cape Bojador, a point just to the south of Morocco. Captain Gil Eannes had been the last to try, and in his official report in 1433 to the prince, he stated that because of the region's extremely rough waters and dangerously rocky coastline Cape Bojador was simply impassable. Finding the captain's excuses entirely unacceptable, Prince Henry ordered him to return to the cape and further instructed him to not even consider returning home until he had succeeded in finding a way around that southern point.

Captain Eannes set sail once more in 1434. Upon his return to Cape Bojador he again encountered one frustrating setback after another in his effort to pass this difficult point. On his fifth attempt to round the cape he decided to try an unconventional approach: instead of sailing close to the shoreline, where he was at the mercy of the treacherous coastal currents, he took his ship far out to sea where the waters were somewhat calmer. Piloting his ship southward in a wide arc he managed to land approximately one hundred miles south of the dreaded cape, at a spot somewhere along the parched shores of the Sahara. Though elated by their amazing achievement Eannes and his crew surely must have been disturbed by the barren sight that stood before them—an ominous sign that perhaps the sun did in fact scorch all the land and dry up all the waters along the equator. Gil Eannes and his wary crew pushed southward for nearly another fifty miles at which point they were greatly relieved by the sight of a far more attractive and verdant land. After scooping up samples of the rich soil and uprooting various specimens of the local vegetation, Eannes and his elated crew sailed back to Portugal.

The glad tidings of Gil Eannes' successful voyage was a truly momentous occasion for Prince Henry. Not only had these brave sailors accomplished what no other Portuguese sailor had been able to do previously, their journey also helped put to rest a number of fears his sailors had about the Dark Continent. Both congratulations and monetary rewards were in store for Captain Eannes, but on short notice Henry ordered him back out to sea once again, this time in the company of Afonso Gonçalves Baldia. According to the court historian Gomes de Azurara, the prince told his bold explorers: "As you have found traces of men and camels (footprints in the sand) it is clear that the inhabited region cannot be far off. Therefore

I intend to send you there again, so that you can do me service and increase your honor, and to this end I order you to go as far as you can and try to gain an interpreter from among those people. It will not be a small gain if we can get someone to give us some tidings of the land." After sailing to Cape Bojador, Baldia broke away to lead his own expedition which eventually, in the year 1436, reached as far as Pedra de Gale. After this voyage of discovery their was a break in Portuguese explorations that lasted for nearly six years. Henry and his faithful sailors had made great strides along the coast of Africa but so far those voyages had failed to discover anything of material value, and because of this fact there were many at court, including his own brother Duarte, who questioned whether it was worth continuing with these expensive voyages.

In August of 1433, shortly before his earthly reign came to an end, King John beseeched his sons to take up the Christian cause once more by leading another crusade against the Moors of North Africa. While Portugal may have still controlled the city of Ceuta it was the Moors who clearly held sway over trade in and around that region. Their strategically placed posts effectively barred all African trade from the city that the Christians had conquered. If that blockade could somehow be broken then Portugal would be in a position to finally tap into the vast wealth of trade that traveled across Africa by way of caravan. The eldest son, Duarte, and his younger brothers, Pedro, Henry, and Fernando, had every intention of honoring their father's final wish but all agreed to postpone such a massive undertaking until they felt the moment was right.

On August 22, 1437, at the behest of their older brother Duarte, who was now the king of Portugal, Henry and Fernando departed from Lisbon at the helm of an impressive Portuguese armada. Sailing across the Strait of Gibraltar, the fleet arrived at Ceuta five days later where they soon met up with the rest of their armed force. The object of their desire this time around was the city of Tangier, a Moorish stronghold lying just to the west of Ceuta. However, the two commanders were disappointed to learn that the force of 15,000 soldiers they had been promised for the invasion was short by approximately 4,500 men. Many of the officers felt that this army was simply too small for a mission as large and as important as this and therefore pleaded with their royal commanders to delay the assault until reinforcements were able to arrive from Portugal. But believing guidance and deliverance would come from above, Prince Henry overruled the objections of his concerned officers.

On the 9th of September, following several days of delay, the Christian soldiers finally began their march toward Tangier. Four grueling days later the entire Portuguese army stood before the gates of the city. Unfortunately for the Christian soldiers, they had now lost the all-important element of surprise. The debate at Ceuta regarding which course of action to take had given the Moors ample time to strengthen Tangier's defenses. When the orders to attack were issued, both Henry and Fernando watched in disbelief as wave after wave of their troops were repulsed by a seemingly impenetrable city wall. Successive assaults proved futile against the staunch defense being put on by the Moors, and in this war of attrition the numbers greatly favored those defending the city. Remembering their success at Ceuta, the Portuguese had planned on and prepared for a quick and decisive conquest. When the battle dragged on into the month of October, the invaders discovered that their precious supplies of food and munitions were dwindling even faster than the numbers in their ranks. The Moors were well aware of the precarious predicament of the Portuguese invaders, and with the tables now turned against him, Henry found himself in the embarrassing position of receiving terms for his immediate surrender from the very forces he had sought to conquer. Prince Henry was told that his remaining soldiers would be allowed to return to Portugal once they promised to lay down their arms, agreed to the release of all Moorish comrades imprisoned both there and abroad, and pledged to surrender the city of Ceuta. At first Prince Henry scoffed at their preposterous proposals, but these conditions became easier to accept once their precious food and water had completely disappeared. Realizing that his situation had become untenable, Prince Henry, on the 16th of October, agreed to all of their terms for surrender. While the Moors allowed the Christian invaders to board their vessels unharmed they could not, however, resist the temptation of a final farewell assault waged more for insult than injury.

To ensure that the Portuguese honored all the terms of this agreement, the Moors stipulated that Prince Fernando was to remain behind as a hostage. Henry had offered to take his brother's place but his officers, and even Fernando, persuaded him to think otherwise. Accompanied by what little remained of his defeated army, Prince Henry sailed back to Ceuta, but once there he had a sudden change of heart and refused to surrender the city back to the Moors, a decision which he justified by averring that "It belongs to God." By reneging on his agreement with the Moors, Henry had condemned his own brother to a lifelong sentence of hard labor and solitary confinement inside a dank Moorish dungeon. This is not to say that Henry made no effort to rescue his brother; in fact, he spent several months at Ceuta trying to raise a ransom for the release of his brother but the Moors made it clear that they would accept nothing less than the keys to the city of Ceuta. Henry returned to Portugal with hopes of raising another army but circumstances at home interfered with his plans for a return to North

Africa. As for Fernando, he was incarcerated at the city of Fez, where he was forced to endure eleven years of deprivation and torture before finally dying.

The devastating defeat at Tangier not only humiliated the noble Prince Henry but it also greatly humbled a proud nation. The problems of Portugal were compounded further by the sudden death of King Duarte in 1438. His six year old son assumed the throne as King Afonso V, with his mother, Queen Leonor, acting as regent. This disruption to the throne forced Prince Henry to attend to numerous affairs at court—a distraction that helps to explain the long gap between expeditions being sent out to probe the coast of Africa. When Pedro, Henry's other older brother, came to power by usurping Queen Leonor's position as regent, he encouraged his brother to return to Sagres so that he might continue with his explorations of the mysterious coast of Africa. Prince Pedro was ousted as regent in 1448 by his political opponents, thereby paving the way for the coronation of Afonso as the new king of Portugal. Pedro passed away one year later, leaving Henry as the sole surviving son of John I. The terrible loss at Tangier would eventually be avenged but not until 1458. In that year a young King Afonso led an imposing armada of 280 ships carrying more than 20,000 troops to a cathartic victory over the Moors. Sailing along as both advisor and interested observer was the king's elderly uncle Henry.

The Dark Continent

PROBING THE GOLD COAST

When the exploration of the African coastline finally resumed in 1441 the explorers sailed aboard the new sleekly designed vessel known as the caravel. Prior to the introduction of this style of ship most of the Portuguese expeditions had been conducted aboard a vessel known as barcha, a relatively small ship which, in addition to its sails, was fitted with oars. It was a caravel that carried Nuno Tristão and his company of men to Cape Bojador; from there they coasted along until they discovered the Bay of Arguin in 1443. While probing a stretch of land between Morocco and Senegal, known as the Rio de Oro, Tristão met up with another expedition led by Captain Antão Gonçalves. Together, these two daring commanders led a shore party on a surprise night raid against an encampment of nearby Arab traders. This Portuguese raid succeeded in capturing all of the personal belongings of these nomadic traders, as well as an African chieftain named Adahu who, along with nine other prisoners, was escorted back to the waiting ships. Following their successful mission it was agreed upon by both captains that Antão Gonçalves would sail back to Portugal, with all the prisoners and plunder they had acquired during this expedition, while Nuno Tristão and his crew pressed on with the exploration of the African coast. Enchanted by the noble demeanor of Chief Adahu the Portuguese crew treated him with the utmost respect during their long voyage home. Gonçalves' return caused quite a commotion at the docks of Lisbon, where large crowds gathered to catch a glimpse of the noble Adahu and the other Negro and Arab prisoners.

During his stay in Portugal, Chief Adahu was accorded all the amenities he required to make his captivity a more pleasurable experience. In return for this kindness, the African chieftain provided his Portuguese captors with a wealth of information pertaining to the extensive trade routes that linked the interior of Africa with the merchants of the Middle East and North Africa. He spoke in great detail about the magnificence of the city of Timbuktu, a place where much of the trade of Africa converged. At Timbuktu, he said, one would find a vast treasure trove of the finest gold Africa had to offer, a great abundance of rare spices and silks from the Far East, and a colossal array of precious gems and jewels collected from all over the world. Adahu's stories of the great wealth that existed in Africa seemed to confirm the tales Prince Henry remembered hearing at Ceuta and therefore strengthened his resolve to find a way to reach these legendary lands. Even though he had been treated well during his time in Portugal, Chief Adahu ached for the sights and sounds of his homeland. The native chief bargained for his return to Africa by offering his captors a promised payment of six Negro slaves in exchange for his freedom and passage back home. Considering all that they had learned from the chieftain, plus the ransom payment he now presented for their approval, Prince Henry and the Crown had no qualms about granting Adahu his request. Captain Gonçalves volunteered to take the noble chief back to the Rio de Oro region along with the other African prisoners he had brought back to Portugal. Once the grateful chief had been returned to his homeland, Gonçalves found that he was willing to part with even more than he had initially bargained for: a hundred African slaves, a number of enormous ostrich eggs, and a fair quantity of gold dust was paid to purchase the freedom of all those who had been captured by the Portuguese.

While these events were transpiring, Captain Nuno Tristão shipped back to Portugal a full boatload of African slaves he had obtained in trade with a number of native tribes along the coast of Cape Branco. These Africans were given a good Christian baptism and then promptly auctioned off to a life of servitude to whoever happened to be the highest bidder. Slavery was a widespread practice amongst many African tribes and Arab communities long before the Portuguese and Spaniards entered into the market, but it was the Iberians who took this barbaric trade to new worlds. In that same year, Prince Henry had been granted a royal charter that entitled him to a monopoly in all Portuguese discoveries made beyond Cape Bojador. Suddenly, the continent of Africa presented an even more enticing prospect, one which could yield the prince a handsome profit. He saw the trade in slaves as a source of revenue that could provide him with capital for future ventures and thereby silence the steady stream of criticism concerning the escalating costs of these expeditions. Unwittingly, Prince Henry, Nuno Tristão, Antão Gonçalves, and Chief Adahu had ushered in one of history's epic tragedies: the European traffic in African slaves.

Fueled by the prospect of earning enormous profits from the sale of human cargo, Prince Henry stepped up the pace of his African explorations. In 1444 alone, three separate expeditions managed to locate and map the islands of Naar and Tider, detect the mouth of the Senegal River, and discover Cape Verde, Africa's westernmost point. The search for Cape Verde was prompted by native tales of greener pastures that lay just to the south of Cape Branco. Up to this point, Portuguese explorers had only viewed a barren desert coastline, but this discovery of vegetation so close to the equator would help dispel the myth that life as they knew it could not possibly exist along the latitudes of the Torrid Zone. With Prince Henry's encouragement Captain Dennis Dias set out from the port of Lagos to learn if these stories were true. It was not until he had sailed well beyond Cape Branco that the sight of jungle vegetation first appeared at the promontory that he would christen Cape Verde, or Green Cape. On that day of discovery, while his ships sailed close to land, a small band of natives who had been watching from ashore jumped into their canoes and began rowing toward the strange sight that had suddenly appeared before them. Once the canoes were alongside their ship the Portuguese sailors reached out and nabbed four of the curious Africans before the rest had time to come to their defense. The remaining natives managed to save themselves from a similar fate by frantically rowing back to the mainland. Captain Dias then returned to Portugal with his prisoners and the glad tidings of greener pastures just beyond Cape Branco. During that same year, Prince Henry strayed from the path of exploration by authorizing an excursion with the sole objective of procuring more slaves to be sold at the auction blocks of Lisbon. Captain Gil Eannes faithfully complied with his royal benefactor's request by returning with a cargo of 235 native Africans.

In the year 1445 Captain Antão Gonçalves returned to Arguin Bay, a spot just south of Cape Branco, with three vessels to discover the whereabouts of a fellow sailor by the name of João Fernandes. Seven months earlier, Gonçalves had granted Fernandes permission to remain behind in order that he might learn more about this mysterious region. As part of a cultural exchange, an elderly Moor, who was eager to satisfy his own curiosity about the homeland of these strangers, was allowed to sail to Portugal with the returning crew. Shortly after Gonçalves and his men set sail for home, the inquisitive Fernandes set off with a friendly desert tribe who had permitted him to accompany them on their travels along the various routes that connected the wealth of West Africa with the lucrative markets of North Africa. While living amongst the nomadic Arabs and Berbers, Fernandes learned that these opportunistic traders were able to obtain most of their necessary provisions and staples by selling captured Africans to the Moors of North Africa.

When the intrepid João Fernandes finally caught up with Antão Gonçalves at Rio de Oro he informed the captain that there was a nearby ruler who was eager to trade goods with the Portuguese. Just as Fernandes had told him, Gonçalves found the local tribal chief willing to part with nine of his Negro slaves and a small amount of gold dust for the usual offering of trinkets that the Portuguese carried with them for this type of trade. While it may have seemed like a small transaction at the time the significance of this trade was not lost on the Portuguese: having stumbled upon gold for the first time in Guinea could only mean that they had finally found a stretch of the celebrated golden trail that had once led Muslim traders directly to the city of Ceuta. Fernandes returned to Portugal to provide Prince Henry with an account of all that he had seen on his extensive travels with the nomads of Africa. His careful and thorough observation of the topography, tribal customs, and trade routes of the western Sahara proved to be invaluable bits of information for future explorers of that region.

By the year 1448 the traffic in African salves had become so large and profitable that Prince Henry ordered the construction of a fortress, which would serve to store and protect their burgeoning commerce in human chattels, on a small island situated near Arguin Bay. Once the Portuguese post was in place at Arguin, Arab merchants and African chieftains traveled from near and far to trade their gold and slaves for a variety of Portuguese goods, with horses and wheat being the most sought after items of exchange. And just how did one measure the worth of a human life during those times? A fully equipped horse in good health could easily fetch a Portuguese trader ten or more healthy African slaves. Commercial intercourse between the nation of Portugal and the kingdoms of Africa would increase greatly during the next decade, especially after Prince Henry began leasing shares of his trade monopoly to enterprising Portuguese merchants in exchange for a hefty percentage of their profits. Regardless of whether they were acquired through way of trade or by means of raids along the coast, African slaves were sent to the trading post at Arguin for processing and from there they were shipped to Portugal for sale in the open market. Exploitation had suddenly taken precedence over exploration. While it is undeniably true that he did profit indirectly from the African slave trade it must be remembered that this pious prince was more concerned with converting "heathens" into "saved" Christians than he was with sentencing them to a life of servitude.

Captain Álvaro Fernandes, a nephew of João Zarco, one of the discoverers of the island of Madeira, extended Portugal's claims well beyond Cape Verde to a point just short of Sierre Leone, a region later known as Portuguese Guinea. His voyage led him to the mouth of a river that he believed to be a tributary of the great Nile River, but what he had actually stumbled upon was a separate river later designated as the Senegal. Since a way around Africa appeared to be beyond the reach of Portuguese ships, many explorers began to think that the more prudent course was to try and find a waterway that cut straight through the Dark Continent. Unfortunately for a great many Portuguese explorers their forays upriver ended in disaster when its winding path caused them to trespass on an established tribal route. Fernandes's own voyage of discovery came to an abrupt halt when the captain found himself suddenly on the receiving end of an arrow dipped in poison. Though he survived the ordeal and returned safely to his homeland, his sailing days were forever at an end.

In 1446 Nuno Tristão embarked on his third expedition along the coast of Africa, a voyage that ultimately proved to be his last. After sailing his caravel past Cape Verde and the Gambia River he came upon the mouth of another river that he decided to explore. Leaving his ship anchored at the harbor, Tristão and twenty-two of his sailors rowed upriver in two longboats. The jungle slowly closed in on the daring explorers and before long the sky above was blotted out by the thickness of the trees. Sighting a native village situated along the water's edge, the explorers expected its inhabitants to be able to provide them with pertinent information about the route of this particular river, and, if they were lucky, they might even have some items of value to trade. But before they were able to reach the banks of the river a dozen canoes raced furiously towards them, each boat filled with armed African warriors issuing menacing screams and offering threatening gestures. The surprised Portuguese sailors suddenly found themselves being greeted with a volley of poisoned arrows that found their marks with amazing and deadly accuracy. Everyone, including Captain Tristão, felt the terrible sting of these lethal projectiles. One sailor dropped dead on the spot, another died during the frantic retreat to their ship, and most of the others died shortly after they were back on board their ship. Captain Nuno Tristão was also to be counted among the dead. As for the two who miraculously survived this terrifying ordeal, the lingering effects of the poison left them too weak to stand and they had no alternative but to rely on the helping hands of five young cabin boys to get their vessel out of harm's way. In order to escape the pursuing African warriors the young sailors had to quickly cut the ship's cable and as the boat drifted aimlessly out to sea the lads desperately tried to get their bearings. After two months of rigorous sailing over savage seas, these young men, along with the aid of a few veteran sailors, amazingly found their way back to Portugal. From then on, the very thought of encountering restive natives armed with poisonous projectiles was enough to strike fear in even the most stout-hearted Portuguese mariner. That fear, however, was not great enough to keep them from continuing on with their exploration of Africa's coast.

THE FALL OF CONSTANTINOPLE

The magnificent city of Constantinople, capital of the Byzantine Empire and a bastion of Christian faith in a land surrounded by the zealous forces of Islam, stood directly in the path of advancing armies of Ottoman Turks who were bent on forging an empire of their own. Rattling their sabers across the Balkans and along the borders of Europe, the Turks, under the command of Sultan Murad II, first laid siege to the city in 1422, but they found it impossible to breach the determined defense put up by the Christians. Constantinople earned a temporary reprieve lasting nearly three decades, a sentence that ended with its fall at the hands of Murad's son, Mohammed II.

Mohammed's army, unlike the previous force sent forth by his father, had at its disposal an explosive technology that would forever change the ways of warfare—gunpowder. Instead of sacrificing wave upon wave of loyal warriors in a sustained effort to wear down the defenses of the city, Mohammed's soldiers could launch a highly destructive attack from a relatively safe distance. The Sultan began his siege of Constantinople in 1452 with a blockade of the Bosporus, the strait that separates Turkey from the mainland of Europe. By April of 1453 Mohammed felt that the city had been weakened enough to where it was now safe to commence with the physical assault.

In addition to an imposing force that numbered close to 140,000 men the Sultan brought to the battlefront a great number of large custom-built cannons, all of which, ironically, had been forged by Christian blacksmiths. Each cannon was capable of hurling shot weighing nearly six-hundred pounds. The stone walls of the great city crumbled under this thunderous and unrelenting bombardment, and just before the end came there were but a mere 7,000 desperate defenders of the faith standing naked before a frenzied onslaught of zealous Turkish soldiers. Mohammed's victory became complete on the 29th of May, a day when his Ottoman armies broke through the shattered fortifications and swarmed into the city. No mercy was asked and none was given. Constantine XI, the last Byzantine Emperor, died while defending his beloved city. After the last remaining Christian soldiers had been brutally butchered where they stood, the wrath of the victors was unleashed upon the now defenseless citizens of Constantinople. As a reward for their glorious victory, the Sultan had granted his men three days to plunder, rape, and slaughter at will, but when he entered the city later that same day and saw for himself the terrible extent of destruction and carnage inflicted by his troops, Mohammed promptly rescinded his previous directive. Order was eventually restored and Constantinople was soon transformed into the city of Istanbul, the capital of the Ottoman Empire.

The fall of Constantinople was a source of great concern to the Christian rulers of Europe and many of them began calling for another holy crusade to take back the city from the infidels. Fearful nobles worried about Ottoman Turks massing along the eastern borders of Europe; an anxious papacy pondered the growing strength of the Islamic faith; and European merchants, especially those hailing from Venice and Genoa, were concerned about the commercial consequences that might arise from this sudden and dramatic turn of events. The Europeans were unable to unite because so many were unwilling to commit either funds or soldiers, and their threat of another crusade soon subsided. As a Christian-controlled city, Constantinople had freely promoted commercial intercourse between the various nations of Asia, Africa, Arabia, and Europe. While trade would continue under Mohammed's rule, it was, however, no longer business as usual. At the Islamic city of Istanbul, it was now Muslim merchants who dictated the terms and costs of doing business abroad. The Venetian merchants managed to negotiate a favored trade status with the new Ottoman rulers while the traders from Genoa struck a beneficial deal that allowed them to keep their profitable trading colony at Pera. Even with these trade agreements the merchants of Italy found that voyages of commercial enterprise were becoming increasingly perilous with the added presence of Turkish pirates who now freely roamed the waters of the Mediterranean in search of ships to plunder.

The fall of Constantinople renewed Prince Henry's determination to discover a direct route to the lands of the Far East. Since Muslim potentates controlled the flow of trade with the East and Italian merchants dictated the distribution of that trade, European states such as Portugal and Spain found themselves at the mercy of foreigners. The rapid spread of the Islamic faith also rekindled the devout prince's longing to locate the legendary Christian kingdom of Prester John.

Where Portugal led, neighboring Spain brazenly attempted to follow. Catching wind of Spain's efforts to establish its own trading posts along the coast of Africa, Portuguese officials immediately lodged a formal complaint before the Pope. Carefully weighing the conflicting claims of these two faithful Catholic nations, the Pope eventually ruled in favor of Portugal. Beginning in 1455 His Eminence issued a series of papal bulls that granted the kingdom of Portugal exclusive exploratory rights to all lands south of Cape Bojador "and past that Southern shore all the way to the Indians." Following these favorable holy decrees Prince Henry commissioned the sailor Diogo Gomes to explore even further along the Guinea coast in search of a passage to the Indies as well as to seek out information regarding the precise whereabouts of Prester John. Accompanied by an interpreter, on the off chance that they should happen upon the elusive Christian kingdom, Gomes set off, but his efforts were continually frustrated by difficult seas. He did, however, explore the Gambia and Geba rivers and along the way he caught a glimpse of the brisk trade that occurred in that region. After negotiating a number of favorable trade treaties with several local African kings, Gomes returned to Portugal to report on fortunes that were just waiting to be had. Embarking on a second voyage in 1460 Gomes discovered the Isle of Santiago, a part of the chain that is collectively known as the Cape Verde Islands. In recognition of the valuable service he had rendered to Portugal, a grateful King Afonso knighted the daring explorer. Gomes was also awarded a new coat of arms that had "a shield with a crest and three heads of Negroes on a field of silver, each with golden rings in ears and nose, and a collar of gold around the neck, and Da Mina as a surname." Years later, after having retired to a life of leisure in the Azores, an elderly Diogo Gomes told his wondrous stories of adventure and discovery to an interested young German cartographer by the name of Martin Behaim.

Prince Henry the Navigator passed away at his Sagres sanctuary on November 13, 1460, at the age of sixty-six. Celibate to the very end, the pious Prince Henry had been the guiding force behind Portugal's assimilation of nautical knowledge and its vast extension of maritime exploration for nearly four decades. During his lifetime he often found himself the object of ridicule and even his own brother, King Duarte, questioned the investment of so much time, effort, and money in expeditions that failed to turn a handsome profit. At the time of his death Henry's estate had amassed an enormous debt estimated to have been in excess of 130,000 pounds. But Prince Henry had set Portugal on a course for greatness. He had inspired a generation of adventurers to look beyond the visible horizon; and in so doing, new lands were mapped, new water routes were charted, new civilizations were discovered, and new earthly rewards were revealed.

THREE

Following the Dream of Prince Henry

Probing the Gold Coast

Following the death of Prince Henry the Navigator, the exploration of Africa's seemingly endless coastline continued under the royal direction and patronage of his nephew, King Afonso V. After concluding that the sharing of information would ultimately result in the sharing of wealth with rival nations, Afonso did everything in his power to deny any foreign power access to Portugal's considerable sum of acquired maritime knowledge. In the interest of national security King Afonso decreed that all discoveries derived from these explorations were the physical and intellectual property rights of Portugal alone and henceforth to remain a well-guarded state secret. All returning ships were required to hand over their maps and logs to a newly established royal commission empowered to review, reveal, and withhold information as they saw fit. Several years later, Portugal's King Manuel would decree that anyone caught sending maps abroad or who was discovered divulging information to any foreign agent would be found guilty of treason—a crime punishable by death. However, such a policy was nearly impossible to enforce, especially once opportunistic sailors began offering their service and allegiance to neighboring nations. Because of this veil of secrecy and the severe devastation caused by a major earthquake that struck the Iberian Peninsula in 1755 the complete records of many explorers during this era of discovery have been lost forever.

Encouraged by the easterly direction to which the coastline of Africa was continually trending, explorers were now of the opinion that they had finally rounded the tip of the Dark Continent and it was only a matter of time before they coasted onto the very waters that washed up against the shores of those lands laden with exotic spices, rare gems, fine silks, and precious metals. By dangling a five year grant of complete commercial control over the region of Guinea, King Afonso succeeded in enticing Fernão Gomes, a wealthy Lisbon merchant, to extend Portugal's claims a minimum of one-hundred leagues each successive year. In addition to having to pay an annual fee for this grant of exclusive trade rights to the region, Gomes was obligated to pledge a small percentage of his profits to the royal treasury. Starting from Sierra Leone in 1469, this monetarily motivated entrepreneurial explorer spent the next five years extending Portugal's claims even further than he had been required, reaching as far south as Cape St. Catherine before his contract came up for renewal.

Portuguese dreams of having finally found a way around the continent of Africa were destined to face a rude shattering in 1472. This was the year that Fernando Póo, after having landed on an island in the Gulf of Guinea, which was to later bear his name, discovered that the coast no longer veered eastward toward the Orient, but once again plunged southward towards the great unknown. Portuguese mariners also discovered that the closer they got to the earth's equator the further the Pole Star descended from their view in the night sky. Since Polaris, or the North Star as it is more commonly referred to, was used to calculate latitude, it was necessary to come up with an entirely new system for determining their exact position in the Southern hemisphere; they later accomplished this by devising tables of declination based on the position of the sun as well as the formation of stars known as the Southern Cross. In the year 1473 Lopo Gonçalves succeeded in crossing the mysterious and imaginary equatorial line without a single sailor's skin broiling to black. The following year, in 1474, King Afonso decided not to renew his contractual arrangement with Fernão Gomes and instead gave the profitable trade concession to his son John, who showed an interest in the further exploration of Africa's coast.

Africa began to reveal to Portugal a little more of her hidden treasures at each newly reached port of call. Prized cargoes of slaves, ivory, and gold soon enriched the coffers of the royal treasury to such an extent that Portuguese officials took to christening the various lands of Africa with titles that corresponded with whatever happened to be their most abundant commodity—the newly christened Slave Coast, Ivory Coast, Grain Coast, and the Gold Coast. The gold of Ghana was, by far, the commodity of choice. Gold, after all, was a tangible asset: a precious metal that could purchase whatever worldly goods or services the Portuguese desired for themselves.

Europe's thirst for gold was absolutely insatiable. However, this sudden lust for items of luxury had come at a time when their meager reserves of gold had begun to dry up. Many European states managed to supplement this dwindling supply by selling their wares at the markets of northern Africa, but their own demands continued to exceed what little they could supply to an increasingly expanding international market. A reversal of fortune finally occurred when the crew of Fernão Gomes stumbled upon a stretch of the legendary gold dust trail, a historic discovery that occurred during the year 1471. In a land they christened the Gold Coast, the present site of the African nation of Ghana, Portuguese sailors encountered natives who seemed to possess an unlimited quantity of gold. While a great deal of their gold was alluvial in nature, with some of it being mined and worked by highly skilled craftsmen, most of the region's gold came by way of trade with tribes located deep within Africa's interior. Since there was, for the time being, more than enough gold to go around, the realization that the Gold Coast was not the source but instead primarily a collection point for the continent's wealth mattered little to the Portuguese. The explorers were more than willing to part with any items that the natives might need or desire; weapons, clothes, food, beads, and wine were bartered for all the gold they could manage to lay their hands on. West Africa quickly became Europe's principal source of gold, supplying an estimated two-thirds of the continent's demand for the precious metal.

The Portuguese explorers were surprised to discover that in many parts of Africa salt was a commodity prized even more than gold, especially amongst the tribes of the interior where it was necessary for human survival in such a torrid climate. They learned that huge blocks of salt were regularly transported by way of caravans to Timbuktu and other cities located in Mali where it was to be traded for either gold or slaves. These large cakes of salt were then transported into the interior of Africa, particularly along the Niger. At predetermined locations the traders would neatly stack the cakes of salt upon the ground and then leave the scene so that the local natives could freely inspect and evaluate the salt. Once they had completed their appraisal of the salt's quality and quantity the timid natives would then deposit what they believed was a fair and equivalent amount in gold next to the pile of salt. Upon their return the next day, the salt traders would inspect the gold offered by the natives and if they believed the quality and the amount was fair they would simply collect the gold and depart. However, if the amount of gold offered seemed too small then both deposits were left undisturbed and the "silent trade" began all over again. This process would continue until both parties were completely satisfied.

In the year 1481 the royal scepter of Portugal passed from father to son, and the newly crowned king, young John II, was determined to carry on Afonso's vision of finding a route to the Indies. Following up on intelligence reports suggesting that his explorers were very near to discovering the legendary realm of Prester John and even closer to locating the ever elusive tip of Africa, King John, in 1482, commissioned Diogo Cam, a distinguished navigator more familiarly known as Diogo Cão, to sail as far as his vessels and provisions would carry him. Convinced that this voyage was destined for success, the king did what no other Portuguese ruler had done before: he dipped into the royal treasury to help finance the expedition. Prior to this voyage, the Crown merely provided its royal blessing to those who were fully capable of paying their own way.

In addition to the usual store of supplies, the Cão expedition carried on board a number of *padrãos* that the captain was instructed to plant at prominent points along the coast of Africa. These seven foot high stone markers were inscribed with the Portuguese coat of arms as well as the names of both the king and the explorer. Previously, explorers from Portugal had staked their claim to new lands by erecting a plain wooden cross or simply etching their distinctive marks on a nearby tree. These *padrãos* also held in place a large cross to signify that this land had been blessed in the name of Jesus Christ, Lord and Savior. Diogo Cão would erect four such *padrãos* on a voyage of discovery that eventually extended Portugal's claims south of the equator as far as the 22nd parallel. Prior to that point, Cão had earned for himself a spot in history by becoming the first European to cruise along the Congo River. He ventured several leagues up the mighty river, which he named the Zaire, before returning to the estuary from whence he had entered. While it surely must have seemed to Captain Cão that the coast of Africa extended all the way to the ends of the earth, he had managed, though unbeknownst to him, to come within a thousand miles of the continent's extreme southern tip. After having erected his last *padrão* in January of 1486 Cão set sail for home only to be robbed of the honors and tribute he so richly deserved by an untimely death at sea before his ship was able to reach the docks of Lisbon.

King John founded a fair number of fortresses along the West African coast during his reign, particularly within the vicinity of the prosperous gold and slave trading regions, in order to protect, preserve, and facilitate Portugal's monopoly in trade. The king planned to eventually use these stone forts as a foundation for colonization of the coastal regions and from there he hoped to move on to exploring the mysterious interior of Africa. But for the time being, the fortresses functioned primarily, and quite effectively, as strategic supply stations for the many commercial vessels that carried on trade along the coast of Africa.

There were a great many missionaries who sailed along on these voyages of discovery. They hoped to carry on the Christian cause by spreading gospel "truths" and invoking "God's word" amongst the "heathen" tribes that resided in these "forsaken" lands. These emissaries of the Church were also sent along to aid the mariners in their search for the fabled kingdom of Prester John. Their determined faith succeeded in converting a great many rulers and the members of their tribes. The most important conversion was that of the Manikongo Nzina Nkuwu in what is present day Angola. These Christian efforts, however, could not compete with the lure of tremendous profit that could be earned from the traffic in slavery. The institution of slavery has been a blemish upon the deeds of many a great civilization, no matter how magnificent their accomplishments may have been, for as far back as history records. The Egyptians, the Greeks, and the Romans all built their monuments, their cities, and their empires upon the backs of slaves. After the fall of Rome, slavery just about disappeared from much of Europe, though one could argue that it simply reappeared under the guise of serfdom during the Middle Ages. However, the slave trade remained an acceptable and profitable practice in most Arabic and African domains. Having cultivated an extensive network of trade with kingdoms and tribes located in the interior of Africa, Arab traders easily found many a greedy ruler willing and eager to barter the lives of his prisoners, and in some cases even members of his own tribe or family, for whatever trinkets the Arabs might have to offer. The purchased slaves were then transported, along with other precious commodities of the region, to the major markets of North Africa, and from there they were auctioned off to the highest bidder. Portugal and Spain were introduced to the slave market by their Moorish overlords, and the institution continued in many parts of the Iberian Peninsula even after the Christian uprising.

When Nuno Tristão returned from his voyage of discovery with a large number of Negroes, he had unknowingly launched Portugal's venture into the financially rewarding business of trafficking in slaves. Though a sordid practice when viewed from our own moral high ground, slavery was clearly an acceptable custom during this era, and as a business, the slave trade was enticingly profitable. Fueled at first by its own demand for labor, slightly more than nine-hundred African slaves were imported directly to Portugal's markets between the years 1444 and 1448. That number increased to an estimated eight hundred annually by 1460 and before long the slave traders found it difficult to keep pace with the soaring demand for imported slaves. Portuguese mariners bartered for an increasing number of slaves but when these efforts failed to produce the required numbers they resorted to capturing slaves by way of violent raids upon unsuspecting villages. The trading posts and forts along the African coast were soon overcrowded with captured and purchased natives waiting to be processed and shipped to an awaiting auction block. But the market for newly acquired slaves was not confined solely to the Iberian Peninsula; many African rulers, especially those of the Gold Coast, were eager to trade their gold and ivory for captives of the Portuguese acquired from other regions of Africa. By the end of the 15th century there were somewhere between 1,200 and 2,500 slaves being exported per year, which meant that the demand for African slaves ranked second only to the demand for African gold.

Envious of neighboring Portugal's newly found source of wealth, Spanish sailors began making a number of daring incursions along the coast of West Africa in search of gold and slaves for their own markets. Around the year 1478, the Spanish sovereigns, Ferdinand and Isabella, sought approval from the Pope to engage in trade along the Gulf of Guinea, but their request was summarily denied. The monarchs were undeterred by the Pope's decision, and clandestine Spanish raids continued with enough frequency to prompt Portugal's newly crowned King John II to seek papal protection from these Spanish pirates. In 1481 the Pope drew up an official edict that granted Portugal a monopoly on trade along all of Africa's western shores. That very same year King John sent Diogo d'Azambuja to Elmina Point to supervise the construction of São Jorge de Mina, a fortress and trade center that was to protect the lucrative traffic in Ashanti gold and serve as a major port of call for Portuguese vessels for the next one hundred and fifty years.

Covilha's Search for Prester John

Portuguese sailors, during the course of these voyages of discovery, on occasion came across tidbits of information pertaining to the supposed whereabouts of the Christian kingdom of Prester John. Though what they heard was often just wishful interpretation, the persistent rumors of his glorious realm seemed to indicate that the priest king and his faithful followers had moved from the furthest regions of Asia and had now relocated somewhere along the continent of Africa. More specifically, the latest intelligence pinpointed his location in the ancient land of Abyssinia, or modern day Ethiopia, a place inconveniently situated on the unknown eastern side of Africa. In a desperate effort to make contact with their Christian counterparts, Portuguese officials came up with a peculiar plan, one which called for the instructing of African prisoners in their language. Once sufficiently fluent in the Portuguese tongue, they were then to be set free at various locations along the coast of the Dark Continent. It was hoped that once released into the wild these natives would make their way into the interior of Africa until they came across the province ruled by Prester John. Needless to say, the plan was a total failure; once these tutored Africans had regained their freedom they simply tried to find their way back home.

Believing that they were close to finally meeting the legendary and omnipotent Prester John, King John II and his advisers began formulating plans for two separate but simultaneous expeditions, one by land, the second by sea, to locate the ever-elusive ruler. King John summoned Pedro de Covilha and Alfonso de Paiva to the royal court where they were briefed about the planned overland expedition. During these secret sessions these two men were supplied with pertinent geographical and scientific information that was supposed to aid them in their completion of this extremely dangerous mission.

Pedro de Covilha was well suited for such an important and perilous assignment. As a young lad he had been sent to Spain where he found himself serving a seven year apprenticeship in the household of the duke of Medina Sidonia, a tutelage which effectively drilled him in the finer points of Spanish elocution and manners. He returned to Portugal in 1474 to serve as a squire at the court of King Afonso V. Following the death of the king in 1481, Covilha was enlisted as one of the body guards for the newly crowned John II. While in the king's service he participated quite admirably in a number of covert operations for the Crown, most notably as a secret agent at the court of Spain's King Ferdinand and Queen Isabella. King John also sent him on intelligence gathering missions to the distant cities of Tlemcen and Fez in North Africa where, as well as learning the customs of the Arab people, he also managed, thanks to a gifted ear for language, to master the Arabic tongue. As for Alfonso de Paiva, there is little known about his past and even less is known about him once he parts company with Pedro de Covilha.

Traveling in disguise, Covilha and Paiva convincingly passed themselves off as Arab merchants who were plying their trade in honey, a scarce and much sought-after commodity that was readily available from lands where they were about to venture. Their secret expedition was financed by letters of credit, which were drawn on a bank in Florence and backed by the treasury of King John II. The two adventurers began their incredible odyssey on May 7, 1487. After crossing the width of Spain to arrive at the port city of Barcelona, Covilha and Paiva boarded a ship that took them first to Naples and then on to the city of Rhodes where they made good on their cover by shipping a large cargo of honey back to Portugal. From Rhodes they sailed to the city of Cairo. During this stopover the two men succeeded in making important contacts within the merchant community, one of which eventually led to an introduction to a group of Moorish traders who had extensive commercial dealings in the Middle East. In the spring of 1488 the two agents of the king sailed across the Red Sea in the company of their new business acquaintances and from there they traveled by caravan to Aden, an ancient port city located at the extreme southern tip of the Arabian Peninsula. Ideally positioned near the entrance to the Red Sea, Aden was a bustling port of call for Muslim vessels returning from trade with the merchants of the Far East and the eastern shores of Africa.

Aden was also a parting of ways for these two intrepid travelers. Alfonso de Paiva was to begin his search for Prester John by crossing over to Ethiopia. Pedro de Covilha, meanwhile, was instructed to journey on to India by boat in order that he might observe and learn more about the arcane Muslim trade connections that existed within the mysterious realms of Asia. It was also hoped that at some point they would both link up with a second expedition led by Bartolomeu Dias, who was going to attempt a rounding of the southern tip of Africa and then sail on up the eastern coast until he found his way to the markets of India.

Boarding a vessel that would cart him across the Arabian Sea, Covilha eventually landed at Calicut, one of the largest and richest cities in all of India. Located on the western side of India, Calicut functioned as a commercial hub for Asian and Muslim traders. Fleets of junks from China and the Indies sailed to its crowded ports, and once docked they unloaded their abundant cargoes of precious gems, spices, silks, and other valuable commodities that were destined to be sold at the local markets. Anxiously awaiting their arrivals were numerous Arab traders willing to pay a handsome price for just about any goods shipped from the Orient. Once purchased, these rich cargoes were then shipped either to the Persian Gulf or the Gulf of Aden, and from there they were distributed to various markets throughout Africa, the Middle East, and even Europe.

During his extended stay at Calicut, Covilha learned a great deal about the many trade routes that the Arabs had managed to conceal so well from the eyes and ears of Christian merchants. He also obtained additional and extremely valuable information concerning the true origins of the exotic spices that exhilarated and enticed the European senses. His reports detailing exactly where peppers, cloves, and ginger came from proved invaluable to the numerous Portuguese mariners who sailed into the Indian Ocean once Bartolomeu Dias had succeeded in discovering a way around the tip of Africa.

While he was secretly uncovering a wealth of information at Calicut, Covilha became increasingly concerned that his covert activities might be exposed at any moment—a detection which would surely have subjected him to the harshest of penalties. When he decided that the time had come to depart Calicut, Covilha made his way northward up the coast as far as Goa, another major port of call also situated along the western coast of India, and once there he boarded a vessel headed to Ormuz, the gateway to the Persian Gulf. After leaving Ormuz, Covilha sailed westward along the waters of the Indian Ocean and then veered southward to explore further along the coastline of East Africa. The Portuguese explorer made stops at many of the major Muslim trading centers, such as Malindi, Mombassa, and Mozambique, all great markets of trade that at the time were completely unknown to the Christians of Europe. Covilha surely must have hoped that at one of these ports of call he would come across either his former partner Alfonso de Paiva or meet up with the expedition under the command of Bartolomeu Dias. At Sofala, the furthest point he reached along the coast of Africa, Covilha discovered, much to his delight, the mysterious source of the gold that supplied the Islamic nations with such enormous wealth. Gold that was mined from the interior of Africa was transported by beasts of burden, which in most instances were enslaved natives, to Sofala where it was exchanged for various Arab wares. Anxious to report his discovery of this gilded land to King John, Covilha began the long journey towards home.

Pedro de Covilha made it safely back to Aden sometime during October of 1490, but before he had a chance to leave the city of Cairo he was approached by two Portuguese special agents, the Rabbi Abraham of Beja and Joseph of Lamego, dispatched by King John II to locate him. It was from these emissaries that he learned Alfonso de Paiva had never returned from his part of the mission and it was presumed that he had perished during his search for the blessed realm of Prester John. The king now wanted Covilha to continue that quest. He was ordered to depart at once for Ethiopia and not to return home until he had made contact with Prester John and successfully concluded an alliance between the two Christian kingdoms. After handing Joseph of Lamego a lengthy letter for delivery to King John, which detailed all the secrets he had uncovered concerning Arab trade interests in the distant regions of Asia and Africa, Covilha and Abraham of Beja journeyed on to Ormuz, a major market for the many unique commodities of India and China. Following a brief stay at Ormuz the two wayfarers parted company; Ibrahim began his long journey back to Portugal by hitching a ride aboard a caravan headed for the Syrian city of Aleppo while Covilha made an unsanctioned pilgrimage to the sacred site of Mecca before attempting to follow in the footsteps of Alfonso de Paiva.

After a somewhat lengthy stay at the holy city of Mecca, Covilha made his way across the Red Sea to an Abyssinian harbor and from there he wandered across the ancient land of Abyssinia until he finally stumbled upon a remote Christian kingdom. After a meeting with the regional ruler, Alexander "Lion of the Tribe of Judah, and King of Kings," Covilha quickly concluded that this was not part of the realm of Prester John but instead the heretofore unknown kingdom of Nubia, whose Christian followers were referred to as Nubians or Nobatians. The Nubians, an ancient tribe of Ethiopia, traced their Christian roots back to the days of King Menelik I and Sheba, queen of Ethiopia. For many generations the isolated Nubians had valiantly and vigorously defended their faith—an interesting mixture of Judaism and Christianity with a unique Ethiopian twist—against marauding heathens and infidels.

King Alexander took an immense liking to this wandering Christian and immediately welcomed him into his inner circle. Encouraged by the king's friendly overtures Covilha sought to forge a mutually beneficial alliance between both Christian kingdoms, but the only benefit this "King of Kings" was interested in was the retention of Covilha's service. Much like Marco Polo at the court of Kublai Khan, Covilha found himself in the employ of a foreign king who would not permit him to leave the country. He was, just like Marco Polo, treated well, in fact like royalty, receiving a large grant of land and a wife for his invaluable service to the "Lion of the Tribe of Judah."

Meanwhile, back home in Portugal, King John II and his courtly advisers poured over the detailed reports supplied by Pedro de Covilha. His rich description of the local markets and vivid details of an intricate international network of trade occurring in that part of the world further strengthened Portugal's determination to find a route that would take them past the great barrier of Africa and across the vast width of the Indian Ocean. As time passed, with no further word concerning the whereabouts of Covilha, everyone at the royal court presumed the worst about the fate of their intrepid secret agent. One can only imagine the astonished look on the face of Rodrigo de Lima, a Portuguese emissary, who, after arriving in Abyssinia in 1520, was greeted by an elderly gentleman who answered to the name of Pedro de Covilha.

A Western Vision

On August 13, 1476, a fierce naval engagement took place off the shores of Portugal and within sight of Prince Henry's famed nautical institute at

Sagres. On that particular day a convoy of Genoese ships loaded with a cargo destined for distant markets in northern Europe and southern England encountered a fleet of French and Portuguese ships on patrol. Ever since Portugal had allied with France in a war against the neighboring Spanish kingdoms of Aragon and Castile there had been heightened tension in the waters off the Iberian coast. The allied commanders, thoroughly convinced that the ships they had come upon were carrying contraband destined for Aragon, immediately opened fire on the Genoese ships. Cannon shot was returned and a raging battle at sea commenced. A deafening bombardment thundered back and forth and as the smoke from the final blast dissipated the full extent of the devastation was revealed: three Genoese ships and four vessels belonging to the alliance had been destroyed.

In an ocean littered with floating debris and dead bodies a lone wounded Genoese sailor managed to keep his wits about him while desperately straining to tread water. Latching on to a nearby oar the young mariner paddled towards the direction of land. After swimming six grueling miles the exhausted sailor finally washed ashore at Lagos, the town located near Sagres Point. Reflecting upon all that had just transpired and interpreting great significance in his landing so close to the site of Sagres, the grateful sailor convinced himself that divine intervention had spared his life in order that he might participate in some greater purpose. From that moment forward Christoforo Colombo, better known to us as Christopher Columbus, decided to dedicate his life to the sea and to God.

Born and raised in the Republic of Genoa, the future "Admiral of the Ocean" struggled hard to rise above his humble origins. His chosen course seems to have been foretold the moment his parents elected to have him baptized in honor of the patron saint of wayfarers, a legendary figure who spent most of his life unselfishly carrying Christian travelers across a wide river, and who is often depicted in art as the carrier of the Christ child. Christoforo was the first child of Domenico Colombo, the son of a wool weaver, and Suzanna Fontanarossa, the daughter of a weaver. Dominico tried his hand not only at the family trade but also at the wine business, but with five children and a wife to support he often had difficulty making ends meet. At one point, his monetary situation became so tenuous, he found himself serving a short stint in jail for failing to fulfill his financial obligations.

While the young Columbus may have come from a family of meager means he was fortunate enough, however, to dwell in one of the richest and most important cities of that time. Though no longer as powerful as the city of Venice, the maritime Republic of Genoa was still a flourishing center of trade, maintaining profitable trading posts at many major Arab markets throughout the Mediterranean basin. The stability of Genoa's overseas trade had been threatened by the fall of Constantinople, but the economic set-back proved to be only temporary, as Genoese officials successfully negotiated with the Ottoman Turks for a resumption of trade.

From his father's shop the young Christopher Columbus could see the towering masts of the many ships docked at Genoa's spacious natural harbor. When his daily chores were done the inquisitive lad would wander down to the wharves at Porta Sant'Andrea to watch the ships drifting in from far away lands or to catch a last glimpse of a departing vessel sailing somewhere beyond the blue horizon. This was a seaport constantly bustling with activity. Here the young Columbus saw stevedores hustling to unload cargo from recently docked boats under the watchful eye of merchants meticulously inspecting their goods; he heard the sounds of pounding and cutting resonating from the tools of shipyard carpenters constructing new boats or making repairs to old ones; he listened to the groans of men as they heaved large casks of water and wine onto ships getting ready to set sail for distant markets; and he overheard sailors swapping tales of strange and exotic lands they had either visited themselves or heard about from other adventurous sailors. These were the enticing sights and sounds that captured the imagination of young Christopher Columbus and ultimately lured him away from following in the path of his father.

At the age of fourteen Christopher became his own man and enlisted as a sailor aboard a local merchant vessel. His first known voyage was as a member of a trading expedition that sailed to the island of Chios, located in the Aegean Sea. Though blessed with a very keen mind, he was unfortunately a victim of his time, an age when only a chosen few were privileged enough to receive any formal education. As a young man aboard a ship manned by veteran seafarers Columbus found himself exposed to men with varying degrees of knowledge. While aboard ship he saw a direct correlation between rank and level of education; basic sailors were generally an illiterate lot who were relied upon to perform the necessary but backbreaking physical tasks required to sail a ship, while the navigational and leadership skills that made for a good officer called for a well rounded education. It was this latter group which inspired Columbus to learn all that he could learn, beginning with the basic skills of reading and writing. He wisely chose to spend his free time studying cartography, reading books, learning how to operate navigational instruments, and most of all, listening and learning from the many voices of experience. Later in life, Columbus embellished his own credentials, just as he would with many of his accomplishments, by claiming to have studied astronomy and geography at Pavia University, but there are no known records which can substantiate his scholarly claims.

During his career in the Genoese merchant marine Columbus had the opportunity to sail to a great many of the ports situated along the Mediterranean basin, seeing firsthand those distant lands he had heard and fantasized about as a small boy back at Genoa. The chance to finally ply the waters of the Atlantic came in May of 1476 when he enlisted aboard a convoy of commercial vessels headed for ports located in Lisbon, London and finally Flanders. After passing the Pillars of Hercules (the Strait of Gibraltar) the ships from Genoa had a fateful encounter with privateers hailing from France and Portugal. The twenty-five-year-old shipwrecked sailor who came ashore at Lagos, somehow managed to find his way to Lisbon. From there, following a delay of several months, he continued his voyage aboard a British vessel bound for England and later on sailed to Iceland.

Christopher Columbus returned to Lisbon in 1479 to take up permanent residence. Here he was known by the name of Cristóvão Colom. There was already at the capital city of Portugal a rather large population of Genoese, and living amongst this close-knit community of expatriates was Christopher's younger brother Bartholomew, who was successfully supporting himself as a mapmaker. The reunited brothers lived together and became partners in a business that made and sold nautical charts. A steadfast dedication to rise above his present station spurred the older brother to learn to read, write, and to speak fairly fluently in the Romance dialects of Portuguese, Castilian, and Latin. Once these skills were mastered he found that he had the ability to mingle comfortably within any social circle, a talent he would later utilize to ingratiate himself with the rich and powerful upper class.

In 1480 Christopher Columbus married the daughter of a deceased nobleman. His beautiful bride was the young Felipa Perestrello, whose father, Captain Bartolomeu Perestrello, was a Portuguese citizen of Italian descent. While serving as a sailor in the service of Prince Henry, Perestrello played a pivotal role in the discovery and colonization of Porto Santo. After having been forced from the island by the rapidly breeding rabbits he had brought with him from Portugal, Bartolomeu later returned to reclaim the island and to serve as its first governor. Columbus was introduced to Felipa Moniz Perestrello while attending services at the Convent of the Saints, a place of worship situated along the banks of the Tagus River. Following a whirlwind courtship the two were united in marriage. Christopher and his lovely wife set up household at Porto Santo and shortly thereafter their blessed union produced a son whom they named Diego. While at his new residence Columbus had full access to the extensive nautical library that once belonged to Captain Perestrello. Here he would find a large collection of maps that plotted the secret Portuguese sailing route that extended down the Atlantic coast of West Africa. Columbus also had access to the captain's private logs and journals, along with numerous other maritime related books and documents.

During his stay at Porto Santo, Christopher Columbus uncovered a wealth of information that helped to rekindle and support a theory he had been formulating for some time regarding the possible existence of a westward sea route to the Indies. He knew that after nearly six decades of determined and exhaustive exploration the brave mariners of Portugal had still not discovered a way around the vast continent of Africa, and it was beginning to appear that maybe there was no end to this enormous land mass. In 1482 Columbus would try his own hand at exploring the Guinea Coast, sailing as far as Elmina, and according to his own recollections, it was a journey that he made on more than one occasion. Witnessing firsthand the numerous difficulties presented by the current direction the Portuguese were taking towards the Indies, Columbus convinced himself, and later others, that sailing westward would be a much less hazardous and far faster route to the great treasures of the Orient.

Columbus's ideas about westward travel were extrapolated from ancient tales of daring voyages to uncharted lands, speculative data regarding the earth's geography, religious allegory, and conjecture which passed for the truth. On board ships and at ports of call he heard varying accounts of bold adventurers who had discovered new lands after sailing off into the sunset. While in England he surely would have encountered fishermen who had sailed westward across the icy North Atlantic to fish off the shores of lands still waiting to be claimed. Any Irishmen he met would have surely boasted that way back in the sixth century one of their own, specifically an Irish monk known to all as Saint Brendan, had explored many lands to the north and west, and whose grand adventures were vividly recounted in the popular medieval manuscript titled *The Voyage of Saint Brendan*. According to this legend the Irish monk and his faithful band of brothers sailed westward across the Atlantic in a quest to find the biblical Garden of Eden. During their search for the lost paradise the monks encountered fallen angels who were now shaped in the likeness of white doves, an enormous whale who allowed them to dock their boat on its back so that they could hold communion, and a shadowy figure who revealed himself as Judas Iscariot. After finding what they were looking for, the monks then spent forty days and forty nights wandering this earthly paradise. Satisfied with their glorious discovery, Brendan and his comrades loaded their ships with a great quantity of precious gems before setting a course for Ireland. Brendan passed away shortly after his return but the legend of his incredible voyage lingered on through sailors' tales and cartographers' maps. However, the precise route to paradise was once again lost to mankind. *The Voyage of Saint Brendan* was a book that very probably found its way into the extensive collection read by Columbus. Columbus's visit to Iceland would not have been complete without hearing a rendering of the oft-told tale of Leif Ericsson's daring and courageous voyage to a place called Vinland. From his adopted homeland of Portugal came the story of seven Christian monks who, in the wake of the Moorish invasion of the Iberian Peninsula during the first half of the eighth century, fled to the sea with a number of faithful followers. It was written that after having found land each monk established an independent city, all of which emerged as cities of tremendous size and enormous wealth. This land was often referred to as Antilla, meaning "the island opposite." Additionally, Columbus, along with most sailors of his time, knew that somewhere to the west of the known world lay the magnificent land which Plato had spoken of: the legendary lost city of Atlantis.

As a learned man, Columbus was fully cognizant of the fact that the earth was indeed a sphere. He had studied the geography of Ptolemy and was intrigued by the ancient geographer's maps that depicted a relatively small gap of water separating the western most point of Europe from the eastern most point of Asia. From the book *Imago Mundi* (*Image of the World*) by Cardinal Pierre d'Ailly he learned that the Atlantic Ocean "is not so great that it can cover three quarters of the globe, as certain people figure," a statement that intimated the Atlantic Ocean was but a narrow divide between the two continents. This conclusion received additional support from the writings of the "prophet" Esdras, who believed that only one-seventh of the earth's surface was water. Armed with these facts it seemed only logical to Columbus that a westward route across the Atlantic would be a much faster course to the Indies than the tortuous path currently being explored along the African coastline.

Christopher Columbus was also an ardent student of Marco Polo, having read and underlined important passages in his own copy of *The Travels of Marco Polo*. He was especially intrigued with the Venetian's vivid details of the incredible amount of wealth that was at the disposal of the Great Khan and his striking description of the island of Cipangu, where the glitter from the golden roofed palace reflected far out to sea. Columbus also made special note of Marco's observation that there were more than 7,000 islands laying off the coast of Asia, a comforting thought to sailors who dreaded being away from the sight of land for any length of time. Once these islands were reached it was just a simple matter of having to sail from one island paradise to another until one finally reached the mainland of Asia.

Perhaps the greatest living influence upon Columbus's vision of a westward sea route to Cathay was exerted by Paolo dal Pozzo Toscanelli. A true

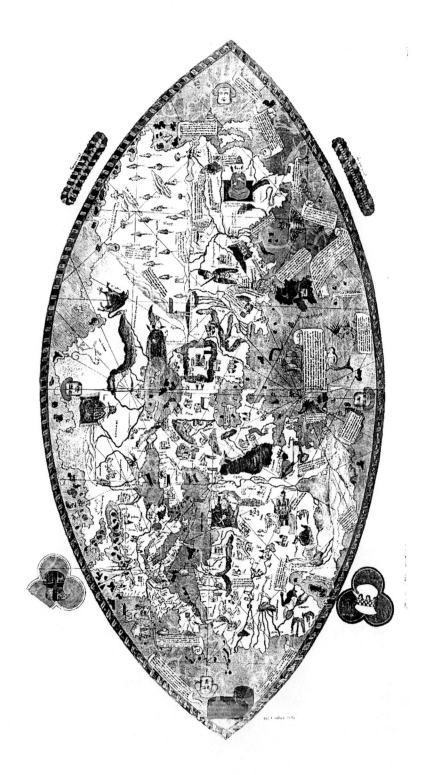

Renaissance man, Toscanelli was a highly respected physician, a brilliant mathematician, and an amateur astronomer, but it was his fascination with geography which brought him great renown throughout many European circles. Having made a financial killing from sound investments in the lucrative spice trade, the Toscanelli family had gone on to become one of the wealthiest households in all of Florence. Such wealth gave Paolo the freedom to actively pursue his many intellectual interests. However, the family fortunes suffered somewhat when the Ottoman Turks captured the city of Constantinople and thereby gained control of the established trade routes of that region. Though the Toscanelli family continued to prosper as merchant bankers and traders, Paolo was consumed by the prospect of plotting a direct sea route that would provide Italian merchants with a way to circumvent the current control exerted by Muslims over the spice and silk trade routes.

In the year 1474 King Afonso V of Portugal expressed an interest in learning more about Paolo's thoughts on a possible western sea passage to the Indies. In a letter dated June 25th of that year, Toscanelli responded to the King's request by elaborating on how a westward route was not only possible but would ultimately prove to be a far more expedient course to the mysterious lands of Cathay, Cipangu, Mangi, and India than the one presently being pursued by Portugal. In formulating his own theory, the Florentine philosopher relied heavily on the recorded descriptions of Marco Polo and the ancient world maps of Ptolemy. We can assume that King Afonso initially subscribed to Toscanelli's theory since in November of 1475 he granted to the sailor Fernão Telles permission to explore this projected path; but unfortunately nothing of note came from such a concession.

When Christopher Columbus learned of this letter written to the King of Portugal he penned his own letter to Toscanelli in which he respectfully requested more information on this topic from the noted scholar. In a cordial reply the eighty-four year old Toscanelli encouragingly stated, "The voyage you wish to undertake is not as difficult as people think; on the contrary, the ship's course is certain, …" and his note went on to estimate that the distance from the Canaries to Cipangu was but a mere 3,000 nautical miles—which in actuality happens to be the approximate distance to the then unknown lands of the Americas. The Italian scholar also enclosed copies of the letter and map he had previously forwarded to the court of

Opposite: **1457 chart created by Paulo dal Pozzo Toscanelli: This Florentine cartographer, astronomer, mathematician, and physician had a profound impact on Christopher Columbus's theory of a westward route to the Indies.**

Portugal's King Afonso. But Paulo Toscanelli did not live long enough to learn of Columbus's journey by the very route he had encouraged him to follow, as he passed away the year following their correspondence, 1482.

Christopher Columbus would extract and manipulate information to conform to his own theories and discard any fact or hypothesis that seemed to contradict his own plans. In an effort to make his proposed voyage more attractive and feasible to prospective backers he whittled Toscanelli's estimate of the distance between the Canary Islands and the mainland of Asia down to a mere 2,400 nautical miles. Of course, Columbus was unaware of the fact that the true distance to Asia was more like 10,600 nautical miles and in between there lay a great land mass that barred the way.

Columbus knew that before his plans could ever move from paper to reality he would have to find a way to obtain financial support as well as royal approval for such a highly speculative venture. It appeared that his persistence was about to pay off when in 1484 the new King of Portugal, John II, granted him an audience before the royal court. Seeking to carry on the work first begun by his great-uncle, Prince Henry the Navigator, and then continued under the direction of his father, King Afonso V, King John II enthusiastically received the unknown sailor from Genoa. His highness listened intently as Columbus laid out his bold plans for an "Enterprise of the Indies," his daring scheme to reach Asia on a route that ran counter to Portugal's current efforts to reach the same destination. In addition to the king's blessing, Columbus requested that the monarch supply him with three fully manned and stored ships for the yearlong voyage he estimated it would take to get there and back. He promised at the very least that he would discover a route to the island of Cipangu for Portugal to claim as her own.

As compensation for the many great risks he was about to undertake and for the vast riches he would soon deliver to the Crown, Columbus set forth the following demands before King John and his courtly advisers: he was to be granted the title of "Great Admiral of the Ocean"; he was to receive a ten percent cut from all future wealth and trade that derived from his discoveries; and he was to be appointed governor of all lands that he discovered. Following a brief moment of silent disbelief, an uproarious round of laughter reverberated throughout the king's chamber. Who was this brazen braggart who made such outrageous demands upon the almighty king of Portugal?

While the Genoese was extremely vague in his details and certainly overly presumptuous in his demands, King John, nonetheless, was intrigued by the presentation made by Christopher Columbus. By the year 1484, the furthest that Portugal's explorer Diogo Cão had reached along the African coast was Cape Saint Mary, and from that point there was still no end in sight to the southerly trend of the African coast. A western route was beginning to sound like the more promising and logical course to pursue. The king relegated the proposal for an "Enterprise of the Indies" to the Junta do Mathematicos, a select panel of experts who advised the court on many matters of great national importance. It seems that the king's advisers took much delight in pointing out the egregious errors and obvious oversights of the Columbus proposal. They disagreed with his calculation of degrees and his measurement of miles, figures which they said grossly underestimated the true nautical distance to Asia. As for the map that he had unfurled before the king, they said it was nothing more than a reworking of the Toscanelli map that was deemed to be highly suspect and overly speculative by the same committee of advisers. Even if they were to approve such an ill-conceived plan, the court members questioned where in all of Portugal Columbus would ever find sailors courageous enough to follow an unknown foreigner to the very ends of the earth. All agreed that the demands and risks for this highly speculative venture greatly outweighed any perceived potential for financial reward.

Christopher Columbus's proposed western scheme was doomed the very moment King John agreed with the conclusions made by his courtly advisers. Shortly thereafter, the king seems to have had a sudden change of heart as he gave his royal blessing to a similar plan presented by a Portuguese navigator. Fernão Dulmo, a sea captain from the Azores, proposed to sail westward until he came upon Antilla, the fabled island of the Seven Cities. What made this plan more appealing than the recent proposal presented by Columbus was that Dulmo, with financial assistance from John Afonso de Estreito, a wealthy merchant from Madeira, pledged to finance the entire expedition with his own funds. King John gave his approval to the venture and promised Dulmo the title to "a great island or islands, or coastal parts of a mainland." Columbus caught wind of their secret agreement, and, as his anger swelled from bitter feelings of betrayal and a sense that perhaps the king had discriminated against him in favor of a native son, he decided to leave Portugal and try his luck elsewhere. As for the self-financed expedition of Fernão Dulmo, there are doubts that such a voyage ever took place. There are some accounts that indicate it did sail in 1487, but his northwesterly course unfortunately led the expedition straight into foul weather and he was soon forced to return home to Portugal.

FOUR

The Spanish Crusade

Courting the Catholic Kings

Spanish Connections

Disappointment and tragedy continued to plague Christopher Columbus throughout the remainder of 1485. Besides feelings of resentment towards the king of Portugal, who he believed had stolen his plan for a westward expedition to the Indies, the sudden death of his beloved wife that same year had left him terribly despondent. Adding to his present woes was the fact that a number of creditors had begun to pressure him for payment of his long overdue debts, and he now feared the very real possibility of having to serve a shameful sentence inside a debtors' prison. Wishing to avoid the same fate that had once befallen his father, Columbus packed up all the personal belongings he could carry, took his young son Diego by the hand, and boarded a ship bound for Spain.

After landing at the port of Palos, Columbus and son traveled but a short distance before reaching the monastery of La Rabida, where they had the good fortune to make the acquaintance of Father Antonio de Marchena. This Franciscan friar, who dabbled in geography and astronomy, took an immediate liking to the Genoan seafarer and his young son. Father Marchena would utilize his considerable influence to gain Christopher Columbus, who was now known by the name of Cristóbal Colón in his newly adopted homeland, an audience with two of Spain's most prominent citizens. One of these persons was Don Enrico Guzmán, duke of Medina Sidonia, a wealthy shipping magnate who controlled much of the fishing trade

80

along the Gibraltar region; but unfortunately he showed absolutely no interest in Columbus's proposal. The Genoan received more welcoming reception from Don Luis de la Cerda, the duke of Medinacelli, who, after listening to Columbus's plan for reaching the fabled Indies, went out of his way to provide sustenance and shelter to the new arrival and his son, as well as to grant Columbus a modest stipend. The wealthy duke, who owned a large fleet of caravels, even contemplated providing Columbus with several of his own vessels for such an expedition; but in the end he decided that a voyage of this magnitude was a matter of national interest and, therefore, would require royal approval and patronage.

When they felt the moment was right, Christopher Columbus and the duke of Medinacelli petitioned the Spanish sovereigns, King Ferdinand and Queen Isabella, for a royal audience. Unfortunately for them, their request happened to coincide with far more pressing matters before the royal court and Columbus was forced to endure a wait that stretched into nearly a year in length. Finally, on May 1, 1486, at the city of Cordova, he stood before the royal couple with his bold pitch to lead Spanish ships manned by Spanish sailors across the waters of the Atlantic to forge a faster and safer passage to the magnificent wealth of the Indies.

While Christopher Columbus was eager to convince King Ferdinand and Queen Isabella that his was indeed a plausible plan, he was, nonetheless, rather apprehensive about revealing too much information—a perfectly understandable reaction when taking into account all that had just occurred at the court of King John. He spoke of how in a mere forty days' sail westward from the coast of the Cape Verde Islands he would unveil to Spain the splendid marvels and great mysteries of the Far East. Columbus, with the visual aid of his own map, played to the Crown's cupidity by promising to find the island of Antilla, the fabled land where seven Catholic monks had fled to found "Seven Cities" of magnificent beauty and enormous wealth. Antilla, he told them, would serve as a way station for the remaining short trek to the "very noble island of Cipangu," a land that many Europeans believed to be "most rich in gold, pearls, and precious stones, and [where] the temples and royal palaces are covered with solid gold." Once Cipangu had been found and explored he planned to then sail on to Cathay, a land of even greater wealth and home to the great and powerful khan.

To further sweeten his proposal, Columbus appealed to the deep religious convictions of the "Catholic kings" with a promise to convert to Christianity the great multitude of heathen souls he was sure to encounter along the way and a pledge that a substantial share of his profits from this expedition would go toward financing another crusade to recapture the Holy

Sepulcher, the tomb outside the city of Jerusalem from which Jesus is said
to have arisen following his crucifixion.

While his demeanor and confidence certainly succeeded in capturing
the attention of the Spanish sovereigns it was, however, Columbus's fervent
passion and powerful elocution which stirred their imaginations. This foreign sailor had laid before them a truly enticing proposal. Spain had long
been envious of Portugal's papally protected preserve of trade along the
extensive western coastline of Africa. There was also a growing concern that
the Portuguese explorers were on the verge of succeeding in their long
quest to round the southern tip of Africa and establish a direct link with
the lucrative trade of the Indies, an accomplishment that would surely make
Portugal one of the richest and most powerful nations in all of Europe.
However, neither Portugal nor Rome had laid claim to the waters that were
directly to the west of Europe. While Queen Isabella was sufficiently
impressed by the plan, King Ferdinand had his reservations, and their divi-
sion over this issue condemned Columbus's proposal to yet another panel
of experts. However, the royal couple did seek to retain the services of
Christopher Columbus by providing him with a small annuity, and later
they would furnish him with royal letters which obligated their Spanish
subjects to provide the esteemed sailor with any food or lodging he might
require.

The select committee of advisers who sat in judgment of Columbus's
proposal was composed of men who were considered to be knowledgeable
in matters of navigation, science, and religion. This particular panel was
presided over by Hernando de Talavera, the bishop of Avila, who also served
as the queen's confessor. The group grilled Columbus for more specific
details on the course he proposed to take but the suspicious sailor continued to remain evasive in the answers he provided to them. The Spanish
committee, much like the previous Portuguese panel, had a difficult time
reconciling the nautical calculations made by Columbus. At that time,
Ptolemy was still the recognized authority on world geography and according to his calculations the continent of Asia was approximately 10,000 nautical miles away, a figure that dwarfed the distance estimated by Columbus.
The committee also called into question the character and experience of
this boastful foreigner, ultimately concluding that he was not qualified to
command such a daring and dangerous expedition. The panel's negative
opinion was reported to Christopher Columbus in August of 1487. Conspicuously absent from the formal proceedings were both King Ferdinand
and Queen Isabella, who were off to do battle with Granada, the last Islamic
bastion dwelling within the borders of Spain.

A HOLY WAR

After nearly seven hundred years of Islamic occupation, the small kingdom of Granada was all that stood in the way of Spain's finally becoming
united under one Christian flag. When the armies of Islam crossed the
Strait of Gibraltar in 711 they were on a holy quest, or jihad, to force the
infidels of Europe to submit to the will of the almighty Allah. The Moors,
who were basically a combined force of Arabs, Syrians, and Berbers, swept
across the land, vanquishing all Christian armies that dared to stand in
their way. The conquest of the Iberian Peninsula was nearly complete by
the year 719, the only exception being a small pocket of Christian forces
who had taken refuge in the mountains to the north.

This invasion by the Moors gave birth to the oft-repeated tale of the
magnificent Seven Cities of Antilla. Fearing the sharp wrath of the Islamic
scimitar, seven Catholic bishops huddled as many devout Christian followers and supplies as they could on board the few small vessels they were able
to charter. The Christian flock then sailed westward onto the unknown
waters of the Atlantic where, after drifting aimlessly for a number of weeks,
they happened upon a large island that they christened Antilla, the "island
opposite" Portugal. It was here that they found for themselves a luscious
garden paradise teeming with an abundance of necessities and luxuries. Large
nuggets of gold, exquisite pearls, and a dazzling array of precious diamonds,
emeralds, and rubies were said to litter the entire landscape. To honor the
munificence of their God, each bishop sought to pay tribute to Him by
building his own magnificent city, designated on many European maps as
the cities of Asay, Ary, Vra, Jaysos, Marnlfo, Ansuly, and Cydone. The wealth
and splendor of the Seven Cities of Antilla was immortalized in books and
maps, and consequently, the legend became embedded in the minds of
those who dared to dream of discovering this mysterious and faraway land.

From their mountain stronghold in northern Spain, a small force of
unyielding Christian soldiers began a long and arduous campaign to reclaim
their homeland from the Muslim invaders. Spanish knights carrying ban-
ners emblazoned with the cross of Saint James, the patron saint of Spain
and their anointed slayer of Moors, rode out to do battle with the enemy.
Rallying behind the shouts of "Santiago!" Spanish warriors fought with
tremendous courage and conviction; summoning an inner strength that
helped to empower them with the might to prevail over vastly superior
numbers, slowly, but steadily, they forced the "infidels" to retreat from the
lands they had long occupied. Following each triumph the devout Spaniards
gave thanks to almighty God for delivering unto them such a glorious victory and pledged to continue the holy war until all of their enemies had

been purged from the land. Christianity was the common bond that united the native people of Spain.

After many defeats and much bloodshed the Moors suffered the loss of most of their territorial claims and before long the once mighty conquerors of Hispania found themselves confined to the small kingdom known as Granada, a small strip of land that faced the Mediterranean Sea and their former homeland of North Africa. The rest of Spain was divided into the independent Christian kingdoms of Aragon, Castile, and Navarre. The unification of Spain, though well under way, was still far from complete, but hope sprung eternal after the union of Princess Isabella of Castile and Prince Ferdinand of Aragon in 1469.

It would be several more years before Spain's royal Catholic couple earned the titles that were to endow them with the authority to consolidate the separate governments, the individual laws, and the divided estates of Spain under one authoritative rule. With the death of her half-brother in 1474, Isabella became queen of Castile and five years later Ferdinand became King of Aragon following the passing of his father. As husband and wife, Ferdinand and Isabella ruled jointly over their domains.

In order to begin instituting the many changes they desired to make, Ferdinand and Isabella needed a common cause their loyal subjects could rally behind, and religion they discovered could be employed as the means to achieve their ultimate political end. As devout Catholics, with Isabella being the more pious of the two, the monarchs sought to merge both church and state into a single body politic. After the head of the Roman Catholic Church assented to their request for the right to make their own clerical appointments, the king and queen quickly gained and exerted control over the influential Church of Spain. His Holiness managed to further their cause with the issuance of a papal bull in 1478 that granted Ferdinand and Isabella the right to establish the Council of the Inquisition, an investigative commission that was answerable only to the royal couple. The Spanish Inquisition, a name forever etched in infamy, unleashed a reign of terror upon tens of thousands of Spaniards who failed to adhere strictly to the sacred tenets of Christianity.

The many barons and knights of Spain, who, by virtue of their enormous landholdings, posed a formidable threat to Ferdinand and Isabella's plans for absolute rule, were forced into submission with the sudden annexation of their estates and castles. As compensation for their material loss the noblemen were granted titles that conveyed great importance, but which, in reality, carried little or no authority. Once they had gained control over the functions of the Church and the properties of the nobles, the Spanish monarchs were finally in a position to assert their complete authority over the affairs of state. With their newly consolidated power base, Ferdinand and Isabella proceeded to the next logical stage, the unification of Spain, and the first step toward that goal was the conquest of Granada. When the Moorish king of Granada refused to pay the mandated tribute of gold to King Ferdinand and Queen Isabella, the Christian rulers were handed a legitimate excuse for commencing their holy campaign to eliminate the last stronghold of the Moors within the borders of Spain. Once again they were aided by the Pope, who declared the war against Granada a holy crusade to wrest the last remnants of power from the Islamic infidels. This call to arms spurred patriotic knights and nobles from both near and far to join the great Christian army commanded by King Ferdinand and Queen Isabella.

THE CAPE OF STORMS

Even though he was greatly frustrated by Spain's recent rejection of his proposal, Columbus refused to abandon his plans for the "Enterprise of the Indies." After all, he reasoned, God would not have spared his precious life just so that he might labor in vain. He knew he was destined for greatness and if he continued to persevere he would, eventually, find his true reward. Shortly after the negative verdict had been rendered by the Talavera commission, Columbus received word from his brother in Lisbon that Diogo Cão, who had recently returned from a second voyage that had begun with great expectations, had been unable to sight an end to the western coast of the African continent. Seeing this as a sign that Portugal might now be more receptive to his plan, Columbus sought to renew his ties with King John II. In a letter addressed directly to the king he wrote of his desire to return to Portugal in order that he might discuss once again his plans for an "Enterprise of the Indies"; but, in that same correspondence, he expressed his fear of possible retribution from unforgiving creditors still intent upon collecting on his outstanding financial obligations. King John extended to Columbus an open invitation to visit him at his royal residence and offered a guarantee of safe passage through the lands of Portugal.

Whether or not Christopher Columbus actually made the return trip to Portugal has long been a moot point amongst historians. However, when taking into consideration this man's steadfast conviction to fulfill a destiny he so fervently believed was ordained by God himself, it seems unlikely that he would have passed on this invitation from King John. Regardless of whether he made the journey or not, Columbus was about to face disappointment once again. If he was at the court of the king he would have been present at the very moment a triumphant Bartolomeu Dias returned to the harbor of Lisbon with the glorious news of having succeeded in rounding the extreme southern tip of Africa. We do know for a fact that Bartolomeo Columbus was an eyewitness to this historic moment and he even made a notation of this epic event in his copy of the *Imago Mundi*.

In August of 1487, a mere three months after Pedro de Covilha and Alfonso de Paiva had embarked upon their secret overland expedition, three small ships under the command of Bartolomeu Dias slipped quietly out of the harbor of Lisbon. The captain's mission, as dictated by King John II, was to complete three successive tasks of paramount importance. First, Dias was instructed to complete what nineteen previous major expeditions had failed to do: discover a way around the southernmost point of Africa's coastline. The second part of the mission called for him to sail up the unfamiliar eastern coast of Africa until he reached the land of Ethiopia and once there he was to link up with Alfonso de Paiva, who, by that time, should have located the whereabouts of the legendary Prester John. To complete the third leg of his mission, Dias would then have to sail across the Arabian Sea to locate Pedro de Covilha in India. By then, Covilha should have gathered a great deal of intelligence pertaining to the secretive Arab trade routes in Asia.

As this was undoubtedly going to be a voyage of great length, it was decided that one of the three ships in Dias's expedition should function solely as a store ship stocked with plenty of food and drink to support the sailors aboard the other two caravels. King John also supplied Bartolomeu Dias with a map, identical in design to the one provided to both Paiva and Covilha, which documented all known information concerning the waters and lands that were part of both Africa and Asia. In addition to the usual provisions for the crew and various selected items intended for purposes of trade, Dias's ships carried three large stone *padrãos* for planting along the coast. Also on board were two African tribesmen who had been captured and taken to Portugal by Diogo Cão, as well as four African women who were originally from the Guinea coast. These African natives were brought along to serve as guides, interpreters, and more importantly, as messengers. At various points along the coast of Africa the natives were, one by one, released by their benevolent Portuguese captors, carrying with them a small amount of gold and silver, some samples of spices, and messages of good will. Dias hoped they would spread the word that the Portuguese were friendly visitors who were eager to carry on trade with the native population.

Bartolomeu Dias had little difficulty following the path that had been blazed by numerous explorers before him. After having passed the furthest point reached by Diogo Cão, and sailing past the Namib desert, where his sailors gazed upon the large mountains of sand which hug a vast and desolate portion of Africa's southwest coast, Bartolomeu brought his ships to anchor at Port Alexander. As a reward for their loyal service and with the hope that they would spread the Christian word amongst the local natives, the two African tribesmen were set free at that very shore. It was also decided that Dias's supply ship would remain behind at this port under the guard of nine sailors while the two caravels continued on with the search for the end of Africa's western coastline.

Struggling against unfavorable winds for the better part of a fortnight, Dias's ships reached a point that was slightly more than five hundred miles from their intended destination when, all of a sudden, they ran head on into wind gusts that increased steadily in their intensity. As these gale force winds pushed the Portuguese ships further and further from shore the weary sailors soon found themselves engulfed in the grip of a violent storm that threatened to plunge both vessels to the bottom of the sea. Only by steering westward towards the deepest depths of the open ocean, well beyond the view of any land, was Dias able to take his ships past the reach of the storm and out of harm's way. Once the waters below had calmed and the skies above had begun to clear the captain gave the order for his ships to turn about and sail in the direction of Africa's coast. However, after several days of steady sailing the crew was still unable to sight the shores of Africa, and many of the men now feared that they were hopelessly lost at sea. Dias endured this latest test of his mettle by altering his course from east to north, and shortly thereafter the crew had cause to rejoice: land was once again visible to them.

The two badly battered vessels pulled into Mossel Bay on February 3, 1488. But once ashore the Portuguese sailors were forced to shield their bodies from a torrential hail of stones flung in their general direction by a large number of hostile natives who had been lying in wait. Taking careful aim with his crossbow, Dias let loose with an arrow that succeeded in finding its intended mark with deadly accuracy. The swift death of one of their own caused the frightened warriors to take flight and just as quickly as it had begun the battle was over. Now that he was able to get a better fix on their present position, Dias took note of the fact that the coastline no longer stretched southward but instead extended eastward. He now realized that somehow, and at some point, his two ships had succeeded in sailing around Cape Agulhus, the southernmost point of the African continent.

Elated by this sudden and unexpected discovery, Dias and his crew continued to sail eastward until they reached Cape Padrone, at which point they went ashore to claim the land for Portugal by erecting a *padrão*. Anxious to find the Indian Ocean, Dias was hurriedly preparing to resume their journey when he was suddenly confronted by a number of his officers and crewmen, all of whom issued demands for the captain to abandon the remaining objectives of the mission. Low on supplies and even lower on morale, the crew believed it was time to stop tempting fate, count their blessings, and return to Portugal with news of their incredible discovery. Showing that he was willing to listen to the concerns and complaints of his fellow sailors, Dias formed a council to discuss the issues at hand. While most continued to agree that it was time to return home, the captain made them an offer that they all considered to be fair. He asked them to give him three more days of steady sailing and if at the end of that time they still had not found what they were looking for he promised to do a turnabout and begin the voyage back home to Portugal. An official document stating the terms of the agreement was drawn up and signed by all parties present. After three days of battling stormy weather and savage seas with nothing new to show for their heroic efforts, Dias was obligated to keep to his end of the bargain and thus set a course for home.

On the 6th of June the explorers sighted the southern cape that had eluded them previously. The crew gazed upon the mighty rock formation known as Table Mountain and landed just long enough to erect another stone pillar. The terrifying roar emanating from storm clouds hovering over the mountaintops of Devil's Peak, Lion's Head, and Lion's Rump prompted Dias to dub this ominous region the Cape of Storms. From this southern point the sailors cruised northward up the west coast of Africa to Luderitz Bay, and after planting the last of their three *padrãos* they sailed on towards their storeship docked at Port Alexander. Dias and his crew were totally unprepared for what they were about to find there. Though the storeship was still intact, six of her nine crewmen were discovered dead on deck, all having died while bravely defending the boat and themselves against bands of marauding tribesmen determined to loot their ship. Another of the valiant guards, worn down by fatigue and illness, died shortly after the return of his comrades. Dias had all of the salvageable provisions and goods on board the storeship transferred to his caravels and once that task was completed he ordered his men to set fire to the empty vessel.

In December of 1488, after having endured a fifteen month long odyssey that had taken them across nearly sixteen thousand miles of ocean, Bartolomeu Dias and his remaining crew finally arrived in Lisbon where they were hailed as conquering heroes by a large crowd of exuberant citizens. Summoned before King John, the courageous Dias told the royal court of how he had come upon the long anticipated route around the southern tip of Africa. Suddenly, after several decades of exploration, the wealth of the Indies appeared to be finally within the grasp of Portugal. The king, though obviously elated by the long anticipated discovery of Africa's end, was, most likely, perturbed by Dias's failure to complete the remainder of his mission. There are no surviving records of honors or rewards being bestowed upon Dias for his epic voyage except for the granting of a small pension, and as for any future expeditions, he continually found himself cast in the role of either an adviser or a secondary commander. We do know that King John decided that his captain's christening of the southern tip of Africa as the Cape of Storms sounded far too foreboding, and he chose to change its name to the Cape of Good Hope, a title that offered up the promise of better things to come.

Realizing that this recent discovery of a way around Africa by Bartolomeu Dias meant that King John would now undoubtedly invest all of his resources in exploring an eastern route to the Indies, the forlorn Columbus brothers decided to begin pursuing other nations that might benefit from their western scheme. While Bartolomeo went to England to pitch their proposal at the court of King Henry VII, Christopher returned home to Genoa with high hopes of finding a financial backer. However, he found that the merchants of Genoa were quite content with their established Asian trade arrangements in the Levant and therefore were unwilling to invest in his plan. Unsurprisingly, a similar response awaited him at the city of Venice. With his options seemingly exhausted, a frustrated Christopher Columbus returned to Spain.

THE CAPITULATION

Finding himself unable to arouse the interest of King Henry VII of England, Bartolomeo Columbus journeyed across the channel to try his luck before the royal court of France. Bartolomeo was able to gain access to King Charles VIII by forging a close friendship with Anne de Beaujeu, the sister of the reigning monarch. In fact, Anne became so infatuated with the Italian cartographer from Spain that she even helped support his stay in France by commissioning several maps from him. While he never did receive a royal commitment to his brother's plan, he was, however, encouraged enough by the initial show of interest to remain in France longer than he had originally planned.

In the meantime, Christopher Columbus returned to Seville, only to find that Ferdinand and Isabella were still preoccupied with their holy crusade against the Moors of Granada. In the summer of 1489, however, it appeared that his luck might have finally begun to change for the better. While Ferdinand was off waging war, Queen Isabella granted him a brief private audience. Columbus was a man possessed of great charm and much intelligence, and he effectively utilized these personal assets to persuade the queen of Castile to reopen his case before the Talavera commission. He walked away from their private meeting with a renewed confidence that the Spanish monarchy would support his grand expedition once this interminable holy war had come to an end.

Spain's long awaited hour of victory finally arrived on January 2, 1492. On that day, Boabdil, the Sultan of Granada, after having suffered through a long and devastating siege, surrendered the city of Alhambra, the last city in all of Spain that was ruled by the Moors, to the Christian armies led by King Ferdinand and Queen Isabella. The peal of church bells resonated throughout the land in mass celebration of Spain's glorious conquest. Christopher Columbus, as jubilant as any Spaniard on that day, knew that once Granada had fallen it was just a matter of time before the Spanish sovereigns would grant their royal blessing to his proposed voyage. He unfortunately left himself open for yet another rude awakening; for in that same month the Crown's advisory committee was to once again reject his plan for an "Enterprise of the Indies." Feeling betrayed by both Isabella and Ferdinand, a dejected Christopher Columbus began making plans to join his brother in France, and surely would have made the journey there had he not stopped first at La Rabida to say farewell to his faithful friend friar Antonio de Marchena. During this visit he also met with Father Juan Pérez, the head of the monastery, and after both men had listened to his woeful tale, the clergymen jointly decided to take up his cause by arranging yet another audience for him with the queen of Castile.

Luis de Santángel, King Ferdinand's keeper of the privy purse, was keenly interested in the plan presented by Christopher Columbus. The finance minister was an astute businessman who had amassed a large personal fortune during his tenure as co-treasurer of the Santa Hermandad, or Holy Brotherhood. This was a secret society of military police established by King Ferdinand, who pledged themselves to ridding Spain of the numerous thieves and murderers that terrorized its citizens. These pursuits were, for the most part, financed by the loot that was confiscated from the bandits they had succeeded in capturing. The long war with Granada had proved costly to the Crown's coffers and Santángel was constantly on the lookout for ways to replenish the rapidly dwindling funds of the royal treasury. Santángel saw in Columbus's proposal for an Enterprise of the Indies the potential for Spain to compete more effectively with her neighboring rival in affairs related to foreign commerce.

The endorsement of such respected men of the cloth as Juan Pérez and Antonio de Marchena helped to sway the court's opinion in Columbus's favor. All that he had to do now was simply set forth his terms for this great service he was about to perform for Spain. Appearing before a royal audience at the town of Santa Fé, Christopher Columbus once again spoke of the magnificent riches his Enterprise of the Indies would soon reveal to Spain. As compensation for the incredible amount of wealth he promised to deliver to the Spanish sovereigns, Columbus demanded, just as he had done at the court of King John, an immediate commission as "Admiral of the Ocean Sea" and appointment as "Viceroy" over all the lands he was sure to discover. As for monetary reward, Columbus stated he would accept no less than ten percent of all revenue generated from the lands he located and claimed for Spain. Both Ferdinand and Isabella were taken aback by these outrageous demands and intimated that perhaps he had overestimated his own worth. As the steadfast conviction of Columbus left absolutely no room for compromise, the sovereigns soon grew weary of his stubbornness and dismissed him from their presence. The proud mariner turned and hastily marched from the royal chamber, mounted his awaiting mule, and then headed down the road to Seville, determined to make his way to France, where he hoped to find patronage in the arms of King Charles VIII.

As Christopher Columbus slowly rode out of town, Luis de Santángel pleaded with Queen Isabella to reconsider the Italian's plan for a westward voyage to the Indies. He reminded the Queen that since Portugal controlled all the trade routes through Africa, and seeing as the Portuguese were now closer than ever to reaching the Indies, it was clearly in the economic interest of Spain to try and cultivate its own trade routes to the Indies. Santángel then appealed to Isabella's strong religious convictions by reminding her highness that Asia was overpopulated with heathens just waiting to be converted to Christianity. His most persuasive point went to the very heart of the matter—the issue of money. He convincingly reasoned that the costs to the Crown would be minimal because nothing would be owed to Columbus unless he actually discovered the Indies, and in that event, his ten-percent commission was but a small price to pay for the enormous wealth that was sure to flow from such a fabulous find. Isabella was deeply moved by Santángel's impassioned defense of Columbus and even offered her own jewels as collateral for a loan to help finance the proposed expedition. Santángel thanked the queen for her generous offer but explained to her that through a combination of private investments and state imposed taxes he would be able to finance the whole venture without having to risk the crown jewels. The finance minister had succeeded in demonstrating that the potential for rewards from this highly speculative venture greatly outweighed any perceived risks, and the monarchs agreed to have Columbus recalled to Santa Fé. A messenger was immediately dispatched who, mounted upon a swift steed, easily caught up with the leisurely Columbus and his mule just four miles away from town. On April 17, 1492, the Spanish sovereigns capitulated to all of the terms previously set forth by Christopher Columbus.

Religious Persecution

THE JEWISH DILEMMA

While under Islamic rule, the Iberian Peninsula had long been a land of ethnic and religious diversity. The Moors, to a great extent, tolerated the beliefs and practices of Judaism and Christianity within their realm. All of that changed under Christian rule: tolerance quickly dissolved under a rigid adherence to orthodox Catholicism. The full wrath of Spanish Christians had been harnessed by a powerful army bent on overthrowing the evil forces of Islam; once this task had been completed, the collective pent-up rage needed an outlet, which it soon found in the persecution of its own large population of Jews. The conquest of the land was but merely an important first step toward conquering the souls of all non–Christians.

Anti-Semitic attitudes governed the thoughts and deeds of most Christian communities in Europe during the period known as the Middle Ages. On many parts of the continent Jews were held in such utter contempt that they were often restricted to living in specially designated areas of the city, commonly referred to as ghettos. They were generally barred from owning land, and those fortunate enough to possess property did so at the risk of confiscation and expulsion by a greedy noble or monarch. The Jews were often portrayed as a vile race of people guilty of committing horrendous atrocities aimed at undermining the Christian faith. It was commonly believed that Jews systematically abducted Christian children for their bizarre ritual sacrifices, and conspiracy theorists even went so far as to blame them for the dreaded Black Death, the horrific plague that wiped out close to one-third of Europe's entire population.

Restrictions upon and exclusion from certain vocations forced many members of the Jewish community to specialize in professions which were commonly deemed unsuitable for a person of good Christian character. One commercial window left open to them was the lucrative practice of lending money for the express purpose of making a profit. The Catholic Church had taken a strong stand against the practice referred to as usury, but Christian merchants starved for working capital simply evaded these religious constraints by borrowing directly from businessmen who were not Christians. Their propensity for making money from money brought great wealth to many Jews and before long a great number of Jewish businessmen were exercising enormous control over a large segment of Europe's commercial affairs.

During the Islamic reign, the Jewish community residing in Spain enjoyed a far greater degree of freedom when compared to the pitiful plight of the rest of their European brethren. Spanish Jews, for the most part, thrived under a grant of religious immunity; many held such prominent positions as physicians, bankers, teachers, scientists, and even a fair number of influential administrative posts. However, their positions in Spain became tenuous under the new Christian rule and grew increasingly precarious under the zealous reign of King Ferdinand and Queen Isabella. Jealous of the Jews' vast accumulation of wealth and considerable assimilation of power, envious Spanish Catholics began lashing out against the Jewish population as a whole. Their outrage soon erupted in violence. Angry mobs of Christians swept through major cities such as Seville and Cordoba, where they proceeded to brutally slay thousands of innocent Jews in the temples where they worshiped, in the buildings where they transacted business, and on the streets where they lived. With Christian vigilantes calling for their immediate expulsion from all of Spain, tens of thousands of Jews sought sanctuary by converting to the faith of their oppressors. While baptism helped to save many lives, the newly converted were generally viewed with suspicious eyes. Many believed that these *conversos* were merely masquerading as good Christians in public while behind closed doors they continued to practice the faith and teachings of Judaism. Bigoted Christians took to labeling converted Jews as Marranos, the Spanish word for swine, and within a short period of time this disparaging epithet became an accepted stereotype applied to all Spanish Jews.

THE SPANISH SOLUTION

Riots aimed directly against the Jewish population broke out once more in March of 1473 at the city of Cordoba and those uprisings quickly spread to many of the neighboring towns and villages. Concerned that many of the converted Jews were still adhering to the practices and beliefs of their old faith, the Spanish clergy persuaded Queen Isabella to appeal to Rome for the reinstatement of the Inquisition to assist them in weeding out those who had strayed from the righteous path of Christianity. Spanish officials had previously utilized the all-powerful authority of the Inquisition during the 13th century as an effective legal means for convicting individuals the Church had accused of heresy, a charge which was viewed as a crime against both God and the state. After that time the judicial powers of this omnipotent institution lapsed until Pope Sixtus IV, in 1478, granted Ferdinand and Isabella the right to appoint three inquisitors of their own choosing to pass judgment in the queen's province of Castile. The right to choose was an extremely important point. Normally, such appointments were made by the clergy at Rome, thereby making it a Holy Roman Inquisition into charges of heresy. But by granting the Spanish monarchs the right to select individuals who were answerable to the Crown and not the Pope, it had now become a Spanish Inquisition. Ferdinand and Isabella would wield the Inquisition as an instrument of terror to help them achieve absolute power within Spain.

The Spanish Inquisition's primary agenda was to investigate charges levied against recently converted Jews who were suspected of secretly adhering to the forbidden practices of Judaism or baptized Muslims believed to have reverted to their banned Islamic beliefs. For those unwilling to confess to their sins, the Spanish inquisitors had at their disposal various devices of torture that excelled at extracting evidence and eliciting the "truth." Those who were found guilty of heresy were usually burned at the stake— a dreadful fate that befell more than three hundred Jews the very year that the Spanish Inquisition was formed. The estates of the condemned were promptly confiscated by the Crown, with part of the proceeds going toward covering the ongoing expenses associated with these holy investigations while the remainder went towards enriching the coffers of the royal treasury.

When reports of the many abuses and atrocities being committed by the Spanish Inquisitors began filtering back to officials in Rome, Pope Sixtus IV attempted to intervene, but His Holiness quickly discovered that King Ferdinand and Queen Isabella were not about to abdicate any powers already subscribed to their precious judicial body. Instead, the Catholic couple, in August of 1483, increased both the breadth and scope of the Inquisition with their appointment of Tomás de Torquemada as grand inquisitor for the Spanish provinces of Castile and Leon. Two months later, the king and queen of Spain, in an additional act of defiance of the Pope, extended the powers of the Inquisition to include the passing of judgment in Aragon, Valencia, Catalonia, and Majorca.

Under the zealous guidance of Torquemada, the Spanish Inquisition instituted a reign of terror against all suspected heretics, blasphemers, witches, moneylenders, and other sinners of the Christian faith. Ironically, this Dominican who had risen through the ecclesiastical ranks to become confessor to both Ferdinand and Isabella, was himself possibly from a family of converted Jews. Torquemada would soon establish tribunals at numerous towns and cities as part of his grand plan to hasten the complete eradication of any potential religious threat to the newly unified Christian kingdom of Spain.

Spanish citizens were encouraged, through promises of spiritual and monetary rewards, to inform the inquisitors of any Marranos or Moriscos whom they suspected of being insincere Christians. Anyone of Jewish or Moorish heritage lived in constant fear that at any moment an angered neighbor, a dissatisfied patron, or an envious business rival might point the finger of suspicion in his direction. It took only the accusation of one person to condemn and subject an entire family to the cruelties of torture as well as the immediate loss of all their earthly possessions. Torquemada made terror a public spectacle with his introduction of an elaborate and gruesome ceremony known as the auto-da-fé (act of faith). Those condemned to death by the Inquisition were paraded to a public spot where, before a usually large assemblage of Christian witnesses, they were given an opportunity to publicly air their sins before the execution of their sentence. Those who failed to confess their sins were burned at the stake, a painfully symbolic taste of the eternal after-life which awaited them in the pits of hell. It has been estimated that during the eighteen year reign of Tomás de Torquemada as many as 10,000 people were sentenced to death, 2,000 of whom were condemned to burn at the stake.

Much of Torquemada's hostility was directed toward purging all remaining remnants of Judaism from Spain's domain. To purify the nation at once, and hopefully for all time, the grand inquisitor presented to Ferdinand and Isabella his final solution to the Jewish problem. He proposed that all Jews be given one last option: either fully embrace the tenets of Christianity, by submitting to the ritual of baptism, or face immediate expulsion from Spain. The Spanish sovereigns agreed with his audacious plan and together they issued an edict on March 31, 1492, that compelled all Spanish Jews to comply with the proposals set forth by Torquemada.

The deadline for complete compliance was set for July 31, 1492. By that date all Spanish Jews should have either been legally baptized as Christians or already departed Spain. Those who chose to flee from religious persecution had only four months in which to dispose of their properties and businesses; the consequent forced selloff provided many Christians with an opportunity to profit handsomely. Since the Jews were forbidden to take any Spanish coin or precious metals out of the country, all proceeds from these forced liquidations had to be converted into bills of exchange. They were, however, allowed to take any personal possessions that they could carry with them. Any assets not liquidated before the established deadline became the sole property of the Spanish Crown.

While an estimated 50,000 Jews fulfilled their baptismal obligation, in order that they might remain as citizens of Spain, a mass exodus of some 170,000 Spanish Jews sought solace in other lands. Gone were the bankers, the teachers, and the businessmen who made up a large and important segment of Spain's middle-class population. While many Spanish Christians celebrated the end of Judaism within their realm, they would later lament the loss of so many men who were knowledgeable in the ways of finance and business.

More than half of the Jews who left Spain during this dark period of the Inquisition took refuge in neighboring Portugal, where there was already a large Jewish congregation. While Portugal's King John II was certainly more tolerant of their religious conviction, he was, however, concerned that such a large influx of non–Christians could prove disruptive to a nation that prided itself on its ongoing missionary efforts to spread the teachings of Jesus Christ abroad. The king had planned to supply these fugitive immigrants with ships to take them somewhere else, but for one reason or another this plan of his never came to pass. They were originally told that they could only stay in Portugal for a period of eight months, after which time they would all have to be beyond the borders of Portugal. Much to the chagrin of this Christian ruler, the Jews stayed on past the date mandated, and even stayed beyond the length of his reign.

When King John II passed away in 1495 the Portuguese crown was handed to his cousin and brother-in-law, the duke of Beja, who took the royal title of Manuel I. The new ruler, who was also a great-grandson of John I, demonstrated his sympathy with the plight of the Jews by rescinding many of the harsh mandates imposed by his predecessor. Just when it appeared that things had finally begun to improve for the Portuguese Jewish community King Manuel began courting Princess Isabella, the daughter of King Ferdinand and Queen Isabella of Spain. The Spanish sovereigns made it perfectly clear to Manuel that they would only bless such a union on the condition that he banish from his kingdom all Jews who refused to receive a proper Christian baptism. Manuel, who had grandiose visions of one day uniting the two Iberian thrones, agreed to their terms for matrimony and shortly thereafter issued his own edict of expulsion in 1496. While a large percentage of the Jewish population, particularly those native to Portugal, chose to convert, there was once again a massive exodus of people seeking to evade further religious persecution. Many of these refugees ended up migrating to new homelands in Turkey, Poland, Germany, Russia, and the Netherlands. Once he had satisfied the demands of his future in-laws, Manuel was free to marry Isabella. But it turned out to be a short-lived marriage as the Spanish princess met with an untimely death in 1498.

Convinced that their plan of forced conversions and expulsions had successfully purged Spain of Judaism forever, King Ferdinand and Queen Isabella then sought to complete the purification of their homeland by unleashing the powers of the Inquisition against the few remaining Muslim communities. The Moors had been allowed to retain their religious freedom following the surrender of Granada in January of 1492, but when Spanish officials called for the expulsion of all unfaithful Marranos just two months later, the faithful followers of Islam knew their day of judgment would soon come.

FIVE

At the Edge
of a New World

Visions of Cathay

THE FIRST VOYAGE OF COLUMBUS

Even after King Ferdinand and Queen Isabella had approved Christopher Columbus's plan for the Enterprise of the Indies, it still took Columbus and Luis de Santángel the better part of a month to obtain the necessary funding for this ambitious undertaking. As he had promised, Santángel used his formidable influence as the treasurer of the mighty Santa Hermandad to arrange a loan of 1,400,000 maravedis for the Crown's contribution to the expedition, and on top of that, the minister of finance added another 350,000 maravedis from his own purse. As for Christopher Columbus, he managed to raise, with the financial assistance of the Bank of San Giorgio in Genoa, an additional 250,000 maravedis towards his own cause. As for the actual outfitting of the expedition, the Spanish sovereigns, with the help of the calculating mind of Santángel, came up with an ingenious plan that would not cost the royal treasury a single maravedi. Citing the port city of Palos for a previous infraction, Ferdinand and Isabella ordered the town to make amends by furnishing Columbus with two fully equipped vessels for his expedition.

It was in May of 1492 that an eager Christopher Columbus, in the company of Father Juan Pérez, traveled to the city of Palos to lay claim to his ships and to begin the process of enlisting a competent crew. Once he arrived at Palos, he presented the royal decree, which he had carried with him, to the mayor of the town who then had it read aloud before an assembly of the city's most prominent politicians and businessmen. The citizens of Palos were given a period of ten days in which to comply with the Crown's order to secure provisions and equip two caravels for the expedition. Once notice had been given, Columbus set himself to the task of recruiting experienced seamen, and since Palos was a bustling seaport that provided steady employment to a great number of sailors, he fully expected to be able to pick and choose from an elite cadre of experienced mariners. As additional enticement for prospective recruits, the admiral placed a large number of gold coins conspicuously atop his recruitment table and then sat back and waited for the sailors to begin lining up. His wait went on for several days without so much as a single sailor signing up for his expedition. Columbus eventually learned that he had become a target of the malicious gossip and superstitious fears being spread by the local townsfolk. They had begun whispering amongst themselves that this foreigner was a madman, and consequently no respectable sailor wanted to play the role of fool to this Italian's folly. Learning of the difficulties that Columbus was encountering at Palos, Queen Isabella tried to help by declaring that a royal pardon would be issued to any convicted criminal who signed up to sail on this venture. Evidently even the convicts thought he was insane, as only four condemned men took advantage of her generous offer to save themselves from the harsh confinement of prison.

What finally rescued the admiral's plan from certain disaster was a timely introduction to the township's favorite sons, the prominent Pinzón brothers. Martín Alonso, Francisco Martín, and Vicente Yáñez Pinzón were all respected navigators and competent men of business who commanded considerable respect and clout amongst the citizens of their hometown. Columbus, who desperately needed the support of the brothers, asked them to join his expedition, and the Pinzóns, who saw in his plans the potential for enormous profit, gladly accepted his offer. With the Pinzóns now at his side, Columbus was finally able to enlist a qualified crew numbering approximately one hundred and twenty men for his epic voyage.

The experienced and knowledgeable sea captain Martín Pinzón made a firsthand inspection of the vessels that had been conscripted for Christopher Columbus, and he found both to be unsuitable for the rigors one would expect to encounter on such a long and grueling voyage. In their search for more suitable craft, Pinzón and Columbus were able to commission from Cristóbal Quintero the caravel christened the *Pinta*, and from Juan Nino they obtained the rights to another caravel which went by the name of the *Niña*. Both Columbus and Pinzón decided to add another ship, a slightly larger vessel which would serve as the flagship for their small fleet. They located a suitable Galician vessel owned by Juan de la Cosa known as the *Marigalante*. However, Columbus felt that the "frivolous Mary" label was an unworthy title for a command ship so he had her rechristened the *Santa María*. By signing on all the owners as crewmen aboard their own ships, Columbus and Pinzón were able to tap into the owners' unique and valuable awareness of each boat's subtle idiosyncrasies. Columbus appointed Martín Pinzón captain of the *Pinta* and his brother Francisco as first mate. Vicente Pinzón was given command of the *Niña*, and Columbus, of course, was to lead the whole expedition from the deck of the *Santa María*.

The next few weeks were spent busily preparing the three ships for their long journey into the vast unknown. There were enough provisions stored on board to sustain the entire crew for a voyage of one year in length. The least perishable foods, such as hardtack, a kind of biscuit, and salted meats and fish were stocked in great quantities. A large number of wooden casks were rolled onto the decks—some contained fresh water while the others were filled with inexpensive wine. Olive oil, an essential ingredient in the preparation of cooked food, was stored in great quantity inside large vats. As Marco Polo's book told of thousands of islands lying off the shores of Cathay and Cipangu, Columbus thought it prudent to prepare for any possible encounters with the uncivilized inhabitants of these remote lands. Brightly colored glass beads and small brass bells, the kind that falconers attach to their birds of prey, were among the many trinkets they brought along for trade with the natives. They also carried aboard their ships small samples of rare gems, exotic spices, and precious metals to visually convey to the island natives the valuable items that they sought to acquire through trade.

Christopher Columbus carried in his pocket letters of salutation from King Ferdinand and Queen Isabella for his expected encounter with the Great Khan of Cathay. To serve as an interpreter for the expedition, he enlisted the services of Luis de Torres, an experienced sailor who was capable of conversing in the Hebrew tongue and, to a limited degree, in Arabic. To record and protect their own interest, the Spanish monarchs appointed Rodrigo de Escobedo as royal notary and Sánchez de Segovia as comptroller of the Expedition to the Indies.

On August 3, 1492, just as the first beams of morning light began to appear over the distant horizon, and immediately following an early celebration of mass, the three ships weighed anchor and sailed westward towards the mysterious realm of the Far East. Their grand adventure had barely begun when a fleet of twenty-five ships passed by them heading toward ports further north, each vessel overcrowded with the solemn faces of the last faithful Jews being expelled from Spain.

MAKING CONTACT

The three Spanish ships pulled into the Canary Islands on the 12th of August to take on additional provisions and to make some necessary repairs to an already damaged and leaking *Pinta*. Columbus had purposely scheduled a stop at the Canaries because a departure from this location had an obvious nautical advantage: most maps of that period showed the Canary Islands lying along nearly the same latitude as both Cipangu and Antilla, and if this were true then all his ships simply had to do was follow a straight course to reach the vast treasures that awaited them on the other side of the world. While they were leisurely soaking in the sights on the isle of Gomera another ship came into port carrying ominous tidings for Columbus and his crew. The captain of that vessel reported that not far behind him were three fully armed Portuguese ships recently dispatched by King John II with explicit orders to capture Christopher Columbus. The admiral had good reason to assume that what he just heard was the truth, for he suspected that the king of Portugal was determined to sabotage his efforts to reach the Indies, and, he feared, the monarch's means to justify this end was to have him arrested and incarcerated for those still outstanding debts.

Not wanting to wait around to verify whether or not this report was the truth, the admiral issued orders for his ships to depart at once from the Canaries. On the 6th of September, after latching on to a gust of wind that was strong enough to swell their white sails emblazoned with the bright red cross of Christ, the three vessels resumed their westward voyage toward the Indies. By adhering to a westerly course along the same latitude as that of the Canaries, Columbus was able to tap into the favorable seasonal winds that helped speed his ships along at a much better than expected pace. Being an experienced man of the sea, Columbus often relied on dead reckoning to determine his bearings as well as his rate of speed. As a precaution on this voyage, he took it upon himself to maintain two separate logs for recording the distances they had traveled. One book, which remained hidden from the rest of the crew and even his own officers, recorded his remarkably accurate measurements, while a second book, which was freely shown to the others, reflected a somewhat lesser estimation. By underestimating his measurements in the latter log Columbus hoped to assuage any concerns that might arise in the event his calculations of the distance between Cathay and Europe came up short.

Ten days into their journey everyone rejoiced over the sighting of "bunches of very green weed," a clear indication that they were nearing land. But their sudden elation soon turned to consternation as the sea, which grew darker as the weeds grew thicker, failed to reveal the outline of any land ahead. They had entered the Sargasso Sea, a vast expanse of still-water in the Atlantic that runs deep with a brownish seaweed known as Sargassum, the plant that provides this body of water with its unique name. Afterwards they continued to see signs that convinced Columbus and his men that land was surely close at hand: a great whale off in the distance, many crabs and dolphins swimming near their vessels, and numerous tropical birds and doves flying directly overhead.

Other than for the disappointment of not having sighted land, the expedition had sailed along quite smoothly. However, this blessing in itself soon took on the appearance of a terrible curse. Observing that there were no storms the men began to worry about how they were going to replenish their drinking water once the barrels ran dry, or, if the winds of this region constantly blew westward how then it would be possible to sail back to Spain by the same route. Columbus and his captains were cautiously concerned that these rumblings of discontent might soon escalate into a full-scale mutiny.

On the 6th of October, Martín Pinzón pulled his boat alongside the *Santa María* in order to suggest to his commander that they just might have better luck finding land if they tried following the path by which the birds flew overhead—a piece of advice which obviously meant that they needed to alter their present course slightly to the south. But the proud Columbus had no intention of following the recommendation of a subordinate officer. Shortly thereafter a frenzy of excitement and anxious anticipation took hold of the entire crew when a sailor cried out that he had sighted land. However, their joy soon turned to sorrow once it was realized that what he saw was but an illusion—a mere marriage of the line of the sea and a distant storm cloud. On the following day, Columbus decided to alter his course after having sighted additional flocks of birds coming from the general direction that Martín Pinzón had spoken of earlier.

Morale amongst the members of the crew was sinking fast and several disgruntled sailors made it known that they wished to return to Spain. There was even a plot to take over one of the ships, a mutiny that might have succeeded had it not been uncovered by Martín Pinzón before it could be set in motion. Columbus managed to placate his discontented crew on the 10th of October with a pledge to return home if land was not sighted within the next several days.

With a promise from the Spanish sovereign of a lump sum reward of 10,000 maravedis to the first man to sight land, each sailor dreamed he would be the one to claim this magnificent prize as his own. Shortly after midnight on the morning of October 12th, Rodrigo de Triana, the lookout perched in the crow's nest of the *Pinta*, cried out "Tierra! Tierra!" The sailors aboard the *Pinta* scurried to the deck and Captain Pinzón fired off a cannon shot to alert the other two ships of their sudden discovery. Columbus quickly emerged from his cabin and was able to catch a faint glimpse of land silhouetted against the dim light cast by the moon above. Though barely able to contain his own elation, Columbus prudently ordered his sailors to wait until dawn before attempting any landing. The admiral would later reward Triana with 5,000 copper coins but denied him the right to the promised prize by claiming it for himself. Columbus would contend that around 10 o'clock the night before he had seen a light off in the distance that could only have been man-made. Much to the chagrin of Rodrigo de Triana, the commander conveniently concluded this was the true first sighting of land.

The first light of dawn confirmed that which they all hoped and prayed would be true. After more than a month of continuous sailing under the shade of blue skies upon a seemingly endless sea they had finally discovered land. Columbus had his ships sail carefully along the coast of the island until he spotted a suitable bay to safely weigh anchor. They had landed at one of the nearly seven hundred islands and islets that comprise the archipelago presently known as the Bahama Islands. The precise island he came across first is still debated to this day, but the general consensus is that his flotilla landed at the island now known as Watling island. Of course, Columbus and his men were absolutely certain they had landed on one of the many islands that supposedly lay off the coast of either Mangi or Cathay.

Landing boats were lowered into the water and the first to reach the beach was the vessel that carried Christopher Columbus and his principal officers. Leaping from his rowboat, the admiral waded the last few feet to the sandy shore of the island, followed closely by his two captains, Martín and Vicente Pinzón. Once on solid ground, Columbus and his entire entourage knelt down in prayer—giving thanks to the Almighty for having safely guided them to this distant shore. The group then proceeded to plant a large cross while Rodrigo de Escobedo, the royal notary, read aloud a proclamation claiming the land, which Columbus had christened San Salvador (Holy Savior), as a Spanish possession.

Christopher Columbus took a moment to reflect on all that he had endured in order to reach this remote uncharted isle in the Atlantic Ocean. After years of painstaking research and meticulous planning; following numerous appearances before various heads of state and their select committees of skeptical scholars; after suffering through the cruel taunts and endless ridicule that spewed forth from the lips of those who lacked his worldly vision; and finally, after having skillfully and courageously navigated his three small ships across a seemingly endless body of water, Columbus

Christopher Columbus: The "Admiral of the Ocean Sea" (kneeling) and his entourage claim the island of San Salvador for King Ferdinand and Queen Isabella of Spain.

took comfort in the knowledge that his place in history was assured. He had proved that there was indeed a western sea route that led to the legendary lands known as the Indies.

While this historic event was unfolding a small band of natives, peering from behind the cover of the island's palm trees, tried as best they could to make sense of all that they had just seen. Curiosity eventually got the better of them and they proceeded to stroll down to the beach for a closer look. Though alarmed at first, the Spaniards soon realized that the naked natives who stood before them were a very gentle and peaceful people. Before long the entire beach was filled with copper-complexioned islanders who were eager to catch a glimpse of the fair-skinned men who had magically floated across the great sea. They took tremendous pleasure in receiving the trinkets that Columbus and his men freely distributed amongst them, especially the tiny bells that tinkled so pleasingly when shaken.

In recording his first impression of the natives, Columbus wrote: "They are very well made, with very handsome bodies, and very good countenances.

Their hair is short and coarse, almost like the hairs of a horse's tail." He also recorded that "They invite you to share anything that they possess and show as much love as if their hearts went with it." Columbus had identified these natives as Lucayans but they were actually Tainos, a tribe whose lineage and language was part of a much larger race of people known as Arawakans. Many years prior, a great number of Arawaks had left their homelands along the coast of South America and rowed great distances across the water to establish new homes amongst the numerous islands of the Caribbean Sea. As history has recorded, it was Christopher Columbus who christened the inhabitants of these lands with the name that persists to this day. Convinced that he was among the many islands that were said to lie off the coast of India, it was only natural for him to conclude that these natives were members of the Indian race.

On the following day the natives returned in full force to resume trading with the Spaniards. Columbus wrote of his second encounter: "They brought balls of spun cotton and parrots and spears and other trifles, which it would be tiresome to write down, and they give all for anything that is given to them. I was vigilant and endeavored to find out if they had gold, and I saw that some of them wore a small piece hanging from holes in their noses, and from signs I was able to understand that in the south there was a king who had large vessels of gold and possessed much of it. I endeavored to make them take me there, but later I saw they had no desire for the journey. I resolved to wait until the afternoon of the following day, and after that to leave for the southwest, for many of them indicated to me that there was land to the south and the southwest and to the northwest, and that those of the northwest often came to attack them. So I resolved to go to the southwest, to search for gold and jewels." This marked the beginning of a pattern that would continue for many years to come—by appealing to the avaricious nature of those who invaded their lands, the inhabitants of the New World found they could easily rid themselves of those Old World intruders with wondrous tales of wealthy kingdoms that lay somewhere just beyond their domain. Thus began the greatest gold rush in all of history.

Elated by the sight of golden ornaments dangling from the faces of so many islanders, Columbus and his men were inspired to search for the source of this wealth. Judging by the poverty of the natives on the island he surmised that this was not Cathay or Cipangu, but ever the optimist, the admiral concluded that he had instead reached the outermost rim of the 7,448 islands that Marco Polo had written about in his book. Taking along six Tainos to serve as guides and interpreters, Columbus set out to see "whether I can come across the island of Cipangu."

The Search for Khan

For the next two weeks the explorers sailed from one island to another, and even though they failed to find any signs of wealth, they did manage to give each new discovery of land a proper Christian name. Columbus's ships finally dropped anchor again on the 28th of October at an island that they all believed to be Cipangu; but in actuality, they had landed at the large island now known as Cuba. This must have been a confusing moment for both the admiral and his crew, for if this was Cipangu then where were the numerous palaces whose roofs were made of gold? When questioned as to where he might find more gold, the island's natives sounded out the name "Cubanacan," which they indicated through gestures was located a considerable distance inland. In their native tongue Cubanacan simply meant the middle of Cuba, but to the hopeful ears of Columbus, it was interpreted as a garbled mispronunciation of the name of the legendary ruler Kublai Khan.

Thoroughly convinced that the royal court of the Great Khan was close at hand, the admiral decided to send Luis de Torres, his appointed interpreter, and Rodrigo de Xeres, a gentleman who once had been introduced to an African king and was therefore somewhat familiar with the proper protocol for a royal encounter, as his emissaries. Armed with letters of introduction from both King Ferdinand and Queen Isabella, Torres and Xeres set out on foot for the imperial city in the company of two native guides who had generously offered to show them the way to Cubanacan. After crossing nearly twelve leagues of extremely difficult Cuban terrain, their journey came to an abrupt halt. The great city that they expected to find turned out to be nothing more than a village of some fifty large huts which were home to nearly a thousand natives. As they entered the village, the two Spanish messengers were escorted to one of the larger huts which, though lavish by the standards of this tribe, was certainly less opulent than they had imagined the Great Khan's palace would be. The local chief, who was referred to as the cacique, honored his unexpected guests with a welcome normally reserved for island royalty. Though Torres and Xeres were greatly disappointed by their discovery, they hold the distinction however of being the first Europeans to come in contact with two indigenous plants that were destined to play an important role in future commerce between the Old World and the New World. One of these items was the tobacco leaf, which the natives skillfully rolled into large cigars and smoked for both ceremonial and medicinal purposes. They were also the first to encounter corn, the main staple of the native diet which the Spaniards described as "a sort of grain they call maize which was well tasted, bak'd, dry'd and made into flour." Torres and Xeres returned from their mission with a report that only served to dampen the spirits of Columbus and his men.

Even before Torres and Xeres had returned from their journey to the village of Cubanacan, Columbus had reworked his maritime calculations and now concluded that they were not on the island of Cipangu after all, but instead had succeeded in reaching the mainland of Cathay. However, with the disappointing news he had just received from his two returning emissaries, the admiral was forced to once again reassess his present position, and he subsequently declared that Cuba, while though still part of the mainland of Asia, was actually the province that Marco Polo and Sir John Mandeville had identified as the province of Mangi. The disappointed sailors continued to sail along the coast of Cuba in hopes of finding the fabled city of Quinsay, but signs of wealth and civilization continued to elude their best efforts. Once again the admiral took to questioning the natives as to the exact whereabouts of precious gold and once more he was told of a far-off land where gold could be found in great abundance. This time the island was called Babeque. Believing all that he had just heard, Columbus set sail in search of this wondrous land of gold, but was forced to return to the island when his ships ran head on into severe winds. On the 21st of November, Martín Pinzón, captain of the *Pinta*, on his own authority, decided to leave the company of the other ships and hunt for the rumored riches of Babeque.

Columbus was not quite sure of what to make of Martín Pinzón's sudden defection. He feared that his second-in-command had either gone off on his own to find fame and fortune, or had returned to Spain to claim for himself all that the enterprise had already discovered. Columbus wandered along the coast of Cuba and then sailed from one island to another in hopes of locating Pinzón but he never caught sight of the missing *Pinta*. Choosing to abandon what was clearly a misguided quest, the *Santa María* and the *Niña* resumed their search for the lands of Cathay and Cipangu.

On the 6th of December the *Santa María* and the *Niña* put in at the harbor of an enormous island that the natives called Quisqueya. The admiral was so taken with the beauty of this island, which seemed to possess a climate and terrain that reminded him of his adopted homeland, that he christened his latest discovery La Isla Española, meaning "the Spanish Island." Before going ashore, Columbus instructed his crew to confine their dealings to only the trade in gold, a simple plan which he hoped would force the natives to lead him directly to their natural supply of precious metals.

The inhabitants of Española proved to be just as warm and friendly as the natives they had previously encountered on the islands of the Bahamas and Cuba. These natives who greeted them with small gifts and great reverence were, just like the other islanders, of Arawakan descent. While Columbus noticed that they were a peaceful race who, much like the other natives he had come across, thrived on the fruits of their bountiful lands, the admiral also learned from them that he would not find every island to be such an earthly paradise. They spoke of a fierce tribe who periodically rowed many miles in canoes, which were large enough to haul as many as eighty passengers, across the water to raid their villages for food, and their favorite food happened to be the tender flesh that cloaks the human body. To the natives of Española these man-eaters were known as Caribs, while other islanders referred to them as the Caniba. Though slightly intrigued by these horrific tales, Columbus was much more concerned with matters currently at hand, namely the source of those golden ornaments which adorned the noses and ears of so many island inhabitants. When he inquired about the gold of Babeque the natives seemed to know of its whereabouts and even added their own tales of nearby islands teeming with golden delights.

Following one particularly grueling day of waging battle against difficult winds off the coast of Española, the exhausted crew lapsed into a deep slumber shortly after having consumed their evening rations. It was Christmas Eve, and all aboard the *Santa Maria*, including the captain, slept soundly while the ship's watch was left to the charge of a lad not yet old enough to be called a man. Columbus recorded in his journal that shortly after midnight, "swells drove the ship very gently onto one of those reefs, on which the waves broke with such a noise they could be heard a league away." When the *Santa Maria* crashed into the reefs Columbus and the crew scurried to do whatever they could to rescue their rapidly sinking ship, but when the situation became hopeless the sailors then frantically turned their efforts toward transferring everything of importance to the deck of the *Niña*. They desperately raced against the relentless pounding of the waves, but the tide eventually turned against them and the *Santa Maria* began to give way totally to the powerful strength of the sea. Guancanagari, the local cacique, came to the rescue by supplying Columbus with a number of tribesmen to assist in the recovery effort. The benevolent cacique also provided the weary Spaniards with sustenance and shelter. Once on solid ground the grateful admiral gave thanks to almighty God for sparing him and his crew, but then he began to ponder over their present and precarious predicament. The *Santa Maria* was wrecked beyond repair, the *Pinta* was still unaccounted for, and the *Niña* was far too small to transport the crew and supplies that belonged to two vessels.

To pay his respects, as well as to give thanks for the generous assistance he received during their hour of need, Columbus traveled to the village that was lorded over by Cacique Guancanagari. It was here that the admiral finally found that which he had longed for—a place overflowing with gold. Everyone seemed to possess at least a piece of this precious metal, and most were willing to part with some or even all that they owned. One cacique was said to have in his possession a nugget of gold the size of his hand which he stubbornly refused to part with as a whole, no matter how much they tempted him; on the other hand, he had no qualms about breaking it into smaller pieces to barter for whatever Spanish trinkets seemed to catch his fancy. Guancanagari showered Columbus with a number of valuable gifts, including masks and rings made entirely of gold. Once again, Columbus began questioning the natives about where he might find even more gold, and just as they had done back on Cuba, the natives pointed inland. This time though, the natives cried out "Cibao," a name that Columbus interpreted to be the elusive Cipangu. Suddenly, God's purpose had been revealed to him.

Columbus clung to the belief that God had once again interceded on his behalf in order that he might be shown the way. In keeping with his blind faith, the admiral further reasoned that the wreck of the *Santa María* was a divine sign that told him, when the time came for his return to Spain, he was to leave a group of his men behind at Española. He ordered the crew to salvage as much wood as they could from the damaged ship, and before long they had succeeded in gathering enough timber to construct a small fort, which the admiral christened La Navidad (Christmas). Columbus appointed Diego de Arana and Pedro Gutiérrez as joint commanders of a garrison that consisted of these two men and thirty-eight other sailors. Most of the forty had volunteered for what they thought would be an idyllic assignment on an island paradise. Besides leaving behind enough provisions to sustain them until he could return with additional supplies and men from Spain, Columbus made sure they had on hand sufficient firepower to command the respect of the natives. It was expected that Diego and Pedro would continue to obtain gold by way of trade with the natives, and it was also hoped that by the time Columbus returned to Española they would have discovered the exact location of the island's rumored fields of gold.

The Right of Way

An Unscheduled Return to Portugal

In preparing for his return to Spain, Columbus had his men load on board the *Niña* a varied sampling of the many exotic treasures he had unearthed on his journey to the other side of the world. There were brightly colored parrots, a great variety of fish, several different kinds of herbs and spices, a bale of cotton, six native Indians, and a fairly sizable quantity of the most precious item of all: gold. Even though he had yet to find the fabulous court of the Great Khan or catch sight of the golden-roofed temples and palaces of Cipangu, the admiral was confident that he was bringing back enough evidence to convince his royal benefactors in Spain that he had truly found the gateway to the riches of the Far East. On January 4, 1493, in the company of Vicente Pinzón and the rest of the crew of the Nina, Christopher Columbus said goodbye to Española, unaware this was to be a final farewell to the comrades he was leaving behind at La Navidad.

On just their second day out to sea, Columbus and his crew came upon an unexpected sight—the return of the missing Pinta and her derelict captain, Martín Pinzón. Not wishing to trade harsh words across the water, the admiral ordered both ships back to the island, and once docked he proceeded to give the disobedient captain a thorough tongue-lashing. In his own defense, Pinzón declared that he had not, as Columbus claimed, abandoned the expedition but instead had sailed on to find Babeque for the admiral. Columbus refused to believe his story. This obviously tense situation quickly escalated to the point where the admiral began threatening to have the insolent captain hanged on a charge of desertion. Martín Pinzón is reputed to have responded, "Is this what I deserve for having raised you to the honor in which you stand?" Pinzón went on to claim that he did eventually find the fabled island of Babeque but what he failed to find was any gold. He said that the natives of this island directed him to Española, the island that Columbus had already discovered. It was at Española, just as Columbus had done before him, that Pinzón traded his inexpensive Spanish wares for a considerable quantity of the natives' gold, half of which he kept for himself. Though the two captains agreed to settle their differences for the sake of the expedition, an air of tension continued to cloud their personal relationship from then on. On the 16th of January, the Niña and the Pinta left Española to begin the long voyage home.

It was pretty much smooth sailing on the waters of the Atlantic for both caravels, that is until the 12th of February. On that day the homeward-bound vessels encountered a storm of considerable magnitude. For the next three days the two small ships were tossed about by gale force winds and raging waters. At the very height of the storm's wrath the crew of the Niña once again lost sight of the Pinta. This time, however, Columbus was certain that Pinzón's ship was forever lost at the bottom of the sea. Fearing a similar fate awaited him and his crew, Columbus made a solemn vow to the Blessed Virgin Mary that if she would deliver them from this terrifying ordeal, then once they reached civilized land they would all march to the site of the nearest church, clad only in their shirts, to pay homage to her. After surviving the savage fury of the wind and the sea Columbus and the exhausted crew of the *Niña* came upon the island of Santa María in the Azores, a Portuguese possession, on the 17th of February.

From the deck of his ship Christopher Columbus could faintly make out the silhouette of a chapel situated some distance inland. In accordance with his promise to the Virgin Mary, the admiral sent part of his crew ashore to begin carrying out their penance. When the first group of sailors failed to return within a reasonable period of time, the admiral began to worry that something was terribly amiss. His suspicions were confirmed the moment he noticed a group of armed men rowing briskly towards his vessel. What followed was an intense confrontation of words between Columbus and a Portuguese captain determined to impose his authority over these impudent Spanish intruders. After informing the admiral that the men he had sent ashore were currently being detained, the captain, who suspected that Columbus's ship was returning from an illegal expedition along the west coast of Africa, ordered him to anchor his ship immediately and to surrender himself, his crew, and his vessel. Columbus scoffed at these brazen threats and ludicrous demands and, in turn, issued his own ultimatum: if they did not release his crew at once he would have no other choice but to bombard them into submission. As they parted company another ominous looking storm began brewing from above, and fearing that his only remaining ship might end up smashed to pieces against the island's coast, Columbus ordered his men to sail out of the harbor.

Once the tempest had passed Columbus returned to the harbor with every intention of making good on his bombastic threat. Fortunately for all parties concerned, the brief passage of time had cooled the temper of the Portuguese captain. Another small boat rowed out to the *Niña*, this time with two priests and a town official aboard. These men were more interested in learning of the admiral's true purpose, and when Columbus produced the royal letters that were signed by King Ferdinand and Queen Isabella of Spain, the Portuguese officials knew they needed to reevaluate their present position if they hoped to avoid a potentially explosive international incident. Once the Portuguese emissaries returned to the island they immediately released all of the Spanish prisoners.

As soon as all of his men were safely back aboard ship the admiral cast off for the final sprint back home to Spain. But once again they ran into foul weather and Columbus was forced to dock his severely weather worn ship at the first available port. As fate would have it, the Spanish crew, on the 4th of March, found themselves seeking sanctuary at a small port town situated along the coast of Portugal, not too far from the city of Lisbon. News of Christopher Columbus's unexpected arrival was quick to reach the ear of King John II and he responded by immediately dispatching an emissary to formally request his appearance before the royal court at Lisbon. Though skeptical about the King's true intentions behind his cordial invitation, Columbus graciously accepted the offer, knowing all too well that it would be unwise to offend such a powerful ruler as King John.

The closer Christopher Columbus got to the city of Lisbon the more concerned he became for his own safety. After all, it was not that long before that a Portuguese fleet purportedly had been sent to intercept him at the Canary Islands, and he was convinced that the king was behind this attempted assault against his person. There were even whispers that King John was luring him to Lisbon to be tried, convicted, and publicly executed. Once he was within the city limits Columbus managed to smuggle out letters to King Ferdinand and Queen Isabella in which he described his many splendid discoveries and how his present and rather precarious situation in Portugal prevented him from bringing this glorious news in person. By whetting the appetite of the Spanish sovereigns, Columbus hoped the royal couple would intercede on his behalf.

Summoned before the royal court on the 9th of March, Christopher Columbus stood proudly before King John II, the same ruler who only a few years earlier had refused to approve his plan for an Enterprise of the Indies. The admiral surely took delight in the knowledge that he had succeeded in reaching the Indies before any of the king's own men could and he took even greater pleasure in reminding the king of this fact. King John II, who received Columbus with honors befitting his Spanish rank, was curious to learn more about these discoveries, specifically, their exact location on a world map. Position was a very important issue, for if his discoveries happened to lie along a latitude south of the Canary Islands then these lands were rightfully a Portuguese possession; however, if their latitude was north of that designation, as Columbus claimed they were, then Spain had full rights to these discoveries. This line of demarcation had been put in place in 1480 with the signing of the Treaty of Toledo by the rulers of both Spain and Portugal. This treaty received papal sanction the following year when Pope Sixtus IV issued a bull that in effect divided all unclaimed worldly possessions between the two Catholic nations of the Iberian Peninsula. Columbus insisted that his path to the Indies followed a line parallel to the Azores and therefore was well within the Spanish half of the sphere. But Christopher Columbus knew this to be a lie, and King John suspected as much. The plain truth of the matter was that each of his discoveries—

the Bahamas, Cuba, Española and the numerous islands in between—were clearly within the Portuguese realm of authority.

The admiral's boastful claim of having found a faster and more direct westward route to the treasures of the Far East was viewed with much suspicion by many of those who were in attendance at the Portuguese court. After all, it was noted that he had failed to locate Cathay, Cipangu, Mangi, or for that matter, any of the fabled cities of the Orient. In addition, he brought no news of the Great Khan nor had he encountered any of the great traffic in spices that was known to take place in that distant part of the world. Many believed that instead of finding the Indies he had instead accidentally stumbled upon the mythical land of Antilla. There were many at court who disapproved of the manner in which this brash foreign braggart flaunted himself before their honorable king, and it is said that a number of King John's faithful men offered to assassinate the admiral before he had the opportunity to return to Spain. The king, however, refused to sanction their murderous plot. Following his meeting with King John, Columbus traveled a short route from Lisbon to pay a respectful visit to Queen Leonor at the Convent of Santo Antônio da Castanheirac. While there he was met by a messenger bearing news that an official escort of soldiers awaited to guard him on an overland journey to Spain. Suspecting a plot against his well-being, Columbus politely declined their offer of protection and returned to the safety of his ship. On March 13th the *Niña* was granted permission to sail for Spain.

A HERO'S WELCOME

Christopher Columbus and his crew managed to safely reach the harbor of Palos just two days later, and once docked he immediately dispatched a messenger to the city of Barcelona, where King Ferdinand and Queen Isabella were presently holding court, to announce his successful return from the legendary realm of the Far East. Shortly thereafter, another caravel pulled into the port of Palos brandishing the same flags and pennants of Spain. Martín Pinzón and the crew of the *Pinta* had managed to weather the powerful storm that had separated them from the *Niña*. In fact, Pinzón and his sailors were quite surprised to learn of the *Niña*'s safe return, for they were thoroughly convinced that she had not survived the full fury of that terrible tempest. The shock of seeing the *Niña* apparently proved too great a strain for the weary Pinzón. Already exhausted from battling the elements, the thought of having to answer to charges of misconduct only served to weaken an already delicate condition. He returned to his house at Palos where on the 20th of March, shortly after having penned a letter in which he professed his utmost loyalty to both Columbus and the Crown, Martín Pinzón exhaled his last breath.

Meanwhile, Christopher Columbus received an enthusiastic reply from King Ferdinand and Queen Isabella that requested his immediate presence at Barcelona. Placing himself at the head of a grand procession, which included many of his crewmen, a great variety of exotic animals, and several natives of the Indies, the admiral paraded through a great number of Spanish towns and villages located along the route to the royal court. At each stop he was received with great fanfare and much ceremony. The length of these numerous celebrations delayed his arrival at Barcelona until nearly the end of April.

In eager anticipation of Columbus's expected arrival, Ferdinand and Isabella spared no expense in lavishly decorating their city in his honor. An enormous crowd hailed the explorer and his entourage as they passed through the gates of Barcelona, and once inside, they received an official greeting from emissaries sent on behalf of the Spanish monarchs. His entrance at the court of the king and queen was no less spectacular. The royal chamber overflowed with everyone who was anyone, each hoping to catch a glimpse of this extraordinary man who was about to deliver to Spain the keys to the Indies. In a solemn gesture normally reserved for only the highest ranking dignitaries, Ferdinand and Isabella rose from their thrones to greet the sailor from Genoa and then seated the admiral in a royal chair near to them.

Christopher Columbus did not disappoint those who had come to hear his incredible tale of adventure and discovery. He spoke of the many islands he had discovered and explored just off the coast of Cathay; of the friendly natives who inhabited those faraway lands; of the exotic flora and unusual fauna indigenous to those distant shores; and of course of gold, all that he had seen as well as all that he had heard about. In a carefully orchestrated display designed to dazzle and delight those in attendance, Columbus brought forth the splendid wealth of the Far East. Large cages that housed parrots and other birds cloaked in their colorful plumage were carried in; giant barrels storing a fabulous array of fish they had caught in those distant waters were pried open; enormous chests filled with aromatic spices and herbs were passed around for all to see; a great number of unusual plants were put on display; and there was even a cage containing a live iguana.

The sight of scantily clad natives caused a tremendous stir of excitement throughout the assembled crowd. Columbus presented these Indians to the royal court as incontrovertible proof that he had indeed landed in the Indies, for after all, Marco Polo had described the people living on the islands between Cathay and Cipangu as those who "have no king or chief, but live like beasts." He also wanted the Catholic monarchs to take into consideration the tens of thousands of natives like them who were just waiting to be brought into the Christian fold. In describing the lands that they inhabited, Columbus painted a picture of such majestic beauty—a virtual paradise on earth—that all in attendance were thoroughly convinced that these were lands truly worthy of being claimed as a Spanish possession.

In saving the best for last Columbus astounded the gathered crowd with a display of what he believed to be the true wealth of the Indies: gold, in all its many splendid forms! Beautifully shaped masks of gold, crudely wrought gold jewelry, large nuggets of gold, and even finely powdered gold was laid out for all to see. Then came the promise of much more to come. The admiral told of the company of men he had left behind on Española who, as he spoke, were busily trading Spanish trinkets of little value for even more gold and, during his absence, were continuing the search for the exact location of the island's supposed enormous fields of gold.

King Ferdinand and Queen Isabella had certainly seen and heard enough evidence to convince them that Christopher Columbus had indeed made good on his promise to find a westward passage to the Indies for Spain. He had placed at their feet a great gift, one which the monarchs hoped would launch a newly united Spain on to future greatness. In turn, the Spanish king and queen made good on their promises and officially appointed him "Admiral of the Ocean Sea" and "Viceroy" of all the distant lands he had surveyed. Later, he was the recipient of 1,000 doubloons (the equivalent of 335,000 maravedis) as a reward for his service to Spain, and on that same day he received the additional 10,000 maravedis that the monarchs had set aside as a reward for the first person to catch sight of land on the other side of the world. Believing that he had been robbed of the prize he so richly deserved by an opportunistic superior, an enraged Rodrigo de Triana, the sailor who had first sighted the Bahamas from the deck of the *Pinta*, shortly thereafter renounced his Spanish citizenship as well as his Christian faith and fled to Morocco to live his remaining years as a Muslim. King Ferdinand and Queen Isabella also pledged to Christopher Columbus their enthusiastic support for an even larger expedition to the Indies under his command.

THE WORLD IS DIVIDED

Now that a path to the riches of the Indies had been discovered King Ferdinand and Queen Isabella took the steps they felt necessary to ensure that this new route remained an exclusive right of Spain's. Just as Portugal's rulers had turned to Rome for papal bulls that granted them exclusive rights "in the Ocean Sea toward the regions lying southward and eastward" in their quest to reach the Indies, the Spanish monarchs now sought special dispensation from the Pope to sanction for them a similar monopoly in the opposite direction.

Fortunately for both Ferdinand and Isabella the new head of the Roman Catholic Church was a creature of the Spanish Crown. The Catholic monarchs had used every means at their disposal, including graft, to secure the election of Spain's own Rodrigo Borgia as Pope Alexander VI. However, there was still one obstacle that they had to overcome in order to make their territorial claim legitimate. A treaty concluded in 1480 between the two Iberian powers had given Portugal territorial rights to all lands south of the Canary Islands. Despite all of their claims to the contrary, Columbus and his patrons were well aware of the fact that the true position of their new finds was south of this extended horizontal line and therefore well within Portugal's sphere of influence. To circumvent Portugal's potential claim to the discoveries made by Christopher Columbus, Ferdinand and Isabella proposed the establishment of a vertical line of demarcation to replace the existing horizontal boundary. The Spanish rulers and the Spanish Pope agreed on a vertical line extending north to south which was one hundred leagues west of the Cape Verde Islands. On May 4, Pope Alexander VI issued the *Inter caetera*, a papal bull, which, much to the chagrin of other European Christian rulers, in effect divided the world between the Catholic kingdoms of Spain and Portugal. Everything west of this imaginary line could be claimed in the name of Spain while everything to the east was a sole right of neighboring Portugal.

Portugal's King John II was absolutely furious over this secret arrangement between Spain and Rome. While the *Inter caetera* had reaffirmed Portugal's rights to its established route along Africa, King John suspected that the sudden change was a conspiracy on the part of the Pope and the Spanish monarchs to deny him access to any western lands that were rightfully his. When his protests to the Pope proved to no avail King John sent an embassy to Spain to register his dissatisfaction with this new vertical line of demarcation. The Portuguese emissaries declared that their king had no intention of agreeing to such terms and intimated that they were already aware of a land in that region which was "very profitable and richer than any other" and that they wished for it to remain within their realm. At this point, both parties agreed that the *Inter caetera* could certainly be improved upon.

However, this present impasse between the two Iberian powers did not prevent Spanish officials from seeking additional bulls from the Pope that further strengthened their claims to the wealth of the Indies. After realizing that the *Inter caetera* had failed to mention the mainland of India specifically, Ferdinand and Isabella procured another bull from Rome which granted them the right to claim those territories lying just off the coast of India. In the same breath, and in what amounted to another affront to the legitimate rights of Portugal, the Pope declared that these new sanctions superseded all previous treaties, bulls, and claims to the Indies. Alexander VI issued his latest proclamation on September 25, 1493, a day that just happened to coincide with the departure of Columbus's second Enterprise of the Indies.

The king of Portugal renewed his complaints regarding this newly brokered deal and let it be known that unless the situation was quickly rectified to his satisfaction he would not hesitate to flex his naval might to take back that which rightfully belonged to him. Negotiations between Spain and Portugal were conducted in secret at the Spanish town of Tordesillas, where they were free from the interference of Rome and the Spanish Pope. It took the ambassadors from each nation until June 7, 1494, to reach a compromise that was deemed acceptable to both sides. In the end Portugal agreed to a vertical line of demarcation on the condition that it was shifted to a position fixed at 370 leagues west of the Cape Verde islands. In exchange, Portugal ceded to Spain the rights to all the islands that had been discovered by Christopher Columbus. While the terms of the Treaty of Tordesillas were honored by both Spain and Portugal once the royal signatures were affixed, the agreed upon arrangement between the two crusading powers of Iberia did not receive official papal sanction until Pope Julius II gave it his endorsement in January of 1506.

SIX

Visions of Cathay

The Second Voyage of Columbus

COLONIAL DESIGNS

Even before Pope Alexander VI had officially granted Spain the right to claim as its own all of the lands recently discovered by Christopher Columbus, King Ferdinand and Queen Isabella had already begun making preparations for an even more ambitious expedition to the Indies. Royal expectations were to be even greater for this second Enterprise of the Indies: not only would Columbus have to make good on his promise to find even greater quantities of gold, he was also expected to make contact with the royal court of the Great Khan, discover even more new lands for Spain, establish a permanent colony at Española, and introduce and convert the heathen hordes to the civilized ways of Christianity.

The conversion of Indian souls was a very important condition of the *Inter caetera* that was issued by Pope Alexander VI. In granting Spain's request, His Holiness had stipulated: "And in addition we order you in virtue of holy obedience to send to the aforementioned islands and mainland learned, God-fearing, experienced and skilled missionaries who will exert all their powers to instructing the inhabitants in the Catholic faith and imbuing them with good morals." To comply with this commandment of the Pope, the monarchs appointed Juan de Fonseca, a deacon of Seville and later the bishop of Burgos, to oversee, from the comfort of his government office in Seville, all Indian affairs in these newly discovered lands. To administer the rites of baptism and to aid in the general welfare of the natives of the Indies, twelve priests were selected to accompany Christopher Columbus on his second expedition. Their missionary efforts were overseen by Friar Bernardo Buil, whom the Pope ordained as "Vicar Apostolic of the Indies." The stage had been set for future conflicts between the high ideals of Catholicism and the pecuniary motives of Spanish imperialism.

It was Juan de Fonseca who laid the foundations of the Royal and Supreme Council of the Indies, a governing body that oversaw all aspects of administration and supervision of matters related to these newly discovered lands across the Atlantic. Answerable only to the king and queen of Spain, the Council of the Indies assumed, and consequently wielded, immense powers over many affairs of state. Personal differences between Christopher Columbus and Juan de Fonseca rapidly deteriorated into an intense dislike for one another; but, in the interests of this expedition, they assumed an air of civility. The admiral also had a run in with Juan de Soria, the royal secretary whom the Catholic couple had appointed to oversee all of the financial affairs of the expedition. It seems that Soria, who apparently begrudged the admiral his success simply because he was a foreigner, had failed to pay Columbus the proper respect he was entitled to, an insult that resulted in a royal reprimand that commanded the royal secretary to "honor and respect the admiral of the Indies, in such a manner as befits his station, and as we desire." Of course, Columbus himself was not without fault. His fiery temper combined with his considerable disdain for bureaucracy and utter contempt toward supervision could, at times, alienate even the most saintly soul.

While the Spanish sovereigns implored both Christopher Columbus and Juan de Fonseca to make haste in their preparations for another Enterprise of the Indies, the sheer size and scope of this expedition made honoring such a request all the more difficult. There were seventeen vessels to fit and nearly 1,500 persons to recruit for this second voyage. Adding to the complexity of the mission was the admiral's determined effort to plant at Española a large colony that would function as a center for trade and a base of operation for further exploration of the Indies. He envisioned a self-sustaining colony which would eventually yield additional revenue for himself as well as his royal benefactors. To aid in the success of his colonial effort Columbus brought along a great number of recognized European staples for planting in these new lands. Wheat, barley, and rice were included among the many grain products that the admiral transported across the waters of the Atlantic. Such fruits as lemons, melons, grapes, and oranges were also brought aboard his ships and stored alongside alfalfa, olives, and sugar cane. There was also a large shipment of livestock that included cattle, horses, chickens, donkeys, goats, sheep, pigs, and cats and dogs. But, in a lesson most likely learned from his deceased father-in-law, there is no mention of any rabbits accompanying this expedition.

The admiral's crew of nearly 1,500 eager seafarers included soldiers, sailors, farmers, craftsmen, laborers, a doctor, and a surgeon. Also signing on for the trip were two of the four convicts who had been granted a full pardon for having sailed on the first voyage. Don Diego, the baby brother of Christopher Columbus, signed on for the expedition as did two future conquistadors of note—Alonso de Ojeda and Juan Ponce de León. Also enlisting for this historic voyage were more than two hundred "gentleman farmers." These were men of means who paid their own way for the chance to experience both an adventure and the enticing possibility of adding to their own fortune. Before setting sail, Christopher Columbus left his son Diego in the care of the royal court, where he would serve as a page to Prince Juan, heir to the Spanish throne.

The Return to the Indies

On September 25, 1493, following many months of careful planning and preparation, the great fleet finally sailed out of the harbor of Cádiz. The admiral made the obligatory stopover at the Canary Islands where a great deal of time was spent replenishing their stores and adding to their wares. The fleet left the Canaries on the 13th of October, steering a course similar to the one Columbus had followed on his first crossing of the Atlantic. Just as before, the admiral was blessed with fair skies above and a good wind at his back, and after only three weeks he was back among the many islands of the Indies. On Sunday, November 3rd a new island was spotted which Columbus, in tribute to the day on which it was discovered, christened Dominica. However, instead of docking at the island of Dominica, the admiral decided to anchor at a sister island that he chose to name Mariagalante, a name that for some strange reason he no longer objected to, in honor of his present flagship bearing the same name.

After finding the island of Mariagalante to be uninhabited the fleet then sailed on until they came upon an even larger island lying just to the north. Columbus ordered one of his captains to take a party of men ashore to conduct a thorough search for any signs of human existence. This expeditionary force soon came upon a small and recently abandoned village; its startled and frightened occupants had chosen to flee the moment they heard the loud lumbering sounds of the approaching Spaniards. During their search of the deserted huts they found little of either value or interest, except for inside one particular dwelling where they saw a sight that made their blood curdle in fear. Piled on the floor were a number of bones that at first glance appeared to be the remains of some wild island animal the tribe might have recently feasted upon. A closer inspection revealed that the flesh from these bones had been thoroughly consumed. Only these were not the bones of some small captured creature of the forest but instead were the gnawed skeletal remains of a human being. Though shocked by this truly horrific discovery, as well as growing ever more fearful for their own safety, the Spaniards managed to muster up enough courage to gather the bones they had found into a bundle in order that they might be shown to their captain—lest he think their tale to be a lie. Once the admiral saw with his own eyes what the sailors had brought him he knew for certain that the tales of fierce man-eaters, whom the natives referred to as either Caribs or Caniba, were fact and not fancy.

Wishing to avoid any further contact with such a barbaric race of people, Columbus quickly sailed away but not before he christened the island Santa María de Guadalupe, thereby fulfilling a hasty promise he had made to the monks of Spain to name an island in honor of the famous Virgin of Guadalupe. The fleet continued to sail amongst the small cluster of isles known today as the Leeward Islands. The next island he sighted was named Santa María de Monserrate and this was followed shortly thereafter by the discovery of Santa Cruz. At the latter island, now referred to as St. Croix, Columbus sent a party of thirty men ashore to search for much needed fresh water. During this quest the shore party unexpectedly came upon a village inhabited by mostly women and children, all of whom, just as the natives of Guadalupe had done, fled to the safety of the surrounding jungle when they heard the sounds of the approaching intruders. The Spaniards stumbled upon more than twenty young girls and two young emasculated boys who had been left behind, all of whom were being held against their will by the native Caribs. Once they were set free the grateful Arawakans proceeded to tell them a chilling tale, one which Álvarez Chanca, a member of the expedition, recorded for posterity. He wrote that the released prisoners "told us about incredible cruelties. The Caribs ate the children they had by them. They raised only those born to mothers of their own stock. The men who are captured alive are taken to the house to be butchered when they are needed. The dead are eaten right away. They say that human flesh is better than anything else in the world." They also told the Spaniards that young boys captured during these raids were usually castrated and then condemned to spend their remaining days as slaves, and those days ended when they were selected to be a particular day's main course. As for young Arawakan girls, they were fattened with food until they were deemed plump enough for a very special feast. The Spaniards also learned from these

Arawakan captives that the male Caribs of this village were currently on another raid for more slaves and food and it might be best for all concerned to leave before their imminent return.

Once they were safely aboard ship these poor tortured souls spoke of the nearby island from where they had been taken against their will, a place they called Borinquén. Columbus vowed to return them safely to their homeland, a promise he fulfilled once his fleet dropped anchor on the 19th of November at an island he would christen San Juan Bautista. He found the natives of this land to be just as friendly as those he had encountered at Española. Other than for the occasional threat of a Carib raid, these Arawakan Indians enjoyed an almost idyllic existence. Their island paradise bore enough tropical plants and the ocean yielded such an abundance of fish that the natives never had a need to labor over the land or to spend time hunting for game in order to satisfy their bellies. While he found San Juan Bautista to be a very inviting island, Columbus was anxious to check on the progress of his men garrisoned at Navidad. After a stay of only two days the fleet weighed anchor, leaving behind the island that future conquistadors would rename Puerto Rico, and set a westward course for Española.

DISAPPOINTMENT AT HISPANIOLA

The admiral's fleet arrived at Española on the 25th of November, an island that we will henceforth refer to by its Anglicized name of Hispaniola. Sailing along the Rio de Oro, the river where their captain had previously found a significant quantity of gold dust, the crew soon came upon a gruesome sight. They spotted the lifeless bodies of two men lying along the river's bank. They noticed that one had his feet bound together while the other had a rope strung around his neck. Since the bodies were so badly decomposed the sailors were unable to determine if they were the remains of their Spanish comrades or of some local natives. The next day they discovered two more bodies, only this time there was no doubt. One corpse still had enough visible hair to reveal the outline of what once had been a beard— a facial growth that the admiral had never seen on any of the natives he had encountered.

These ominous sightings certainly cast a giant shadow of doubt over the crew's grand expectations of what awaited them at Hispaniola. Everyone now stood on full alert as they sailed towards Navidad. When the fleet finally anchored along the reefs close to the site of the fort, the admiral had his sailors fire off several volleys of shot to announce their arrival. When no return signal came from the fort, a concerned Columbus organized a shore party to go and survey the situation. Their worst fears were soon realized. Sifting through the charred remains of what was once Fort Navidad, the sailors found no sign of the Spanish soldiers who had remained behind from the first expedition. In the nearby native village they came upon their first clue—the discovery of the shipwrecked *Santa María*'s anchor.

The search party found the native village entirely deserted. Apparently, when the fleet fired off its signal of arrival, the panic stricken natives had fled inland to hide from the unexpected returning Spaniards. A number of villagers were rounded up for interrogation by the admiral and eventually they led him to a spot where eleven more dead comrades were found hidden underneath some tall grass. Judging by the vast degree of decomposition it was clearly evident that these men had been dead for at least several months.

Upon further cross-examination of the captured natives Columbus managed to piece together the grim series of events that climaxed with the massacre of his men and the burning of Fort Navidad. The Indians told him that the men of the fort had begun quarreling amongst themselves as soon as he had departed for Spain. Pedro Gutiérrez and Rodrigo Escobedo, the men whom Columbus had appointed as joint commanders, placed ever increasing demands for more food, more women, and more gold upon the nearby villagers. When the natives failed to satisfy their lustful demands the Spaniards took to cracking their whips and brandishing their swords to take by force that which they desired. At some point, Gutiérrez and Escobedo, after having brutally murdered one of their own soldiers, abandoned the fort, along with nine other men to search for the island's legendary fields of gold. In the company of their native mistresses the soldiers scoured the island until they came upon a region lorded over by a cacique named Caonabo. Learning that Caonabo's domain was rich in gold the renegade Spaniards attempted to extort a tribute from the native ruler. Unfortunately for them, this would prove to be their final demand. The outraged cacique ordered his warriors to slay each and every one of these insolent Spanish soldiers, a command they complied with in an expedient manner.

Once all of these Spaniards were put to death, Caonabo appealed to the caciques of the other tribes to join him in an assault against the remaining soldiers stationed at Fort Navidad. Just a few days after having spilled the blood of eleven Spaniards, Caonabo and his warriors marched toward the settlement currently defended by Diego de Harana and a handful of loyal soldiers. Arriving during the night the warriors commenced with their attack by setting fire to the fort. As the Spanish soldiers and their native concubines ran screaming from the blaze that quickly engulfed their wooden shelter they were vigorously pursued by Caonabo's armed warriors.

A number of Spanish souls sought sanctuary in the surrounding ocean only to face death by drowning while those who remained on solid ground were eventually hunted down and butchered. Some of the corpses were carefully hidden but most were left to rot at the very spot where they were slain.

Suddenly nothing appeared as Christopher Columbus had promised. The crew of this second expedition had expected to arrive at an island paradise where friendly natives were anxiously waiting to receive them with open arms. At Navidad they expected to be greeted by fellow Spaniards who had passed their time busily preparing the foundations for a fruitful colony and unearthing even greater amounts of precious gold. But few could have felt more disappointment than Columbus himself; all that he had envisioned had, both literally and figuratively, gone up in smoke. Once he had managed to regain his composure, the admiral issued orders for the dead to be given a proper burial and for the settlers to search the surrounding area for any treasure that might have been hidden by the Spanish garrison. When an exhaustive search failed to uncover any concealed gold left behind by the previous occupants of the fort a number of the men called upon Columbus to lead an army to avenge the savage deaths of their fallen comrades. The admiral refused to comply with their request. Though disappointed to discover that these natives, whom he had come to admire for their gentle and passive nature, were capable of such atrocities, he was wise enough to understand that their sudden aggressive behavior had been provoked by the wrongful actions of his own men.

Seeking Cibao

Once all of the dead had been given a proper burial, Columbus decided that it would be better to build a new settlement at another location rather than to attempt to rebuild over the charred remains of Navidad. When taking into consideration all that had occurred at the previous site, it was certainly a prudent decision on the part of the admiral. His fleet sailed slowly along the coast of Hispaniola in an easterly direction and after nearly a month of probing and exploring Columbus finally found a spot that he considered suitable for his new colony. A camp was set, a site was cleared, wood was gathered, and before long the colonists had erected for themselves nearly two hundred huts, all of which formed a village that the admiral christened as the colony of Isabela. Columbus had now begun to lay the groundwork for the self-sustaining agrarian-based colony he had long envisioned for Hispaniola. Unfortunately for the admiral many of the settlers, especially the gentlemen farmers, were far more interested in prospecting for gold than in tilling the soil. They had joined this expedition expecting to line their pockets with significant finds of gold: quantities great enough to allow them to retire to a life of luxury back home in Spain. To ensure that the colonists remained focused on the many tasks at hand the admiral proclaimed a ban on all independent gold prospecting during specified periods. Columbus found this to be a difficult rule to enforce and one that even he had trouble abiding by.

Regrettably, Christopher Columbus had failed to plan for the unexpected. No sooner was the settlement of Isabela up and functioning than an illness of unknown origin began to run rampant throughout the colony. Whatever the sickness was, and most likely it was malaria, it took a terrible toll on the inhabitants of the colony. The general laborers appear to have been hit the hardest and problems quickly arose when some of the soldiers and the gentlemen farmers refused to perform what they deemed to be work too degrading for their lofty stations. Grumblings of discontent were overheard when all were compelled to perform tasks, no matter how menial, as assigned by the admiral during this period of crisis.

Despite all that had gone wrong on this expedition Columbus was still determined to find the legendary gold mines that the natives had spoke of on his first landing at Hispaniola. This time, however, the admiral understood that the land the natives constantly referred to as Cibao simply translated into "the rocky land" and therefore was not a jumbled reference to the elusive realm of Cipangu. Columbus sent forth two separate expeditions—one headed by Alonso Ojeda, the other by Ginés de Gorbalán—both of which were guided by Indians who claimed to know the way to Cibao. By the end of a fortnight the two individual expeditions had returned with evidence of gold and news of even greater fields of gold that were waiting to be found just slightly beyond where they had searched.

Elated by such seemingly promising reports, Columbus immediately began drawing up plans for a much larger expedition, one that would be under his personal command, to locate the golden realm of Cibao. But before setting out he decided the time had come to send word back to Spain regarding his present progress, and of course, the terrible tragedy that had occurred at Navidad. On the 2nd of February the admiral sent Antonio Torres to Spain as his bearer of news to King Ferdinand and Queen Isabella. Torres would sail home in the company of twelve ships, each of which Columbus had loaded with as many precious items as possible in the hope that they would help assuage any concerns his royal benefactors might have concerning the disaster that had occurred at Navidad. Upon the ships' arrival at Cádiz the stevedores carted off a substantial quantity of spices, a great many more exotic creatures, and a large sum of gold worth an estimated 30,000 ducats. Also emerging from the boats were several more Indians, twenty-six to be exact, three of whom were members of the fierce man-eating Carib tribe.

While Ferdinand and Isabella were disappointed that Columbus had failed to send back news of his having located either Cathay, Cipangu, Mangi, or the Great Khan, they were extremely disturbed by the news of what had happened at Navidad. As for the many items that the admiral had sent back, there was little on board that the Spanish sovereigns had not seen before. The most intriguing exceptions were undoubtedly the three savage Caribs who were presented before the monarchs. Members of the royal court were mesmerized by Torres's tale of the barbarous nature of these natives. He spoke of Carib warriors who rowed hundreds of miles in fleets of large canoes to attack the relatively docile inhabitants of other islands. Torres went on to tell of how these fierce fighters massacred whole villages, killing all the men and most of the women, reserving only the most beautiful females for the return journey. The Spaniards were horrified to learn that these attacks were not for the purpose of conquest, a quest that they could appreciate; but instead, these assaults were motivated by a basic need for food. The eating of another human being for sustenance and the absorption of their inner spiritual strength were extremely difficult and truly revolting concepts for the civilized European mind to grasp. The citizens of Spain became so fascinated with these terrifying exploits that they soon took to calling the tropical sea where they lived the Mar Caribe, or as it is now known, the Caribbean Sea. From the name Caniba, the other name that the Taino tribe called the Caribs, came the word cannibal, a universal term used to identify a person who feasts on the flesh of humans.

Stories of primitive people who took an unusual delight in the consumption of human flesh had circulated throughout Europe long before the arrival of the Caribs. One such tale came from Niccolò de Conti, a Venetian merchant, who, while disguised as an Arab trader, spent nearly a quarter of a century traveling between the major cities of the Middle East as well as India and many of the islands that are a part of the vast Indonesian archipelago. Upon his return to Venice in 1441 he told his grand tale of adventure to Poggio Bracciolini, a personal secretary to Pope Eugenius IV, who recorded the events for posterity. Conti spoke of having visited the Andaman Isles where he encountered such a barbaric practice: "In one part of the island called Batech, the inhabitants eat human flesh, and are in a state of constant warfare with their neighbors. They keep human heads as valuable property for when they have captured an enemy they cut off his head, and having eaten the flesh, store up the skull and use it for money. When they desire to purchase any article, they give one or more heads in exchange for it according to its value, and he who has the most heads in his house is considered to be the most wealthy."

Meanwhile, back at Hispaniola, Christopher Columbus was busy organizing his expedition to find the golden region known as Cibao. His preoccupation with visions of wealth took the admiral away from the mundane affairs of governing Isabela, an oversight which further fueled a growing discontent that was beginning to fester throughout the new settlement. Shortly before his designated date of departure, the admiral happened to uncover the emerging plans of a rebellion being organized by none other than the expedition's royal inspector, Bernal de Pisa. The admiral had this royal official seized, fettered, and confined aboard the fleet's flagship. After having forestalled this potentially explosive situation Columbus returned to his plans for a march on Cibao, the land where natives told him that gold was "born." On the 12th of March the admiral left Isabela at the head of an imposing army of five hundred men while his younger brother Diego remained behind to govern the colony during his absence. The expedition spent the next several weeks overcoming rugged terrain and enduring constantly foul weather without encountering any signs of the legendary land of Cibao. After a march of approximately twenty-seven leagues from Isabela the expedition came upon a tribe of Tainos who seemed to posses an infinite supply of gold. While he found the natives to be quite friendly, Columbus was more interested in the fact that they were extremely eager to trade their valuable gold nuggets for his meager Spanish trinkets. It was at this spot that they began to build a trading post, which they called Santo Tomás, and in a matter of a few days the Spaniards found themselves rewarded with a treasure of gold weighing in at more than twenty pounds.

Once he felt confident that Santo Tomás was fully capable of functioning without his direct supervision, Columbus decided to return to Isabela with news of the expedition's good fortune. After selecting fifty-six men to remain behind under the command of Captain Pedro Margarit, the admiral and the rest of his army began the long and difficult march back to the colony. However, his arrival at Isabela was not the glorious triumph he had expected. During his absence a fair number of the sick had succumbed to the lingering effects of their illness and now, upon his return, he found the remainder of the settlers on the brink of starvation. Shortly thereafter came the disturbing news from Captain Margarit that trade with the Indians had come to an abrupt halt amid rumors that Caonabo, the mighty cacique who had orchestrated the massacre at Fort Navidad, was planning an immediate attack against Santo Tomás. Columbus responded to Margarit's desperate plea for help by sending Alonso Ojeda and an armed force of just under four hundred men to bolster the defenses of his new settlement.

COLONIAL DISCONTENT

Believing that the problems of native unrest and colonial discontent had been brought under control thanks to swift and decisive action on his part, Columbus decided to renew his search for Cathay and the imperial court of the Great Khan. Leaving Isabela once again to the charge of his brother Diego, the admiral sailed away on April 24, 1494, with three of his five remaining ships. Setting a course for Cuba, a region that he was sure was part of the mainland of Cathay, he came within sight of this large island just after five days of sailing. Columbus and his crew were to spend the next five months traversing from one island to another in a frantic search for the ever elusive kingdom of Cathay. During this period of exploration the admiral discovered the island of Jamaica and many of the islands that are a part of the Lesser Antilles, but his search failed to reveal any signs of the fabulous wealth and elegantly refined civilizations that Marco Polo had so eloquently described in his book.

Frustrated by his own inability to locate the court of the Great Khan, Columbus decided to continue this quest at another time and on another voyage. However, just before returning to Isabela, Columbus had an official document drawn up by the ship's notary which declared that they had in fact landed upon the shores of Asia. Each sailor was asked to attest to this claim by affixing either his signature or his mark to the official document. Those who doubted this finding were given the opportunity to be persuaded otherwise by the admiral himself. Since none of these sailors had ever seen an island as big as Cuba and since their journey had stopped just short of its westernmost point, where it would have been revealed to them that this was but an island, most of the crew felt comfortable with the conclusion made by their admiral. In addition to their signature each sailor swore an oath to this finding and anyone who recanted his testimony would not only face a stiff fine of 10,000 maravedis but would have to forever endure the loss of his tongue.

During the return voyage to Isabela the admiral contracted a fever that soon caused him to become delirious. His condition grew steadily worse and eventually he lapsed into a coma. Fearing that their admiral was near death the crew hastened their pace towards the island of Hispaniola. By the time the ships made it back to Isabela on the 29th of September there had been a very noticeable improvement in the admiral's health but the lingering effects of his debilitating illness forced him to remain bedridden for much longer than he had hoped. His spirits were lifted by the unexpected surprise of seeing his other brother, Bartolomeo, who had sailed to Isabela at the head of three ships fully loaded with sorely needed provisions. Bartolomeo

Columbus had decided to join his brothers, Christopher and Diego, at Hispaniola after Antonio Torres had arrived at Spain with the disconcerting news of the terrible massacre that had taken place at Fort Navidad. Their joyful reunion, however, was disrupted by the fact that the colony had fallen into disarray during the admiral's prolonged absence. Unable to live off the fruits of their own labor a great number of settlers had taken to freely roaming the island in search of both food and gold, often resorting to violent measures against any natives who failed to meet their impetuous demands. Now that the peace had been broken, a number of tribes took to launching counterattacks against their Spanish oppressors. This reign of terror led to the abandonment of the Santo Tomás settlement while back at Isabela a number of colonists began preparing to sail back to Spain to complain about the sad state of affairs that currently existed under the Columbus regime.

Just when it seemed that the escalating crisis at Hispaniola had extended beyond the control of the three Columbus brothers, Antonio Torres returned from Spain with four ships stocked with desperately needed supplies, and, much to the delight of this male dominated colony, a fair number of women. Torres also brought news from the Spanish sovereigns concerning the signing of the new Treaty of Tordesillas and that they both expressed a desire for the admiral's return to Spain to discuss how this new line of demarcation would impact upon his many discoveries in the Indies. Still weak from his illness and slightly embarrassed by what little he had to show for his efforts, the admiral decided he would send his brother Diego in his place.

As his strength began to return, Christopher Columbus slowly began to assume a more active role in the governing of his own colony. In retaliation for the several dozen Spaniards who had been killed by recent Indian raids, the admiral sent forth an army empowered to use any and all means necessary to restore order to the island. He had, in effect, declared war upon the natives, and his soldiers did not hesitate to engage the enemy in battle. While the natives greatly outnumbered the Spanish force, they were certainly not strong enough to defend themselves against such superior weapons and tactics. After having suffered much loss of life the rebellious natives reluctantly laid down their arms. The victorious Spaniards then marched back to Isabela with nearly sixteen hundred prisoners in tow.

This war with the natives had only delayed the inevitable. The time had come for Columbus to report back to King Ferdinand and Queen Isabella on his progress. With very little gold to send back and absolutely no news concerning the precise whereabouts of the Great Khan, Columbus concocted a scheme that he hoped would momentarily appease his royal

benefactors. He selected five hundred and fifty of his healthiest looking
Indian prisoners for shipment back to Spain as slaves in spite of the fact
that the monarchs had already declined his previous plan to ship Caribs
back to Spain for sale at the slave market in Seville. To Columbus it was
all just a matter of semantics and legal interpretation. The admiral's justification for their enslavement was that this particular shipment of Indians
happened to be prisoners of war and therefore were no longer protected
under the sacred conditions of the *Inter caetera* that had been issued by the
Pope.

Columbus once again sent his trusted officer Antonio Torres back to
Spain, only this time he was accompanied by the admiral's brother Diego.
Torres's four vessels left Isabela on February 24, 1495, carrying on board
captive Indians in lieu of the expected shipment of gold. Of the five hundred and fifty Indians being transported across the Atlantic, two hundred
perished at sea, while those who survived the voyage were eventually auctioned off at the markets of Seville.

Back at Isabela, Christopher Columbus received news sometime around
mid–March that Cacique Guatiguana was planning to launch an assault
against his Spanish settlement. Now fully recovered from his illness, Columbus led a force of several hundred Spaniards and an unknown number of
allies in a preemptive strike against these restive natives. After a march of
ten days inland the Spaniards encountered a widely scattered army of warriors estimated at ten thousand strong on the open field of the Vega Real.
The Spanish force consisted of two hundred soldiers, a cavalry of twenty
horses led by Alonso Ojeda, and twenty hounds for hunting. The noise and
smoke of gunfire, the deadly accuracy of the crossbow, and the terrifying
charge of soldiers on horse threw the assembled Indian forces into mass
confusion. In a matter of minutes the engagement had turned into a full
scale rout, but the slaughter of countless panic-stricken natives attempting
to flee in every direction continued for quite some time.

Such an easy victory encouraged Christopher Columbus to continue
his advance with the expectation that he just might capture Caonabo, the
rebellious cacique who was the guiding force behind most of these Indian
uprisings. Their mission met with a successful conclusion when Alonso de
Ojeda caught up with and managed to trick this Indian chieftain into submission without the slightest bit of a struggle. Entering the cacique's camp
with only a few men, Ojeda succeeded in convincing Caonabo that the
Spaniards sought a peaceful resolution to their differences and that he had
been sent by the admiral to escort the great chief back to Isabela for the
signing of a treaty. Convinced that there was truth in these words, Caonabo agreed to be escorted by Ojeda to a private meeting with the admiral.

Once they were well beyond the sight of Caonabo's village, Ojeda produced a set of shiny new shackles which he told the cacique were items similar to those worn by the great king of Spain, but only during the celebration of special ceremonies or in the observance of sacred holidays. Believing this to be a great honor, Caonabo consented to the attachment of these irons to his ankles and wrists. Once the chains were securely in place, the entourage of Indians who accompanied the chief on this journey were brutally butchered before the disbelieving eyes of the cacique. Caonabo was then returned to Isabela where he languished in a small prison cell for nearly a year before being shipped to Spain as a prisoner of war.

Now that Caonabo was his prisoner, Columbus had become the new lord of Cibao, and as such, he expected and demanded that his subjects pay him a fitting tribute. Every Indian was ordered to pay a quarterly tax, an amount equivalent to one hawk's bell full of gold dust. These instruments of measurement were the same bells that the Spaniards had once handed out freely to the natives as tokens of their friendship and, until recently, had used to barter with the Indians for their precious gold. Though it came at the great expense of the natives, Columbus soon learned that Cibao was not the "birthplace" of gold after all, and eventually came to realize that there was, in fact, not nearly as much gold as he had imagined there would be on the island of Hispaniola. The great fields of gold he had envisioned turned out to be nothing more than a meager trickle of alluvial deposits. As for the native population, instead of tending to the needs of the tribe and their families, they now spent each day desperately searching for gold in order that they might appease their new Spanish overlords. When the time came to ante up, Columbus discovered that very few Indians were able to meet their established quotas, and rather than face further punishment for their obvious shortcomings, many Indians chose to abandon their homes and seek sanctuary from their oppressors by hiding amongst the hills of Hispaniola. In an attempt to ease their burden, the admiral agreed to reduce their quarterly tribute by half, but even this proved to be more than they could hope to achieve. Frustrated by these paltry results, Columbus took to ruling the natives with an increasingly heavy hand, ultimately condemning most of them to a life of servitude.

Sometime during June of 1495 Columbus bore witness to a strange and truly terrifying sight—a vision that no known European had ever encountered before him. While preparing for his return to Spain, to report that order had once again been restored to the colony of Isabela, the admiral noticed a peculiar looking ring encircling the sun. At the same time there appeared an ominous formation of clouds taking shape in the distant horizon. When he inquired about these peculiar events the natives told him that a frightful storm, known as a *huracán*, was heading towards the island. As the day wore on the winds began to steadily increase in their intensity. The approach of nightfall brought a torrent of rain accompanied by howling winds so strong that the Spaniards found it difficult to even stand. Surging waves of water slammed against the ships anchored in the harbor with a force strong enough to send three of them to a permanent watery grave. Many of the Spaniards feared that this was the dreaded "Day of Judgment" and that their final fate had been rendered by God himself. When the storm finally blew over and blue skies reigned once again above, the settlers took stock of what little remained in the wake of the storm's fury. The only surviving ship was the *Niña*—the very same caravel that had served him so well on his first voyage—so consequently the admiral had another legitimate excuse for postponing his requested return to Spain.

THE RETURN TO SPAIN

The mounting problems that confronted Christopher Columbus were further compounded and complicated by the sudden return of Antonio Torres in October of 1495. The reports that Torres and Diego Columbus had submitted to Ferdinand and Isabella regarding the progress of this second Enterprise of the Indies had been overshadowed by the numerous complaints that had filtered back from the disgruntled colonists at Hispaniola. While the monarchs permitted Torres to return to Hispaniola with four ships fully loaded with more necessary supplies for the colony, he was also required to provide passage for an appointed royal inspector by the name of Juan Aguado. His mission was to determine if there was any truth to the charges currently circulating concerning the horrendous conditions existing at Isabela. Unfortunately for Columbus, the royal inspector had arrived at a time when relations with the natives were sorely strained by his burdensome gold tax and while a great many of the colonists were still stricken by a seemingly incurable illness. Aguado also found it troubling that so many healthy colonists ignored their duties to the settlement and were instead busily scouring the countryside for gold to fill their own pockets. None of these findings proved more disturbing to the royal inspector than the sight of Indians being openly employed as slaves within the colony. Queen Isabella had clearly stipulated that these natives were her "subjects and vassals" and therefore were to be treated with the utmost respect. One of the principal objectives of this expedition was to convert heathens to Christianity, and as far as Aguado could see the admiral had strayed far from the righteous path. The disparaging reports sent back by Aguado to

King Ferdinand and Queen Isabella were so critical of Christopher Columbus that the sovereigns saw no choice but to issue orders for the admiral to return to Spain at once.

Distraught over this sudden and dramatic turn of events, Christopher Columbus spent the next few weeks sulking while he sailed among the numerous islands he had discovered and claimed for Spain. Hoping to recapture his past glory the admiral desperately sought to strike gold or find the elusive kingdom of the Khan, but he was willing to settle for any discovery that might prove worthy enough to return him to the good graces of King Ferdinand and Queen Isabella. Once he finally realized his search was in vain, the humbled admiral began making preparations for his long voyage back to Spain. Just before his departure he handed over command of Hispaniola to his brother Bartolomeo along with instructions to abandon the cursed site where Isabela stood and to establish a new settlement elsewhere on the island.

The admiral prepared two vessels, one of which was the *Niña*, for his return journey. Two hundred and twenty disillusioned and homesick settlers crammed on to the decks of the two ships along with thirty natives, including the infamous Caonabo. The ships set sail on March 10, 1496; Columbus sailed aboard the *Niña* while his latest nemesis, Juan Aguado, was a passenger on the other caravel. It took the two vessels nearly three months to cross the Atlantic, a voyage which, in the end, proved too difficult a journey for Caonabo to survive. This time, however, there were no royal emissaries to receive them, no cheering crowds to greet them, no parades to salute them, and no towns lavishly decorated in their honor. All that stood before them was a long and lonely ride to the royal court, currently in session at the town of Burgos.

In July, a humbled but still proud Christopher Columbus stood before King Ferdinand and Queen Isabella. After being put at ease by the gracious manner of the monarchs the admiral willingly provided them with answers to their many questions. His well rehearsed responses managed to assuage most of the royal couple's lingering fears and concerns. He reminded his benefactors of all that he had already accomplished and all that he could still achieve if granted the time and opportunity to do so. He told them that Cathay and the court of the Great Khan were well within his grasp, and he conjured up wondrous visions of the magnificent wealth which awaited them at the journey's end. With their faith in Columbus restored, the Spanish sovereigns dismissed all the charges and allegations levied against him and reinstated all his titles, privileges, and then some. Hoping to capitalize on their generosity, Columbus wasted no time requesting royal approval for a third expedition to the Indies. Ferdinand and Isabella concluded their meeting by agreeing to help fund yet another voyage for the admiral.

Columbus had returned to Spain with little in the way of commercial value, but his men, on the other hand, brought back something that was entirely unforeseen. Sailors from both voyages had enjoyed intimate relations with the native women, who, for the most part, gave themselves freely to the Spaniards. The mild strain of syphilis, which was common to the natives of these islands, was easily transmitted to their new Spanish lovers. The sexually gratified Spaniards did not know what to make of the lesions and rashes that soon began to appear on their bodies. They probably thought nothing more of their physical ailments once these symptoms went into hibernation—most likely blaming their condition on the severe tropical climate. Unwittingly, the returning sailors introduced the chronic and highly infectious disease of syphilis to an unprepared Europe, where over the course of the next century, it reached epidemic proportions.

SEVEN

The Spice Monopoly

The Voyage of Vasco da Gama

FOLLOWING THE CHOSEN COURSE OF DIAS

The triumphant return of Bartolomeu Dias in the year 1488 had given the tiny nation of Portugal great cause for celebration. His successful voyage around the southernmost point of the African coast had unlocked for a future generation of explorers the long sought-after gateway to the Indian Ocean and those mysterious lands which lay beyond. Though certainly elated by the success of this mission the king was clearly disappointed that his explorer had not ventured further than he had. Nevertheless, King John immediately began making preparation for a grand expedition that would finally complete the journey to India. Unfortunately the king's plans encountered a succession of serious setbacks and countless delays, all of which were sufficient in total to cause the postponement of his proposed expedition until the summer of 1497.

An initial cause for delay was the Crown's concern over the precise whereabouts of Pedro de Covilha and Alfonso de Paiva, the two agents dispatched by King John to learn more about the ancient and arcane trade routes of the Middle East and to discover the location of the noble Prester John. The king of Portugal anxiously awaited their reports, confident that the information they had secretly uncovered would prove beneficial to the upcoming expedition. It would take until 1490 before dispatched Portuguese agents were able to catch up with Covilha at the Egyptian city of Cairo, and by that time they already knew that Paiva had failed to complete his part of the mission.

135

Of course the biggest setback to King John's planned expedition was the seemingly successful voyage to the Indies by Spain's commissioned explorer Christopher Columbus. His claim of having reached islands that belonged to the Indies by simply sailing westward was destined to become a highly debated and hotly contested issue between the two Iberian kingdoms. By citing Columbus's failure to locate any of the great cities known to exist in the kingdoms of the Far East, King John alleged that this celebrated sailor had merely discovered a chain of islands that had no connection whatsoever to the Indies. Portuguese officials even took to calling his discoveries Las Antillhas, a reference to the mythical lands believed to lie across the Atlantic in the general direction Columbus had sailed in. Spain's rulers held fast to the belief that their admiral had in fact reached the outer chain of islands that were a part of the Indies and submitted that Portugal was simply jealous that Spain was on the verge of making contact with the wealthy rulers and merchants who resided in that part of the world before they had.

While this war of words continued to escalate between the two Iberian powers, King John found himself caught off guard when King Ferdinand and Queen Isabella contrived with the Pope to alter the direction of the previously established line of demarcation. The drawing of a new boundary line was followed by additional papal decrees which served to strengthen Spain's claims at the expense of Portugal's rights. Negotiations between Spain and Portugal over these disputed boundary issues continued until the signing of the Treaty of Tordesillas in June of 1494. In the end, King John acknowledged the many discoveries of Christopher Columbus as part of an emerging Spanish empire. While he had certainly succeeded in keeping Spain as far away as possible from the coast of Africa, the king of Portugal had also managed to coax them into moving the recently established imaginary vertical boundary further to the west—a move that provided Portugal with an opening by which they might encroach upon the Spanish West Indies.

Selecting a qualified commander for this epic expedition apparently presented its own set of unique problems for King John. While Bartolomeu Dias had been received with great fanfare upon his return, he was, for reasons still not entirely certain, not appointed to lead the much anticipated follow-up expedition. Dias was, however, retained as a consultant for the upcoming expedition, a role which he fulfilled quite admirably. To pass through the gateway discovered by Bartolomeu, King John selected a gentlemen by the name of Estêvão da Gama to take over the helm. Estêvão was well known and highly regarded within the king's inner circle, and at the time of his appointment he was serving as the civil governor of the port city of Sines. But King John's plans were once again disrupted, this time by the untimely passing of Estêvão da Gama. Stepping forward to fulfill his father's appointed role was the dutiful son, Vasco da Gama. An experienced sailor in his own right, Vasco had served with great distinction in Portugal's navy. While most of the king's advisors were quick to point out the young man's lack of experience and qualifications to lead a mission of this magnitude and importance, the king overruled their objections and entrusted the command of this expedition to Vasco da Gama. Clearly, Vasco had made a favorable impression upon King John, who saw in the younger da Gama a man possessed of a keen mind and a strong will, qualities that he deemed essential in a leader for such a challenging voyage.

In 1495, just when it seemed that Portugal was finally on track for its own "Enterprise of the Indies," King John passed away, having succumbed to the painful effects of dropsy at the early age of forty. Since King John's only legitimate male son and heir to the throne, Prince Afonso, had suffered an accidental death in 1491, he was succeeded by his twenty-six year old cousin, Manuel I, later known as "the Fortunate"—a reference to his good fortune in inheriting not only the crown but also the benefits of the work first begun by Prince Henry and then carried on by John II. As the new king, Manuel I made it clear that he wished to keep the course undertaken by his predecessor by confirming the appointment of Vasco da Gama as the leader of the expedition to India.

While Vasco da Gama spent much of his time honing his navigational skills as well as perusing the reports sent back by Pedro de Covilha, Bartolomeu Dias was busily supervising the construction of two prototype vessels, the *São Gabriel* and the *São Rafael*. These ships were specifically designed to withstand the rigors associated with the rounding the Cape of Good Hope and then some. Known as *nãos*, these vessels of more than four hundred tons were just as maneuverable as their sister ship the carrack, but their larger size and sturdier construction made them better suited for a voyage such as the one they were about to embark upon, especially for navigating the turbulent waters which steadily swirl around the Cape of Good Hope. Da Gama's fleet was comprised of four vessels: besides the *São Gabriel*, designated the flagship of the expedition and captained by Vasco da Gama himself, and the *São Raphael*, commanded by Vasco's brother Paulo, there was the *Berrio*, a caravel under the charge of Nicolau Coelho, and a 300 ton store ship whose name has been lost to the passage of time, supervised by Gonçalo Nunes. As for the pilots, Pedro de Alenquer, a veteran sailor who had accompanied Dias on his epic voyage, was aboard the *São Gabriel*; João de Coimbra steered the *Rafael*; and Pedro de Escobar navigated the *Berrio*. The ships were manned by a crew of one hundred and seventy men and fully stocked with provisions that were carefully calculated to satisfy the needs of a voyage for as long as three years. Also stored on board were a great number of trinkets, such as the glass beads and the hawks' bells that had served them so well in bartering with natives along the west coast of Africa. In addition, these ships carried a vast quantity of striped cotton cloth, sugar, olive oil, and other assorted items, all of which they hoped to trade for valuable spices at the great trading markets that Pedro de Covilha had so vividly described in his reports to the king. For protection, as well intimidation, each of Vasco da Gama's ships were armed with twenty cannons. While his primary mission was to find a direct sea route to India, his principal directives, once he reached the mainland, were to establish diplomatic relations with the rulers, forge commercial ties with the merchants of this wealthy region, and obtain that which was even more precious than gold itself: a vast and varied quantity of delectable spices.

Following nearly two years of intense preparations, Vasco da Gama's expedition was finally ready to set sail for India on July 8, 1497. Public announcements of their intended destination drew a large crowd to the harbor of Lisbon to watch the fleet cast off on their historic voyage. To observe the performance of the ships that he had helped design and to also provide da Gama with last-minute navigational advice, Bartolomeu Dias was permitted to travel with the expedition, but only as far as the Cape Verde Islands where they would then part company. While da Gama sought fame and glory in completing the journey paved by so many others who sailed before him, Dias would seek piece of mind as the new commander of the São Jorge de Mina, the Elmina fortress that he had assisted in the construction of while a junior officer under the command of Fernão Gomes.

Vasco da Gama wisely chose to follow the sailing recommendations made by Bartolomeu Dias, and as he came within the vicinity of Sierra Leone he guided his vessels away from the harsh currents of the African coast. Just like Dias before him, da Gama steered his vessels westward, out into the deep of the Atlantic, and then veered south once he latched on to the strong westerly winds that would propel his ships around the southern tip of Africa. Such a wide arc into the Atlantic also provided the Portuguese explorers with an opportunity to probe the waters that, as stipulated by the Treaty of Tordesillas, had been designated as part of their realm. There has even been speculation that Vasco da Gama may have sighted the coast of Brazil during this stretch of the voyage, a supposition that seems all the more plausible when taking into account the subsequent route followed by Pedro Cabral, a path which ultimately led to the European discovery of this unclaimed land.

After thirteen long weeks away from any sight of land—a full eight weeks longer than Christopher Columbus had gone between landfalls on his first voyage—the crew broke out in a chorus of cheers the moment the coast of Africa came back into view. Three days after spotting the continent the fleet landed at St. Helena Bay, some 300 miles northwest of the Cape of Good Hope. Da Gama was disappointed by his own miscalculation; he had hoped that his course would have swept them past the point that Dias had ominously named Cabo Tormentoso, or Cape of Storms. Making the best of his present situation, da Gama took this opportunity to overhaul and repair his weather-worn vessels. The boats were carefully run aground so that the crew could scrape off the barnacles and burn off the seaweed that clung to the underside of their hulls. It was here at St. Helena that the Portuguese had their first encounter with the Hottentots, a tribe native to South Africa. Though they appeared friendly at first, the mariners managed to incur the full extent of their wrath when they strolled uninvited into a nearby Hottentot village. The Portuguese quickly learned that they had inadvertently overstepped their bounds. Startled and angry native warriors attacked the Portuguese interlopers without warning or hesitation, injuring a great number of them including Vasco da Gama, who suffered the pain and the indignity of a spear thrust into his leg.

Concluding that the Hottentots were not a people to be reasoned with, Vasco da Gama and his men hurriedly patched up their vessels and proceeded to sail toward the Cape of Good Hope. Their voyage around the spectacular sight offered by this grand promontory was made all the more difficult by the contrary winds and choppy waters that constantly swirl around this cape. On November 25, 1497, after nine days of battling the elements the fleet finally managed to safely drop anchor at Mossel Bay. Da Gama granted his men a brief respite before venturing back into the unfamiliar waters of the Indian Ocean. While at Mossel Bay the Portuguese carried on trade with a local tribe eager to exchange ivory bracelets for the Europeans' tiny brass bells. Cordial relations between the parties came to an abrupt end when the villagers accused the Portuguese of stealing their precious water. When the natives began assembling in a manner which da Gama perceived as threatening, the captain ordered the firing of several warning shots, deafening blasts that sent their accusers scurrying in the opposite direction. While at Mossel Bay, da Gama decided to dismantle his storage ship but not before redistributing its cargo amongst the three remaining vessels. The crew then watched from the safety of their respective ships as what was left of this vessel was put to the torch. Just before leaving Mossel Bay a *padrão* was erected on a small island in the bay but as da Gama and his men sailed away they watched in helpless disbelief as the natives came out of hiding to demolish their sacred stone cross and pillar.

THE MYSTERIOUS COAST OF AFRICA

Da Gama's fleet returned to the sea on the 8th of December, sailing past the Great Fish River—the furthest point reached by Bartolomeu Dias— and then continued on until it arrived at the Copper River on January 11, 1498. After five uneventful days at this location the adventurers resumed their voyage up the unknown eastern coast of Africa. Reaching the Rio de Bons Sinais on the 25th of January, Vasco da Gama erected another *padrão* and then made the decision to give his crew and the ships a much needed and well deserved rest.

After a month's stay at Rio de Bons Sinais the expedition resumed its northerly course along the coast. Once they had passed the southernmost point visited by Pedro de Covilha, the fleet hugged the unfamiliar coastline until it came upon the town of Mozambique on the second day of March. This ancient port city was unlike any African village the Portuguese were accustomed to; instead of simple huts they saw before them elaborately built homes and elegantly designed mosques. This was, in fact, their first brush with civilization since having left the Cape Verde Islands. As they leaned over the sides of their ships the sailors took notice of the visibly recognizable Islamic influence evident in the architectural design of the city's structures and marveled at the bright colors and graceful attire of the Mozambique people. This bustling city by the sea was one of the southernmost trading posts in an extensive network of trade that had been carried on between African, Arab, and Asian merchants for many centuries prior to the arrival of the Europeans. At Mozambique's enormous marketplace traders from many lands converged to deal in a vast array of precious commodities. Some of these commodities were completely unknown to the Portuguese, but many were familiar because eventually they had found their way to the myriad markets of Europe by means of trade along the Mediterranean basin. Here, just as they did at other Islamic centers of trade, Arab and native traders haggled over the price of African ivory, Indian spices, Chinese porcelain, and Arabian dates, as well as the going rate for honey, coconuts, pearls, gemstones, cotton, silk, leopard skins, and of course, gold.

The Portuguese explorers found the Bantu natives of this region exceptionally hospitable and kind enough to supply them with most of what they requested. In fact, their friendly demeanor inspired many of the sailors to unofficially christen this site Terra da Boa Gente—the land of the good people. However, they soon learned that appearances can be deceiving. While the residents of Mozambique had never seen vessels such as those belonging to Vasco da Gama at their port before, they merely assumed that these Portuguese sailors were but strangely attired Muslim traders, a misconception that da Gama and his men hoped to use to their advantage. Luckily, one of the expedition's sailors spoke Arabic well enough to act as a translator and through his linguistic efforts they were able to learn much about Muslim trade activities in this region and the even larger ports of call that lay just to the north of Mozambique. They were also informed of the fact "that Prester John resided not far from this place; that he held many cities along the coast.... The residence was said to be far in the interior, and could be reached only on the back of camels." But da Gama was even more intrigued by the news of four Arab vessels that were currently docked in the harbor, each of which was purported to be laden with a precious cargo of spices, jewels, and a great amount of silver and gold.

Hoping to mix business with politics, Vasco da Gama invited the sultan of Mozambique to dine with him aboard the *São Gabriel*. When he felt the moment was right, the Portuguese commander presented the sultan with a gift—a small sampling of the various items that he intended to trade at the magnificent markets of Mozambique. Much to his surprise, the sultan became highly enraged over the tribute being offered to him. This was a ruler who was accustomed to receiving presents of great value, usually precious stones or metals, and when he saw the cheap trinkets da Gama had laid before him he demanded a more fitting tribute. But the Portuguese sailors had nothing better to offer. As his scheme to win the sultan's favor had backfired, the Portuguese commander decided to leave the city, hoping for better success at ports lying directly to the north. The Sultan generously provided them with two experienced pilots, the ostensible motive being to help guide da Gama and his ships through the treacherous waters of the Indian Ocean. When one of the Muslim pilots discovered that the men he was sailing with were actually Christian infidels he immediately abandoned the cause. Placing their trust in the remaining Muslim pilot, the crew soon learned of the true intentions of the sultan of Mozambique. Having been insulted even more than the Europeans had realized, the offended ruler had ordered his pilots to navigate these beggarly traders to Mombasa, then the largest town along the eastern coast of Africa. Once there, they were to be taken by force and held as prisoners until their scheduled day of execution. Arriving at Mombasa on the 7th of April, the Portuguese sailors were greeted that very night by one hundred hired thugs who attempted to board their vessels. After successfully fending off their attackers, da Gama had the sultan's pilot put to a test of torture—droplets of boiling oil that painfully seared his flesh—until his forced confession confirmed what they already suspected.

Leaving Mombasa behind them, the expedition ventured onward until they dropped anchor on the 14th of April at the splendid city of Malindi.

Located along the coast of present day Kenya, Malindi was a favorite port of call for traders bringing their wares from across the Indian Ocean. Unlike their host at their previous port of call, the sultan of Malindi, who had an ongoing rivalry with the powerful sultan of Mozambique, welcomed the Portuguese with open arms. However, with the bitter experience at Mozambique and Mombasa still fresh in his mind, the Portuguese commander understandably chose not to risk going ashore. Since da Gama would not come to him, the sultan broke with the traditional protocol and presented himself before the Portuguese captain. As a token of his friendship, the monarch presented the visitors with a small but significant portion of the precious spices they cherished just as much as gold: cloves, pepper, nutmeg, and ginger.

Da Gama was particularly interested in obtaining from the sultan of Malindi the services of an experienced pilot who could navigate his ships across the unknown waters of the Arabian Sea. The navigator selected for this task, Ahmad ibn Majid, the most renowned Indian Ocean pilot of his time. Known to many as the "Lion of the Sea of Fury" he was also a noted and respected author of a great number of books on sailing the large body of water that separates Africa from Asia. By most accounts, the sultan of Malindi freely offered the services of ibn Majid to his Portuguese guests, but another telling of this story paints a very different picture of the exchange between Vasco da Gama and the ruler of Malindi. According to this version, the sultan had no intention of parting company with his famous royal navigator. The Portuguese commander responded to this royal refusal by abducting one of the monarch's favorite servants. By choosing extortion over diplomacy, by ransoming the life of this trusted domestic for the skilled services of the famed navigator, the Portuguese captain obtained what he desired.

CALICUT

After their newly acquired navigator had plotted an easterly course that would take them directly to the city of Calicut, the three Portuguese ships weighed anchor on the 24th of April. While the final leg of this voyage was to be the long anticipated climactic journey's end for the Portuguese explorers, to ibn Majid, this was simply just another voyage across the waters he had traversed so many times before. Guided by Majid's knowledge and propelled by the powerful thrust of the seasonal monsoon winds, the fleet made excellent time, and they sighted the coast of India after only 23 days of sailing. On May 20, 1498, Vasco da Gama and his crew became the first

Europeans to dock a ship at the port of Calicut. Upon receiving news of their arrival, the zamorin, or king, of Calicut immediately dispatched an emissary to greet Vasco da Gama and to extend an invitation to him to visit his royal palace at once.

Unlike at Malindi, da Gama had no qualms about going ashore. Taking along thirteen of his most trusted officers and sailors he set off to meet with the zamorin of Calicut. Leaving his brother in charge of the anchored fleet, Vasco instructed Paulo to sail directly for home if for any reason he should fail to return when expected. Da Gama and his men were escorted through the streets of Calicut with great fanfare by a large retinue sent by the ruler. The sounds of blaring trumpets, banging drums, and the blasting of firearms attracted an enormous crowd eager to catch a glimpse of these strange looking Europeans. At several points along this procession da Gama and his men had to forcibly shove their way through a mob of curious onlookers. The city of Calicut certainly exceed all their expectations, appearing even more splendid and luxurious than Pedro de Covilha had described it in his detailed report to King John II. During their stroll through the streets of the city they happened upon a Hindu temple, and in mistaking its religious symbols for those of their own faith, the Portuguese officers concluded that they had stumbled upon a Christian community that might very well be a remote portion of the legendary realm of Prester John. Alvaro Velho, a sailor who kept a personal journal about his many experiences on this voyage, paints a vivid picture of this supposed "Christian" church:

> The body of the church is as large as a monastery, all built of hewn stone and covered with tiles. At the main entrance rises a pillar of bronze as high as a mast, on the top of which was perched a bird, apparently a cock. In addition to this, there was another pillar as high as a man, and very stout. In the center of the body of the church rose a chapel, all built of hewn stone, with a bronze door, and stones leading up to it. Within the sanctuary stood a small image which they said represented Our Lady. Along the walls, by the main entrance, hung seven small bells.
>
> Many saints were painted on the walls of the church, wearing crowns. They were painted variously, with teeth protruding an inch from the mouth, and four or five arms. In this church the captain major said his prayers, and we with him.

While most of Calicut's citizens were in fact Hindus, it was the relatively small but wealthy Muslim population that governed the important affairs of commerce of this city.

When Vasco da Gama and his entourage finally reached the royal palace they were disappointed to learn that they would not be received right away by the zamorin. Unfortunately for the Portuguese explorers, a group of prominent Muslim merchants, representing the very faction that dominated the commercial concerns of Calicut, had managed to get to the ruler first. Desiring to protect their established markets from any and all forms of European intrusion, the jealous Arabs, whose presence at the city of Calicut dated back as far as the 7th century, did their best to convince the zamorin to be wary of these Portuguese sailors bearing gifts. When da Gama was finally granted an audience with the mighty ruler, he presented him with a letter from the king of Portugal, one which conveyed the proper respect required for forging a mutually gratifying trade accord. However, Vasco da Gama managed to once again sabotage his own cause with the offering of a meager tribute that was deemed an insult to a ruler of such magnificence and importance. A member of the captain's crew recorded that da Gama presented to the King of Calicut: "... four scarlet hoods, six hats, four strings of coral, a case containing six wash-hand basins, a case of sugar, two casks of oil, and two of honey." Da Gama would never recover from his latest faux pas. Try as he might, Vasco failed to reach any sort of trade accord; the only concession that the zamorin would grant to him was the right to purchase whatever food items he might need for his long journey back to Portugal.

Disappointed but not entirely discouraged, Vasco da Gama and his men secretly tried their hand at bartering the expedition's meager wares in the hectic marketplace of Calicut. At first the Arab and Indian merchants refused to trade with these Portuguese paupers, but eventually they relented and began trading, provided that it was on their terms. Three months of bickering and bartering yielded da Gama a fairly large cargo of spices that included peppers, cinnamon, cloves, nutmeg, and ginger, along with a sampling of precious stones, but when taking into account the exorbitant price his men had paid for these items it was but a pitiful showing for all of their efforts. Da Gama had learned firsthand just how shrewd and calculating these Muslim merchants and traders were when it came to matters of business.

Realizing that nothing more could be accomplished at Calicut, the Portuguese explorers began making preparations for their lengthy voyage home. Da Gama sent Diogo Dias as an emissary, in the protective company of several other sailors, to inform the zamorin that they were now ready to return to their homeland and to petition the ruler for the right to purchase a greater quantity of spices. In addition to refusing their request the zamorin demanded that the Portuguese pay him the customary fee for the privilege of docking at his port. To make sure that he received that which he was entitled to the zamorin made Dias and his comrades captive guests at his royal palace. When da Gama learned of this outrageous ransom demand the

Vasco da Gama: Da Gama (with upraised left hand) is granted an audience with the zamorin shortly after having become the first European captain to sail into the harbor of Calicut.

enraged captain ordered the capture of a number of Calicut citizens to barter for the exchange of his detained sailors.

To complement his cargo of spices and gems Vasco da Gama smuggled aboard his ship a half dozen native Hindus for presentment to King Manuel. His return voyage, however, would have to be made without the guidance of master pilot Ahmad ibn Majid, who had managed to escape from his service under the Portuguese during their stopover at Calicut. Da Gama's ships pulled out of the harbor on the 29th of August, sailing northward along the Malabar coast in hopes of finding more amicable centers of trade before attempting a return to Portugal. Instead, all they found was backwater regions with little to offer in trade except for rice and coconuts. At one of these stops the captain gave the orders for his boats to be beached so that they could be given another thorough overhaul before endeavoring to cross the combined waters of the Arabian Sea and the Indian Ocean.

By mid–October they were ready to navigate the great gulf of water which divides Asia from Africa. Unfortunately, Vasco da Gama's decision to sail at that particular time of the year would prove to be disastrous. This was still the tail-end of the season when the blusterous monsoon winds blow steadily towards India. Already weary from having weathered a tough battle against powerful headwinds, the small fleet was soon forced to contend with the subsequent calms. Instead of following a straight southwest course back to Africa, the explorers were forced to zigzag, or, to use the proper nautical parlance, to traverse, across the water in a desperate search for favorable winds and currents. They had planned on a return voyage similar in duration to their outward voyage, storing just enough provisions and water to last them for a journey of one month in length. But without the guidance of the pilot Majid and the aid of a favorable breeze their journey turned into a horrendous three month long nightmare for the crew.

When their food and fresh water began to run low, the sailors found themselves confronted with one of the horrors commonly associated with long voyages at sea: the dreaded disease known as scurvy. A vitamin deficiency resulting from a lengthy absence of fresh meat, fruits or vegetables in one's diet, scurvy is a debilitating disease that will, if left unchecked, lead to a prolonged and excruciatingly painful death. Though sailors were then uncertain as to the exact cause of scurvy, most captains knew from experience that the first visible signs of such an illness meant it was time to reach land as quickly as possible. But in Vasco da Gama's case there was no land in sight.

The symptoms of scurvy spread rapidly aboard the three ships. Already weakened from malnutrition, the afflicted sailors were horrified to notice blood beginning to ooze from their painfully swollen gums. As their gums continued to rot and soften the teeth of the infected sailors no longer had a firm place to take root and consequently began to fall from their diseased mouths. As the sickness progressed, dark blotches began to appear on their arms and legs and before long those sores spread to the rest of the body. Over time these unsightly lesions turned gangrenous. When the disease reached its final stages a stricken sailor could do little more than lie on the deck of the ship and anxiously await death as a final relief from what had become a wretched existence. Thirty of Da Gama's crew found a final resting place at the bottom of the sea during this terrible leg of the voyage. Thanks to the privilege of a better diet, most of the officers managed to escape the more severe effects of this devastating disease.

With barely a handful of men still strong enough to handle the rigorous tasks required aboard each ship it appeared that their situation had become utterly hopeless. One crew member spoke of their desperate plight in his diary. "I assure you, that if the state of affairs had continued for another fortnight there would have been no men at all to navigate the ships." Their perseverance eventually prevailed, however, and on January 7, 1499, Vasco da Gama's three ships manned by a skeleton crew drifted into the port of Malindi. The sultan of Malindi harbored no ill will toward the

Portuguese sailors and, in fact, he showed tremendous compassion when he learned of the crew's wretched condition. The kindly potentate sent out a generous supply of fruits, meats, eggs, and fresh water to the docked boats, and the emaciated crew slowly feasted their way back to health. However, even with the near full recovery of his crew, da Gama realized that there were simply not enough men to handle all three ships effectively. The commander resolved this dilemma by beaching the *São Rafael*, the vessel that he had deemed the least seaworthy, and then condemned her to a fiery ending. Just before the Europeans left Malindi, the sultan favored Vasco da Gama with a majestic tusk of ivory to take back to Portugal as a gift for King Manuel and even granted him permission to erect one of his *padrãos* at Malindi.

On their homeward voyage, Vasco da Gama made it a point to steer clear of the hostile ports of Mombasa and Mozambique. On the 20th of March, the two vessels safely maneuvered around the Cape of Good Hope, and from there they continued on until they reached the islands of the Azores. The island of Terceira would serve as the final resting place for Paolo da Gama, the commander's brother. Having never fully recovered from the lingering effects of scurvy, Paulo's condition grew steadily worse during the return voyage. After they had rounded the Cape of Good Hope, Vasco made a mad dash for the Azores once it had become painfully obvious that his brother would never make it back to Portugal. Once they landed at Terceira, Vasco dispatched the *São Gabriel* on ahead to Lisbon while he remained behind to comfort his ailing brother. The expedition's flagship returned to the docks of Portugal in July with the varied and valuable samplings of gems, precious metals, and assorted spices they had acquired from the distant markets of India. One day after landing at Terceira, Paulo succumbed to his illness and was buried on the island by his grieving brother.

Finally, after having sailed some 27,000 miles of ocean on an odyssey that took more than two years to complete, the two ships were reunited at Portugal in the early part of September. The expedition had taken a heavy toll on the courageous crew that had served under Vasco da Gama. Of the one hundred and seventy men who initially set out on this journey, only fifty-four were to set foot again on Portuguese soil. Scurvy was the scourge of their voyage home, laying claim to the lives of nearly a hundred brave souls. Da Gama and his shipmates reached Lisbon on the 9th of September but because he still needed more time to mourn the loss of his beloved brother as well as additional time to reflect on all that he had endured and accomplished, he delayed his grand entrance into the city for another nine days. Once he had regained his composure Vasco da Gama proceeded directly to the court of King Manuel to offer his official report. If he had any apprehensions about the king's reaction to his not returning with a signed trade agreement or a more profitable cargo of goods, those concerns were immediately put to rest. King Manuel paraded da Gama and his crew through city streets crowded with enthusiastic citizens who turned out to cheer and celebrate the tremendous accomplishments of Portugal's newest national hero. To show his gratitude for all that Vasco had accomplished for the nation of Portugal, Manuel conferred upon him the title of "Dom," endowed him with an annual pension of one thousand cruzadas, and granted him the town of Sines, the village of his birth, to lord over. The last appointment however was strongly objected to by Jorge de Lencasstre, duke of Coimbra, an illegitimate son of King John II, and grand master of the Order of Santiago, who refused to relinquish his title to the town. After a lengthy and bitter legal battle, Vasco da Gama finally agreed to settle on the honorary title to the town of Vidigueira. During this period he married Catherine de Ataide, and this union produced six sons.

After Vasco da Gama succeeded in finding a passage to India, King Manuel proclaimed himself the "King by the grace of God, of Portugal and of the Algarve, both on this side of the sea, and beyond it in Africa, Lord of Guinea, and of the Conquest, Navigation, and Commerce of Ethiopia, Arabia, Persia, and India." Future historians simply shortened his title to "the Fortunate." Manuel also took great satisfaction in flaunting the success of this expedition before the other European heads of state, especially those of neighboring Spain. Ever since Christopher Columbus had returned from his first voyage, King Ferdinand and Queen Isabella had continually boasted about how their "Admiral of the Ocean Sea" had discovered a faster route to the islands of the Indies and how they were on the verge of reaching the mainland of Asia. Manuel could now gloat that Vasco da Gama had actually reached the land that Christopher Columbus was still trying to find. These daring voyages made by Portugal's Vasco da Gama and Spain's Christopher Columbus helped launch a thousand other such voyages, which, in turn, ushered in the great age of exploration and a brand new era of commercial enterprise.

Portugal's Conquest of the Indies

THE VOYAGE OF PEDRO CABRAL

Plans for a second expedition to the distant shores of India were immediately set in motion following the return of Vasco da Gama. This expedition, however, was to be much greater in size and far grander in scope than its predecessor. Pedro Álvares Cabral, a distinguished nobleman with no previous sailing experience, was chosen to lead an armada of thirteen vessels and twelve hundred men. His mission was twofold: First off, by following a course plotted by Vasco da Gama himself, Cabral was to take an even wider westerly sweep into the Atlantic to find out if there was anything worth claiming on the Portuguese side of the boundary that had been established by the recently ratified Treaty of Tordesillas. Following this foray into uncharted territory, Cabral was to continue on to India, where he was to establish trade relations with the zamorin of Calicut. By sending a larger and more heavily armed fleet, Manuel clearly intended to deliver a strong message to the ruler of this city: either commence to trading with Portugal or face the full fury of Portuguese ships capable of pounding his great city into submission.

On March 9, 1500, exactly six months after Vasco da Gama's triumphant return to Lisbon, the expedition under the command of Pedro Cabral set sail for India. Even King Manuel was amongst the enthusiastic crowd of well-wishers who came to watch their celebrated departure. Also sailing on this epic voyage was the forgotten explorer who had paved the way for both Vasco da Gama and Pedro Cabral, Bartolomeu Dias. Finally being offered the opportunity to complete the voyage he had long been denied, Dias was give the command of a vessel in Cabral's fleet.

A short while after having sailed past the Cape Verde Islands the fleet met with its first disaster: one of Cabral's ships was reported as missing and presumed sunk. The arc of their course put the armada within sight of land at a point just slightly further to the west of where da Gama had previously sailed. After adjusting their course, Cabral's ships finally dropped anchor on April 22, 1500, at the body of water later named in honor of its discoverer, Cabralia Bay. Once they had determined that this site did in fact lie within King Manuel's domain, Cabral, finding himself without a *padrão* to plant, erected a large wooden cross and proceeded to claim the land for Portugal. Originally known as Terra de Vera Cruz, or Land of the True Cross, Portugal would rename the territory Brazil after discovering that the land contained a great abundance of brazilwood—a tropical tree that produces a bright red dye that was of enormous commercial value to the Portuguese. Encouraged by the willingness of the local natives to participate in their celebration of Mass, the sailors gave a number of the Indians small tin crucifixes to wear around their necks. Afterwards, Cabral dispatched three of his ships to Portugal under the command of Gaspar de Lemos to bring news of their fabulous discovery to the king, an act that lends credence to speculation that they already were aware of land in this region and that part of Cabral's mission was to confirm the existence of such. After a stay of ten days Cabral was anxious to resume his voyage to India, but before their departure he selected two men, both conscripted convicts on this voyage, to remain behind to reconnoiter the region of Brazil now known as Bahia. The two lost souls were condemned to this strange land with only a measly ration of supplies, and few expected to ever see or hear from them again.

While Cabral and his crew were certainly the first Europeans to claim this land they were not, however, the first Europeans to gaze upon those shores. That distinction belongs to the Spanish navigator Vicente Pinzón, the same Pinzón who commanded the *Niña* on Columbus's first voyage of discovery. Granted command of an expedition of his own, his search for gold and pearls had led him to the coast of Brazil a mere three months prior to Cabral's historic landing. His four caravels sailed as far as present-day Recife—the point where the coast of Brazil begins to angle southward, and it was there that he touched land on January 26, 1500. Since he never bothered to lodge a claim to these lands, one can speculate, with some degree of certainty, that Pinzón must have known he was on the wrong side of the demarcation line. From this location Pinzón navigated northward until he sighted the mouth of the Orinoco and from there the Spanish expedition sailed straight to the Spanish colony of Santo Domingo.

Just off the Cape of Good Hope, Cabral's fleet sailed into one of those sudden storms which had given the cape its notoriety. Shortly after they were struck by stormy seas some of the sailors spotted a bright comet in the sky, a sighting which they took to be a portent of impending doom. This ominous prediction rang true when hurricane force winds suddenly slammed into their ships, causing them to pitch and roll and ultimately to scatter in every direction. Unable to withstand the brunt of the storm's fury, four of Cabral's vessels capsized and then plunged to their deep watery grave. Tragically, Bartolomeu Dias, the explorer who christened this point the Cape of Storms, was forever denied the opportunity to reach India, as he was among the many who went down with their ships during the tempest that occurred on May 29, 1500.

Once the storm had finally subsided, the remaining vessels resumed their voyage toward India. Sofala was reached on the 16th of July, Mozambique on the 20th, and Kilwa on the 26th. Their reception was less than inviting at each of these ports of call, and once it became clear that the merchants of these towns had no intention of trading with them the explorers quickly moved on. Just as it had been for Vasco da Gama, the port city of Malindi proved far more hospitable, and just like da Gama, they were able to procure the services of a pilot who could steer them across the vast breadth of the Indian Ocean. As a token of his gratitude, Cabral bestowed upon the ruler of Malindi a great number of gifts, the most lavish of which was a solid silver saddle complete with silver spurs and stirrups.

Much to the disappointment of the Muslim community at Calicut, Portuguese flags could once again be seen waving in their harbor. Cabral's squadron pulled into port on September 13th and immediately petitioned for an audience with the zamorin. Not surprisingly, their request was denied. Offended by the worthless tribute paid to him by his predecessor, Vasco da Gama, the mighty ruler of Calicut had no intention of wasting his valuable time on traders hailing from such an obviously poor nation. Fortunately for Cabral, da Gama's bitter experience at Calicut had taught them to bring along trade items of far greater value. By cleverly greasing the right palms, Cabral managed to cajole his way into a meeting with the reluctant zamorin. For the next three months the Portuguese commander pleaded his case before the king of Calicut: he told him that Portugal was a great and powerful nation willing to pay a handsome price for an exclusive right to trade directly with his wealthy kingdom. Each time they met, Cabral presented the zamorin with a splendid array of gifts, most of which succeeded in appealing to the extravagant taste of the ruler.

Cabral's persistence eventually wore down the sovereign's determined resistance and he finally agreed to grant the Portuguese a trade concession. Besides giving them permission to trade directly with local merchants, the zamorin also allowed the Portuguese sailors to set up a depot in the harbor. Seventy of Cabral's men were assigned to this warehouse to bundle, store, and safeguard the numerous spices they were sure to accumulate in trade. While the Muslim merchants objected to this Christian intrusion, they did, for the most part, honor the zamorin's decree and carried on commerce with the Portuguese.

Blinded by the lavish tribute paid to him by Pedro Cabral, the zamorin issued a ruling that would cause an already tense diplomatic arrangement to explode in bloodshed. To satisfy the Portuguese request for full boatloads of spices, he granted them the right to acquire as much cargo as their six vessels could possibly hold. Only able to procure enough goods to fill just two of his ships, Cabral complained to the zamorin that certain hostile factions were conspiring to impede his efforts. Siding with the Christians on this issue the Hindu ruler of Calicut decreed that no Muslim ships were to be loaded until the remaining Portuguese vessels were filled to capacity. The zamorin also gave Cabral the authority to confiscate the cargo of any Muslim ship which failed to comply with his royal edict. When Cabral put these powers to the test by seizing a supposedly disobedient Muslim ship on the 16th of December, enraged merchants took to rioting in the streets of Calicut. As the mob marched toward the Portuguese compound, it grew larger in size and greater in anger, and by the time they reached the depot they were an army of nearly three thousand vigilantes bent on exacting a terrible revenge. The Portuguese workers at the compound defended themselves as best they could, but there were simply too few to withstand a force of so many. In the end, fifty-one of Cabral's warehouse workers, including the foreman Ayres Corres, were savagely butchered while the remainder of the crew narrowly escaped a similar fate by diving into the harbor and swimming to safety aboard their nearby anchored ships. Infuriated by this deadly assault Cabral retaliated without hesitation. Capturing ten ships in the harbor he showed the Muslims just what Portuguese will was capable of; for each murdered Christian he mercilessly executed ten "infidels." After imposing the death sentence on more than five hundred captives, Cabral had the cargo from each captured ship loaded onto his own and once this task was completed he ordered his men to set fire to the empty vessels. Convinced that the zamorin secretly supported the Muslim assault on his depot, Cabral then turned his cannons towards the direction of Calicut and proceeded to unleash a deafening bombardment upon the city.

Following this deadly altercation, Cabral's fleet sailed south until it reached the city of Cochin. A rival port of Calicut situated along the Malabar Coast, Cochin was renowned for its spice trade, especially its traffic in peppers. The rajah of this city was openly receptive to Cabral's generous overtures and granted him a great number of trade concessions. Just as he had done at Calicut, Cabral established a depot that was to serve as both a center for commerce and a storage facility for the precious commodities he acquired in trade. The establishment of such a depot meant that future Portuguese traders would no longer have to worry about bartering for goods in a foreign market, and instead, would simply deal directly with the commandant of the Portuguese trading post. After taking on board a substantial supply of peppers, Cabral left a number of his men behind to maintain the depot while he continued to explore along the Malabar Coast. Sailing to Cananor he stopped long enough to take on a load of ginger and then decided that the time had come for him and his men to return to Portugal. While on the way home one of his remaining ships ran aground and was unable to continue the voyage. Since all of his ships were already overloaded with cargo, Cabral decided to burn the disabled ship and its entire contents so as to avoid any possibility of these precious spices falling into the hands of rival Muslim merchants.

Pedro Cabral made his celebrated return to Lisbon on June 23, 1501, and even though his arrival was marred by the return of only four of the thirteen ships he had originally set out with he had succeeded in bringing back a cargo of spices that more than compensated for the venture's losses in both manpower and materials. What became of Cabral after his return to Portugal is uncertain, as there are no records of his doings and whereabouts after this date, and many historians speculate that after profiting handsomely form his grand adventure, he simply embraced a sedentary lifestyle in his remaining years. The significance of Cabral's journey was soon revealed to all of Europe; after having been at the mercy of exorbitant rates tacked on by Arab and Italian spice merchants for as long as anyone could remember, Portugal was now in a position to buy directly from the source, thereby making it the new middleman for the prosperous European spice market. Italian merchants could only look on in trepidation as Portugal, shortly after Cabral's return, established its own exchange at Antwerp to market its imported spices to the rest of Europe. Shortly thereafter merchants and bankers from Germany and Italy began to descend upon the city of Lisbon to establish their own offices at Europe's newest epicenter of trade.

Pleased at the prospect of being able to reap tremendous rewards from Portugal's newly forged trade agreement with Cochin, Manuel the Fortunate was quick to dispatch a flotilla comprised of four vessels under the command of John da Nova following Cabral's return, and another trading expedition set sail the following year. However, there was still a score to settle with Calicut.

THE RETURN OF VASCO DA GAMA

To ensure that Portuguese trade overseas continued to flourish and to guarantee the safety of his many men and vessels doing business abroad, Manuel was determined to use every means at his disposal to purge all elements of Islamic influence from the affairs of trade in India. While he never made an official declaration, the king had, in effect, declared a war over control of the spice-laden Indies. To avenge the massacre at Calicut he enticed Vasco da Gama back into service by bestowing upon him the grand title of "Admiral of the Indian Sea" and offering him a generous trade concession, which, following the successful completion of the mission, held the promise of making him an exceedingly wealthy man.

In addition to settling Portugal's differences with Calicut, Vasco da Gama was expected to make his presence known at any port on the way to India that, in the past, had been less than cooperative with the demands of Portugal. Once the subjugation of Calicut was complete, da Gama was expected to return to Lisbon with as large and as varied a cargo of spices as his fleet of ships could possibly store. To carry out this mission, da Gama was provided with an armada of fifteen vessels, which he guided out of the harbor in February of 1502. Deciding that the expedition might be in need of additional support, King Manuel dispatched another five ships in April to join up with the Admiral of the Indian Seas.

At Kilwa, located in present-day Tanzania, Vasco da Gama forced the city's sultan to acknowledge the sovereignty of King Manuel and to honor him by pledging to pay an annual tribute to Portugal. Kilwa was a city of spectacular splendor, a place that was overflowing with many types of expensive Eastern luxuries—items that the citizens could easily afford thanks to a natural abundance of copper and ivory. From Kilwa, da Gama sailed on to India.

As their fleet approached the Malabar Coast the Portuguese came upon a large dhow transporting a rather large contingent of faithful Muslims returning from a sacred pilgrimage to Mecca. In an act of sheer piracy, Vasco da Gama had his men board the vessel and demand that the passengers hand over all of their valuables. This was certainly a very profitable heist, netting him close to twelve thousand ducats plus a nearly equivalent amount in confiscated goods. Once his men had collected all that they could, the Portuguese commander issued the order to burn the ship along with everyone on-board. The high-pitched screams and cries of three hundred and eighty men, women, and children rose above the roar of the flames that rapidly engulfed the dhow and the captive occupants, but their cries failed to touch the hearts of their persecutors.

By the end of October Vasco da Gama's fleet was strategically positioned off the shore of Calicut. The admiral issued an ultimatum to the zamorin: either expel every Muslim resident from the city at once or prepare to suffer the gravest of consequences! Hoping to find a way to appease the Portuguese commander, the ruler of Calicut sent several envoys out to his ship to try to negotiate a peaceful settlement. Da Gama told them that his demands were nonnegotiable, and to further emphasize the extreme measure of his resolve he sent back a gruesome message intended to instill terror in the hearts and minds of Calicut's citizens. After having captured a number of small fishing and merchant vessels sailing in the harbor, da Gama had each member of the crews hanged at once and then ordered his men to dismember the lifeless bodies. Severed heads, hands, and feet were tossed in a small boat, and once filled it was cast toward the shore of Calicut. Adding further insult to this already grisly gesture, Vasco enclosed a note in Arabic proposing that the zamorin use the enclosed body parts to make a special curry dish for himself. Infuriated by this barbaric act perpetrated against his people, the zamorin immediately dispatched a mighty fleet to engage the admiral's ships, but they were simply no match for the superior firepower of the Portuguese. After he had destroyed the entire fleet, da Gama turned his cannons toward the city and continued the bombardment until the zamorin of Calicut surrendered the city to him.

Once all remnants of Muslim control had been purged from the city of Calicut and Portuguese authority reigned in its place, Vasco da Gama sailed south to check on Pedro Cabral's trading post at Cochin. With word of his ruthless actions at Calicut having preceded him, the admiral, from then on, encountered very little resistance to his terms for trade along the Malabar Coast. He established new trading posts at Cananore and Quilon in addition to rebuilding the depot that had been destroyed at Calicut. During this trek along the coast of India the admiral continued to confiscate the cargo of any Arab ship having the grave misfortune of crossing his path. When da Gama decided the time had come for him to return to Lisbon he left behind a squadron of five ships, under the command of his nephew, to protect Portugal's commercial interests in the Indies. The admiral arrived home in September of 1503 with the greatest cargo of spices and treasures that had ever been unloaded at a Portuguese dock. After being bestowed with honors and titles which celebrated and glorified all that he had accomplished in the name of Portugal, Vasco da Gama retired to his estate where he lived quite comfortably off the continuous flow of profits that resulted from his trade concession in India. But India would beckon Vasco da Gama back for one more visit.

EIGHT

Those Who Trespass Against Columbus

The Expeditions of John Cabot

THE FIRST VOYAGE

Born one year before fellow native Genoan Christoforo Colombo, Giovanni Caboto was consumed with a similar passion for learning more about the world around him. At some point during his formative years his family moved to the rival Italian republic of Venice, and in 1476, at the age of 26, Giovanni became a naturalized citizen of that cosmopolitan city-state. During his stay at Venice he became an ardent student of geographical and navigational matters. He would continue his education with hands-on experience as a spice merchant plying his trade along the great Mediterranean trade basin. According to his own recollections these affairs of trade took him to exotic locations such as Mecca, the bustling Arabian trade center that was, and still is, the most sacred of Islamic holy cities.

Giovanni Caboto's exposure to the great trading centers of the Levant gave him cause to ponder the many intricate and arcane commercial alliances that existed between merchants of the Middle East and those of the Far East. Anxious to journey to these mysterious regions that he had heard mention of, but fully aware of the fact that it was next to impossible to penetrate the protective barriers that barred European travel to the East, he began to speculate about possible alternative routes to these forbidden lands. Just like Christopher Columbus, he conceived of a westerly course to these lands that were said to be overflowing in spices and wealth, and, like Columbus, Caboto needed the services of a noble patron who was willing and able to back such a daring venture. He was wise enough to realize that he would never find such support in Venice. For after all, the merchants of Venice made their great fortunes wheeling and dealing in the Muslim controlled markets of the Levant, and they were not about to back any proposal that might offend their Arab trade partners and ultimately jeopardize their extremely delicate but highly lucrative business arrangement.

Caboto's continual quest for a wealthy benefactor landed him in England sometime around 1484. Accompanied by his wife and three sons, Lewis, Sancia, and Sebastian—who later became a celebrated explorer in his own right—Giovanni first settled at Blackfriars but later moved to the bustling seaport town of Bristol. He was quick to adopt England as his new homeland, and to demonstrate his appreciation, and of course, to enhance his own acceptance within English circles, he Anglicized his name to John Cabot. He was convinced that most of the exotic spices that Europeans craved so dearly originated from regions located in northern China and openly maintained to potential benefactors that the sole reason Christopher Columbus could not find the mainland of China, the Great Khan, or an abundance of spices and precious metals was that the explorer was simply searching too far to the south.

England was a relatively poor nation at the time of John Cabot's arrival. Internal strife had long hindered her economic well-being while ongoing wars for glory and gain had mostly succeeded in draining the Crown's limited coffers. Fortunately, England was blessed with one commodity that would help keep her fragile economy afloat: wool. Both at home and across the channel, there existed a tremendous demand for all kinds of woolen products, a need that many English merchants were quick to capitalize upon. The export of raw wool turned a tidy profit for many a merchant and those earnings increased dramatically once they began exporting fine woolen cloth woven by England's own weavers.

A flourishing cloth trade brought commercial prosperity to a fair number of English towns, most notably the port city of Bristol. Having established itself as a center for the wool trade with Ireland as early as the 11th century, Bristol eventually expanded its market to the European continent and before long its fine products began to reach the great markets located along the Mediterranean trade basin by way of the merchants of Italy. As part of a concerted effort to broaden their market horizon, Bristol merchants eagerly sought to finance trade expeditions, even underwriting speculative ventures in search of legendary lands thought to exist to the west of England's shores. The tale of Saint Brendan's voyage, the discovery of a placed called

Vinland (land of wine), and the ancient legend of the lost city of Atlantis were among the many stories swapped by sailors that captivated the imaginations of seamen and merchants alike along the docks of Bristol.

Henry VII, who was crowned King of England in 1485, deserves much of the credit for restoring financial soundness to the land that he ruled. His frugal approach toward government expenditures in conjunction with various schemes for increasing revenue paid off by replenishing a nearly empty treasury. Intent on improving England's position within international markets, Henry enacted legislation that helped to promote English manufactures and to stimulate the export of those novel products. King Henry was also receptive to novel approaches for locating new markets and even briefly entertained a proposal submitted by Bartolomeo Columbus, on behalf of his brother Christopher, for a westward expedition to the Indies. Even though he hesitated to invest in Columbus's Enterprise of the Indies, the proposal, at the very least, instilled in him the idea that such a voyage was possible.

It was around the time of Bartolomeo's visit to England that John Cabot began proposing his own scheme for a westward expedition to the Indies. He had managed to win the support of a number of Bristol merchants but without the blessing of King Henry their proposed patronage was of little consequence. His situation did not improve until after Christopher Columbus, while in the service of Spain, had completed his second westward voyage and news had arrived of a proposed eastward expedition by Portugal, under the command of Vasco da Gama, to reach the Indies.

Armed with the advantages of more impressive credentials and a more convincing plan, John Cabot emerged as the winner for the king's favor. On March 5, 1496, Henry VII granted John Cabot and his three sons letters of patent that authorized them to seek out new lands, and, hopefully, discover new markets for England. Since the Crown's own coffers were still somewhat limited, funding for the expedition was left to the responsibility of Cabot and his many Bristol supporters. The sovereign conceded to them the rightful claim to any lands that Cabot discovered, but in exchange for this privilege they were obligated to pay the crown a one-fifth share of any profits that were derived from this venture. With the signing of this agreement, England had officially entered the great spice race.

John Cabot's momentous occasion was put off until May 2, 1497. On that morning a large and enthusiastic crowd lined up along Bristol's quay to catch a glimpse of their adopted hero setting sail for unknown places with familiar names. Desiring to keep the expedition small, Cabot outfitted only one ship, a small bark he called the *Matthew*. His crew of only eighteen seamen reputedly included his youngest son Sebastian. After receiving last minute encouragement from his Bristol fanciers, Cabot cast off in search of a new way to Cathay.

Careful to avoid any possible intrusion into the recognized sailing routes belonging to Spain and Portugal, Cabot plotted a course that took him and his crew around the southern coast of Ireland, and after making a slight northerly adjustment he steered a straight line westward across the North Atlantic Ocean. They finally reached land on the morning of the 24th of June, and once ashore, John Cabot took possession of his discovery by planting an English flag, and to honor his former homeland, he flew the Venetian colors alongside the English banner. As all logs and maps from this epic journey have disappeared, and without his having left a permanent or recognizable imprint behind, the exact location of John Cabot's landing still remains a mystery. Taking into account his given trajectory, a landing at Newfoundland, Nova Scotia, Labrador, or Cape Breton Island is all well within the realm of possibility.

Convinced that he had found the mainland of Asia, Cabot sailed along the coast in search of any noticeable trace of civilization. What he mostly saw was a dense forest of towering trees and a vast ocean teeming with schools of sturgeon, cod, and salmon. Unable to locate any visible signs that could substantiate his initial conclusion he simply reasoned that he had stumbled upon the northernmost fringe of the vast Asian continent—a region heretofore unknown to the cartographers of Europe. Just like Columbus before him, John Cabot deluded himself into believing he was on the outer rim of lands known to Marco Polo and therefore, he was nearly within reach of the great wealth of Cathay. With this thought in mind, Cabot made the decision to return to England in order to get approval for a much larger fleet, one which would be capable of hauling back the enormous amount of treasures he would undoubtedly find on the next voyage.

A SECOND JOURNEY

Returning to the banks of the Avon on the 6th of August, John Cabot and his crew carefully maneuvered the *Matthew* the relatively short distance upriver to the awaiting docks of Bristol. There he found nearly all of the townsfolk gathered to celebrate his triumphant return. Though there surely must have been some initial disappointment over his failure to return with any gold, silk, spices, or even any natives, Cabot managed to temper those concerns with wondrous tales of what he saw and what he expected to see on their next voyage. He reported that he had sailed a great distance along the northern shore of Asia, just far enough to determine that this was indeed a land mass of considerable size. He eloquently spoke of a place similar in climate to that of England, from which sprouted a vast forest of tall trees suitable for manufacture; and off shore, there was an abundance of fish great enough in quantity to satisfy the bellies of every European many times over. As for those magnificent cities of Asia that he had failed to sight, Cabot reassured the skeptics that they were but a few day's sail from the farthest point he had just explored.

Having successfully convinced the merchants of Bristol that he was on the right path to the great wealth of Cipangu and Cathay, John Cabot set off for London to personally report his marvelous findings to the king. Pleased by the news presented to him, Henry rewarded Cabot with a payment of ten pounds and the pledge of a yearly pension that was to total twice that amount. Believing that his nation was on the verge of reaching the court of the Great Khan ahead of Spain and Portugal, the frugal King Henry agreed to become a financial partner with the wealthy merchants of Bristol in Cabot's next expedition. Reveling in his newfound celebrity, John Cabot took to calling himself the "admiral."

Returning to Bristol, Cabot immediately set about the task of preparing for his follow-up voyage to Asia. Common talk among the idle townsfolk centered around the supposed exploits of the Italian immigrant. There were rumors that he had already located the legendary Seven Cities founded by seven seafaring Portuguese monks, as well as gossip about his having also set foot on the magnificent lands lorded over by the Great Khan. Everyone just knew it was only a matter of time before the docks of Bristol overflowed with untold treasure from the distant kingdoms of the Far East. The question on everyone's mind was when would Cabot set sail?

By most accounts, Cabot assembled a crew numbering approximately two hundred men to sail aboard the five boats that were set to embark on this second voyage of discovery. Sometime in May of 1498—the exact date continues to remain a subject of debate—before an even larger crowd filled with even greater expectations, Cabot's fleet cast off for the Indies. From the very outset the expedition was beset by numerous problems, the most significant being the terribly foul weather and bitterly cold conditions that conspired to hamper his second attempt at a northwest passage. A sudden storm proved severe enough to disable one of his ships, forcing it to seek a safe harbor in Ireland while the rest of the fleet continued on its way. In the early part of June, the ships rounded the southern coastline of Greenland and sailed along the icy waters of the Davis Strait. Coasting down to the shores of Labrador, it has been speculated that Cabot carried on trade with the local tribes of that region. After having explored the North American coast as far south as the Chesapeake Bay without encountering so much as a single town, or port, or even a solitary wandering trading vessel, the crew's tolerance finally snapped. Frustrated by his many unfulfilled promises and concerned about their dangerously low provisions, the crew demanded that the ships return to Bristol at once. Fearing that a refusal on his part would be a sure prescription for insurrection, Cabot reluctantly acquiesced to their demands and set a course for home.

One can only imagine the terrible shame felt by John Cabot and the bitter disappointment he must have faced upon his return to the docks of Bristol. His vessels, all of which were supposed to be laden with precious spices, gems, and metals, unloaded only a starving and extremely weary crew. Visions of vast riches, which had preoccupied the thoughts of his wealthy Bristol backers for so many months, were suddenly replaced with the stark reality of impending financial doom. Public disdain and disgrace surely followed him from this point on, and unfortunately, all we know for certain of John Cabot after his return to England is that he received his promised pension payment for the year 1499. There are some accounts that claim Cabot and his men never returned from the second voyage, but this theory does not stand up to what little we do know. It is generally believed that he died shortly thereafter, taking with him, though only momentarily, English desire for any more adventures overseas. In fact, following this debacle, English exploration was, for quite some time, confined to bold fishermen who followed Cabot's path to catch fish off the Grand Banks of Newfoundland. For many years to come, John Cabot was merely remembered as the father of the renowned explorer Sebastian Cabot. Today, however, we have reconsidered John Cabot's deeds by recognizing him as the modern discoverer of North America. But was he?

THOSE WHO CAME BEFORE JOHN CABOT

Bjarni Herjolfsson (also spelled Biarni Heriulfson) was a merchant Norseman who made his living swapping wares between the residents of Norway and Iceland. When Bjarni reached the shores of Iceland with his latest cargo of items in A.D. 986 he was surprised to learn that his father had recently disposed of all the family property there and headed for the supposedly more verdant pastures of Greenland, a new land promoted by its discoverer, Erik the Red, as an idyllic place to live. A quarrelsome and quick-tempered man, Erik the Red had been banished from Iceland, the colony founded by his father, for having killed a man during a dispute—his second such offense during his stay there. As they sailed in search of Greenland, Bjarni and his crew encountered a severe storm that swept him and his Viking crew far from their intended course. Once the tempest had subsided, the weary sailors found themselves encased in a thick fog that limited their visibility to but a few feet in every direction. Drifting aimlessly for several days, Bjarni and his fellow sailors finally saw off in the distance an unfamiliar "well-wooded" land formation, most likely a stretch of the Labrador coastline. While many aboard were eager to explore this newfound land, Herjolfsson was only interested in finding his way to the settlement at Greenland. Upon his delayed arrival at Greenland, Bjarni, along with his family, gave up sailing and settled down to a more comfortable agrarian lifestyle. However, their tale of misadventure intrigued another settler by the name of Leif, who just happened to be the son of Eric the Red.

Sometime around A.D. 1000, Leif Ericson, also known as Leif the Lucky, after having purchased the same long boat, or, in keeping with the proper Norse vernacular for a vessel of this design, the *knarr*, used by Herjolfsson and his crew, organized his own expedition to seek out the unknown distant land that Bjarni and his comrades had stumbled upon. In his attempt to retrace the course of Herjolfsson's previous voyage, the intrepid Norsemen, along with his crew of thirty-five stout-hearted men and several head of cattle, may have touched land at Baffin Island and Labrador, but he chose to settle for the winter at a place they called Vinland. The exact location of Vinland has been contested for some time; there are those who say it was located in Nova Scotia, some believe it was an island just off the coast of New England, while others cite Newfoundland. With the arrival of spring the Norsemen sailed back to Greenland with a fair sampling of the fermented grapes that produced the intoxicating wine for which they had named the land. Leif Ericson's grand adventure inspired other Norse expeditions seeking to establish a permanent colony, but those efforts were frustrated by native attacks that soon managed to drive these European intruders from their precious homeland. Eventually, even the Greenland colonies were forsaken, leaving for future discoverers only the rubble of abandoned settlements and sagas of bold exploits as proof of what the original explorers had accomplished during their lifetimes.

The memory of these daring Norsemen's deeds across the waters of the Atlantic lived on in the many mariners' tales that circulated in the numerous European seaports. Christian I, king of a united Denmark, Norway, and Sweden, had taken a keen interest in such stories and sent forth an expedition led by his admiral, a man by the name of Didrik Pining, a captain named Pothorst, and a pilot known as either Johannes Scolvus or Skolp. Also accompanying them on the search for the lost colonies of the Vikings was João Vaz Corte-Real, a Portuguese sailor whose quest for fortune and adventure had led him to ports far north of his homeland. The expedition left Iceland sometime between late 1472 and the early part of the following year and, by many accounts, managed to reach the island of Greenland. The explorers may have ventured as far westward as Newfoundland before finally returning home. Corte-Real was rewarded for his service with his own captaincy in 1474—another milestone in a distinguished seafaring career that ended with his death in 1496. Ultimately, he served as a source of inspiration for his sons. As for Admiral Pining and Captain Pothorst, they were later convicted of committing acts of piracy and were hanged for their heinous crimes. There are sufficient reasons to doubt that Pining, Pothorst, Scolvus, and Corte-Real actually sailed together though most historians agree that each of these men did in fact sail westward at some point in time.

The news of John Cabot's search, by way of Arctic waters, for the treasures of Asia caught the attention of the Portuguese navigator Gaspar Corte-Real. Whether his plans for a voyage along a similar route were prompted by a personal desire to reclaim territory he believed to have been discovered previously by his father, or a self-assurance that he could succeed where John Cabot had failed, remains unclear, but more likely than not, both factors played a part in his decision to launch such an expedition of his own. We do know for sure that Gaspar Corte-Real submitted a proposal for such a northwest voyage, a request that would receive the royal stamp of approval from King Manuel on May 12, 1500.

Anxious to get under way, Gaspar Corte-Real had two caravels loaded, manned, and readied by the beginning of that summer. Casting off from the docks of Lisbon the two small ships made their way to the Portuguese colony at Terceira, the second largest island of the Azores. After taking on additional provisions, his ships continued on a northerly course until they finally made landfall at some undetermined point along the eastern coast of Greenland. Carefully coasting around Cape Farewell, the Corte-Real expedition sailed along the western shore of the island before darting across the water to gaze upon the shores of both Labrador and Newfoundland. By his own account, Gaspar dropped anchor at several points along the coast and during the course of his thorough reconnoitering he came across a number of natives who draped their bodies with the hides of various animals of the forest. The ships then continued up the strait that separates the two land masses until the appearance of very large ice floes made such a course exceedingly perilous.

Gaspar Corte-Real and his crew were back in Portugal before the end of the year with the glorious news of having rediscovered the long forgotten Greenland as well as the many other lands that had been explored by his father. With the aid of his brother Miguel, Gaspar began preparing for an even more extensive exploration of the lands he had recently surveyed. Three small ships set sail from Lisbon in the spring of 1501 on a course that carefully retraced Corte-Real's previous route. Unfortunately for Gaspar and Miguel, a significant number of massive icebergs now barred the way, so instead of maintaining a heading for Greenland they were forced to alter their course in the general direction of Newfoundland. Once there, they came across a great many natives, a population sizable enough to turn the sailors thoughts away from exploration and toward visions of financial gain at the slave markets back home in Portugal. Resorting to slave raids along the coast, the Portuguese mariners hauled in sixty men and one woman, a handsome catch that Gaspar entrusted to his brother to bring back to Portugal. The Indians enslaved by the Corte-Real expedition were from the Beothuk tribe, natives who were eventually hunted into extinction by future French and English settlers. The three Portuguese ships separated sometime during the month of September; Miguel assumed command of the two homeward bound vessels, while Gaspar continued to explore southward aboard the remaining craft. Assuring his brother that he would rejoin him shortly at Lisbon, Gaspar set off to determine where exactly his discovery would lead him.

Arriving safely at Lisbon in October of 1501, Miguel immediately applied for royal permission for both him and his brother to continue their search for a northwestward route to Asia. While his request was pending and after his valuable cargo of natives had already been disposed of, all Miguel could do was wait for Gaspar to return with news of his marvelous findings. But Miguel's anxiety continued to mount with each passing day that his beloved brother failed to reappear. The days soon turned into weeks and when those weeks passed into months, Miguel felt obligated to sail in search of his long-lost brother. With three vessels under his command, Miguel departed Lisbon on May 10, 1502, making great haste toward the very spot where the two had parted company. After they made landfall at Newfoundland sometime towards the end of June, it was decided that each ship would search in a different direction, with all three reporting back to the same spot by no later than the 20th of August. Unsuccessful in their efforts to locate Gaspar's missing ship, two of the search and rescue boats anxiously awaited at the designated rendezvous site for the return of the ship carrying their leader, Miguel Corte-Real. When he failed to appear on the designated day, or the day after, a frantic search was undertaken to find the man who had sought to rescue his brother, but their desperate efforts were to no avail.

The remaining ships eventually returned to Portugal, where King Manuel was informed of the sorrowful news that yet another member of the

Corte-Real family was missing and presumed dead. Manuel, who knew the brothers well and held each in the highest esteem, commissioned two vessels, at a considerable expense to his own purse, to learn of their true fate. In the meantime, their older brother, Vasqueanes, began preparing his own expedition to search for his missing brothers, but the king was not about to lose another Corte-Real to such a quest. Refusing to grant him leave, Manuel was able to console the despondent Vasqueanes with his assurance that the expedition he had just dispatched would surely learn of their whereabouts. Unfortunately, the expedition returned empty-handed; the final resting places of Gaspar and Miguel Corte-Real remain a mystery to this day.

The daring expeditions of both John Cabot and the Corte-Real family were not forgotten by another group of entrepreneurial seafarers: the fishermen. From 1500 on a great number of English and Portuguese fishermen ventured across the Atlantic to cast their nets into the cod-rich waters off the coast of Newfoundland. The scent of fish in these waters soon attracted fishermen from Spain and France. Many of the mariners, particularly those from Portugal and England, took to staying on land so that they might dry their fish before returning home with their rich haul. These wooden shelters, though primarily a seasonal residence, marked the beginning of Europe's settlement of the North American continent.

Fall from Grace

THE THIRD VOYAGE OF COLUMBUS

Tidings of John Cabot's discovery of lands to the northwest and Vasco da Gama's current expedition to India were disconcerting bits of news to the ears of Christopher Columbus and his royal patrons. With England treading near to the islands of the West Indies and neighboring Portugal on the verge of reaching the mainland of India, there was a sense of urgency to launch yet a third Spanish Enterprise of the Indies. Ever since his homecoming in March of 1496, Columbus had busied himself with preparations for a return voyage, but with many courtly advisors now having serious doubts about his ability to govern as well as his seeming inability to locate the vast riches of the Orient, the admiral found his efforts to get under way constantly being undermined by bureaucrats. In addition to these concerns, a number of individuals, especially those in positions of authority, had begun to question exactly what it was that the admiral had discovered, believing that perhaps these lands were not part of Asia after all. Financial problems also plagued his plans to set sail. King Ferdinand and Queen Isabella had pledged a generous endowment for his third expedition, but as of February 1498 he had received only a one-fifth share of this promised money. The monetary discrepancy was eventually settled with the proceeds from a loan, secured by the sovereigns, along with profits obtained from the sale of the surviving native slaves the admiral had brought back to Spain.

After having spent nearly two full years in Spain, Columbus was finally ready to embark on his third voyage of discovery. Prior to his departure, the admiral decided to put his personal affairs in order by drawing up his will. Since the titles and privileges bestowed upon him by the Spanish sovereigns were hereditary rights, Columbus hoped to put to rest any future claims against his estate by making his eldest son, Diego, heir apparent to all his worldly possessions. On May 30, 1498, Columbus led his fleet of six ships out of the port of Sanlúcar de Barrameda for yet another voyage across the Atlantic. To aid in the growth of his colony the admiral also brought along on this journey thirty good Christian women eager for marriage. Once at sea the fleet made straight for the Canary Islands, at which point Columbus decided to divide his fleet and set them on divergent paths to the Indies; three vessels were to sail the familiar route across the Atlantic while the admiral and his three ships continued south toward the Cape Verde Islands. Eventually, the fleet would reunite at the Spanish settlement on Hispaniola.

After touching at São Tiago, Columbus plotted a westerly course just north of, but parallel to, the line of the equator. The admiral had good reason for following such a course. The ancient Greek philosopher and scientist Aristotle had theorized that all lands along the same latitude produced similar natural products. Since gold had been discovered near or along the equatorial line that passed through Africa it was easy to conclude that any lands along parallel lines would also be a birthplace of gold. Unfortunately for the admiral and his crew, this new route selected by Columbus led the fleet directly into the equatorial doldrums, a region where the wind can suddenly slip into a long dormant state. From the 13th of July to the 22nd of that month his three ships drifted ever so slowly under the blistering beams of an unrelenting sun. The admiral's dire predicament was further complicated by a sudden onset of gout, a condition that impaired both his physical and mental state for much of this voyage. A saving gust of wind finally put the ships back on a westerly course, and from then on Columbus, ever fearful of the intense heat and the motionless seas of this region, made no further attempts to sail along the line of the equator. Running low on food, water, and patience, Columbus quickened his pace to find a suitable site to land his ships. His efforts were finally rewarded on the last day of July with the sighting of three mountainous peaks off on the distant horizon. Once he was able to ascertain that these were mountains belonging to just one land mass, Columbus, once again seeing divine intervention at work, christened the land Trinidad, in tribute to the Holy Trinity.

Once he had sailed far enough to determine that Trinidad was but an island the admiral then spent the next two weeks probing the extensive coastline that adjoins the Gulf of Paria. At the great Orinoco delta he observed the powerful surge of fresh water that pours into the ocean, a sight which prompted him to conclude, quite correctly, that he had happened upon a land of significant size, perhaps even a continent. His own words even suggest that he was beginning to question whether or not this was in fact the Indies: "I have come to believe that this is a vast continent, hitherto unknown. I am greatly supported in this view by the great river and the fresh water of the sea, and I am also supported by Esdra, who in Book 4, Chapter 6, says that six parts of the world consist of dry land, and one part of water.... And if this be a continent, it is a marvelous thing, and will be so among all the wise, since so great a river flows that it makes a freshwater sea of 48 leagues." In the end, however, he cast aside his own doubts by reasoning that he had simply reached a part of Asia heretofore unknown to Europe. He was unaware of the fact that he was the first European to gaze upon the coast of South America, a vast continent later named in honor of an explorer who followed in the wake of Christopher Columbus.

While he did encounter a great number of natives on this voyage the admiral often had great difficulty finding ways to communicate with them. On one occasion, a score plus four of local inhabitants paddled toward his vessel in a rather large canoe and once alongside they began to whoop and holler at the curious sailors aboard the Spanish ship. Whatever it was that the natives were attempting to convey was clearly beyond the comprehension of Columbus and his crew. When their own efforts to communicate with the natives came to nothing the admiral attempted to demonstrate their friendly intentions by ordering a sailor to strike up a beat on the tabor. The peculiar sight of Spanish sailors gesticulating to the strange rhythm of a small drum seemed to offend the Indians, who apparently interpreted their spontaneous jig as some form of war dance directed at them. The volley of arrows unleashed by the natives sent the dancing sailors scurrying for their own weapons. By the time the Spaniards retrieved their crossbows and took aim the natives of Trinidad had already begun paddling back towards the safety of their island.

Columbus had far better success with the native inhabitants of the mainland. While anchored off the coast of Venezuela the admiral noted that "Some of the natives came out to the ship at once in their canoes and asked me, on behalf of their king, to go ashore. And when they saw that I was not inclined to do that, they came out in hordes to the ship, and many of them wore pieces of gold on their breasts, and some had pearls strung around their arms. I rejoiced greatly when I saw these things, and spared no effort to find out where they obtained them, and they told me that they got them there, and in a land further north." Columbus eventually went ashore but, much to his dismay, the precious pearls and gold that he hoped to obtain through trade never materialized. However, the stories that he brought back about the great pearl fisheries of this region would entice a wave of future explorers who desired to continue the search for these lustrous gems of the sea.

RETURN TO SANTO DOMINGO

With the crew's morale beginning to waver, the ship's provisions dwindling at a rapid rate, and his own health steadily deteriorating, Columbus abandoned his plans for any further exploration of these newly discovered lands and made great haste for the familiar surroundings of Hispaniola. On the last day of August, after nearly a fortnight of sailing, the fleet arrived at the new settlement of Santo Domingo. Founded and named by Bartolomeo, in tribute to the memory of their father Domenico, shortly after his brother had departed for Spain, Santo Domingo rested along the banks of the Ozama river on the south side of the island and in close proximity to the recently discovered gold mines of Hispaniola. Other than expressions of delight over being reunited with his brother, Bartolomeo had few encouraging words for the ailing admiral. The mysterious illness that had plagued the settlement of Isabela continued to torment and claim the lives of many colonists at Santo Domingo. Also adding to their worries was the unsightly epidemic of itchy rashes and oozing chancres—the effects of the sexually transmitted disease we now know to be syphilis. As disturbing as this situation was to the admiral, the news of open resistance to the direct authority of Bartolomeo and Diego Columbus was of much greater concern to him.

The leader of this rebellion was Francisco Roldán, a man whom Christopher Columbus had appointed as "alcalde" of Isabela just prior to his departure for Spain. Since such a position is synonymous with mayor, Roldán was under the opinion that he was endowed with administrative authority on par with the siblings of the admiral. However, he soon learned otherwise. When the move to Santo Domingo failed to improve either his position or the condition of the colonists, Francisco had little trouble rallying supporters to his own cause. Roldán and his band of malcontents were presented with an opportune moment to settle their differences when Bartolomeo Columbus decided to travel inland to collect the admiral's precious gold tax from the Indians and left the reigns of power in the unskilled hands of his brother Diego. The younger Columbus learned of the plot to sail back to Spain on a ship currently beached along the coast and ordered a halt to the preparations for desertion. When the conspirators refused to heed his authority, Diego dispatched a messenger to summon his older brother back to Santo Domingo. Bartolomeo's return put an end to Roldán's plan to leave the island of Hispaniola but failed to stop him from abandoning the settlement with nearly seventy rebellious colonists.

Forging an alliance with several of the island's discontented caciques, Roldán began making preparations for an armed assault against a Spanish fortress situated between Santo Domingo and the former colony of Isabela, but his plans were foiled by the sudden arrival of two supply ships from Spain. Besides unloading a cargo of much needed provisions, the ship also brought news that Christopher Columbus was busily preparing for his return to Hispaniola. With these tidings, Francisco Roldán and his followers retreated to Xaragua while the unruly native faction returned to the safety of their villages. But Bartolomeo Columbus was in no mood to forgive and forget. At the head of his own army, Bartolomeo attacked and set fire to a number of native villages and in the process managed to capture Guarionex, the cacique who had lent the support of his people to the notorious Spanish traitors.

Just when it appeared that Roldán's insurrection was about to be extinguished for good, an unexpected stroke of luck helped to breathe new life into it. The three ships that Columbus had sent ahead to Hispaniola after having reached the Canary Islands arrived unexpectedly at a harbor very near to the rebel base. Unaware of these current events, the captains of the vessels granted permission for many of their sea-weary sailors to go ashore. Hoping to commandeer these ships to go back to Spain, the persuasive Roldán succeeded in enlisting the vast majority of the men who came ashore to his cause; but the most important part of his plan failed to materialize when those still on board ship caught wind of his scheme and immediately sailed away to Santo Domingo.

Such was the state of affairs when Christopher Columbus finally returned to the shores of Hispaniola on August 31, 1498. Instead of dealing forcefully with the insurrection, as Bartolomeo had been doing, the admiral sought a peaceful reconciliation with Francisco Roldán. Unfortunately for the admiral, this course of action merely made an already tense situation even worse. In his rush to settle their differences, Columbus made a great number of concessions that favored the cause of Roldán and his band of rebels: they were to be provided with two ships and enough provisions to sustain them on their long voyage back to Spain; they received a pledge that entitled them to continue receiving wages until they left the island; and they were issued a letter addressed to the Spanish sovereigns that exonerated them from any potential charges of misconduct.

After they had been granted all that they had demanded, many of the rebels began to have second thoughts about leaving Hispaniola. Most of these men had left Spain for a chance at a better way of life, which meant that for many of them there was little incentive to trade the remote possibility of finding wealth at Hispaniola for the certain poverty that awaited them at Spain. Also, there were a number of criminals among the rebel force who had managed to escape a trip to the gallows by agreeing to sign on for this most recent expedition to Hispaniola, and they had no desire to face the dangling noose of the executioner once again. Roldán negotiated another pact with Columbus that gave them the right to remain at Hispaniola. As a reward for their renewed allegiance, Columbus granted each rebel who agreed to stay on at the colony a plot of land to call his own, absolved them of all their past transgressions, and reinstated Francisco Roldán as alcalde, or mayor.

TROUBLE IN PARADISE

Prior to this latest pact with Roldán, Christopher Columbus had sent two of his ships back to Spain with news of the many marvelous new lands he had discovered, a fair sampling of beautiful pearls, a small amount of gold, some cotton, and another shipment of Indian slaves, as well as a report of the uprising that had erupted at Hispaniola during his absence and his effective efforts at restoring order to the settlement the moment he arrived. But in his letter to the sovereigns, the admiral had unintentionally admitted to his own inability to resolve this current crisis by requesting that an experienced judge be sent to Hispaniola on the returning fleet. This was a disturbing situation to Ferdinand and Isabella, for while they still believed Columbus to be a good admiral both rulers now had grave concerns about his ability to govern.

In choosing an arbitrator to resolve the delicate situation at Hispaniola, King Ferdinand and Queen Isabella turned to Francisco de Bobadilla, a soldier and statesman whom both held in the highest esteem. As a crusading knight, he had served with great distinction in the holy war to reclaim

Spanish lands from the Moors, and for this valuable service he was rewarded with the governorship of several Andalusian towns. In keeping with the request of Columbus, the monarchs initially appointed Bobadilla as a chief magistrate to mete out Spanish justice at Hispaniola. His authority, however, increased significantly following the unexpected arrival of Alonso de Ojeda and fifteen of the rebels who had chosen to return to Spain. After hearing their additional complaints against the admiral, the monarchs, following much consultation and deliberation, concluded that the time had come for Christopher Columbus to be replaced as governor of the island he had discovered and colonized. In May of 1499, Bobadilla, in addition to his responsibilities as chief magistrate, was proclaimed the new governor of Hispaniola. Curiously, in spite of all the sudden concern over the admiral's competency to command, the remainder of the year slipped by before Francisco de Bobadilla set sail for Hispaniola.

While these events were unfolding in Spain, the situation at Hispaniola continued to worsen. Even though Columbus had managed to settle his differences with Roldán, the numerous concessions made by him were perceived by many as a sign of weakness on his part—a flaw in command that a great number of other disaffected colonists attempted to exploit for personal gain. The colony itself was in utter disarray; malaria and syphilis ran rampant, and those who remained healthy spent less time tending to community chores and more searching for gold. The listless Columbus, who was still recuperating from his own illness, became an object of scornful ridicule and many took to calling him "Christopher Columbus, Admiral of the Mosquitoes." Even the natives no longer respected his authority and showed their disdain by ignoring whatever new demands he placed upon them. When it became evident to the colonists that Hispaniola had little to offer in the way of wealth, a few Spanish malcontents secretly plotted to overthrow the Italian triumvirate.

Luckily for Christopher Columbus these latest threats against his authority coincided with the return of his health, whereupon the admiral resolved to put an end to these insurrections once and for all with an impressive show of strength. Leaving Don Diego behind to govern the affairs of Santo Domingo, the admiral advanced inland toward Concepción de la Vega at the head of an impressive army while his brother Bartolomeo led his own armed force to subdue the region of Xaragua. This rebellion, unlike the one staged by Francisco Roldán, was dealt with in the harshest manner; captured rebel leaders were marched back to Santo Domingo in order that they might be given a proper public execution. When the fleet of Francisco de Bobadilla finally arrived at Santo Domingo on August 23, 1500, the newly appointed governor of Hispaniola was greeted by the appalling sight of seven Spaniards swinging from the hangman's noose. Hoping to impress Bobadilla with claims that the rebellion was nearly under control Don Diego boasted that five more rebels were slated to hang from the gallows the next morning. The thought of Italian mercenaries hanging Spanish subjects did not sit well with the zealously patriotic Bobadilla. Convinced that the situation at Hispaniola was much worse than he had been led to believe, Francisco de Bobadilla retired to his boat to begin making plans for an orderly and complete transfer of power.

On the 24th of August, shortly after having attended Mass, Francisco de Bobadilla had a crier read aloud to an assembled crowd the royal letter of patent that proclaimed him to be the chief magistrate of Hispaniola. As his first order of business, Bobadilla demanded that the younger Columbus turn over any information relevant to his official inquiry into the insurrection, a request which included the immediate transfer of all prisoners, especially those who had been sentenced to hang. When Don Diego refused to comply with his demands an angered Bobadilla stormed back to his boat to ponder his next move. The following day, and once again after Mass, Bobadilla read aloud the royal decree that appointed him governor of the island of Hispaniola and to show that he meant to exercise his declared authority he unveiled the ship's heavy artillery, all of which was pointed directly at the settlement. This time, when Diego refused to hand over the condemned prisoners, Bobadilla had him placed under arrest. With Santo Domingo now under his jurisdiction the new governor made himself at home in the abode that belonged to Christopher Columbus. Rifling through the admiral's personal possessions and extensive notes, Bobadilla impounded anything he believed to be even remotely related to his inquiry. Messengers were dispatched to La Vega and Xaragua with orders for both the admiral and Bartolomeo to return at once to Santo Domingo.

Christopher Columbus did not return to Santo Domingo until the middle of September, and as one would expect, given the current crisis, his meeting with Bobadilla was less than amicable. The admiral adamantly refused to acknowledge Bobadilla's authority and not even a royal letter addressed to him personally from King Ferdinand and Queen Isabella, which implored both him and his brothers to honor this appointment, could sway Columbus from his stubborn stance. Frustrated by the admiral's unyielding and arrogant manner, the new governor of Hispaniola had the former governor imprisoned alongside his brother Diego. When news of their incarceration reached Bartolomeo Columbus at Xaragua, his first reaction was to rescue his brothers by launching an assault against Bobadilla, but he had a change of mind following the receipt of a letter from his older brother beseeching him to avoid an armed conflict with the chief magistrate.

Respecting the wishes of the admiral, Bartolomeo returned peacefully to Santo Domingo. But once inside the settlement he was immediately placed under arrest, shackled, and lodged with his brothers in prison. Shortly after having been reunited, the three brothers suffered the indignity of being paraded in chains through the colony to a vessel destined to transport the disgraced trio back to Spain.

NINE

Same Planet,
Different Worlds

The New World According to Vespucci

A BUSINESS OPPORTUNITY

There was yet another son of Italy who was fated to play a important role in the discovery and exploration of lands located to the west of Europe. Born in Florence in 1454, Amerigo Vespucci, the son of Stagio and Elizbetta, had the good fortune to come from a family of some social standing in a city that flourished in the arts and prospered from commercial intercourse abroad. With the benefit of an excellent education and the influential aid of his father's many important political and business connections, the young Amerigo landed a respectable assignment as the private secretary to Florence's ambassador to France. After a two-year stint in the diplomatic corps he returned to the city of Florence to help manage the family's business affairs but resigned three years later when he was offered a promising position at a prestigious firm owned and operated by the enormously wealthy Medici family.

The Medicis dabbled in just about any trade that showed a promise of profit; wine, fish, tapestries, grain, and silver wares were but a few of the many commodities that passed through their accounting ledgers. They had commercial ties with nearly every major port of the Levant as well as important business connections at most European ports of call and major centers of commerce. This vast network of overseas trade, combined with their rapidly growing and highly lucrative banking operations, helped to transform the city of Florence into the financial capital of Europe and, in the process, made the Medici clan one of, if not *the* most powerful and wealthy families of that era.

Though the young Amerigo Vespucci was hired at first as a mere clerk, his keen mind and shrewd business manner quickly caught the attention of both Lorenzo and Giovanni Medici, and before long he was entrusted with the responsibility of managing a great many of their business affairs. Such dealings often brought him into direct contact with the rugged sailors who plied the waters of the Mediterranean for a living; and it was their intriguing tales of adventure that undoubtedly awakened in him a latent interest in navigation. From then on, much of Vespucci's free time was consumed with learning as much as he could about the piloting of ships, the positions of the stars, and the geography of the world.

The Medicis, at some point towards the end of the year 1491, transferred Amerigo to their subsidiary office situated near the busy docks of Seville. His arrival happened to coincide with the launching of the great spice race, a pursuit that was creating a dangerous divide between the Iberian kingdoms of Spain and Portugal. Consequently, this obsessive quest to reach India or China by way of the seas had made the Iberian Peninsula a region of boundless opportunities for anyone with a skill or an interest in maritime affairs. Unlike the prosperous Italian city-states, which were primarily concerned with maintaining their longstanding and profitable trade relationship with Muslim merchants operating in the Mediterranean basin, both Portugal and Spain were intent on finding a way to bypass the control of the Arab middlemen by sailing directly to the source of the numerous commodities that they and all the rest of Europe craved so dearly.

While stationed at Seville, Vespucci came under the tutelage of Giannetto Berardi, the manager who supervised the Medicis' maritime supply contracts in that city. Berardi was one of the many agents contracted to assist in the furnishing of supplies and provisions for Christopher Columbus's historic first voyage of discovery, and as his new assistant, Vespucci probably played a small role in this undertaking. We do know for sure that both Vespucci and Berardi secured victuals for a ship that sailed as part of the fleet on the admiral's second Enterprise of the Indies. When Columbus returned from his latest voyage in the summer of 1496, Berardi had passed away and the fully capable Vespucci now assumed the title and duties of manager at the busy Seville office. Under his shrewd direction this Medici branch office became the leading supplier for vessels sailing from Spain, and consequently his firm was the one that Columbus hired to outfit a number of ships for his upcoming third voyage to the Indies. Over the course of their business dealings, Columbus and Vespucci acquired a mutual respect for one another, and just before the admiral's departure each had begun to take the other into his confidence.

Throughout his movement into the ranks of management, and despite the accompanying constraints that the burgeoning affairs of business placed upon his personal time, Amerigo never abandoned his interest in exploration. Fortunate that both his vocation and his passion lay in the same direction, Vespucci used, but never abused, his position to uncover knowledge pertaining to the many Spanish and Portuguese voyages of exploration. His own studies and calculations eventually led him to the conclusion that his good friend Christopher Columbus had not discovered the Indies by sailing west, but exactly what lands the admiral had stumbled upon would continue to occupy his thoughts for the remainder of his life.

THE KNOWN VOYAGES OF VESPUCCI

In the year 1499 Amerigo Vespucci put his own interests first and effectively utilized his business connections to earn himself a prominent position aboard an expedition being led by the veteran explorer Alonso de Ojeda. As one of the admiral's former lieutenants, Ojeda had distinguished himself on the second expedition to the Indies by capturing the rebellious cacique Caonabo on the island of Hispaniola. Though he planned to follow in the path of his former commander, Ojeda's interests were, however, far more pecuniary than exploratory. Alonso enjoyed the benefits of a close relationship with Bishop Fonseca, Spain's minister of affairs for the Indies, and because of their friendship he was able to obtain a peek at Columbus's confidential report that described the many discoveries made during his third voyage across the Atlantic, as well as the accompanying charts sent to the king and queen that happened to pinpoint a region rumored to contain an abundance of pearls just waiting to be harvested. Anxious to explore the rich possibilities of this region, Ojeda requested and ultimately received permission from Juan Fonseca to lead his own expedition across the Atlantic. Until recently, such a request would have been unthinkable: Christopher Columbus was at the height of his popularity and, in addition, he was, by royal decree, "Viceroy" of all the discovered lands he had set foot upon. But since the admiral had failed to make good on all that he had promised, the authority to explore and exploit the islands of the Caribbean was slowly being granted to others, in the hope that they might have better luck in finding the vast riches that seemed to constantly elude Christopher Columbus.

While he was initially hired as a representative of the expedition's financial backers, Vespucci's extensive maritime knowledge earned him the respect of both the officers and the crew, and before long he found himself assuming many of the duties normally associated with command. Another sailor of note on this voyage was the pilot Juan de la Cosa, also a veteran of Columbus's second Enterprise of the Indies and later a cartographer of some renown. Depending on which account one reads, either four or six ships sailed from Cádiz on May 18, 1499, under the command of Alonso de Ojeda. After a brief stopover at the Canaries the fleet sailed across the Atlantic until landing somewhere along the coast of the future site of French Guiana. Realizing that they had arrived at a point considerably south of where Columbus had explored on his most recent voyage, Ojeda was anxious to steer his fleet northward toward the "Coast of Pearls." Vespucci, on the other hand, was more interested in sailing the virgin coastline further southward to determine whether or not it led to the legendary land of Cathay. After much discussion it was agreed that they would divide their forces in order that each might pursue his own quest.

Captain Alonso de Ojeda led his half of the fleet north to the island of Trinidad, then he steered westward towards Margarita, and soon afterwards his expedition happened upon the great pearl fisheries of Cubagua, the legendary land that had escaped the admiral's notice nearly a year earlier. After amassing a small fortune in pearls by way of trade with the natives, Ojeda sailed on in hopes of finding even greater treasure, but none would ever match the magnificent discovery he had made at Cubagua. However, another memorable find did occur further along the coast of Lake Maracaibo. It was here that he found native huts resting on large wooden beams that safely suspended their homes high above the surface of the water. It was a sight that was slightly reminiscent of a European city of enormous stature that just so happened to be structured in a similar style. Ojeda and his crew honored and romanticized this strip of land by christening it Venezuela, a name that means "Little Venice."

While Ojeda searched for treasure, Vespucci and his half of the fleet sailed southward to explore the great unknown. Clinging to the notion, just as Columbus had done before him, that this was the mysterious southeast coast of Cathay, Amerigo anxiously searched for Cattigara, the fabled port city that had been charted by the ancient geographer Ptolemy. During the course of this journey he discovered the great gulf of water that is the mouth to the mighty Amazon River—a site also encountered during an expedition led by the Spaniard Vicente Pinzón. As Vespucci continued to probe just below the line of the equator it became clear to him that this was truly a land mass of considerable length and with its coastline continually tracking toward the east he surely must have realized at some point that the region extended on into the Portuguese hemisphere. By now his ships were suffering terribly from the devastating effects of the teredos, little worms that thrive in the warm tropical waters of the Caribbean Sea and wreak havoc upon wooden vessels by attaching themselves to the hull and slowly, and unrelentingly, boring their way through the ships' planks. Though he certainly desired to continue on, the leaks caused by the teredos forced Vespucci to abandon this quest and instead seek out immediate sanctuary for his troubled ships.

Following along the same path that had recently been sailed by Alonso de Ojeda, Amerigo and his crew soon came upon Trinidad and the great Gulf of Paria that separates this island from the mainland. As he sailed back to the coast of Venezuela, Vespucci had an opportunity to gaze upon the majestic mouth of the Orinoco, the very same delta that had given Columbus cause to question whether or not such a region existed in the known Indies. Believing that the westward trend of the shore would eventually lead them to a passage to India, the expedition continued on until it reached La Guaira. Coming ashore to explore the land and to replenish their rapidly diminishing stores the sailors came into contact with natives who did not take kindly to strangers treading upon their homeland. After a number of his men were struck by arrows Vespucci retaliated with an armed assault against the village that he deemed responsible for this unprovoked attack. A vicious battle ensued and quickly ended with the incineration of the entire village and the slaughter of one hundred and fifty of its inhabitants. Shortly after this deadly conflict the badly damaged ships under Vespucci's command slowly limped their way toward the island of Hispaniola.

On September 5, 1499—long before Amerigo Vespucci ever considered sailing to Hispaniola—Alonso de Ojeda and his small fleet turned up at the Spanish settlement governed by his former commander. Ojeda's sudden arrival was an unforeseen event that greatly troubled the admiral; for this was a clear signal that he no longer had the full confidence of King Ferdinand and Queen Isabella, and if they were willing to sanction this rogue expedition that trespassed on his claims then surely more were soon to follow. While Columbus still had the authority to chase away his former lieutenant, there was little he could do about the many other treasure seekers who were destined to follow in the wake of Alonso de Ojeda.

Amerigo Vespucci and his weary crew were fortunate enough to benefit from a more cordial climate at Hispaniola. Christopher Columbus permitted them to linger long enough to complete the necessary repairs to their badly battered ships, replenish their nearly depleted provisions, and to take some time to refresh themselves before setting sail once more. Departing from Hispaniola sometime towards the end of November, Vespucci and his crew spent the next few months searching amongst the numerous islands and islets of the Bahamas for signs of material wealth, but no such sight ever revealed itself to them. Before long Vespucci's sailors did what sailors are often prone to do: they began to grumble, and with good cause. It had been nearly a year since the fleet sailed from the docks of Cádiz, and while they had seen many strange and wonderful sights they had very little to show for their time and trouble. The crew's many complaints soon manifested themselves as a loosely united demand for an immediate return to Spain, and such a request placed Amerigo in a precarious position: to ignore the wishes of his men would surely give rise to a mutiny, while, on the other hand, to return home with empty cargo bays would certainly anger the venture capitalists who expected him to return with nothing short of a profit. In an effort to satisfy his contractual obligation Vespucci and his crew resorted to slave raids amongst the many villages of the island inhabitants. Only after they had captured more than two hundred natives did Vespucci capitulate to the demands of his crew and set a course for their return to Spain.

As soon as he was safely back on Spanish soil, Amerigo Vespucci began preparing for yet another voyage across the Atlantic. Still convinced that he had sailed along the extreme edge of Cathay, Vespucci was certain that this next expedition would locate the elusive strait which emptied into the Indian Ocean. He even took time to write to the Medicis about his confrontation with the fierce Caribs: "When we had sailed four hundred leagues along the coast, we commenced to find people who did not desire our friendship, but stood waiting for us with weapons, which they held in readiness, and when we approached the shore in the boats, they resisted our landing, so that we were forced to combat with them. At the end of the fight they broke from us with loss. Since they were naked, we made a great slaughter of them, and at the end we routed them and massacred many of them, and pillaged their houses."

Unfortunately for Vespucci, he found the Spanish monarchs to be less than enthusiastic about his proposed enterprise. Concerned that he may have inadvertently crossed the established line of demarcation that separated Spanish and Portuguese claims in that distant part of the world, King Ferdinand and Queen Isabella decided to avoid risking a potentially explosive international incident by declining his request for another expedition. This unfavorable decision by the Catholic sovereigns failed to deter the Italian explorer from pursuing other means of support. Unencumbered by thoughts of national allegiance, Vespucci, during the latter part of 1500, simply left the service of Spain and sought the royal patronage of neighboring Portugal. Amerigo had managed to arrive at an opportune moment, for this was the

AMERICO VESPUCIO GRAN PILÓTO.

Amerigo Vespucci: Though he has often been credited with voyages he never undertook and discoveries that had already been made by others before him, Vespucci still deserves recognition as one of the greatest European explorers of his era.

same time when the ships dispatched by Pedro Cabral had returned with news of his discovery of a western land they had christened Terra de Vera Cruz, and the king was now eager to learn more about this unknown region that clearly fell within his domain. Elated at the prospect of having in his employ an explorer who already had sailed to these faraway lands, King Manuel provided a royal reception for Amerigo Vespucci and then proceeded to seduce him into his service by bestowing upon him the grand title of "Royal Geographer for Portugal" and offering him a pledge that he would be permitted to accompany the second expedition, already in the planning, to this "Land of the True Cross."

Serving under the command of Gonzalo Coelho, Amerigo Vespucci sailed aboard one of the three ships that cast off from the docks of Lisbon on May 13, 1501. The expedition ventured first to the Cape Verde Islands where they had the good fortune of meeting up with Pedro Cabral's spice laden homeward bound fleet. A friendly exchange of information surely aided Coelho in setting his bearings for Terra de Vera Cruz, and very possibly, judging by their description of the true Indies, may have convinced Amerigo that the land that they were about to sail to was not a part of Asia after all.

After leaving the Cape Verde Islands the Portuguese expedition followed a southwesterly course until it made landfall near Cape São Agostinho, a spot that was in close proximity to the coordinates previously established by Pedro Cabral. Captain Coelho sent two men ashore to meet with the natives in hopes of establishing friendly trade relations. After five days passed without the men on the ships seeing or hearing from their two comrades, a great number of nubile native girls appeared suddenly along the shore. Gonzalo Coelho sent one of his young sailors, a handsome lad whom the captain expected would be able to work his endearing charm on the local women. As the young attractive native girls seductively caressed the sailor into a state of arousal an older tribeswoman crept up from behind and proceeded to savagely bash the sailor's head with a large wooden club. The shocked Portuguese sailors were kept at bay by concealed native archers who let loose a volley of arrows aimed in their general direction. The dead sailor was then dragged up to a nearby hill where they cooked his carcass over an open fire. There, in full view of the horrified sailors, the natives sat down to feast upon their fallen comrade. The captain, sensing that the two other sailors had met with a similar fate and, not wanting to risk the lives of any more men, decided to sail away to a nearby safer spot.

Once they had ascertained beyond all doubt that this land truly was within the hemisphere that belonged to Portugal, the explorers then set their sights on uncovering any material wealth this promising land might yield. After cutting down and storing a large quantity of tropical trees that resembled the hard red wood imported into Europe by way of the Indies the sailors continued their journey southward along the coastline of the continent. It was at Port Seguro that both Coelho and Vespucci unexpectedly came upon the two convicts Pedro Cabral had left behind nearly a year earlier to scour the land in search of civilization. While the two men entertained their rescuers with wondrous tales of adventure and survival, which included an encounter with natives who appeared friendly at first but who they later discovered were the infamous and ravenous cannibals who inhabited this region, both unfortunately had little else of interest to report. They had never encountered any signs of civilization, they had never met anyone who knew or had even heard of the Great Khan, they had never sighted any trading vessels sailing across the waters, and they had never seen any caravans hauling great cargoes of valuable commodities across this God-forsaken land.

Coelho, Vespucci, and crew sailed into the bay of Guanabara on New Year's day of 1502, and in observance of that date they christened their discovery Rio de Janeiro. From this point southward the coastline veered steadily toward the west, an angle that soon carried them across the recognized line of demarcation and therefore into the hemisphere that rightfully belonged to Spain. Choosing to ignore their obvious transgression the explorers sailed on in hopes of finding either a way around or a passage through this seemingly endless land formation. This excursion took them beyond the Plate River—some fourteen years before it was "discovered" and claimed by the Spanish navigator Juan Solís—and they may have even reached as far south as the Gulf of San Julian before deciding to return to Portugal. They finally docked at Lisbon on the 22nd of July, 1502. Of all the many discoveries they had made on this voyage the most significant was certainly the realization that none of the geographical evidence at hand could support the prevailing theory that this land was connected in any way, shape or form to the continent of Asia; and from his own observations Vespucci was able to conclude, quite correctly, that this was indeed a "New World."

Sufficiently impressed by the abundant and increasingly valuable cargoes of brazilwood brought back from these ventures across the Atlantic, Portuguese officials decided to change the name of Terra de Vera Cruz to simply Brazil. Despite its commercial promise, Brazil would always take a back seat to Portugal's commitment to control trade along the waters of the Red Sea and the Indian Ocean. Anxious to continue the importation of brazilwood but unwilling to dip into the royal treasury, the Crown concocted a familiar scheme that would achieve both aims: they offered brazilwood concessions to willing and financially able Portuguese entrepreneurs. The first such concession was awarded in 1503 to Fernão de Noronha, a converted Jewish merchant, who agreed to assume all risks associated with this venture in exchange for the opportunity to profit from the harvesting.

Meanwhile, Spanish authorities were anxious to learn of the reasons behind Portugal's growing interest in these lands to the west and who better to learn that information from than Portugal's residing "Royal Geographer," Amerigo Vespucci. Having succeeded in luring the venerable Vespucci back to Spain in 1505, Spanish officials wasted little time in summoning him before the royal court where he willingly provided them with detailed testimony about these enticing faraway places. Desiring to retain his services once again, the Crown offered Vespucci a prominent position with the Casa de Contratación in Seville, the tribunal that oversaw all of Spain's commercial affairs in the West Indies. Accepting their generous offer, Amerigo took up permanent residence at Seville and shortly thereafter became a naturalized citizen of Spain.

Amerigo Vespucci's stature grew even greater with his appointment in 1508 as the very first "piloto mayor," or pilot-major, of Spain. This newly created position carried with it a great number of responsibilities, but Vespucci proved he was more than qualified to handle such a Herculean task. He immediately instituted standards of training for every pilot; established strict licensing procedures for all navigators; assisted in the preparation of new expeditions and even charted their routes across the Atlantic; and, following each new sighting or discovery, meticulously revised Spain's official map of the West Indies. In just a few short years, Vespucci had managed to transform a respectable but relatively small fleet into a mighty naval power that was capable of rivaling the savvy seafaring skills of their Iberian brothers. In 1512, while in the midst of planning one more expedition of his own to the New World, Vespucci passed away, a victim of the malignant malaria he had contracted from an earlier voyage.

THE CANTINO AFFAIR

With the race to reach the Indies by way of the sea taking on ever greater economic and political importance, it becomes easier to understand why both of the Iberian powers became increasingly guarded as to their respective trade routes. In Spain, all official charts were maintained in a strongbox secured under dual lock and key: one key being in the sole possession of the pilot-major, the other retained by the royal cartographer. In Portugal it was officially deemed an act of treason, a crime punishable by death, to divulge any information, especially to a foreigner, concerning the now established sea routes to the Indies. As hard as these two nations tried to shroud their expeditions in a veil of secrecy they could not hide from the rest of Europe the fact that they were reaping tremendous dividends from these overseas expeditions. Foreign merchants—the eyes and ears of their respective homelands—saw firsthand at the docks of Lisbon and Seville the tremendous amount of exotic treasures being unloaded from the hulls of these returning fleets. Foreign sailors arriving at Portuguese and Spanish ports often enjoyed a lively session of swapping stories with other sailors about their grand adventures to distant and exotic lands. But the greatest threat to national security came from the fact that many sailors and officers were suddenly willing to sell their experience and allegiance to other nations, provided the price was right.

Italian merchants were closely monitoring the ongoing efforts of Portuguese and Spanish mariners to reach the ports of India, and the closer they came to reaching their intended destination the more anxious the Italian business community became. Their concern was certainly understandable when one recalls that Italy's financial well-being was almost entirely dependent upon their longstanding favored trade status with Muslim merchants, who, as middlemen, were themselves dependent upon their longstanding trade relationships with merchants from both Asia and Africa. Fearing that their livelihood might very well be in jeopardy should Portugal ever succeed in its determined quest, Italian merchants and noblemen desperately sought to learn more about these voyages. The most accurate way to chart Portugal's progress, without arousing her suspicions, was to somehow obtain a copy

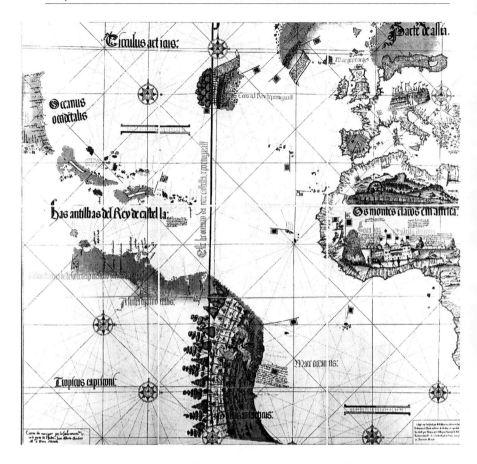

The Cantino Map: The infamous map, which was illicitly purchased and then smuggled out of Portugal, charts many of the western discoveries made by explorers from both Spain and Portugal.

of the Portuguese *padron*—the official royal map that marked every route followed and every discovery made by these numerous expeditions. While many tried, and many failed, one such scheme did meet with success.

By the beginning of the 16th century nearly all of Europe was fully aware of the fact that the Portuguese had succeeded in finding their way to the fabulous treasures of India. While word of Vasco da Gama's voyage was certainly disconcerting news to the many merchants of Italy, tidings of the following voyage undertaken by Pedro Cabral sent shock waves throughout the many markets situated in the Levant. While da Gama had certainly set the course to India his expedition had returned with but a meager measure of material value. Cabral, on the other hand, demonstrated that Portuguese captains had no reservations about using force to obtain what they desired, and in so doing, he managed to bring back an exceedingly rich cargo of spices. Anticipating even greater hauls from their future expeditions, Portuguese officials took the next step toward cornering the market on the European spice trade with the establishment of their own spice exchange at the prominent trade center of Amsterdam. Concerned about the growing threat to his homeland's dominance over the lucrative trade in rare spices, Ercole d'Este, the Italian duke of Ferrara, sent Alberto Cantino, a cartographer by trade, on a covert mission to the city of Lisbon.

Masquerading as an important Italian ambassador, Alberto Cantino had little trouble making the right connections at Lisbon. Eventually he came across a fellow cartographer who had access to the information he desired, and for the price of twelve ducats, a considerable sum for that era, the man promised to provide Cantino with a copy of Portugal's official *padron*. The finished product turned out to be even better than what he had initially bargained for. Cantino received an updated and detailed map that plotted not only the routes sailed by the likes of such renowned Portuguese explorers as Diogo Cão, Bartolomeu Dias, Vasco da Gama, and Pedro Cabral along the continent of Africa, but one which also outlined the numerous discoveries made by both Portugal and Spain on their westward voyages across the Atlantic Ocean. Once their clandestine transaction was concluded Alberto managed to find a way to smuggle the map back to his employer in Italy. This map, forever after known as the Cantino map, was in the hands of the Duke of Ferrara sometime toward the end of 1502. However, by this time it was too late for either Italy or any other nation to stop what had already been put in motion by the two Iberian superpowers.

The Final Voyage of Columbus

RESTRICTED FREEDOM

The sight of Christopher Columbus, "Admiral of the Ocean Sea," imprisoned below deck in chains, his wrists confined by manacles and his feet restrained in fetters, was simply too much for Alonso de Vallejo, captain of the *La Gorda*, to bear. Once they were out of sight of land and far from the uncompromising character of Francisco de Bobadilla, the benevolent Spanish captain offered to remove the shameful irons that the admiral wore, as well as the chains that bound his two brothers. The proud Columbus declined his generous offer. Since he had been placed in chains by an appointed emissary of the Spanish sovereigns, he reasoned, it was they alone who held the key to his freedom. Not surprisingly, Bartolomeo and Diego joined with their brother and respectfully declined Vallejo's generous gesture. Their solemn journey across the Atlantic took the better part of October to complete and once docked at Cádiz the three Columbus brothers were paraded off deck in full view of all who had gathered in anticipation of their arrival. Forced to endure a gauntlet of ridicule from the assembled crowd the three Italians were then marched to a cell where they were forced to await their day of judgment.

At some point during his lengthy incarceration the admiral managed to get off a message to King Ferdinand and Queen Isabella, who were currently holding court at Granada, which told of his present predicament at Cádiz. Shocked by this unforeseen turn of events the monarchs sent word to Cádiz that the three prisoners were to be released at once. Requesting their immediate presence before the royal court the monarchs provided the brothers with two thousand ducats, a more than ample amount to cover any expenses they might incur along the way. On December 17, 1500, the admiral and his brothers stood before Ferdinand and Isabella. Humbled by his recent experiences and haunted by thoughts of having disappointed his royal benefactors once more, a penitent Christopher Columbus dropped to his knees and broke down in tears. Once he had regained his composure, the admiral offered up a number of excuses for his failures and then begged for their forgiveness. Moved by his sincere and unsolicited act of contrition, the sovereigns expressed to him that they were willing to forgive and forget the past, but as for the present, his future with Spain remained uncertain.

Christopher Columbus spent the next several months petitioning the court for the restoration of his titles and for the king and queen to grant him authorization to lead yet another expedition to the Indies. His constant requests went unanswered. Forced to idly sit back and watch as other sailors sailed to the lands he had discovered and claimed for the greater glory of Spain caused him to remark bitterly: "They all made fun of my plan then; now even tailors wish to discover." Perhaps the biggest blow to the admiral's ego was the news that Portugal had surpassed Spain in the great race to reach the shores of Asia. Vasco da Gama's successful voyage to India and back had cast a giant shadow of doubt over the admiral's claim to have reached the outlying islands of the Indies. As compelling as this new evidence was, Columbus still refused to be swayed from his convictions. Conceding only the fact that his contemporary had reached the mainland of India first, the admiral, as a means of distinguishing his discoveries from those made by

Vasco da Gama, merely took to calling his many discovered lands the West Indies.

Strangely enough, Portugal's good fortune worked to Columbus's advantage. Eager to capitalize on Vasco da Gama's discovery, King Manuel I soon sent out an even larger expedition under the command of Pedro Cabral to retrace the newly discovered route to India. It was during this voyage that Cabral came upon lands lying to the west that fell within the hemisphere claimed by Portugal. Elated by his discovery, the captain dispatched three ships for home to relay the good tidings to the king. But news of this nature was extremely difficult to suppress. Knowledge of their newfound land was soon in the hands of the proper authorities in Spain, and once the Spanish were able to reconcile these coordinates with those plotted earlier by their own explorer Vicente Pinzón, there was a general concern that Portugal now had ambitions westward as well as eastward. Afraid of losing even more ground to their competitive neighbor, Ferdinand and Isabella decided to reconsider the admiral's request for another opportunity to find the enchanted realm of Cathay.

No longer in a position to dictate terms, Christopher Columbus had little choice but to agree to a great number of restrictions regarding the general direction of his fourth voyage, which he called *El Alto Viage* (The High Voyage). He also had to accept the decision that he would no longer be entitled to the governorship of any lands that he discovered for Spain. The monarchs even went so far as to forbid Columbus, under any circumstance, to return to the island of Hispaniola. However, this latter decision by Ferdinand and Isabella was not intended as a vindication of the harsh judgments imposed by the man they had sent to replace Columbus as governor. Convinced that Francisco Bobadilla had grossly overstepped his bounds when he issued the order to place the admiral and his brothers in chains, the Catholic monarchs, in September of 1502, appointed Nicolás de Ovando as his replacement as governor and chief magistrate for all of the Spanish West Indies.

Grateful for the opportunity to sail once again, Christopher Columbus vowed to redeem himself by locating the Strait of Malacca—the passage that Marco Polo had sailed through on his return from the court of Kublai Khan. Once he had discovered a safe passage to India, he would remain there just long enough to barter for boatloads of spices as well as other rare and exotic goods, and once his business was completed he would return to Spain by way of the Cape of Good Hope. In other words, the bold Christopher Columbus proposed to become the first man to circumnavigate the earth. Hopeful that this fourth voyage of the admiral's would end in the long sought-after success, the king and queen provided him with royal letters of salutation and introduction for presentation to Vasco da Gama in the hope that their expeditions crossed paths in that distant part of the world.

Anxious to get under way, Columbus set out for Seville in October of 1501. Once there, the admiral immediately began to scour the docks for seaworthy vessels and a competent crew to sail them. Unfortunately for him, nearly every good vessel and practically every experienced sailor had already been spoken for, most having been recruited into service for the grand fleet commissioned to transport the newly appointed governor across the Atlantic. The best that he could do, given the limited selection at hand, was the purchase of four caravels similar in size to that of his previous ship the *Niña*. The *Capitana* was selected as the admiral's flagship, while the *Gallega*, the *Vizcaína*, and the *Santiago* rounded out the rest of the flotilla. All four vessels had already seen much service, and consequently each required extensive repairs before being deemed worthy enough to withstand the rigors commonly associated with a voyage of such length. Columbus fared much better with the crew, eventually enlisting one hundred and forty-six men, a count that included his brother Bartlolomeo and his second son, Fernando. Laboring under the delusion that his success was clearly preordained, Columbus, in February of 1502, sent a letter to the Pope in which he pledged his personal profits from this voyage to the Church, with the understanding that these funds would be used to help raise, for the sake of all Christendom, another crusade to reclaim the Holy Land.

On February 13, 1502, following several months of exhaustive preparation, Nicolás de Ovando set sail at the head of an imposing armada of thirty-two ships and twenty-five hundred men to lay claim to the governorship of Hispaniola. Three months later, on the 9th of May, Christopher Columbus set sail on a similar course, but at the helm of a significantly smaller fleet.

STORM WARNINGS

Nicolás de Ovando assumed full command of the colony of Santo Domingo the very moment he stepped off the boat. Upholding a promise made to Christopher Columbus by both King Ferdinand and Queen Isabella, the new governor, acting on the admiral's behalf, restored the title to all properties that Francisco Bobadilla had wrongfully confiscated from the former governor. Bobadilla offered no opposition to these orders; any resistance would have been an act of suicide given the fact that Ovando's force outnumbered the present population of the colony by more than eight to one. The new governor had ambitious plans for molding Santo Domingo into a productive and self-reliant colony, but his lofty aspirations were quickly shattered by a series of unforeseen obstacles. Disease-carrying mosquitoes and an oppressive heat made for a deadly combination that conspired against Ovando's grandiose plans. The death toll grew greater with each passing day and those who still had some measure of strength spent most of their energy digging the more than one thousand graves needed for those who never recovered.

For the majority of those who signed on for this journey, the idea of laboring for the fruits of the earth could never quite equal the tantalizing appeal of prospecting for precious gold. Every colonist was acquainted with tales regarding the magnificent fields of gold that awaited them at Hispaniola, and such stories filled their heads with dreams of returning to Spain as men endowed with enormous wealth. Unfortunately for them, the stark reality of their situation soon sobered such fanciful thoughts. Hispaniola never had that much gold to begin with, and what little gold there was had already been, for the most part, collected and shipped back to Spain. The realization that gold was not quite as accessible and plentiful as they had been led to believe certainly didn't dash their dreams of finding wealth, it merely meant they would have to search a little longer and dig a little harder. But manual labor was seen as an unsuitable line of work for someone who envisioned himself a gentlemen of means, and as they fancied themselves superior to the indigenous population, the Spaniards simply took to forcing thousands of idle Indians into hard labor, compelling them to dig wherever they thought gold might be hidden from plain sight. Such strenuous labor inflicted a terrible toll on the Arawakan people: hundreds of natives died daily from the heavy burden they were forced to bear. With death and desertion on the rise, Ovando set out to replenish his work force by conquering other villages, and he even went so far as to hang Princess Anacaona on a charge of treason when she made the fatal mistake of attempting to intercede on the behalf of her own people.

While these terrible events were unfolding at Hispaniola, Christopher Columbus was making rapid headway across the waters of the Atlantic. Having left the Canary Islands on May 25th, his small fleet continued on a southwesterly course until reaching land twenty-one days later at a small mountainous island inhabited by the fierce Carib tribes. After christening his latest discovery Matinino—an island now known as Martinique—the admiral, in direct defiance of a royal decree, sailed straight for Hispaniola. His seemingly blatant act of insubordination was not without reasonable cause. The *Santiago* had proved to be an extremely poor sailing vessel and the admiral hoped to replace it with the purchase of one of the many ships that had sailed over with Governor Nicolás de Ovando. Upon his arrival at Santo Domingo on the 29th of June, Columbus took note of the ominous signs from high above which foretold the coming of a terrible storm, the kind that the natives referred to as a *huracán*. Fearing a possible confrontation with Governor Ovando, Columbus decided to send Pedro de Terreros, the captain of the *Gallego*, in his place to bargain with the governor for a new ship and to forewarn him of the coming storm.

At the time of the admiral's arrival, the new governor was attending to last-minute preparations for the return of twenty-eight of his vessels to Spain. His fleet was all set to cart home a cargo that included as much gold as he was able to locate and as many native slaves as he could possibly do without. This was the excuse given by Nicolás de Ovando when he told Pedro de Terreros he could not spare a single ship. The governor even went on to add insult to injury by refusing to grant Columbus permission to anchor his ships in the Ozama estuary. Snubbed by his replacement at Santo Domingo, the admiral had little recourse but to cast off in search of a harbor that might provide sanctuary from the fury of the oncoming storm. Compelled by a moral obligation to warn fellow sailors of the danger that was rapidly heading their way, Columbus appealed to the commander of Ovando's fleet to postpone his departure until the storm had passed. The captain of this expedition had good reasons for choosing to ignore the admiral's prophecy of doom: one of the passengers aboard his fleet was the recently deposed governor, Francisco Bobadilla. Taking into account their past differences, along with the fact that the sky overhead was clear and the water below was calm, it becomes easier to understand why Bobadilla failed to heed the admiral's dire forecast.

Having done all that he possibly could to ease his own conscience, Columbus sailed westward along the coast of Hispaniola while the fleet bound for Spain sailed eastward, directly into the path of the rapidly intensifying hurricane. The awesome power of this terrible tempest slammed into the armada with incredible force and devastating results. Blackened skies unleashed a torrent of rain; howling winds spun the mighty vessels out of control; and waves of frightening proportion slammed into the creaking wooden hulls of the ships. Twenty four vessels and more than five hundred passengers fell victim to the rage of this truly horrific storm. The list of the dead included such notable figures as Antonio de Torres, commander of the fleet; Francisco Roldán, leader of the rebellion at Isabela; the cacique Guarionex, an imprisoned tribal chief; and Francisco Bobadilla, the former governor of Hispaniola. Also settling at the bottom of the sea were some two thousand pounds of gold earmarked for deposit in the Spanish treasury. Of the four surviving vessels, three badly battered ships managed to find their way back to Santo Domingo while a fourth ship, the *Aguja*, miraculously survived the dreadful ordeal with enough strength to complete the long journey back to Spain. Ironically, the *Aguja* was the caravel that had been commissioned by the admiral's faithful friend Alonso Sánchez de Carvajal to carry home four hundred and five pounds of gold that rightfully belonged to Christopher Columbus.

After safely weathering the storm in a cove located on the far eastern end of Hispaniola, Columbus took advantage of the ensuing calm to make the repairs his vessels drastically needed before he could resume his search for the Strait of Malacca. Once his ships were deemed seaworthy enough the admiral cast off in the general direction of Jamaica, the island that he had discovered on his second voyage across the Atlantic. Shortly after sailing past Jamaica, Columbus was forced to make yet another brief stopover, this time at an island just off the coast of Cuba, in order to administer further repairs to his sea-worn vessels. Afterwards, the fleet sailed on a southwesterly course, a direction that eventually brought them to the coast of present-day Honduras, a stretch of the lengthy isthmus that bridges the divide between the two great continents of the New World. Inspired by the notion that he had discovered a section of the Malay Peninsula, Columbus spent the next six months probing for a nonexistent strait that supposedly emptied directly into the Indian Ocean. Cruising south along the coast, the admiral had to contend with the mutinous rantings of a crew that had grown extremely weary of their constant struggles with contrary winds and violent storms. However, the sailor's thoughts of insurrection quickly subsided once the ships dropped anchor at a breathtakingly beautiful island known to the natives as Quirivi but renamed La Huerta, or "The garden," by Columbus.

Less than a league away, on the mainland, the explorers arrived at a large native village known by its inhabitants as Carai. Alarmed by the sudden approach of strangers from the sea, the natives of Carai, along with reinforcements from neighboring villages, assembled in great numbers along the shores in anticipation of having to forcefully defend their sacred homeland. Once they understood that the Spaniards had come in peace, they immediately laid down their weapons and warmly welcomed them into their village. The Spaniards were, at first, dazzled by their beautiful jewelry and numerous animal figurines which glimmered with gold; upon closer inspection, though, they were able to determine that these items were made from a very poor grade of gold. When the explorers inquired as to where "real gold" might be found, the natives led them to believe that a golden land lay just a short distance to the south. The prospect of having finally come across a coast flowing in gold inspired the ever optimistic admiral to christen the region Costa Rica, the rich coast. They stayed there for a period of eleven days, much of their time being consumed with attending to the numerous leaks brought on by ship worms relentlessly burrowing through the wood of their submerged hulls. Once the ships were adequately restored, the crew took on additional stores of food and fresh water and Columbus enlisted the services of two Carai natives to serve as both guides and interpreters on their voyage.

To his great delight, the admiral soon discovered that the natives had spoken the truth. After just a day of sailing the small fleet came across a group of islands just off the mainland inhabited by a seemingly less civilized tribe, but one, nonetheless, in possession of "real gold." In describing his encounter with the natives, Columbus noted in his journal: "The people go naked and wear golden mirrors round their necks. But they will not sell them, or give them in exchange. They give me the names of many places on the coast, where they said that gold could be found, and mines. The last name was Veragua, which is about 25 leagues off." They also spoke of a place called Ciguare, another golden land lying in the interior of Costa Rica. The admiral chose to continue his voyage in the direction of Veragua.

Gold now consumed the admiral's every thought and deed. In a letter intended for King Ferdinand and Queen Isabella, Columbus remarked: "The Genoese, the Venetians, and all other people who have pearls, precious stones and other things of value carry them to the ends of the world to trade with them and turn them into gold. Gold is a most excellent thing; he who possess gold may do all that he wishes in this world, and may also lead souls into Paradise. The lords in these lands, in the country of Veragua, when they die, I am told that their gold is buried with them." These were powerful words that not only captured the imaginations of the Spanish sovereigns but also the thoughts of a future generation of explorers whom we have come to collectively refer to as the conquistadors.

The admiral spent all of November and December of 1502 hunting for either the gold of Veragua or a passage that would lead him and his men straight to India. After becoming frustrated with his own inability to find the Strait of Malacca, Columbus decided to double back along the coast of Panama and to instead concentrate his efforts on locating the legendary gold mines of Veragua. His search for the passage to Asia ended at Limon Bay which, ironically, is nearly the exact spot that many years later was to become the entrance to the man-made Panama Canal. On January 6, 1503, the sacred day of Epiphany, the ships anchored at the mouth of a river which, in paying homage to the birthplace of Christ the Savior, Columbus named Betlem, a place that now retains the name of Belén. The following month, and a little less than a league away from Betlem, they finally found what they had been searching for: the Veragua River. Convinced that he had at last discovered a land that was home to an abundant supply of gold, Columbus decided to establish a colony that he would call Santa María de Betlem. The admiral intended to leave his brother Bartolomeo and eighty additional men behind to mine for the plentiful gold of Veragua while he sailed back to Spain to obtain additional supplies and colonists. After selecting what seemed to be a suitable site along the west bank of the river, his men proceeded to clear the land and then erect eight wooden homes thatched with palm leaves. While the Spaniards were busy constructing their settlement and making additional repairs to their ships a large group of curious natives, led by a cacique named Quibian, dropped in for a visit with their new neighbors. They were friendly enough at first, even offering to trade gold with them, but their mood changed dramatically the very moment they learned that the Spaniards were there to stay.

Wishing to rid his land of these intruders, Quibian began making plans for an all-out attack against the Spanish settlement. It was Quibian's wish to have his warriors massacre every Spaniard and for them to lay waste to all of the structures that desecrated his land. When his faithful interpreters informed him of Quibian's murderous plot, the admiral decided to launch a preemptive strike against the cacique's village. Catching the natives by surprise, the Spaniards had little trouble conquering the village and taking Quibian, along with a great number of his chieftains and their respective families, as their prisoner. To the Spanish victors went the spoils of "golden mirrors, eagles, small golden cylinders which they string round their arms and legs, and braided gold which they wear on their heads like crowns, about 300 ducats worth." Quibian and his entourage were taken aboard the *Capitana* for transfer downriver to their Spanish settlement, but the wily cacique, with the aid of his loyal subjects, managed to elude his captors and returned to the safety of his village. As for the rest of the chieftains and their families, a few more eventually escaped, but the majority chose death, hanging themselves from the rafters below the deck of the ship on which they were imprisoned, as their means of escape from the clutches of the Spanish soldiers.

Once back at his village, Quibian rallied his warriors and attacked the Spanish settlement, which was guarded by only a small force under the command of Bartolomeo Columbus. Seven Spaniards lost their lives during the first attack and a great many more were seriously wounded, including Bartolomeo. Shortly after the admiral came to their rescue, Captain Diego Tristán and three other soldiers were ambushed and killed while searching for fresh water for their comrades. It was now painfully clear, even to the ever optimistic Christopher Columbus, that a Spanish colony could not survive under such hostile conditions. The order to evacuate was issued and all of the admiral's men and supplies were crowded onto just three ships; the *Gallega* was deemed to be beyond repair and consequently scuttled at the river's edge. Forced to abandon his dream of founding a golden empire, Columbus set sail on April 16, 1503, to search one more time for the elusive Strait of Malacca.

MAROONED

The plight of Christopher Columbus and his weary crew became even more desperate once they reached Puerto Bello. It was here that the *Vizcaína* began taking on water so badly that the admiral had no choice but to simply let her sink. Now the two remaining vessels, the *Capitana* and the *Santiago*, had to support a crew totaling one hundred and thirty in number. The explorers bravely continued on as far south as Cape Tiburon, situated at the border of Panama and Columbia, before Columbus decided the time had come to abandon his fruitless quest. Recurring disasters coupled with bitter disappointments had plunged the morale of the crew, as well as the admiral's, into the deepest depths. The voyage also took a terrible physical toll on the aging admiral: his gout had returned with severe crippling effects; fever, probably malarial, fogged his state of mind; and an infection of the eyes blurred his vision. On the 1st of May, he set sail for Santo Domingo, hoping against all hope that the governor would permit him to dock just long enough to prepare his ships for the return voyage to Spain.

With the prevailing winds and currents dictating their direction, Columbus found himself on a heading for the island of Cuba. Along the way they discovered two small islands that were nesting grounds for giant sea turtles, hence the name Las Tortugas, or Turtle Island. While the admiral desperately tried to alter their course, the crew frantically fought to keep both ships afloat. No matter how hard they pumped or how fast they bailed they could not stem the rapid rise of water in the ship's holds. Having lost the battle to the teredo worms, the admiral suddenly found himself in a desperate race to make landfall before his ailing ships became completely submerged below the surface of the water.

Columbus and his crew managed to safely reach St. Ann's Bay along the northeast coast of Jamaica on the 25th of June. At a point just short of the shore the two badly battered ships were run aground at a site that was to become their final resting place. The crew continued to utilize the damaged vessels as shelter but when the food began to dwindle, a party was sent ashore on a trading mission with the local natives. Sustenance aside, rescue was the foremost thought on every sailor's mind, especially the admiral's. As their ships could no longer sail, and since it was very unlikely that any Spanish ship would purposely journey to Jamaica, a bold and daring scheme was concocted for their own rescue—someone would have to row across the vast body of water that separates the islands of Jamaica and Hispaniola.

Two of the admiral's captains, Diego Méndez and Bartolomeo Fieschi (the latter's friendship with Christopher Columbus dated back to when the two were small boys growing up in Genoa), volunteered to lead this dangerous mission. To carry them across this vast stretch of water the captains selected and bartered for two mid-sized canoes from the natives, which they proceeded to rig with makeshift sails. On the 17th of July, fourteen men, a group that included several natives, boarded the two canoes and set off for the colony of Santo Domingo. With the aid of favorable winds and the powerful push of their paddles, they completed the lengthy voyage in a mere five days, an amazing feat when considering the fact that they had to cross one hundred and twenty-five miles of open sea. This is not to say the voyage was without peril. One Indian guide died from thirst and had they not arrived at Hispaniola when they did, all would have surely suffered the same fate. After making landfall at the extreme western end of Hispaniola, Captain Fieschi desired to return to Jamaica to inform the admiral of their success, but no one, except for the captain, was willing to face that horrendous ordeal again. While Fieschi and his weary crew remained where they had landed, Captain Méndez and his crew continued to paddle an additional three hundred miles along the coast of Hispaniola until finally reaching the colony of Santo Domingo where they then confronted Governor Nicolás de Ovando about the terrible plight of Christopher Columbus and his crew.

Meanwhile, back at Jamaica, the hope of ever getting off the island lessened with each passing day. After the days and weeks on the island slowly turned into months, it was generally assumed that their brave comrades had perished at sea. Bartolomeo Columbus assumed many of the daily duties of command during the admiral's weakened physical state, relying on a strict regimen of work to ward off the crew's thoughts of despair. But a growing sense of hopelessness caused many to question his authority, and those seeds of discontent soon gave rise to an open rebellion. Most of the crew deserted Columbus and his brother and switched their allegiance to two other brothers, Francisco and Diego de Porras. The mutineers planned to follow in the wake of Fieschi and Méndez, and sail for Hispaniola with a fleet of canoes. Three times they set sail and three times they were repulsed by the overpowering strength of the sea. Following their last futile attempt to escape the island the rebel force, unwilling to fend for themselves, forced their way into a nearby village where they spent their days idly living off the fruits of the natives' hard labor.

Because of the many atrocities committed by this renegade band of Spaniards, the natives retaliated against Christopher Columbus and his men by announcing that they would no longer swap their food for his shiny beads of glass or those tinkling bells made of brass. Since the Spaniards relied on this simple trade for their daily ration of food, the admiral pleaded with them to reconsider, but they refused to yield their position. Unable to reason with them, Columbus resorted to a bit of chicanery to get the natives to submit to his will. He had in his possession an almanac containing an astronomical chart that foretold the occurrence of a lunar eclipse on the night of February 29, 1504, a date that was but a mere three days away. Summoning the caciques to his camp on that fateful evening, Columbus proceeded to verbally assault his guests, ranting on about how their selfish behavior had offended the almighty God of the Christians. The admiral then told them that as punishment for their terrible sins, his God was about to snatch the moon from the heavens above. With impeccable timing the admiral motioned to the night sky at the very moment the earth's shadow began to darken the moon's edge. The sight of the radiant moon beginning to disappear before their very eyes caused the natives to scream out in horror, and they begged Columbus to put an end to the wrath of his God. At the height of their fear, and just before the eclipse became total, Columbus exacted from the caciques a promise of food for his starving men before he called upon his God to restore the moon to its proper place. Once they had agreed to all his terms the benevolent Columbus made good on his promise and the frightened but ever so grateful caciques made sure they upheld their end of the bargain.

The sudden appearance of a small caravel towards the end of March helped lift the sunken spirits of Columbus and his stranded crew. However, much to their dismay, this ship had not been sent from Hispaniola to rescue the marooned men but instead to deliver a message to the admiral. A letter from Captain Diego Méndez provided Columbus with the glad tidings of their successful crossing but contained few other words of encouragement. Méndez wrote of his meeting with Nicolás de Ovando and how the governor displayed a total disregard for their desperate plight by steadfastly refusing to sanction any rescue mission to the island of Jamaica. In closing, Méndez told them to keep the faith and promised that he would somehow find a way to get them off the island. The captain of the ship, a messenger sent by Governor Ovando, took pity on the stranded Spanish compatriots and left behind a cask of wine and a small quantity of pork before heading back to Hispaniola that same day.

With a renewed sense of hope that their rescue was close at hand, Columbus sought a reconciliation with the mutineers. The admiral offered them amnesty, his only conditions being that they return peacefully and obediently to his command. However, Francisco de Porras set forth his own conditions for their return, and his unwillingness to compromise ultimately led to an armed conflict between the two Spanish camps. After his loyalist army emerged victorious over the larger rebel force the magnanimous Columbus granted pardons to all of the surviving rebels, all except Francisco de Porras, whom he had imprisoned in chains. Two rescue ships, both hired by Méndez, finally arrived at the end of June and on the 28th of that month, and after having had to endure a dreadful stay of more than a year on the island, Columbus and his remaining crew of one hundred and fifteen men sailed for the colony of Santo Domingo.

Arriving at Santo Domingo on the 13th of August, Christopher Columbus was unexpectedly treated to a cordial reception by the governor and was even allowed to stay at his royal residence. But the admiral sensed that treachery was afoot and those suspicions were confirmed when Ovando released Francisco de Porras from his chains and publicly announced that he would punish whoever was responsible for his wrongful arrest. Hiring the services of another ship, Columbus set sail for Spain on the 12th of September, accompanied by his brother Bartolomeo, his son Fernando, and twenty-two seamen who remained loyal to him. The majority of those who elected to stay behind were the original group of mutineers who feared the admiral would renege on his pledge of a full pardon once they returned to the shores of Spain.

The admiral's final crossing of the Atlantic was marred by a violent storm, which came close to ending the voyage prematurely, and a sudden relapse of his debilitating ailments. When they finally docked at Sanlúcar on November 7, 1504, the admiral was so weak from his illness he had to be carried off the ship by means of a stretcher. He was then transported to Seville where it was hoped that a brief period of rest would allow him to regain his strength before paying his respects to the joint rulers of Spain. Upon his arrival at Seville, Columbus wrote to the king and queen to inform them of his return and then anxiously awaited their reply, assuming that he would soon be summoned before the royal court to tell of his latest adventure. He soon learned the reason for his being allowed to linger so long at Seville: Queen Isabella, his most ardent supporter at court, had passed away on November 26, 1504, less than three weeks after his return.

Though greatly saddened by the news of Isabella's death, Columbus continued to press the Crown for reinstatement of his titles, restoration of his claims upon the Indies, and reimbursement of the funds he believed were still owed to him. Amerigo Vespucci, who had recently returned to the service and the good graces of the Spanish Crown, visited with the ailing Columbus on the 3rd of February. Always a great admirer of the admiral, Vespucci offered to help in any way that he could. Greatly moved by this gesture of kindness, Columbus wrote to his son Diego: "I have spoken with Amerigo Vespucci, the bearer of this letter. He is going to court, where he has been summoned in connection with points of navigation. He has always been anxious to please me. He is a very honorable man. Fortune has been against him, as against so many others." Unfortunately, not even the esteemed Amerigo Vespucci could sway the court's current unfavorable opinion of Christopher Columbus.

Diego Columbus represented his father's interests as best he could before the royal court, but when Ferdinand continued to ignore his requests, the admiral concluded that his presence was needed to change the king's unyielding position on this matter. It was not until May of 1505 that Christopher Columbus felt strong enough to make the lengthy overland journey to Segovia, where the king was presently holding court. Ferdinand gave him a warm reception but still refused to honor any of his demands. He did, however, appoint an arbitrator to assess the validity of Columbus's numerous claims against Spain. These negotiations succeeded in restoring his claim to one-tenth of the one-fifth proceeds nominally set aside for the Crown but not to the many titles and possessions that once belonged to him. As a concession, the king offered him property in Spain, but it was an offer that the proud Columbus refused to even consider.

When the court moved to the city of Salamanca in October of 1505, Columbus was there, once again pleading his case, but to no avail. In April of the following year he followed the royal court to Valladolid, but Ferdinand, having grown weary of his repetitious requests, refused to even grant him an audience. His health, however, continued to deteriorate during his stay at Valladolid and once again he was confined to what would soon prove to be his deathbed. On May 20, 1506, in the presence of his loving sons, his brother Diego, and his loyal captains Diego Méndez and Bartolomeo Fieschi, the "Admiral of the Ocean Sea" was summoned to his eternal rest.

Contrary to popular belief, Christopher Columbus happened to be a very wealthy man at the time of his death. Points of principle and pride, not desires for selfish gain, were the factors that motivated the admiral in his seemingly obsessive quest to restore his good name. While many may have questioned his capabilities as a governor none could match his extraordinary abilities as a navigator; and while he may not have been the first European to reach the New World, he was certainly the first to chart a path which others could clearly follow; and while he never did discover a route to Asia, he did lay claim to new lands that would eventually make Spain the wealthiest and most powerful nation on the face of the earth. He was and always should be remembered as one of mankind's greatest visionaries.

Mundus Novus

While death certainly deprived Christopher Columbus of the knowledge that he had found an exciting New World it also spared him the indignity of having to witness another explorer being honored as the discoverer of these new lands, even though that credit went to his good friend and colleague Amerigo Vespucci. After returning from his last voyage across the Atlantic, Vespucci took time to write to family and friends in Italy about his extensive travels abroad. In these letters he not only described the many spectacular sights he had gazed upon but also provided the reader with some insight into his own conclusions about the lands he had recently explored. To Lorenzo de Medici, his longtime benefactor, he wrote: "We arrived at a new land, which, for many reasons ... we observed to be a continent." Many of these private letters, including the one sent to Medici, eventually found their way into general circulation, titillating the local public's fancy with phrases such as "These regions we may rightly call ... a New World, because our ancestors had no knowledge of them."

Vespucci's letter found a much larger audience once his writings were translated into Latin, and that audience grew to nearly all of Europe once those letters found their way onto the pages being churned out by the new and improved printing press. Movable type, an innovation of the German goldsmith Johannes Gutenberg, gave the world a new technology, one that quickly proved to be the most effective and efficient means of spreading the word of man. Suddenly, knowledge was within reach, but not necessarily the grasp, of the masses. In the beginning, bibles and the classical works of ancient Greece and Rome were steadily reproduced in print shops, but later those same presses began churning out books about the faraway exotic lands being discovered by daring sailors who ventured forth from the Iberian Peninsula. The public could not get enough of these stories. Whether these tales were fact or fiction was of little importance, so consequently fiction frequently substituted for fact in these publications. Amerigo's letters were often plagiarized and embellished by writers eager to publish their own adventurous tale set in the mysterious New World. One publisher, in 1505, went so far as to circulate a phony letter that described a voyage that Vespucci never even made.

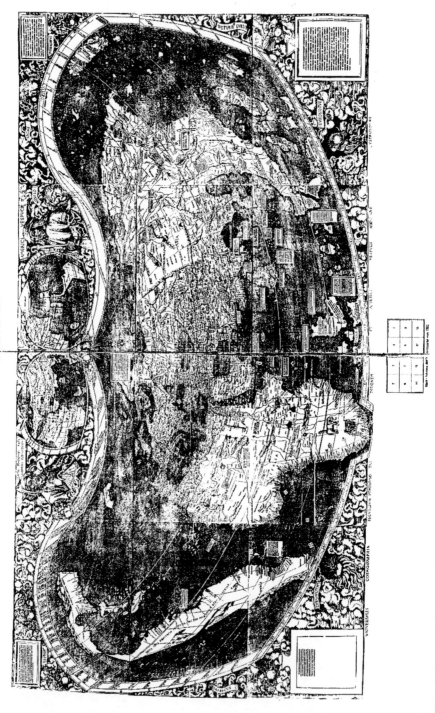

DIE WELTKARTE VON 1507.

Just as Amerigo Vespucci's letters were beginning to circulate throughout Europe, a group of German clergymen and scholars residing at the cathedral of Saint-Dié, located in the Vosges Mountains of northeastern France, were preparing to print a new and elaborate edition of Ptolemy's *Guide to Geography*. A printing press had been donated to the group in 1500 by Walter Kudd, a canon endowed with great wealth and a keen interest in seeing his own work published. But it was Martin Waldseemüller, a priest with a passion for geography, who led the push to print a world atlas based on the work of Ptolemy. However, this ambitious project came to an abrupt halt after a member of the group came across a copy of a French letter titled "Four Voyages," which told of Amerigo Vespucci's many voyages of discovery. (Amerigo has often been credited with as many as four voyages across the Atlantic, but given the evidence at hand, historians can only accurately account for two such expeditions.) It was, however a Latin version of Vespucci's letter with the intriguing title of "Mundus Novus," or New World, which gave the group cause to reconsider Ptolemy's view of the world.

After concluding that "Another fourth part (of the inhabited earth) had been discovered by Americus Vespucious...," Martin Waldseemüller abruptly abandoned the Ptolemy project and commenced working on a new world atlas, one which would show all the discoveries known to have been made by the many explorers who sailed under the flags of Portugal and Spain. The *Cosmographiae Introductio* was published and released by the group in April of 1507. Penned for the most part by Waldseemüller, this world map gave all of Europe a new and very different perspective of the earth. The discoveries made across the Atlantic were shown in great detail and for the first time they were depicted as lands not part of Asia but instead as parcels of land, which, when viewed as a whole, formed the outline of a "New World." In defense of his dedication of the new continent located in the Southern Hemisphere to the man he had come to admire, Waldsemüller stated: " ... I see no reason why anyone should justly object to calling this part Amerigre, i.e. the land of Amerigo, or America, after Amerigo its discoverer, a man of great ability." Demand for the book was so great that a second edition had to be published in August of that same year. As for the name America, it met with such widespread acceptance that it was

Opposite: **The 1507 Martin Waldseemüller map of the world. Convinced that Amerigo Vespucci was the legitimate discoverer of the New World, this German mapmaker christened these lands in honor of the explorer. Once he realized his mistake Waldseemüller published a new map that renamed the region as Terra Incognita.**

eventually extended to include even the other vast continent situated in the Northern Hemisphere.

When Martin Waldseemüller learned that a false date had been ascribed to Amerigo Vespucci's discovery, most likely by the printer, he took immediate steps to right a great wrong. In his new map of the world, which he drew up in 1513, the name America is erased from the southern continent and replaced with the simple title of Terra Incognita. But it was too late; his own printed words had proved too difficult to retract. Right or wrong, the power of the press had been firmly established and, in this case, it credited the wrong man as the discoverer of this "fourth part" of the world. The name of Christopher Columbus, the true European discoverer of these lands, was saved from obscurity thanks mostly to the dedicated efforts of his faithful sons Diego and Fernando. Diego, the admiral's eldest son from his marriage to Felipa Moniz Perestrello, spent the rest of his life trying to restore all of the privileges and titles that had been stripped from his father. Fernando Colón, a progeny of the admiral's torrid love affair with the young and beautiful Beatriz Enriques de Harana, wrote a splendid biography that served as a reminder to future generations of the great deeds and numerous accomplishments of his illustrious father.

TEN

The Grand Prize

Manuel's Scheme to Corner the Spice Trade

After having finally discovered a path to the great wealth of Asia, the small kingdom of Portugal, a nation that was at the time home to less than a million citizens, suddenly found itself thrust onto center stage of European commerce. In a letter dispatched to King Ferdinand and Queen Isabella immediately following Vasco da Gama's celebrated return from the true Indies, a confident King Manuel of Portugal revealed his grandiose plan for the conquest of the region: "We hope with the help of God that the great trade which now enriches the Moors of those parts ... shall, in consequence of our ordinances, be diverted to the natives and ships of our own kingdom, so that henceforth all Christendom in this part of Europe shall be able to provide itself with these spices and precious stones."

In 1501, following Pedro Cabral's return from India with a rich cargo of spices, Portuguese officials established for themselves an exchange at the bustling port city of Amsterdam. Since they were no longer burdened with the costs of having to deal directly with Arab middlemen, Portuguese merchants were able to drastically undercut the prices of their competitors, principally the Venetian merchants, by as much as eighty percent of the current market price. Their dominance over the European spice market occurred with such swiftness and completeness, they unexpectedly found that their vessels could not return fast enough to meet the soaring demand for these splendid spices. Recognizing a sudden shift in economic power, other nations, such as Germany and Italy began sending more of their merchants and more of their ambassadors to the city of Lisbon.

In 1503, the same year that Vasco da Gama returned from his second
voyage to India with a tremendous haul of valuable goods, Afonso Albuquerque, a veteran navigator and soldier, sailed from Lisbon with an armada
consisting of twenty-two ships to procure even greater amounts of treasure
from the shores of the Malabar Coast. Using diplomacy to gain the favor
of the rajah of Cochin, Albuquerque was eventually granted permission to
build a complex which would serve as both a factory for trade and a fort
to ensure the protection of that trade, and in so doing, he laid the foundation for a Portuguese commercial empire that would eventually extend
throughout much of Asia and the Orient. Afonso Albuquerque returned
home to Portugal in July of 1504 with a large cargo of spices that added
greatly to Portugal's steadily growing fortune.

The intoxicating effects of all this newly acquired wealth, along with
the respect and power that accompanied it, made Portugal's King Manuel
thirst for even greater fortune, a craving which he believed could be quenched
only after he had gained complete control of the many trade markets that
were situated along the path of the Indian Ocean. But standing in the way
of the king's avaricious aims were several centuries of harmonious trade
relations between the nations of the Far East and those of the Middle East,
and Arab traders had no interest in sharing their handsome profits with
Christian merchants from Portugal. Deciding to sever those ancient ties by
means of force, Manuel once again enlisted the services of Afonso Albuquerque. Leading a squadron of five heavily armed warships attached to
yet another large fleet bound for India, this time under the command of
Tristão da Cunha, Albuquerque's mission was to seek out and destroy any
Muslim strongholds that stood in Portugal's path to India. Once they had
safely rounded the Cape of Good Hope, Albuquerque and da Cunha
attacked, without mercy, any African port city that participated in trade with
Muslim merchants. Eventually, but not until after they had jointly conquered
and plundered a number of cities along the eastern coast of Africa, the two
commanders went their separate ways: Tristão da Cunha sailed across the
Indian Ocean in the direction of the Malabar Coast while Afonso Albuquerque continued to make his presence known and feared as far north as
the Persian Gulf.

In 1507 Albuquerque succeeded in capturing Socotra, a relatively large
island near the mouth of the Red Sea, and shortly thereafter his ships managed to seize control of Hormuz, an island of even greater economic and
strategic importance. Situated near the Persian Gulf and the Gulf of Oman,
Hormuz was one of the principal Arabian markets for the vast array of merchandise regularly brought over from India. With the capture of these two
islands, the Portuguese were well positioned to enforce an effective embargo

on Arab trade. A quick counteroffensive, however, returned Hormuz to the Arab fold and, for the moment, put an end to the Portuguese threat against their economy.

While Albuquerque and Tristão da Cunha were wreaking havoc along the coast of Africa, King Manuel was busy preparing to send an even larger fleet to lay claim to all of the Indies. He appointed Francisco de Almeida, a veteran from the conquest of Granada, as Portugal's first viceroy of India and supplied him with a mighty armada of twenty-two ships and twenty-five hundred men to help impose his authority. Several of his merchant ships belonged to the Fuggers and the Welsers, two prominent German merchant banking families who had forged close financial ties with both Iberian kingdoms. Volunteering to sail aboard this grand fleet was a young sailor by the name of Fernão de Magalhães, a man whom we know better as Ferdinand Magellan.

Privileged by his noble birth, even though his family was from the ranks of the lesser nobility, the young Ferdinand was entitled to opportunities that offered him the prospect of a better way of life. Seeking to improve his son's future station, Rue de Magalhães sent twelve year old Ferdinand to Lisbon where he would serve as a page to Queen Leonor, wife of King John II. The lad was provided with a well-rounded education during his stay at the royal court, and he showed a particular interest in the studies of astronomy and navigation—two courses which helped to steer him in the direction of his chosen profession. Ferdinand was present at the time of Vasco da Gama's celebrated return from India, and, like many citizens of that day, he stood in awe of all that this great man had endured and accomplished in the service of his country. Though he would never know it, his own exploits would one day eclipse even those of the great Vasco da Gama.

When the opportunity to sail to lands explored by such illustrious mariners as Vasco da Gama, Pedro Cabral, and Afonso Albuquerque presented itself, the twenty-five year old Ferdinand Magellan and his good friend Francisco Serrão immediately signed on for the expedition commanded by Francisco de Almeida. Setting sail on March 25, 1505, the fleet followed the now standard sailing route around the Cape of Good Hope and on up the east coast of Africa. Along the way, Almeida made full use of his naval might to eliminate any Muslim resistance or influence that he happened to encounter. To make sure that Portugal maintained a permanent presence in this distant part of the world, Almeida built a number of small forts on the route to India to help preserve and protect their economic interests.

The African coastal towns of Sofala and Kilwa were the viceroy's first conquests, with Kilwa actually being a reconquest for Portugal. In 1502, during his bloody second voyage to India, Vasco da Gama had stopped at Kilwa just long enough to force the ruler to recognize the king of Portugal as his sovereign. As a conquered people they were expected to pay an annual tribute to Portugal, but such a demand was immediately forgotten the moment da Gama's sails disappeared beyond the horizon. Bitter memories of Portuguese aggression were relived three years later when Francisco de Almeida docked in the same harbor with an even larger fleet. The sight of so many Portuguese ships and men struck such terror in the mind of Kilwa's sultan that he immediately abandoned his throne and his city in an effort to save himself. Almeida appointed a new sultan to rule in his place and then built a fortress to ensure that the citizens of Kilwa remained forever loyal to the kingdom of Portugal.

After settling all accounts with Kilwa, Almeida sailed north to the wealthy port city of Mombasa. His vicious and merciless assault against Mombasa was entirely premeditated; it was retribution for the Africans' unsuccessful plot to capture Vasco da Gama and his men when they stopped there on their peaceful mission of trade. Almeida settled the score by crushing the sultan's army, laying waste to much of the city, and pillaging as much treasure as his many ships could carry. Now that he had instilled fear and respect for Christian will and might, the Portuguese armada sailed away, not even bothering to leave a fort in their wake.

Francisco Almeida continued northward until he arrived at the island of Socotra where he then began his westward crossing of the Arabian Sea. Once they reached India, he continued to fortify Portugal's position with the addition of military compounds on the island of Angediva, just off the shores of Goa, and another at Cananor. Almeida made the city of Cochin his headquarters for the launching of an aggressive campaign to rid the Indies of both Muslim commerce and influence. A Portuguese fort had already been established at Cochin in 1503 by Afonso de Albuquerque, the naval commander who one day would relieve Francisco Almeida of his command.

The viceroy ordered his captains to rid the neighboring waterways of all Arab trade, and they faithfully complied by attacking, looting, and destroying any vessels suspected of doing business with the Arabs. One of Almeida's captains, Nuno Vaz Pereira, promoted Ferdinand Magellan to the rank of pilot's assistant aboard a barge specifically designed and equipped for attacking the fast moving dhows that roamed these waters. The young officer displayed an uncanny prowess in naval warfare, sinking more than two hundred Arab vessels over a fifteen month period. Almeida's orchestrated reign of terror succeeded in eliminating much of the Arab trade along the Malabar Coast but his string of victories were soon beset by two tragedies, one professional, the other very personal.

Both father and son had sailed together on this campaign to India. Lourenço de Almeida managed to distinguish himself before his father's eyes by leading his own expedition that succeeded in discovering Ceylon, a large island just off the coast of India. The viceroy's son was fortunate enough to have stumbled upon a very valuable find for Portugal; Ceylon had the distinction of being the principal source of the world's supply of cinnamon, and cinnamon was one of the most sought-after spices throughout the markets of Europe. Lourenço's next excursion proved to be most unfortunate. At Chaul, located near the city of Bombay, his fleet encountered a massive armada of Egyptian ships on a search and destroy mission. Feeling threatened by Almeida's tightening grip on the regional spice trade, the sultan of Egypt, in conjunction with a number of other resentful Muslim leaders, had organized a large fleet to seek out and eliminate the Portuguese naval threat. Lourenço was killed and his fleet annihilated in the ensuing naval engagement. While the elder Almeida was still grieving over the loss of his beloved son, Afonso de Albuquerque arrived at Cochin with a fleet of ships under his command. As a reward for his numerous victories, King Manuel had appointed Albuquerque the new viceroy of India. But Francisco de Almeida had other plans, none of which included his having to relinquish his governorship of India. When Albuquerque produced his royal commission, Almeida responded by having this pretender to his title of viceroy arrested and thrown in prison. Having reaffirmed his absolute authority, Almeida assembled a fleet, which included not only his ships but also those that had sailed under the command of Albuquerque, and then set off to avenge the death of Lourenço.

Francisco de Almeida's fleet left a trail of death and destruction all up and down the western coast of India. The city of Chaul, the site of Lourenço's demise, was doomed to suffer the harshest punishment of all. To pacify Almeida's wrath, every man, woman, and child of Chaul was slaughtered, and once this terrible holocaust was complete the entire town was then burned to the ground. In February of 1509, just near the northern island of Diu, Almeida finally caught up with the Egyptian fleet he had been desperately seeking. The captain of the Egyptian armada was more than willing to oblige Almeida's overture for a naval engagement; after all, from his point of view, this appeared to be an act of suicide on the part of the Portuguese commander. The Muslim fleet consisted of two hundred gigantic dhows carting a mighty military force estimated at twenty thousand strong while the Portuguese could only muster a fleet of nineteen ships carrying a crew numbering less than two thousand men. What the Egyptians failed to take into account was the superior battle experience of the enemy and the blind rage of their battle-hardened commander. Against those odds, the Muslims were doomed to suffer a swift and devastating defeat. Nearly half of their fleet was sunk before the Egyptian captains turned sail and retreated to the safety of their home shores. Almeida's incredible victory at Diu not only avenged the death of his son but also guaranteed Portuguese supremacy over the traffic of the Arabian Sea. Even though their victory was great, the losses they suffered were significant. A great number of Portuguese sailors lost their lives that day, including captain Nuno Vaz Pereira, and many of the survivors suffered serious wounds, including Ferdinand Magellan.

When the victorious Portuguese fleet made its return to Cochin, Ferdinand was transported to a hospital, where he would spend the next five months recuperating from his wounds before he was declared fit enough to return to active duty. Francisco de Almeida continued to pursue his claim to be the viceroy of India while the royally appointed Afonso Albuquerque was forced to languish in his prison cell. Almeida eventually surrendered to the inevitable, but only after another fleet sent by King Manuel arrived at the docks of Cochin in November of 1509. After assuming his rightful position, Albuquerque had Almeida placed on board one of the three vessels departing for Portugal on the first day of the last month. Three months later, after having rounded the Cape of Good Hope, the returning ships put in at Table Bay for much needed fresh water. While tending to the task at hand the sailors were suddenly surprised by a band of Hottentot tribesmen, the same race of people who had shown their hostile side to Vasco da Gama during a brief encounter on his first voyage, and a heated exchange escalated into a violent confrontation. Sixty five Portuguese sailors lost their lives that day, including Francisco de Almeida, who fought bravely alongside his fellow countrymen. Before returning home, the victorious surviving sailors gave the former viceroy of India a proper Christian burial at the very site where he fell in battle.

As the new viceroy of India, Albuquerque inherited authority over a vast tract of the rich Malabar coast, but this did not mean that he exerted control over all of the ongoing spice trade. Many of the spices sold at the great markets of India were shipped over from the Moluccas, a group of islands that are a part of the Malay Archipelago. These were the legendary "Spice Islands," the lands which all of Europe fantasized about and a place that Portugal and Spain had searched long and hard to find. On the west coast of the Malay Peninsula lay the magnificent port Malacca, a city that served as a central distribution point for nearly every spice known to man. It was here that fleets of large Chinese and Malayan vessels, known as junks, docked and unloaded their fragrant cargoes of pepper, cloves, cinnamon, and nutmeg for exchange at the city's great marketplace. Many of these exotic spices were purchased by Indian merchants who then shipped them back to their own markets along the Malabar coast, where they were then sold to Arab merchants. From there the spices were shipped by means of dhows to various centers of trade, including the Middle Eastern cities of Ormuz and Aden, as well as the cities of Mombasa, Mozambique, and Sofala along the eastern coast of Africa. Malacca was where the great natural resources of the Far East were exchanged for the wealth of the Middle East.

Realizing that Portugal could never completely monopolize the spice trade until it had gained control of the markets at Malacca, Albuquerque dispatched five ships under the command of Diogo Lopes de Sequeira on a reconnaissance mission to learn of the city's strengths and weaknesses. Also sailing along on this expedition were a fully recovered Ferdinand Magellan and his good friend Francisco Serrão. Once the ships had reached the harbor at Malacca, the Portuguese commander sent a large and well-armed party ashore to meet with the ruler of the city. Sequeira was apparently confident that such a show of force, limited as it was, would be enough to make the Muslim sultan of Malacca submit to the will of the Portuguese. Guessing at their ulterior motives, the crafty sultan provided Serrão's emissaries with a warm reception while he secretly schemed against them.

It was an alert Ferdinand Magellan who was the first to notice that trouble was brewing. While stationed on deck he happened to notice a great number of Malayan vessels moving swiftly towards their ships. His timely warning to the Portuguese commander of this impending attack helped to save the entire fleet from a hostile takeover and its crew from an almost certain death. But this was only part of an orchestrated attack. At the same time, the sultan's soldiers descended upon the party of men who had come ashore. Caught by surprise, several Portuguese sailors were savagely hacked to death before anyone had time to react to what was happening. While the sailors mounted a courageous defense there were simply too many warriors for so few men to overcome. A Malayan victory seemed assured once they had forced the weary sailors to retreat to the water's edge. Once again, Magellan would come to the rescue. Now that the attack by sea had been repulsed, the victorious sailors aboard ship helplessly watched the grisly battle that was taking place on land. Refusing to stand by idly while his comrades desperately fought for their lives, Magellan rushed to their aid by rowing ashore in a small boat. He arrived just in time to rescue a boatload of men, including his friend Francisco, but he was too late for the sixty others who were either already dead or had been taken prisoner by the Malayan warriors. Once Magellan and the survivors were back on board, Sequeira pulled anchor and quickly sailed his ships out of harm's way. While the Malayans had clearly won the battle on that day, the determined Portuguese would soon return in greater numbers to win the war for control of the markets at Malacca.

On their journey back to Cochin, Diogo Lopes de Sequeira's squadron of ships was attacked by Chinese pirates who were patrolling the waters for easy prey to loot. When the Chinese junk came alongside the Portuguese ship, a ferocious hand-to-hand battle ensued, with the combatants battling one another aboard each other's decks. Once they realized that the Portuguese were unlike the compliant victims they were normally accustomed to, the Chinese buccaneers withdrew from the engagement. Unfortunately for Francisco Serrão and several of his comrades, the Chinese retreat occurred while they were still clashing swords aboard the pirate vessel. Viewing Serrão's latest dilemma from the safety of their ship, Magellan and four other seamen sprang into action by jumping into a rowboat and rapidly racing after the escaping pirate ship. Once they caught up with Chinese junk and had managed to board her, Magellan and his men fought with such desperate determination and savage fury, they eventually forced the pirates to lay down their arms and surrender. Showing his mettle in combat once more, Magellan not only managed to rescue Serrão from certain death for a second time but also succeeded in capturing a vessel laden with a vast treasure trove of stolen spices, gems, silks, and precious metals. While their mission had met with only a modicum of success, an appreciative Albuquerque recognized the valor of both Magellan and Serrão by appointing each a captain of his own vessel.

A Monopoly of the Spice Market

The viceroy of India decided to postpone any plans for a major assault against Malacca until after he had completed his conquest of the Malabar Coast. At that time Calicut and Goa were the two largest centers of commerce along the west coast of India, and Albuquerque knew that once he gained control of those lucrative markets, then all of the remaining smaller marketplaces along that coast would subsequently fall under his thumb. Albuquerque's fleet attacked Calicut in January of 1510 but his navy was unable to breach the city's steadfast defense. Undeterred by this setback to his plans, the viceroy simply regrouped his forces and set his sights on conquering the ancient city of Goa. Just two months after his failure at Calicut, Albuquerque stood victorious at Goa in a conquest which occurred with such suddenness and ease that it caught even the viceroy by surprise. Unfortunately for both Albuquerque and his troops there was precious little time to savor their glorious victory.

Three months after the fall of Goa, a determined Yusif Adil Shah returned with an army of sixty thousand zealous Muslim soldiers to reclaim his city. What Albuquerque had failed to take into account was the fact that Goa was more than just a city of enormous commercial importance, it was also a very sacred site, a place where the faithful Muslims of India gathered to begin their pilgrimage to the holy city of Mecca. Greatly outnumbered, the Portuguese force retreated to the safety of their ships anchored in the harbor. It was there that they spent nearly the entire summer, due in part to an effective blockade put in place by the shah but mostly because of the miserable weather conditions brought on by the rainy monsoon season. When the weather finally cleared in August the Portuguese fleet sailed away from Goa only to return with a vengeance a mere three months later.

After having enlisted the aid of every available Portuguese ship and sailor, Albuquerque returned to Goa with a much larger fleet in November. Though the evidence is inconclusive, Magellan more than likely participated in what turned out to be one of the bloodiest campaigns ever conducted in that part of the world. The Muslim forces mounted a brave and resolute defense of their fair city but it was simply not enough to keep the determined Christian armada at bay. Even when their victory was assured the Portuguese conquerors continued to vent their rage against the defenseless remaining citizens of Goa. More than eight thousand men, women, and children were reportedly massacred during a single afternoon of carnage carried on by Albuquerque's vengeful soldiers. Once the conquest was complete, Goa replaced Cochin as the Portuguese seat of power in the Indies. Shortly thereafter, Calicut, the city which had repulsed Albuquerque's earlier advancement, surrendered to the viceroy without even a struggle.

Now that he had firmly established control over the numerous markets along the Malabar Coast, Afonso Albuquerque was ready to turn his attention to the conquest of what was arguably the richest city in the world: Malacca. Commanding an imposing fleet of nineteen heavily armed warships, the viceroy returned in the early part of August to the very harbor where Sequeira, Magellan, and Serrão had met with an embarrassing defeat. Anticipating the return of these Portuguese infidels, the sultan had bolstered Malacca's defenses with an army of twenty thousand soldiers and the strategic placement of nearly three-thousand cannons. Following the firing of the first shot a deafening roar of cannons thundered back and forth but it was the city of Malacca which proved to be the much larger and easier target to find. Portuguese cannonballs battered the city's fortifications, obliterated hundreds of buildings, and left its many streets littered with thousands of dead bodies. After suffering through twelve days of incessant naval bombardments the city of Malacca finally surrendered to the Portuguese fleet.

It was only after they had entered the city that the Portuguese conquerors were able to grasp the enormous extent of wealth they had just inherited. Few, if any Europeans had ever laid eyes on such a treasure trove of sparkling diamonds, rubies, emeralds, and sapphires. But even this princely sum of jewels paled before the splendor of the extraordinary amount of precious gold that Malacca would yield to them. Not surprisingly, much of this vast accumulated fortune had found its way into the possession of the sultan, an observation substantiated by Albuquerque's discovery and subsequent confiscation of some sixty tons of gold cast in various forms and shapes, all of which was stored at the royal palace. As for the rest of the city, there was more than enough wealth to go around for all who had participated in the conquest. As part of his reward, captain Ferdinand Magellan became the owner of a teenage Malayan slave whom he called Henrique. Henceforth, Henrique would follow wherever his master sailed, and he even accompanied Magellan on his bold but ill-fated attempt to become the first man to sail around the world.

Shortly after the conquest of Malacca, Albuquerque dispatched an expedition to search for the legendary spice producing islands, now known to be part of the chain of islands in the Malay Archipelago and collectively referred to as the Moluccas. Under the command of Antônio de Abreu, three ships set sail from the harbor of Malacca just before the end of 1511. Abreu, who commanded the flagship *Catarina*, was accompanied by Francisco Serrão as captain of the *Sabaia*, while Ferdinand Magellan was at the helm of a third caravel whose name is no longer remembered. To help steer them safely in the direction of the splendid islands that produce much of the world's supply of pepper, cinnamon, nutmeg, and cloves, a number of Javanese pilots were conscripted into service. Carefully navigating the shallow channel of the Strait of Malacca the explorers soon learned that the spice trail extended for a very great distance. Their southeasterly course took them past the numerous and thriving commercial ports located in Sumatra, Java, and Borneo before they arrived at the Sunda Islands, a chain which includes the exotic lands of Bali, Lombok, Sumbawa, and Flores. After they arrived at Flores, the pilots from Java altered course. Sailing along a northeasterly setting the Portuguese flotilla soon arrived at the southern islands of the Moluccas.

Much to their delight, the Portuguese explorers found the largely Malayan population of Amboina, Banda, and the Ceram islands warmly receptive and extremely eager to swap goods with them. After filling his cargo bays with nutmeg and various other rare spices, Antônio de Abreu decided the time had come for him and his men to return to Malacca. However, on the return voyage the ships ran into a bit of bad weather which resulted in Francisco Serrão's ship sustaining damage severe enough to force its separation from the other vessels. Serrão and his crew barely managed to make their way back to Amboina. After his ship was patched and deemed seaworthy once again, Serrão decided to forgo a return to Malacca and instead continue exploring the breathtakingly beautiful islands of the Moluccas. Eventually they landed at Ternate, a small island which, due to its natural abundance of clove trees, had grown comfortably rich off the overseas demand for the aromatic buds it produced. To Serrão the island of Ternate was a tropical paradise, and having succumbed to the friendly charm of its people and the picturesque beauty of the land, he willfully spent all his remaining days living a life of leisure in the service of the sultan. From his new home Francisco Serrão wrote to his good friend Magellan: "I beg you to join me here, that you may sample for yourself the delights which surround me."

Because of this voyage as far east as Ambon and Banda that Magellan was a part of and his subsequent western voyage to the islands of the Philippines, historians and authors can state with a relative degree of accuracy that he was the first man to circumnavigate the globe. However, whether or not Magellan ever actually sailed to the Moluccas has been a subject of frequent debate amongst historians.

As for the two ships commanded by Abreu and Magellan, they eventually found their way safely back to the harbor of Malacca. Their magnificent cargo of spices was all the proof needed to convince everyone that they had indeed found the way to the long sought-after "Spice Islands." A wave of Portuguese expeditions to the Moluccas soon followed, and these voyages eventually led to the establishment of forts and factories at a great many of these islands. Even Ternate, the island paradise of Francisco Serrão, was eventually invaded by these commercial expeditions and proved itself accommodating enough to later become the permanent residence of the Portuguese governor of the Moluccas.

With Albuquerque's victory at Malacca and Abreu's discovery of the way to the Moluccas, the dreams and desires of King Manuel and his royal predecessors had finally been fulfilled. Portugal had as near a monopoly of the lucrative spice trade as any nation could ever hope to achieve. Direct access to the spice growers of the Moluccas meant the Portuguese had peeled away that last layer of burdensome costs tacked on by miserly middlemen, and with control of the great market at Malacca they had positioned themselves as the new middlemen of trade and now had the power to manipulate and dictate market prices as they saw fit. The tiny nation of Portugal had suddenly become the wealthiest and most powerful nation in all of Europe.

Afonso the Great

Afonso Albuquerque stayed at Malacca long enough to erect a fairly sizable fort, appoint a governor to oversee the operations of Portugal's newest possession, and dispatch an exploratory expedition to find the legendary Spice Islands. Once he was satisfied that the city had been thoroughly cleansed of any further Muslim threat (most of the Muslim merchants fled to nearby Borneo when the city was conquered), the viceroy prepared to return to his headquarters at Goa. While he planned to sail back with only four ships, leaving the majority of the fleet behind to protect Portugal's interests in Malacca, he was, however, determined to return with every ounce of treasure he could possibly store aboard his fleet. The boats were loaded with hundreds of chests, each of which was stuffed with an incredible array of precious gems and jewels, as well as all of the gold and silver they had confiscated from the city. Albuquerque stripped the city of so much coin and precious metal that after his departure the conquered citizens of Malacca had to resort to minting coins out of tin to serve as their circulating currency.

Promising to send additional supplies and reinforcements the moment he reached the Port of Goa, Albuquerque set sail with the bulk of the sultan's treasured gold stowed aboard his flagship, the *Flor de la Mar*. Unfortunately for those who sailed along with Albuquerque, this was an expedition destined to fall victim to both circumstance and the viceroy's avaricious nature. On just their second day out to sea the ships sailed directly into the path of a very powerful storm. Two of the grossly overloaded boats sank almost immediately to the bottom of the sea, taking with them their entire crew and all of the valuable treasure they contained. Shortly thereafter, a badly crippled *Flor de la Mar* struck a reef near the island of Sumatra and began taking on water at an alarming rate. Albuquerque volunteered himself and five other officers to row out in search of the only remaining ship, and once it had been found, he promised to return for those he had left behind. The viceroy did manage to find the other ship, but instead of returning to the aid of the sailors aboard his flagship he continued on towards Goa. As for the fate of the *Flor de la Mar*, crashing waves tore apart her hull just hours after Albuquerque had abandoned her. The mighty flagship then sank, along with the magnificent treasure that once belonged to the sultan, to her deep watery grave. Out of a crew of some four hundred men only three exhausted sailors survived this terrible ordeal by swimming to the safety of a distant shore.

Afonso Albuquerque finally landed at Goa with his sole surviving treasure ship in September of 1512, arriving just in time to put down a serious uprising aimed at overthrowing his regime. Once order had been restored to Goa, Albuquerque launched another massive assault against existing Arab trade routes along the Red Sea. In 1513 his fleet attacked the port city of Aden, a major Muslim center of trade located at the southern entrance to the Red Sea. But the city was heavily defended and therefore able to temporarily repulse the viceroy's best effort to advance Portugal's commercial interests in that area.

After he had adequate time to recover from his disappointing defeat at Aden, Albuquerque took to preying upon towns that were situated along the Arabian coast. He terrorized several settlements into submission by capturing any local vessel that had had the grave misfortune of having crossed his path. The viceroy ordered his men to cut off the nose of any female passenger and to chop off the hands of every male passenger aboard ship. Once this grisly deed was done he had his men send these butchered victims, along with their severed body parts, back to land. A slightly less gruesome yet still extremely effective Portuguese method of persuasion that Albuquerque liked to employ at hostile ports of call was the shocking display of the bloody and rotting corpses of recently executed Muslim captives hanging from the ship's yardarms. Albuquerque's campaigns of terror eventually wore down Arab resistance at Aden and also allowed him to recapture the island of Hormuz in 1515, thereby giving Portugal control over most of the major shipping lanes in that distant part of the world. The addition of fortresses at Aden and Hormuz to the list of existing bases along the Malabar Coast and at Malacca enabled the Portuguese to effectively exert control over most of the spice traffic that flowed between the lands of the Far East and those of the Middle East.

The viceroy's bitter hatred of all Muslims was so consuming that he even formulated an audacious scheme to turn a large portion of the Islamic realm into a barren wasteland. Sailing his fleet up the Red Sea, Albuquerque stopped at Abyssinia in order that he might send a proposal to the Christian king of this land—a ruler whom many still believed to be the omnipotent Prester John—requesting that they join forces in the digging of a giant canal which would drain the water of the Nile into the Red Sea: a diversion which would ultimately turn all of Egypt into a vast desert. The viceroy never had the opportunity to put his plan into motion, for he was soon summoned back to Goa to deal with a completely different kind of threat. Albuquerque had committed the political sin of having done his job too well. His string of successful campaigns in the Far East elicited calls from a number of envious men at the royal court of King Manuel to appoint someone to replace him as viceroy of the Indies, a request that the king acceded to in the latter half of the year 1515. When he returned to Goa there was already a ship from Portugal waiting in the harbor to deliver a message summoning him back home. What made the news even more unbearable for Albuquerque was the fact that the king had appointed Lope Soarez, a man whom he detested greatly, as his successor. On December 15, 1515, just a few days after having been relieved of his command, a distraught Afonso Albuquerque died aboard his ship. His body was immediately returned to Goa for burial, and there his remains lay until they were finally brought home to Portugal some fifty years later.

The new King of Portugal, John III, son of the union between Manuel the Fortunate and Maria, the daughter of Spain's Ferdinand and Isabella, had become concerned about numerous reports of corruption amongst Portuguese officials residing in India. Seeking answers to this problem the young king turned to the counsel of Vasco da Gama. Having profited greatly from his investments abroad, as well as from his pension from the Crown, and his appointment as count Vidigueira by a very grateful monarch, Vasco da Gama enjoyed the many comforts that were the rewards of his being one of the richest noblemen in all of Portugal. Unable to resist the call of another adventure, a much older Vasco da Gama set sail once again, more than twenty years after his celebrated second voyage to the Malabar Coast, as the newly appointed viceroy of India. He arrived at Cochin in the fall of 1524 and even though he succeeded at weeding out much of the corruption that plagued the region the rigors of such a long voyage coupled with the many duties of command weighed heavily on the elder statesman. On Christmas Eve of that same year the great explorer passed away in the land he had discovered and conquered for Portugal.

A Redistribution of Wealth

Portugal and Manuel the Fortunate were both the beneficiaries of all that Afonso the Great had accomplished for them. His conquests in India and Malacca provided Portugal with direct access to the many markets of the Orient, and the string of forts he constructed along the coasts of Africa,

Arabia, and Asia ensured that those ports remained safe within their fold. Arab dhows that once hauled valuable cargoes across the Indian Ocean were suddenly replaced by Portuguese carracks and nãos carrying similar freight. Large fleets of these enormous vessels now departed Portugal on a regular basis. While some were destined for ports along the coast of India and others sailed further on to Malacca and the Moluccas, nearly all returned home with their hulls fully loaded with the many splendid treasures of the Indies. Precious items carved from jade or ivory; valuable articles cast from silver or gold; priceless works woven out of delicate silk; trunks filled with rare gems, pearls, and jewelry; and crates containing beautifully crafted and intricately designed porcelains were among the many marvels that Portuguese stevedores unloaded from returning vessels docked at the city of Lisbon. These same ships also brought back a great number of plants and minerals such as aloe, borax, camphor, musk, and sandalwood whose medicinal value greatly exceeded the value of their weight in gold. But the most valuable cargoes of all were the numerous spices that European tastes had grown accustomed to: nutmeg, cinnamon, pepper, ginger, cardamom, saffron, and cloves had, by this time, become essential ingredients of European continental cuisine. Because of their proven qualities in the preservation of food, especially meat, and their perceived therapeutic value in staving off diseases such as the Black Death, cloves were perhaps the single most sought-after product of the Far East.

The establishment of a relatively safe sea route to the East Indies had assured Portugal of its own financial well-being. Money that once flowed so freely into the purses of the Italian merchants was suddenly redirected into the pockets of merchants who hailed from Portugal. Choosing to invest wisely in his nation's future, Manuel enlarged his merchant fleet in order to accommodate even greater quantities of goods from the markets of Africa, India, and the Orient which, in turn, produced even greater profits for Portugal. To ensure that his treasure ships returned safely to the ports of Portugal the king also increased the number of warships in his navy. Manuel also used his fortunes to revive Portuguese interest in art, science, and literature, and in the process he managed to transform the city of Lisbon into one of the great cultural centers of Europe.

Every boatload of rare and exotic goods received from the markets overseas was preceded by a large shipment of European bullion from the docks of Portugal. Gold and silver, but especially gold, was being shipped abroad at such an alarming rate that there was a growing concern that the existing supply of European metals would one day become depleted due to this insatiable demand for foreign products. The means to pay for the many items of Asia and the Orient would soon become the driving force behind the

Iberian search for additional sources of gold, an eternal quest that eventually took both Portugal and Spain to the far ends of the earth.

Another factor that contributed greatly to Portugal's desperate need to procure more gold was the soaring costs associated with her ongoing and expansive efforts to monopolize the spice trade. It cost a great deal of money to construct and operate Portugal's numerous forts and factories overseas; to build and maintain a massive merchant fleet and an accompanying armada of warships; and to pay the salaries of the thousands of men who served as soldiers, sailors, and workers in Africa, Asia, and the Far East. There were some years during the height of Portugal's power that the costs of operating, enforcing and preserving their monopoly actually exceeded the amount of money that was derived from their overseas operations, but these were, for the most part, the exception to the many years of astronomical profits they earned for themselves.

Europe's primary source of gold, either directly or indirectly, had always been the mysterious continent of Africa. A vast interlocking system of African trade gravitated either northward to markets along the Mediterranean basin or eastward towards markets on the Indian Ocean. It was from these various ports of entry that the precious products of Africa were exchanged for essential goods transported from Arabia, Europe, Asia, and the Far East. While items such as ivory, timber, slaves, and shells were in great demand, it was, however, the gold of Africa that attracted traders from many parts of the world. The brisk trade conducted along the coast of East Africa was predicated on a single basic fact: Arab and Indian traders knew they could exchange their spices, their silks, and their pottery for pure African gold.

Portugal caught a glimpse of Africa's wondrous wealth after having conquered the Moroccan city of Ceuta. It was there that a young Prince Henry learned about the great "ships of the desert" that carried overland the riches obtained from the inner regions of Africa. Africa was also where Henry first heard about the gold trade of Senegal and Ghana, tales that helped to launch the epic Portuguese voyages of discovery. While the legendary land known as the Gold Coast was not reached until shortly after the death of Prince Henry the Navigator, its discovery, however, enriched the royal coffers enough to convince a previously skeptical Crown that such expeditions along the Atlantic Coast were certainly in Portugal's best interest. After circumnavigating the tip of the continent, Portuguese mariners were astounded by the vast differences in the way of life that existed between the societies of East and West Africa. For many centuries, African tribes along the Indian Ocean had carried on extensive trade with Arab and Asian merchants and it was this exposure to the outside world which helped to form the great civilizations that existed at Mombasa, Malindi, and the legendary city of Timbuktu. These places were a striking contrast to the prim-itive cultures that the Portuguese had come into contact with during their trek down the Atlantic coastline of Africa. Up to that point they had encountered only peoples and lands that, because of their isolation from the rest of mankind, were completely untouched by progress.

After having gained control of the major markets situated along the coast of East Africa, Portuguese explorers desperately tried to tap into the gold trade of that region. At Sofala they heard spectacular stories of a great inland empire ruled by a mighty king who controlled most of the gold traffic of Zimbabwe and Mozambique. Once they had founded a settlement at Sofala, the Portuguese dispatched several expeditions in search of the wealthy and powerful chief known to all as Monomotapa. By forging a treaty with this omnipotent ruler of Africa's interior, Portuguese officials hoped to uti-lize his empire as a central collection point for gold to be dispersed to ports located at Angola and Mozambique, thereby linking the two opposite coasts of Africa by means of a gold route. Sometime around the year 1511, Anto-nio Fernandes became the first European to set foot in the kingdom of Monomotapa only to discover that this once great empire was now in a rapid state of decline, a victim of numerous losses resulting from an ongo-ing war with the neighboring Bantu tribes. Thus, Portuguese dreams of exploiting the abundant gold of Africa's interior never materialized.

Portugal enjoyed much greater success probing the seas of the Orient in voyages of discovery that eventually brought them to the legendary lands of Cathay and Cipangu. Tomé Pires managed to reach the mysterious realm of China in August of 1517 but was forced to endure a lengthy wait of three years at Canton before he was finally granted an audience with Emperor Wu-tsung. With grand expectations of establishing diplomatic relations and a favorable trade status with China, Pires journeyed to Peking with a letter of introduction from his sovereign, Manuel the Fortunate. These expecta-tions were quickly shattered when it was determined by Chinese court officials that the letter from the king of Portugal failed to convey the proper respect required for an introduction to the almighty emperor of China. Pires was then sent back to Canton where he was imprisoned for a brief period. Despite an official rebuke of their initial overture to establish a mutual trade accord, Portuguese merchants still carried on a profitable, though dangerously ille-gal, trade with Chinese merchants eager to sell their merchandise, provided the price was to their liking. Even after the arrival of Tomé Pires at Canton, it still took a long time before most of Europe realized that Cathay and China were one and the same place. Portugal finally solved the mystery concern-ing the whereabouts of Cipangu when one of its trade expeditions unex-pectedly landed at the islands of Japan.

ELEVEN

Colonization
of the Caribbean

The Commonwealth of Spain

Following in the wake of both Christopher Columbus and Amerigo Vespucci were a great number of private adventurers who sailed to the West Indies bent on discovery for fortune's sake alone. Their avaricious nature was fueled by Christopher Columbus's tidings of great wealth still waiting to be uncovered on the many islands of the Caribbean and Vespucci's report of having sailed to a rich and beautiful land now recognized as being part of a New World. Those who ventured forth at their own expense did so only with a license of approval from Spain's Council of the Indies and an understanding that the Crown was entitled to a one-fifth share of all gold or silver they discovered, confiscated, or acquired on these expeditions.

At Hispaniola, the colony of Santo Domingo functioned not only as the administrative center for Spain's slowly emerging colonial empire in the Caribbean but also as a launching point for a growing number of private expeditions in search of gold and glory. Following the paths previously blazed by Christopher Columbus, Spanish explorers sailed from one island to another in hopes of finding either the gold, pearls, or spices that had eluded the admiral on his previous expeditions. Sailing westward, this new wave of explorers scoured the islands of Cuba and Jamaica; to the south they landed at the southern isthmus of Central America and the northern coast of South America, a stretch of land later referred to as the Spanish Main; to the east they found the island of Puerto Rico; and to the north they explored the extreme southeastern tip of North America. A great number of these expeditions around the Caribbean led to the discovery of significant amounts of gold and silver, a fifth of which always found its way back to Spain.

The sight of so much Caribbean gold being unloaded at the docks of Seville and Cádiz was enough to entice Spaniards from all walks of life to risk a voyage across the vast breadth of the Atlantic Ocean. The New World gave new hope to the less fortunate, provided that they were blessed with Castilian lineage—all others knew it was not worth their while to apply. It was Queen Isabella who had set this uncompromising condition, that only Castilians could colonize the Americas, but with the rapid expansion of settlements in the West Indies the needs of the colonies soon outweighed her desire to enforce racial purity amongst the colonists. Beginning in 1511, seven years after the passing of Queen Isabella, the freedom to emigrate to the Indies was extended to all Christian Spaniards. The removal of the ban on non–Castilians proved to be a successful means of attracting able-bodied men to the colonies, but, in turn, it also made it easier for a great number of Spain's less desirable characters to reach the shores of the Caribbean. Murderers, rapists, robbers, and debtors were among the many Christian fugitives from justice who found a new lease on life simply by sailing to the West Indies.

Diego Columbus, the devoted eldest son of the admiral, continued to press the family's claims to all titles and lands in the West Indies long after the death of his father. He did everything he could to improve his position at the royal court, including courting and marrying Doña María Álvarez de Toledo, a relative of King Ferdinand. Diego's efforts were finally rewarded in 1508 when the king appointed him "Admiral of the Ocean and Governor of Hispaniola." While the son may have felt vindicated by the king's decision to restore his father's titles to the family, the privileges that had once been bestowed on the admiral were an entirely separate matter and Diego was therefore impelled to carry on a legal battle that unfortunately he could never win. Reaching Hispaniola the following year, Diego relieved Nicolás de Ovando of his title as governor of the island. The loyal son certainly demonstrated a much better flair for administrative affairs than his father ever did, an inference based on the fact that Diego remained governor of the island until his death seventeen years later. However, nearly half of his term was spent in Spain either defending himself against spurious charges or pursuing his endless legal claims against the Crown. His wife remained behind to govern Hispaniola during his frequent and extended absences. When Diego died in Spain on February 24, 1526, his hereditary title passed to his son Don Luis. Sadly, the grandson of the great Christopher

Columbus proved so incompetent as a governor that even his own mother
was forced to broker a deal with the king that granted her son a dukedom
in Veragua in exchange for the family's claim to all governing titles in the
West Indies in perpetuity. With this arrangement, mother and son relin-
quished all that the deceased Diego Columbus had fought so long for.

It was during Diego's term as governor of Hispaniola that most of the
islands of the Caribbean were explored, conquered, and settled. Juan Ponce
de León, who sailed to the New World as a member of the admiral's second Enterprise of the Indies, was selected to lead an armed force against
the fierce cannibals of San Juan Bautista, an island just to the east of Hispaniola. It was from this island, which the conquering Spaniards later
renamed Puerto Rico, that the Caribs continued to terrorize the shores of
Hispaniola with their periodic canoe raids in search of Arawak victims to
serve as either slaves or sustenance. Armed with superior weaponry, Ponce
de León and his army easily slaughtered hundreds of island natives, thereby
eliminating the Carib threat to the inhabitants of Hispaniola. In recognition of the great service he had rendered to Spain, Juan Ponce de León was
appointed governor of the island in 1509 and granted all rights to any gold
he might discover, except, of course, for the obligatory royal tribute. It was
from the natives of Puerto Rico that the Spanish conqueror heard wondrous
tales of an island just to the north called Bimini, which, besides being a
land of immeasurable wealth, was supposedly home to a legendary fountain
that had the power to restore youth to anyone who drank from its water.
Ponce de León surely must have believed that the Indian tales he heard
were undeniable proof that the legendary "Well of Youth," which Sir John
Mandeville had described in his book of worldly travels, did in fact exist.
It was an elderly Ponce de León who twice led expeditions in search of this
mystical fountain of youth, each time arriving at a land which he called
"Pascual Florida" (flowery Easter) because he had first sighted it on Easter
Sunday. It was on the second voyage that Ponce de León suffered a mortal
wound, obtained during a fierce engagement with Indians determined to
drive the unwelcome Spaniards from their homeland. Retreating to the
safety of nearby Cuba, Juan Ponce de León died shortly after his arrival at
the city of Havana.

The island of Jamaica was conquered and colonized by Juan de Esquivel in 1509, while the conquest of nearby Cuba was begun in 1511 under
the direction of Diego Velázquez de Cuellar and his faithful henchman,
Panifilo Narváez. While gold was surely the most sought-after treasure, it
was not, however, the only precious attraction of the New World. Learning of riches discovered by Alonso de Ojeda and Nino Pearlonso, both
veteran mariners who had served under Christopher Columbus, a great num-

ber of expeditions sailed from Santo Domingo for the shores of Venezuela where many an adventurer hoped to harvest a fortune from the pearl producing waters that encircle the islands of Margarita and Cubagua. Columbus's tales of vast treasures waiting to be discovered along the southern isthmus of Central America inspired many a fortune hunter to explore the dense jungles of Nicaragua, Costa Rica, and Panama.

Before the sudden arrival of the Spaniards, most of the natives of the Caribbean had lived quite contentedly on their respective islands, living their lives according to the laws dictated by their natural habitats. Fertile lands and a bountiful sea meant they never wanted for food; social order was maintained by an understanding that the needs of the group outweighed the needs of the individual; warfare, with the exception of the occasional Carib raid, was usually a last resort for settling tribal disputes; and death, for the most part, was but an end result in the natural order of life. Their idyllic lifestyle underwent a radical transformation once they were introduced to the deadly sins of the Spaniards: greed, envy, lust, and wrath. These were entirely foreign concepts to the aboriginal inhabitants of the New World, and their cumulative effect, in conjunction with the Christian effort to save the heathen from himself through means of forced conversions, resulted in the near extermination of an entire race of people.

It was Christopher Columbus who set the tone for future relations between the settlers from Spain and the natives of the West Indies. The sight of small pieces of gold dangling from the noses of several natives sent the admiral and his men on a frantic search to locate the main source of gold in this part of the world; they believed that this most precious of all metals must have derived from one of the many splendid cities located within the realm of the Great Khan. Unable to locate the great wealth of Cathay or Cipangu and under tremendous pressure to show a profitable return on his expedition, the admiral imposed a tax that every Indian was required to pay in gold. When his tax plan failed to produce the desired results he then turned the natives into human chattels by shipping many of them to Spain for the express purpose of being auctioned off as slaves. His attempt at establishing a profitable slave market was abruptly halted by the pious Queen Isabella, who was determined to save her new subjects from eternal damnation by subjecting them to the strict tenets of the Catholic Church. A "pound of flesh" served as down payment for their Christian salvation. It was determined that the Indian's lot was to labor over the land that once was theirs but which now belonged to Spain. The native population was expected to perform any function deemed too demeaning for a Spaniard, and most of those chores centered around laboring to provide food and wealth for their Spanish masters.

The ruthless exploitation of the Caribbean Indians increased greatly following the death of Queen Isabella, their self-anointed protector. During his role as the sole monarch of Spain, Ferdinand permitted his colonies in the New World to institute the *repartiemento*, a system whereby the natives were commended to a Spanish colonist, often referred to as an *encomendero*. It was the responsibility of the *encomendero* to care for both the physical and spiritual well-being of those natives apportioned to him. In return for these services, the congregated Indians were expected to show their gratitude by rendering unto the Spaniards that which the Spaniards believed they were entitled to—food and gold being the most often requested forms of tribute. While the Spanish Crown did its best to deny the fact, the *repartiemento* system was but merely a legal justification for institutionalized slavery.

Foremost on the minds of nearly every Spaniard who settled in the New World was the tantalizing prospect of being fortunate enough to discover an abundant quantity of gold. Many of those who made the trek across the Atlantic envisioned themselves discovering a land literally paved with gold, where all one had to do was simply choose from an infinite assortment of golden nuggets conveniently strewn across the island. It was widely believed that within a short period of time and with only a minimal amount of effort, any Spaniard was capable of finding enough gold to return home to live the leisurely life that was reserved for only the most fortunate. Reality soon conjured up a rude awakening for anyone who harbored such thoughts. While it was true that the natives found most of their gold along the river beds, the fact was, as Columbus had discovered previously, the island's total amount of alluvial gold was but a trifle.

Though frustrated at first by the apparent lack of gold on the surface of the island, the Spaniards resolved to try their hand at unearthing the precious metal from various underground sources. Gold mining operations sprang up wherever the Spaniards decided to dig, but the actual physical act of digging was a chore reserved primarily for the native population. Thousands of Indians were forced to toil in the mines, and thousands would lose their lives in the exhaustive effort to extract ever greater quantities of gold for their Spanish overlords. The Indians working the mines at Hispaniola perished at such a rapid rate that the colonists had to resort to kidnapping natives from other nearby islands in order that the excavation of gold could continue as scheduled. It has been estimated that by the year 1512 the mines of Hispaniola were yielding gold at an annual rate of nearly one million dollars. However, they soon discovered that the island's supply of gold was not inexhaustible, a costly lesson learned at the terrible expense of the island's indigenous population. When Columbus first arrived at Hispaniola in 1492 there were an estimated two hundred and fifty thousand native Tainos living on the island, but by 1513, at the height of the island's mining operations, the population had, by some accounts, plummeted well below the twenty thousand mark.

Gold was certainly not the only precious item that proved to be a source of eternal misery for the natives of the West Indies. At the islands of Cubagua and Margarita, Spanish fortune hunters forced the native Caribs to make endless dives into the ocean to retrieve bushels of valuable pearls. When the Carib death rate began to affect profits at their pearl fisheries, the Spaniards at Cubagua and Margarita, just like the Spaniards at Hispaniola, began raiding other islands for additional slave labor. Their search took them as far as the Bahamas, where they discovered that the Lucayans were even better swimmers than the Caribs. Consequently, the islands of the Bahamas became a favorite source for divers, so much so, that within the space of just a few years, the entire population was shipped from their homeland and relocated to wherever their services were needed the most. These same Indian divers also provided another valuable service for Spain. It was not uncommon for a treasure ship attempting to sail back to Spain to fall victim to the inclement weather or the treacherous waters which plagued the Caribbean. When such vessels sank close to port the Spaniards were able to recover much of their sunken treasure by employing the aquatic skills of these Indian divers.

Not every tribe of the West Indies readily submitted to the will of the Spaniards, but most, however, were eventually subjugated by them. The island Caribs resisted the Spaniards' attempts to enslave them as best they could, but their best efforts could not prevent their near annihilation. Even the generally submissive Arawaks of Hispaniola revolted against Spanish tyranny only to see their rebellion quickly fail, not because they were outmanned, but because they were outgunned. The devastating effects of war, pestilence, hard labor, and prolonged abusive treatment were all contributing factors to one of history's most horrific holocausts. Many Indians elected to choose death on their own terms, often taking the lives of their families and then themselves as a means of escape from a life of Spanish oppression.

The South Sea

THE MOSQUITO COAST

The Spanish search for gold, pearls, spices, and slaves amongst the many islands of the Caribbean Sea eventually led them to the narrow isthmus that connects the two continents of the Americas. In 1501 the Spaniard Rodrigo de Bastidas, a wealthy Spanish official who was granted permission to explore and exploit the lands recently discovered by Christopher Columbus, led a small expedition that explored much of the Atlantic coastline of present day Panama and Colombia, a stretch of land later identified as part of the infamous Spanish Main. The chief pilot for this expedition was Juan de la Cosa, a sailor who, by virtue of his previous voyages with Columbus and Alonso de Ojeda, had an extensive knowledge of the Caribbean region. Also sailing on this expedition was a young sailor by the name of Vasco Núñez de Balboa, who, like so many other Spaniards of that era, hoped to find his fortune in the West Indies. Blonde haired, well-proportioned, good natured, highly intelligent, and an excellent swordsman, Balboa was well-liked by men and adored by women. After a year filled with many exciting adventures but which yielded only a meager amount of material wealth, Bastida decided to cut his losses and head home to Spain. They were forced to alter their course toward the direction of Hispaniola after discovering that their boats had sprung major leaks brought on by the insatiable wood eating teredos. Shortly after reaching the island their ships sank, forcing most of the survivors to book passage on the next vessel headed for Spain. Balboa was among the few who elected to stay behind at Hispaniola. Thankful for such a willing and healthy colonist in his company, Governor Nicolás de Ovando provided him with several acres of land to call his own.

The region explored by Rodrigo de Bastidas and his men probably would not have received any further attention had it not been for the subsequent expedition of Christopher Columbus in 1502 that covered much of the same ground. On his fourth and final voyage to the Caribbean the admiral had encountered natives along the isthmus who had in their possession a small quantity of gold but spoke of places they called Veragua and Ciguare, which were inland regions where gold supposedly exceeded even the infinite imaginations of the covetous explorers. While he never did find the rich lands that they spoke of, Columbus kept those tales of golden provinces alive by christening the region Costa Rica. When other adventurers returned to Hispaniola with reports of having found gold and pearls at the eastern most point of present day Panama a great number of Spanish fortune seekers sought an official sanction that would empower them with the right to claim these lands as their own.

In 1508 King Ferdinand granted to two of his loyal Spanish subjects the exclusive rights to explore, conquer, and settle those lands previously explored by Bastidas, Balboa, and Columbus. The strip of land that stretches from Cape Gracias a Dios to the Gulf of Darien was bequeathed to Diego Nicuesa while, at the same time, Alonso de Ojeda received an adjacent land grant that extended on into the South American coastline, into modern-day Colombia. The ambitious Nicuesa had sailed to the West Indies aboard the same fleet that had brought Nicolás de Ovando to Hispaniola, and while he was stationed at Santo Domingo, Nicuesa managed to distinguish himself under the watchful eye of the new governor. Alonso de Ojeda, a veteran of many adventures in the New World, had faithfully served under the command of Christopher Columbus, sailed along with Amerigo Vespucci, and on his own had explored much of the region in which he was now given a colonial appointment.

While Diego de Nicuesa's departure was temporarily delayed due to an ongoing dispute that centered around the hereditary claims of Diego Columbus, Alonso de Ojeda and his crew of nearly three hundred men quietly slipped out of the port of Santo Domingo and sailed across the Caribbean to the coast of Columbia where they hoped to establish the colony of New Andalusia. Landing at the harbor that was destined to become the future site of the city of Cartagena, Ojeda and his crew immediately set out to conquer and enslave the local Caribs whom they were counting on to provide the manual labor for the building of their settlement. After they had ransacked a fair number of nearby villages the Spaniards soon learned just how formidable a foe the Caribs could truly be. Pushing further into the dense jungle with seventy of his soldiers, Ojeda and his troops suddenly found themselves scurrying for cover from an onslaught of arrows that rained down upon them. Their initial fears turned to pure terror once they realized that the arrows that succeeded in piercing their armor and bodies had been dipped in a poisonous solution that made death an even more painful and certain proposition. This deadly concoction was a strange brew of various ingredients that included certain roots, a variety of fruits, along with an odd assortment of toads, spiders, ants, bats, venomous snakes, and poisonous fish, all of which were combined in large vats and cooked over an open flame, far from their own village. It is said that the natives knew their mixture was finally complete when the individual assigned to watch the fires keeled over from the effects of the deadly fumes. All of the Spaniards, except for Ojeda and one other sailor, were killed during this terrifying altercation. Some of Ojeda's men were captured alive, only to be saved for an even more gruesome fate. Juan de la Cosa, the navigator and cartographer who had sailed twice with Columbus and twice with Ojeda, was seized by the Caribs and tied to a tree in order that he might serve as a target for Carib warriors competing to measure their skill with the bow and arrow. Ojeda was wounded, though not mortally, and once he and the other surviving sailor found their way back to the ship the remaining crew immediately cast off in search of a more hospitable location.

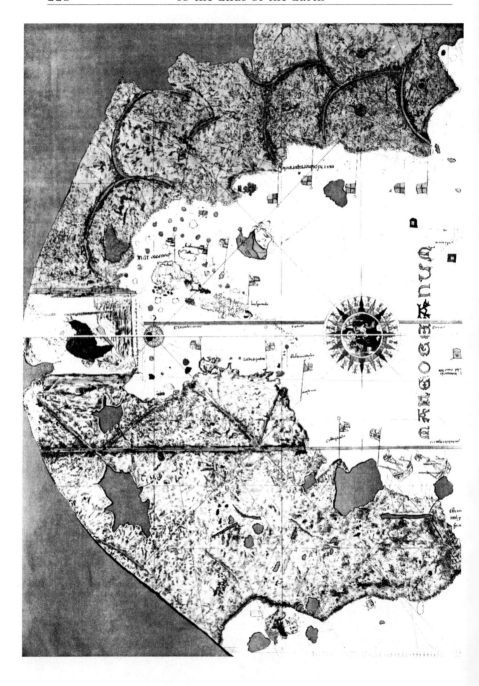

Ten days after Ojeda's expedition sailed from the docks of Santo Domingo, Diego de Nicuesa embarked on his mission to establish a colony that he intended to call Veragua. Following a similar course, but sailing with a much larger force comprised of seven hundred and forty-five men stowed aboard five large ships, Nicuesa had little trouble crossing the waters of the Caribbean. However, coming ashore proved to be a much more difficult task than he had ever anticipated. Harassed by hostile natives wherever he attempted to land, Nicuesa sailed on until he finally found a safer spot at the Cape of Gracias a Dios. Along the way, Nicuesa's crew hooked up with Ojeda's fleeing fleet, and as a combined force they launched several attacks against the local villages. The cumulative effects of their prolonged exposure to battle, the sweltering heat, yellow fever, and starvation not only dwindled their numbers but also drained the Spaniards of their will for adventure. Eventually the two commanders, who detested one another equally, jointly decided to go their separate ways. While Nicuesa and his men continued to search for the gold of Veragua, Ojeda and his men sailed to the Gulf of Uraba where they attempted to establish the colony of San Sebastián. Unfortunately for both parties, they not only continued to come under the constant attacks of the fierce Carib warriors, they also found themselves completely defenseless against the unrelenting swarms of blood-sucking mosquitoes.

At some point during Ojeda's miserable ordeal at San Sebastián a Spanish desperado by the name of Bernardino de Talavera, who, along with seventy of his marauding followers, stopped to barter some of his ill-gotten contraband. A man of highly questionable scruples, Talavera was one of the first in a long line of notorious buccaneers who made his living attacking and plundering other vessels and settlements on the waters of the Caribbean. Enlisting the services of Talavera, Ojeda proposed a return voyage for himself to the colony of Santo Domingo, ostensibly to obtain more supplies and recruits for his settlement; but more likely than not, he had simply grown weary of his many disappointments on this voyage and his still painful wounds. After turning over his command to Francisco Pizarro, a middle-aged soldier who had recently sailed to the West Indies, Ojeda cast off in the company of Talavera and his motley crew. Instead of sailing directly for Hispaniola, Talavera continued along the coast of the isthmus, presumably to carry on more illicit raids, before setting back out to sea.

Opposite page: **Juan de la Cosa's 1500 map of the Western Hemisphere: A professional pilot and an accomplished cartographer, de la Cosa sailed with Christopher Columbus on the second Enterprise of the Indies as well as with Alonso de Ojeda and Amerigo Vespucci.**

When it became apparent that their badly leaking vessel was no longer sea-worthy the sailors made a mad dash for the nearest shore, which, in their case, turned out to be the island of Cuba. With their boat damaged beyond repair and the likelihood of another ship passing that far west extremely remote, the stranded sailors decided to hike to the east end of the island where they might have a better chance of being rescued. To reach their intended destination the Spaniards had to hack their way through several hundred miles of thick jungle growth and by month's end, when they finally reached the other side of the island, there were only about a dozen men, including Ojeda and Talavera, who were still standing. To their great relief, a passing vessel under the command of Panfilo de Narváez happened to sight the shipwrecked survivors and brought them aboard his ship. The rescue turned out to be only a brief respite for some of the survivors. Rec-ognized for his many past transgressions, Talavera was taken to Jamaica where he would soon swing from the end of a rope. As for Ojeda, he even-tually made it back to Santo Domingo only to die shortly thereafter at the settlement's hospital.

THE COLONY OF SAN SEBASTIÁN

Alonso de Ojeda managed to live long enough to confide in his per-sonal lawyer, Martín Fernández de Enciso, about the many brave soldiers he had left behind at San Sebastián and of their urgent need for additional provisions. In executing the last wishes of his good friend and client, Enciso placed himself in command of a hastily organized expedition that consisted of one hundred and fifty men charged with the task of providing relief for the starving settlers of San Sebastián. After they had sailed far beyond the sight of Santo Domingo's harbor, Captain Enciso was surprised to learn that there was a stowaway aboard his ship.

After he had returned from the failed fortune-seeking mission com-manded by Rodrigo Bastidas, a disheartened Vasco Núñez de Balboa embarked on a less risky way of earning a living by setting himself up as a gentleman farmer. Unfortunately for Balboa the business end of farming proved to be much more difficult than he had envisioned and in order to keep his business afloat he was forced to borrow from anyone he could per-suade to lend him money. Balboa's financial affairs continued to worsen and before long his numerous creditors were threatening to have him thrown into debtors' prison for failing to fulfill his contractual obligations. His mounting monetary problems nearly came to a climactic conclusion when several lenders attempted to have him apprehended. The destitute

Balboa managed to escape their clutches by hiding in a barrel that was supposed to contain grain earmarked for the starving colonists at San Sebastián. Rolled on board Enciso's flagship, Balboa waited quietly inside the cask until he felt comfortable that the ship had reached a point of no return, a spot far enough out to sea where the captain would not entertain the thought of returning him to the docks of Santo Domingo. Emerging from his hiding place, Balboa immediately presented himself before the captain, pleaded his desperate case and then threw himself on Enciso's mercy. Possessed of a charismatic personality and described by one observer as "of gallant mien, and handsome ... tall, clean-limbed and strong," Balboa succeeded in winning the captain's favor. From then on this stowaway from Hispaniola was accepted as a full-fledged member of the Enciso expedition.

While these events were taking place, Francisco Pizarro was doing the best he possibly could to keep the colony of San Sebastián intact. His noble efforts were hindered by constant attacks from hostile Caribs, starvation, and illness, all of which had conspired to dwindle his ranks down to a measly force of just sixty men. Giving up all hope that Alonso de Ojeda would ever return as promised, Pizarro began making plans for the evacuation of this dismal domain; but unfortunately their only means of conveyance was two vessels entirely too small to carry that many men. Too weak to march, Pizarro and his men simply waited for nature to take its course, and once their numbers had been sufficiently thinned they then attempted a bold escape by way of the sea. The boat that carried Pizarro and his crew was able to sail away safely, but the crew of the other vessel were less fortunate. Their boat quickly sank, but luckily for them they were not too far from shore.

The path of Francisco Pizarro and Martín Enciso soon crossed and together they sailed back to see what remained of the San Sebastián colony. Besides finding a few survivors there was little else worth salvaging. Uncertain as to what was now the best course to follow, the captain sought the counsel of his crew. Most of the disheartened men simply desired to return to Hispaniola. It was at this point that Balboa stepped forward to inspire and rally the men with an eloquent speech of the vast riches which were just waiting to be found. A new leader had suddenly emerged; while Enciso still held rank over the expedition it was Balboa who now commanded the respect of the men. Captain Enciso managed to contribute to his crew's growing sense of despair by sailing too close to shore, a maritime miscalculation that resulted in his crashing and permanently disabling his flagship on a sandbar. This was merely one of many blunders the self-appointed commander was doomed to commit in a very brief period of time. Following a hostile encounter with natives that not only claimed the lives of several

Spaniards but which also forced those who survived to endure the stench and humiliation of being pelted with human excrement belonging to their enemy, Enciso decided to take the offensive by leading his own raiding party. The captain lost what little respect he still commanded over his men when he cowardly ran for cover after an attack by tribal warriors whose sum total numbered but three. When it became clear to everyone, except of course for Enciso, that the captain lacked the essential qualities to lead in the face of adversity, the disgruntled soldiers switched their support to the man who they felt best exuded an air of leadership, the stowaway from Santo Domingo, Vasco Núñez de Balboa. Relishing his newfound respect, Balboa seized the reigns of power from the incompetent commander, and together with Francisco Pizarro, he led the expedition away from the hostile region of Urabá. An enraged Enciso was placed under arrest but was released shortly thereafter on the condition that he would respect the new chain of command and promise to leave the new colony of Santa de la Antigua peaceably.

Relocating their troops from the mainland of South America to a spot situated along the eastern coast of the isthmus, an area later known as Panama, Balboa and Pizarro founded the colony of Santa María de la Antigua del Darién, a settlement that commonly went by the abbreviated name of Darién. Finding the natives of this region to be less hostile and the food more plentiful the Spaniards were able to lay the foundations of a flourishing colony. Their new settlement also benefited greatly from the support of Diego Columbus, the governor of Hispaniola, whose official support of Balboa's right to govern helped keep at bay the repeated efforts of Martín Enciso to reclaim his lost command. But most of the credit for the colony's initial success belonged to Vasco Balboa. Instead of waging war against the natives the new leader paid homage to the local tribal chiefs. It was this show of respect and kindness towards the indigenous population that paved the way for a mutually beneficial peace accord.

The colony of Darién received an unexpected visit from a man who most Spaniards assumed had perished somewhere in the dense jungles of Panama. Arriving in a boat manned by what little remained of a once impressive army, Diego de Nicuesa not only sought to lay claim to Balboa's command but brazenly demanded that the colonists turn over to him all gold currently in their possession. After having concluded his partnership with Alonso de Ojeda, Nicuesa and his band of marauders had continued to travel up the coast of Panama until they stopped long enough to found the colony of Nombre de Dios, on a site where the city of Colón now stands. Unfortunately for Nicuesa and his men, the colony of Nombre de Dios was doomed to an even worse fate than its sister colony of San Sebastián. Native uprisings, disease, and starvation all claimed their deadly toll, and those who managed to avoid death were reduced to vanquishing their terrible hunger by feasting upon the strewn bodies of the dead. Leaving behind hundreds of their fallen comrades, Nicuesa and his remaining crew had sailed off in search of safer shores.

Since Balboa and his band of followers had trespassed upon a stretch of territory that he had been appointed governor of by King Ferdinand, Diego de Nicuesa was well within his rights to claim command of the colony of Darién. However, Balboa and his men did not relish the idea of turning over the settlement they had labored so long and hard to construct or the vast amounts of gold they had accumulated by way of trade to the likes of man as notoriously greedy and tyrannical as Nicuesa. Fortunately for the settlers of Darién, Nicuesa did not have the strength to back up his threats and claims; they were able to easily chase the governor and his men back to their ship. Forced to cast off at once, Nicuesa planned to sail directly to Santo Domingo to seek redress from the governor, but his boat and all aboard were fated to become yet another casualty of the turbulent waters of the Caribbean Sea. As for the deposed Martín Enciso, he was allowed, shortly after the banishment of Diego de Nicuesa. to sail away with the few men who still remained loyal to him. Enciso eventually found his way back to Spain where he complained to King Ferdinand, and to anyone else who would listen, about how he had been wronged by a man whom he had graciously spared from a confinement inside a debtors' prison.

By coming to the aid of the powerful cacique Comaco in a battle against an enemy tribe Balboa earned for both himself and his men the respect and support of many of the tribes that surrounded Darién. Even the cacique named Caret became so enamored with the dashing Spaniard that he offered him the hand of Ceretita, his young and beautiful daughter. This was a proposal which Balboa, in the best interests of international intercourse, willingly accepted. The commander of Darién also forged a strong friendship with Prince Panciaco, the eldest son of Comogre who was the omnipotent ruler of Comogra. Father and son both showed their gratitude to Balboa and his men for their loyal support by rewarding them with an extremely generous amount of gold dust and a great many wicker baskets filled with golden items forged in the likeness of the various creatures who shared the land with them. The Spaniards could scarcely believe their own eyes when they were presented with such a bountiful tribute of gold—an amount estimated to have weighed some five hundred pounds. Other than for decorative purposes, gold was simply of little practical value to native Americans; but to the Spaniards, this brightly colored metal was the ultimate symbol of pure wealth. It was these conflicting perceptions of value that ultimately forged an impassable divide between two very different civilizations. Both Comogre and Panciaco caught a glimpse of the sickness they believed infected the European mind when the Spaniards began to argue and fight amongst themselves while attempting to weigh and divide their golden treasure into even shares. Disgusted by this vulgar display of greed, Panciaco struck his fist against the Spaniard's scale with a force strong enough to send gold flying in every direction. Now that the prince had their undivided attention he proceeded to lecture the Spaniards in a stern voice: "If this is what you prize so much that you are willing to leave your distant homes, and risk even life itself for it, I can tell you of a land where they eat and drink out of golden vessels, and gold is as cheap as iron is with you." Needless to say, the Spaniards wanted to learn more about this "Golden Land."

A First Glimpse of the South Sea

Vasco Núñez de Balboa had hoped to receive an official appointment as governor of the land he had settled for Spain but King Ferdinand would only grant him an interim governorship of Darién, a tenuous title that he hoped to rectify by appealing to the Crown's lust for gold. Balboa had shipped the obligatory royal fifth of gold back to Hispaniola as proof that this was indeed a land of great wealth. But this treasure ship never reached Hispaniola. The ship had sunk somewhere between ports, a fact which was unknown to Balboa and his men. After a long period of time had passed without any word from Hispaniola the colonists at Darién began to suspect that the captain and his crew had absconded with the Crown's gold. Balboa sent forth another messenger who sailed directly to Spain to report directly to King Ferdinand of a mysterious "Other Sea" which the natives had spoke so often of, and of the magnificent kingdoms to the south that might very well present Spain with another golden opportunity. He also gave notice to the king that he intended to march across the isthmus to determine whether such tales were fact or fancy. Balboa had convinced himself that such a discovery would earn him the respect and the gratitude he believed he was entitled to. But, in the end, it was his own words which would ultimately betray him.

Balboa's report eventually reached Spain, but not before the ousted Martín Enciso had arrived home to offer his account of the traitorous soldier who had usurped his command. Vowing revenge against the man whom he viewed as a Judas Iscariot, Enciso utilized every means at his disposal to bring about the downfall of Balboa. His obsessive quest eventually landed him an audience with Ferdinand, which, in turn, earned him the fervent support of Bishop Juan Rodríguez de Fonseca, whose position on the Council of the Indies afforded him considerable influence over all matters that concerned the West Indies. Balboa's account of another sea, which many thought might very well be the ever-elusive western passage to the Far East, and his tale of nearby cities where gold flowed freely and abundantly, clearly captured the attention of King Ferdinand. However, when all was said and done, it was Bishop Fonseca who commanded the ear of his royal highness. With visions of gold and spices reigning supreme, plans were immediately drawn up to replace the colony of Darién with a much larger settlement to be called Castilla del Oro (Golden Castile). Unfortunately for Balboa, he did not figure in the new scheme of things. At the instigation of Enciso and the behest of Father Fonseca, it was decided that a nobleman by the name of Pedro Arias Dávila would replace the deceased Diego de Nicuesa as the new governor of this Spanish territory.

Learning of the Crown's plan to replace him as governor of Darién, Balboa decided to proceed with his proposed expedition while he still had the opportunity and the authority to make such a decision. On September 1, 1513, in the company of his trusted lieutenant Francisco Pizarro and one hundred and ninety Spanish soldiers, or nearly half the strength of Darién, Balboa set out on his historic march across the isthmus of Panama. Also accompanying the Spaniards in the supporting roles of guides and porters were several hundred natives graciously provided by Cacique Chima. Their Indian guides informed them that it was but a mere six days' march westward before they would come upon the "Other Sea." Unfortunately for Balboa and his entourage, their chosen path plunged them into a jungle fraught with peril. Besides having to hack their way through every step the exhausted Spaniards and natives were forced to contend with man-eating crocodiles submerged under the waters of the swamps and rivers, blood-sucking leeches and vampire bats, venomous snakes and scorpions, the powerful sting of frighteningly large centipedes, and the inevitable confrontations with native tribes bent on protecting their homeland. Upon entering one of the villages that had the grave misfortune of being situated along their route the Spaniards were shocked to find men cohabiting as though they were man and wife. Disgusted by the sight of men parading around dressed as women, Balboa and his troops purged the village of its sinful ways, butchering a great many of those who dwelled there.

The treacherous fifty mile trek across the narrow isthmus took Balboa and his men more than three weeks to complete and by the time they reached their intended destination the hazards of the journey had claimed the lives of more than half the members of the expedition. It was on September 25, 1513, that the Indian guides brought the weary Spaniards to a peak high enough where one could catch a glimpse of the still distant Gulf of San Miguel. While his men waited below, Balboa climbed to the top of the hill and it was from this vantage point that he became the first European to gaze upon the "Other Sea" that washes up against the shores of the Americas. While taking a moment to inhale the spectacular view before him, Balboa surely must have pondered over the prospect of what might lie beyond this vast sea in front of him. He soon motioned for his men to climb up and join him, and once they were reunited at the top the grateful soldiers knelt in unison to offer up a prayer of thanksgiving. The commander then proclaimed, "There you see, friends and companions, the object of your desires and the reward of your many labors. As the notices of another sea given us by the son of Comogre have turned out to be true, so will the words of Panciaco be fulfilled concerning the great riches of the lands to the south."

After setting up a base camp below this peak, Balboa selected twenty-six able bodied soldiers, including Pizarro, to accompany him on the last leg of this march to the sea. Even from that spot it still took the Spaniards and their native companions another four grueling days to reach the coast. Once they arrived at the bay they christened in honor of Saint Michael, Balboa waded out into the water with the flag of his homeland in one hand and his unsheathed sword in the other to claim the ocean and all the lands that it touched for his sovereign, King Ferdinand. After formally staking claim to the Other Sea, Balboa turned to face the shore and motioned for his comrades to come join him. They all tasted of the water, and its salty nature confirmed that this was indeed an ocean much like the Atlantic. The Spanish explorer gave his discovered Other Sea a proper name: El Mar del Sur (the Southern Sea). As excited as they surely must have been about their amazing discovery they could not help but be struck by the sobering realization that Asia was still a very long way off. Balboa's expedition confirmed what many had speculated for quite some time: the Indies that Columbus had discovered and a great many Spaniards had explored since were not the Indies proper. There was still another ocean of indeterminate breadth to be crossed before they could even begin to lay their hands on the true wealth of Asia.

Balboa's sole saving consolation was the titillating news that he was not very far from the golden kingdoms located somewhere to the south of that point. The explorers hastily reassembled the parts of the boats that had been carried across the isthmus on the backs of their Indian porters. However, their attempt to sail to the nearby Pearl Islands was thwarted by a sudden and violent storm that forced the small fleet back to the mainland. After much discussion, Balboa elected to postpone such a voyage until the coming of spring, a time the natives told him when the turbulent waters of this region were much calmer. They marched back to Darién with dreams of a later return with much sturdier ships that could carry them to those wondrous lands where the rivers ran rich with gold.

THE EXECUTIONER

Vasco Balboa and the remainder of his expeditionary force returned to the colony of Darién on January 19, 1514, but before he had an opportunity to embark on a second expedition to the Sea of the South the new colonial governor Pedro Arias Dávila, or Pedrarias as he is more commonly known, arrived along with his wife to stake his claim to the vast fortunes of the New World. An armada of twenty Spanish vessels with nearly two thousand colonists aboard and loaded with all necessary provisions for the establishment of a thriv-

VASCO NUÑEZ DE BALBOA.
Descubridor del Mar del Sur. Nació en Xerez de Estremadura en el año de 1475 y fué muerto en Acla en 1517.

Vasco Núñez de Balboa: His discovery of the "Other Sea" proved that the West Indies were still an ocean apart from the true Indies.

ing new colony landed at Darién in July of that same year. Included among those who sailed with Pedrarias were a number of future conquistadors who would leave their mark upon the New World, a list which included such notable men as Francisco Vásquez Coronado de Veldes, Hernando de Soto, and Bernal Díaz del Castillo. What disturbed Balboa and his loyal troops even more than the arrival of Governor Pedrarias was the unwelcome return of Martín Enciso, their former commander, who had sailed to Darién to assist in the founding of Castilla del Oro.

By graciously surrendering his command and pledging his complete allegiance to the newly appointed governor, Balboa managed, much to the disappointment of a vengeful-minded Enciso, to momentarily gain the favor of Pedrarias. He did not hesitate to inform his superiors of their discovery of the Southern Sea and the rumors of a great and powerful civilization that could be reached by way of this newfound body of water. Pedrarias was somewhat perturbed by the news that Vasco had already discovered the Other Sea—a glory which he felt should have been reserved for him alone. By cunningly appealing to the governor's enormous ego and avaricious nature, Balboa not only saved his own neck but also the lives of all the other men who had participated in the rebellion that deposed and deprived Enciso of his command, including Pizarro.

It did not take very long for Balboa to realize that Governor Pedrarias was a man who possessed few, if any, admirable traits. At the advanced age of seventy, Pedrarias certainly seemed to be an unlikely choice for such an important and demanding position, but like so many men placed in positions of power he had made the right royal connections to earn himself such an important appointment. In Pedrarias's case opportunity arose in part because of his previous military service against the Moors at Granada and North Africa, but mostly it came about because of his marriage to Doña Isabel de Bobadilla y Peñalosa, who had been Queen Isabella's lady-in-waiting. As for Balboa, Pedrarias first stripped him of his command and then confiscated all of his personal property, items which were later dispersed amongst Martín Enciso and all who had a complaint against him. Even Balboa's home was seized in order that it might serve as the permanent residence of the new governor. Enciso sought to exact his revenge by having Balboa placed under arrest on a charge that he had grossly overstepped his authority when he banished Diego de Nicuesa from the settlement. His accuser alleged that this was a wrongful act that contributed to the premature death of the rightful governor of this land. The newly appointed chief judge who had sailed over with the new governor's fleet objectively weighed all the evidence at hand and after careful consideration dismissed all the charges brought against Balboa, a decision that obligated an outraged Enciso to release the prisoner at once. Balboa was then permitted to rejoin the military but only as a demoted member of the rank and file.

The new governor's first order of business was to amass as much gold as possible from the natives and he was willing to use any means available to achieve this objective. Failure to comply with Pedrarias's covetous demands either condemned the Indians under his jurisdiction to a lifelong sentence of Spanish servitude or, as was often the case, a swift but brutal execution. The use of torture was condoned by the governor for the explicit purpose of discovering the precise whereabouts of more gold. A great number of natives were either roasted alive, suffocated at the end of a rope, or fed to ravenous canines not only as a means to elicit information concerning the precise location of more gold but also to serve as a form of entertainment for the bloodthirsty Pedrarias. The peaceful and rewarding alliances that had been forged previously with the local caciques were effectively voided by these barbaric acts perpetrated by Pedrarias and his soldiers. Even Balboa commented that the Indians were suddenly transformed into "fierce lions" who waged war against the harsh policies of the acting governor.

When the news of Balboa's discovery of the Other Sea reached Spain a grateful King Ferdinand rewarded him with the title of "*Adelantado* [Advancer] of the Southern Sea" and deeded him a vast tract of the land he had already settled. Anxious to return to El Mar del Sur, Balboa began making plans for another march to the sea, and once he had returned to those shores he proposed to sail south in search of the legendary "Kingdoms of Gold." Jealous of the titles and accolades that were suddenly bestowed upon Balboa, Pedrarias did everything in his power to make sure his junior officer received no further favors from the Crown. The governor was adamant in his refusal to grant Balboa any soldiers for his expedition and when the stubborn Pedrarias refused to listen to reason the *adelantado* simply appealed directly to King Ferdinand for help. In his letter to the king of Spain, Balboa wrote of how Pedrarias continually found ways to impede his efforts to return to the Southern Sea; in addition, he provided a detailed account of the many horrendous atrocities that had been committed against the Indians by direct order of the governor. Not to be outdone, Pedrarias wrote his own letter to the Crown filled with words carefully crafted to discredit the deeds, as well as to assassinate the character, of Vasco Núñez de Balboa. Ultimately, King Ferdinand ruled in favor of Balboa and ordered Pedrarias to furnish him with whatever provisions or men the *adelantado* might require for his return journey to El Mar del Sur. As a gesture of his newly found goodwill Pedrarias betrothed to Balboa his daughter, who at that moment still resided in Spain. But this was nothing more than a ruse, contrived in conjunction with Pedrarias's wife, to momentarily gain Balboa's trust.

Now that the way to the Southern Sea was more familiar to them, Balboa and his men had a much easier trek across the narrow isthmus that separates the world's two great oceans. Hundreds of natives once again accompanied him on the journey, and on their backs were carried the many parts needed to construct four sailing vessels of rather respectable size. Shortly after their arrival at the shoreline of El Mar del Sur, Balboa's expedition came across a group of Indian traders who had knowledge of a magnificent empire to the south. They claimed that the residents of this land lived in elegant houses, dressed themselves in elaborate and colorful clothing, and drank from cups and ate off plates made of pure gold. The natives even drew for the *adelantado* and his men a picture of a llama, which to Spanish eyes resembled the familiar camel, the beast of burden commonly used by Arab traders to transport the magnificent treasures of Africa, Asia, and the Middle East. Spurred on by these fabulous tales of wealth, Balboa and his men hurriedly reconstructed their ships; once this task was completed, they set sail on a southern course for the great empire of gold. Even with these larger and sturdier boats, Balboa once again could not overcome the ill winds and strong currents inherent to this region. No matter how hard they tried, the Spaniards could not navigate past the Pearl Islands and after many attempts they were forced to return to the mainland. Reluctantly admitting defeat, Balboa abandoned his ambitious quest and led his men back to the Spanish settlement.

Meanwhile, Governor Pedrarias, who could never quite bring himself to forgive his son-in-law for writing to King Ferdinand about his various indiscretions with the natives, conspired with a number of his officers and appointed officials to have Balboa arrested on a trumped-up charge of plotting to lead an armed rebellion to overthrow the present regime. Luring the unsuspecting Balboa to a meeting at the settlement of Acla, Pedrarias awaited his arrival with a squadron of soldiers under the command of the crafty Francisco Pizarro, a soldier who was always aware of which was the right hand to kiss. When Balboa reached out with open arms to embrace his father-in-law, Pedrarias gave an orchestrated nod to Pizarro, who in turn issued a signal to his men. The soldiers quickly seized the *adelantado* of the Southern Sea; then they placed him in chains, informed him of his many crimes, and proceeded to march him back to Darién to await what was already a preordained fate. Tried for treason before a select jury of the governor's most loyal servants, Balboa found it impossible to mount a defense that could save either himself or his four comrades from the cavalcade of accusations hurled at them by their accusers.

The trial, the sentence, and the execution of said sentence all occurred with amazing swiftness. Pedrarias was determined to conclude this matter before any of Balboa's loyal soldiers had a chance to come to the *adelantado*'s aid. Found guilty of treason, Balboa and his comrades were ordered to be executed that very evening. On January 12, 1519, just as the sun began to set, Vasco Núñez de Balboa and the four other captured Spaniards were led to the public square to face the sharp blade of the executioner's ax. The bloody torsos of the five men were left to rot in the open courtyard so that the buzzards might enjoy the opportunity to feast upon them. Their severed heads were impaled on long poles and prominently displayed to serve as a gruesome reminder of the harsh penalty one could expect for having displeased the governor.

Shortly after Balboa's execution, Pedrarias moved his headquarters to the Southern Sea side of the isthmus where he transformed a small native village into the city of Panama. It was fear, more than respect, that instilled an intense loyalty in the soldiers who served under Pedrarias. The mere mention of the name of this elderly conquistador was enough to cause even the most battle-hardened soldier to tremble in his armor. Everyone knew of the terrible and swift wrath of this merciless man, and none could ever forget the harsh punishment he had exacted from his own son-in-law.

Showing absolutely no interest in the fabled cities that had captured the imagination of Balboa, the governor sought to satisfy his insatiable greed for gold by concentrating his efforts on conquests to the north. His armies stormed their way through Panama, Costa Rica, Nicaragua, and Honduras, looting every village and killing or enslaving every native they happened to encounter along the way. Their trail of death and destruction eventually led them to another band of conquistadors who were creating a similar path southward. A long and bloody war soon ensued between the armies of Hernán Cortés, the conqueror of Mexico, and the armies of Governor Pedrarias for control of Central America.

Unfortunately for his enemies, and they numbered many, Governor Pedrarias outlived most of them, clinging to life until finally expiring at the ripe old age of ninety-one. As for Francisco Pizarro, he found his path to fame and fortune by continuing the quest first begun by Vasco Núñez de Balboa. In the year 1532 Pizarro landed at Peru, and, after having ascertained that the tales spoken of by the Indians at the shores of Panama were indeed true, he led an army numbering less than two hundred men across the towering peaks of the Andes Mountains to conquer the golden kingdoms of the Incas.

TWELVE

The Voyage of Magellan

Wounds That Never Heal

After nearly seven years of faithful service in the naval campaigns that were waged to gain control of the lucrative East Indies trade, Ferdinand Magellan returned home to his native Portugal. During his illustrious overseas career he had proved himself, on many an occasion, to be a sailor of extraordinary skill as well as a man possessed of great courage, in both character and deed. Convinced that this was now an opportune moment to renegotiate what he believed to be his true worth to the Crown, a confident Captain Magellan presented himself before the royal court at Lisbon to submit his applications for a promotion in rank and an increase in salary. He also sought the right to command his own expedition to the Moluccas, where he hoped to join up with his good friend Francisco Serrão, who was leisurely basking in the warmth and wealth of the island paradise of Ternate. The captain's pride, however, was cut to the quick when King Manuel the Fortunate denied each and every one of his requests and adamantly refused to entertain any of his subsequent demands for another audience.

Seeking solace from the unexpected cold shoulder of an ungrateful king, Ferdinand Magellan enlisted in Portugal's latest ongoing struggle to drive the Moors out of North Africa. Entertaining the notion that he might capture the king's favor by once again distinguishing himself in battle, Ferdinand sailed in 1513 aboard the fleet that participated in the bloody Battle of Azamor. While the Moroccan stronghold there eventually fell into the hands of the Portuguese there were minor skirmishes with the Moors that continued for sometime thereafter. During one such episode Magellan was struck in the leg by the sharp lance of an attacking Moor, a penetrating thrust that was severe enough to cripple him for life. Once he was capable of returning to duty, the slightly lame Ferdinand was given an assignment as the officer in charge of prisoners and confiscated plunder. When a number of horses mysteriously turned up missing, Magellan was held accountable. The incident armed his envious enemies who spread malicious rumors that he had pocketed money by selling guarded property back to the enemy. These accusations received an official sanction when Magellan's superior officer issued an order calling for his immediate court-martial.

Refusing to allow his good name to be sullied by these outrageous criminal charges, Magellan ignored the authority of the military court and sailed directly to Lisbon to personally address his grievances to the king. However, preceding his arrival at court was a letter sent by Magellan's commanding officer that fully detailed the serious nature of the charges levied against him along with the additional charge that the officer in question was now officially A.W.O.L. from his post. Refusing to grant the insubordinate officer an audience, King Manuel ordered Magellan to return at once to Morocco to stand trial. Compelled by a sense of duty to comply with the king's order Ferdinand immediately sailed back to Africa to face his accusers. Upon his arrival he found that the commander had a sudden change of heart and was now willing to forgive and forget the charges of theft, desertion, and trading with the enemy. But the proud Magellan demanded a forum by which he could vindicate himself of these spurious charges. It was a request that his superior honored by reinstating the court-martial proceedings against him. Speaking on his own behalf, Magellan put on a stalwart defense that succeeded in convincing everyone sitting in judgment that he was innocent of all the charges brought against him.

Ferdinand Magellan returned to Lisbon in the early months of 1516 to renew his petition for greater recognition and a larger share of money for his many years of dedicated service to Portugal. Magellan's perseverance eventually gained him an audience before King Manuel, but this personal appearance before the monarch fared no better than any of his previous attempts to gain the king's favor. The monarch, in successive order, declined Ferdinand's request for a promotion in rank, an increase in allowance, and a reassignment to the Moluccas. Their obvious clash in personalities came to head when Magellan asked Manuel for permission to offer his services to another sovereign. Such an unexpected request managed to arouse the king's anger; with great disdain in his voice, he told Magellan to do as he pleased for it mattered little to him. Before withdrawing, Magellan, in a final gesture of respect, bent to kiss the royal hand but the obviously annoyed Manuel refused to even offer it to him. Rising from this final rebuff, Ferdinand turned his back on the king and stormed out of the royal court.

During his stay at Lisbon, Magellan had made the acquaintance of Rui Faleiro, a mathematician who had recently been rejected for the position of royal astronomer of Portugal. It was Faleiro who opened Magellan's eyes to the possibilities of reaching the Indies by sailing westward across the recently discovered "South Sea." By his calculations this body of water was but a few thousand miles across—a much shorter and, very probably, a far safer route to the Indies than the long and treacherous trek around the vast continent of Africa. In order to reach the East Indies by sailing westward all Magellan would have to do was either find a way around or locate a passage through the extensive land barrier known as the New World. Magellan also concluded, on the basis of Faleiro's figures, that Portugal did not have the right to claim the spice laden Moluccas as their own because they were actually situated in the hemisphere that belonged to Spain, as ordained by the 1494 Treaty of Tordesillas. Such reasoning helps to explain Magellan's eagerness to seek the patronage of another king and why Spain became his kingdom of choice.

Deciding to accept an open invitation that had been extended to him by a pair of estranged Portuguese sailors who had taken up residence at Seville, Magellan crossed over to Spain, never to set foot again on his native soil. In October of 1517 he arrived at the home of Diogo Barbosa, a seasoned sailor who had been to the shores of Brazil and who was now an important official involved in the oversight of Spanish voyages to the New World, and his son Duarte, who like Magellan, had served in the royal navy under Francisco de Almeida. Also following in the footsteps of Magellan was his new-found partner and friend, the scholar Rui Faleiro. While at Seville, Ferdinand met and fell in love with Beatriz Barbosa, the daughter of Diogo, and following a whirlwind courtship the two were united in marriage.

In January of 1518, Magellan, along with his bride Beatriz and his associate Faleiro, set out from Seville for the royal court currently in session at Valladolid. Once he had managed to convince Juan Rodriguez de Fonseca, the bishop of Burgos and the founder of the Council of the Indies, as to the soundness of his westward plan to sail to the Indies, Magellan had little trouble gaining an audience with the Spanish monarch. Spain now had a new king, the young Charles (Carlos) I who had inherited the throne following the death in January 1516 of King Ferdinand, his maternal grandfather. Magellan stood before the king's council with a leather globe of the world that was a near exact replica of the Nurnberg globe constructed by the famed German cartographer Martin Behaim and secured under lock and key inside the royal map room at Lisbon. Pointing to a strait that was painted on his globe, Magellan showed how this secret passage, which flowed from the great Atlantic Ocean to the recently discovered Southern Sea, would finally give Spain access to the real Spice Islands. Faleiro furthered their cause by explaining how his calculations proved that Portugal knowingly laid claim to islands that clearly resided within the territorial waters of Spain. Besides giving testimony of his own rewarding experiences in that part of the world, Magellan brought along a letter from his good friend Francisco Serrão, who was still stationed at the Moluccas, to further emphasize just how bountiful these lands truly were. He read aloud carefully selected excerpts that provided the assembly with a vivid firsthand account of the abundant wealth and beauty that was just waiting to be claimed by Spain.

Ferdinand Magellan: Motivated by a desire to reunite with his good friend Francisco Serrão, who had settled on one of the Spice Islands, the Portuguese sailor switched his allegiance to neighboring Spain to obtain the necessary support for his epic voyage.

The presentation made by Ferdinand Magellan and Rui Faleiro certainly caught the attention of the Spanish court. However, there were still a number of skeptics who remembered, and made it a point to remind the young king, that it was not all that long ago that another charismatic foreigner had made a similar promise to the Catholic monarchs that he could reach the riches of the Orient by sailing in the direction of the setting sun. What concerned many Spanish officials the most was the fear that Magellan's proposed sailing route would tread upon the already established Portuguese trade routes of that region, and in so doing, he might unintentionally set off an international incident. Visions of great wealth and the powerful influence of Bishop Fonseca, respectively, outweighed and overcame these concerns of the royal court, as well as the protest being lodged by incensed Portuguese diplomats, thereby clearing the way for young King Charles I to approve Magellan's plan to sail to the Spice Islands.

On March 22, 1518, Magellan and Faleiro were presented with a con-

tract to sign that authorized them to hunt for a Spanish route to the Moluccas. The Crown agreed to provide the explorers with five ships and whatever funds they needed to fully equip the expedition. As an added incentive
for the successful completion of their mission, Magellan and Faleiro were
to receive a substantial share of the profits that everyone expected them to
earn from this voyage, as well as the governorship to any unclaimed islands
they happened to discover along the way. As expected, Magellan was named
as the commander of the fleet, an appointment that endowed him with the
highly respected rank of captain-general.

Magellan's Strait

PROBING FOR A PASSAGE

The Casa de Contratación, or the India House as it was sometimes
referred to, was charged with the task of furnishing Ferdinand Magellan and
Rui Faleiro with five fully stored and manned ships for their daring voyage.
Financing for this grand venture was to be supplied in part by the wealthy
Jakob Fugger II. The two explorers were pleased to learn that the ships that
they were to be provided with were Spanish nãos, spacious vessels that could
easily accommodate the large amount of precious cargoes that they fully
expected to haul back to Spain. However, a closer inspection by Magellan
revealed that all of the five ships granted to him were vessels well past their
prime and therefore would require extensive repairs before they could be
deemed seaworthy for such a long and arduous voyage. Though his discovery of the true condition of these vessels was certainly disappointing, it
should not have come as a surprise to Magellan that the Crown was less than
willing to relegate any of its superior ships to an expedition fraught with
such uncertainty.

Recruiting a competent and reliable crew presented its own unique set
of problems for Ferdinand Magellan. As part of their effort to conceal the
true nature of this expedition from neighboring Portugal, the Spanish
Crown carefully avoided any public mention of their mission. This shroud
of secrecy was even extended to the crew, as recruits were asked to sign on
for a two year tour of duty to a destination that would only be revealed
once the ships were well out to sea. Unfortunately, their little ruse failed
to fool everyone, especially a number of prominent Portuguese officials who
promptly issued a dire warning to Magellan and the Spanish Crown that this

voyage had better not encroach upon "the demarcation and limits of the most serene king of Portugal." Magellan's associates clearly fared much better at keeping their own countrymen in the dark, and Magellan, just like Columbus before him, found very few Spaniards willing to follow a foreigner into the vast unknown. Forced to recruit mostly from a supply of men who had sailed under the flags of other nations, the commander eventually succeeded in mustering a crew of two hundred and sixty-five able bodied men. His cosmopolitan crew was comprised of a number of Greeks, Germans, Italians, French, Malays, Africans, Basques, Flemings, Dutch, Spaniards, Portuguese and even one Englishman. Thirty-seven of the enlisted men were fellow Portuguese, including his brother-in-law Duarte Barbosa. The large number of Portuguese sailors recruited by Magellan was a cause for some concern at the Spanish court. Fearing that once out to sea these fellow Iberians just might forget their newly sworn fealty, several members of the king's inner circle insisted on the appointment of full-blooded Spanish officers to sail along on this voyage. Magellan had little say over the appointment of Gaspar de Quesada, Luis de Mendoza, and Juan de Cartagena as captains aboard three of his ships.

Also included on the fleet's roster was a Venetian by the name of Antonio Pigafetta who, after considerable persuasion on his part, received Magellan's permission to sail along as an unpaid observer. Pigafetta was a wealthy gentleman who had an almost obsessive fascination with the daring sea voyages being undertaken by sailors who hailed from the shores of Portugal and Spain and longed to join in on such a grand adventure himself. By some accounts, Antonio Pigafetta was a spy sent by the merchants of Venice to learn more about Spanish efforts to establish trade relations with the kingdoms of Asia. Regardless of what was his true motive for joining the expedition the Venetian quickly gained the respect and acceptance of both the crew and his commander by pulling his own weight during the journey. His tremendous regard for Ferdinand Magellan can be seen in the detailed journal he kept about their long voyage, a daily diary from which he later penned *Primo Viaggo Intorno al Mondo*, or the *First Voyage Round the World*, a classic work that provides a firsthand account of one of mankind's greatest adventures.

Conspicuously absent from the list of those who sailed on that day was the name of Rui Faleiro. Magellan's partner suffered from a mental illness that had become more pronounced during their extended period of preparation. Obsessed with the thought that others were attempting to steal his plans, as well as being plagued by ominous premonitions of his own death on this voyage, Faleiro had begun to slip into the dark realm of insanity. When word of Faleiro's deteriorating mental state reached the ears of the royal court, Magellan's trusted associate was ordered to remain behind. Faleiro's condition would continue to worsen and many of his remaining days were spent either in jail or inside institutions for the insane until his death in the year 1544.

After eighteen months of repairs, recruiting, stocking, and planning Ferdinand Magellan's fleet was finally ready to set sail for the Spice Islands. In addition to dealing with Portuguese agents bent on sabotaging his efforts, Magellan had to contend with prejudicial bureaucrats determined to minimize his authority during this extensive period of preparation. The five ships were loaded with enough victuals calculated to last the crew for a voyage of precisely two years in length. In addition to the necessary food and provisions the boats carried tremendous stores of items to be used for barter with local inhabitants at their intended destination, the Moluccas. Twenty thousand hawk bells, five hundred pounds of glass beads, four hundred inexpensive German knives, hundreds of brass bracelets, five hundred small hand mirrors, a vast quantity of velvet, and nearly two thousand pounds of quicksilver (mercury) were included in their inventory for trade with the natives of the Spice Islands as well as any other lands they might happen upon. Each of Magellan's ships towed a batel, or long boat, as well as several small boats stored aboard deck.

At the Crown's behest, Ferdinand Magellan and his ships finally departed from the docks of Seville. However, the small fleet sailed down river only as far as Sanlúcar de Barrameda where they stopped to take on more provisions. Magellan remained there for another five weeks before leaving the mouth of the Guadalquivir River. The principal reason for their extended stay at Sanlúcar de Barrameda was the disturbing discovery that unscrupulous suppliers at Seville had sold them rancid meat and inedible biscuits. He rectified the bad food problem but it was not until they had reached the coast of South America that he learned that many of these suppliers had short-changed him on the weight of his provisions. Instead of enough food to sustain the crew for an additional eighteen months at sea they discovered that they had enough victuals for but six more months. On the 20th of September 1519 the flotilla finally floated onto the waters of the Atlantic. Magellan led the way aboard his flagship the *Trinidad*, and was closely followed by the *Santiago*, the *Victoria*, the *Concepción*, and the *San Antonio* which were under the respective commands of João Serrão, Luis de Mendoza, Gaspar de Quesada, and Juan de Cartagena. From Sanlúcar the expedition sailed south to the Canaries before heading on a southwestward course to locate the strait that would empty their ships into the sea that Vasco Núñez de Balboa had recently claimed for Spain.

It was customary on voyages such as this for captains to bring their vessel alongside the designated flagship at the approach of evening in order to pay their proper respect to the fleet's commanding officer and to learn of any new directives. When the *San Antonio* pulled alongside the *Trinidad*, the Spanish captain Juan de Cartagena failed to address Ferdinand Magellan in the required manner. The customary greeting was "God keep you, sir Captain General and master, and good company." But Cartagena had committed two serious omissions of proper salutation. He sent in his stead a junior officer who, in accordance with the orders of his own captain, purposely omitted the rank of general in his greeting to Magellan. This oversight elicited a prompt and strong rebuke from the captain-general. Magellan told Cartagena that henceforth he expected to be properly greeted by the captain himself. But on the following evening an arrogant Cartagena willfully omitted the proper salutation once again, and after he repeated this offense on the third successive evening, Magellan decided the time had come to teach this disobedient Spanish captain the meaning of respect.

On the fourth day Magellan called for a meeting of all his captains aboard the *Trinidad*. Magellan calmly listened to Cartagena's feeble excuses and his list of complaints, that is until the Spanish captain proclaimed that he would no longer follow Magellan's orders. Anticipating such a response from Cartagena, Magellan signaled to Gonzalo Gómez de Espinosa who, along with Duarte Barbosa and Cristóbal Robelo, pointed their unsheathed swords at the insubordinate captain. The captain-general stripped Cartagena of his command and then placed him under arrest. To dispel any suspicions of prejudice, Magellan appointed another Spaniard, Antonio de Coca, as interim captain of the *San Antonio*. The commander then turned the prisoner over to Luis de Mendoza, the Spanish captain of the *Victoria*. While many of the Spaniards were displeased with Magellan's seemingly draconian measures against an insubordinate officer, they all knew this was not the proper time or place to challenge his authority: a more opportune moment was sure to present itself on a voyage of such length.

On the 8th of December, nearly two months after having cast off from the Canary Islands, Magellan and his crew finally caught sight of land. The ships dropped anchor at the easternmost point of Brazil, very near to where the present city of Recife now stands. Fearing to linger too long at what was clearly territory that belonged to Portugal, Magellan made only a brief stopover before continuing southward in search of a passage to the "Other Sea." Five days later, on the 13th of December, the flotilla sailed into a breathtakingly beautiful harbor they named Santa Luzia, unaware of the fact that this bay had been explored and christened with the name of Rio de Janeiro several years earlier by Gonzalo Coehlo and Amerigo Vespucci. Besides the spectacular view, Magellan and his crew found other reasons to extend their stay at the Bay of Rio de Janeiro. Shortly after their arrival the explorers encountered the native Guaraní Indians, whom they found to be both cordial in their manner and extremely generous in their trade with them. To the great delight of Magellan's crew the Guaraní were willing to swap female companionship for just about any kind of Spanish trinket. The cheap German knives they had brought along were offered as tribute to the brothers and husbands of the Guaraní women who consented to having sexual intercourse with the love starved members of the expedition. Most of the crew, including the priests on board, save for Magellan, indulged in repeated sexual delights for close to a fortnight. While they certainly enjoyed the hospitality of their generous hosts the Spaniards were horrified to learn of the Guaraní tribal custom of feasting upon the flesh of their enemies. Antonio Pigafetta would record in his journal: "They did not eat the whole body of the man taken but eat it piece by piece. They cut him up in pieces, which they put to dry in the chimney, and every day they cut off a small piece and ate it with their ordinary food to call to mind their enemies."

Anxious to resume his mission, Magellan led his fleet out of the Bay of Rio de Janeiro on the 26th of December and continued southward in search of the elusive *paso*. Every bay and every river they came upon was thoroughly explored either by ship or long boat to determine whether or not it was the passage that would take them to the other side of the world. Again and again they discovered little more than their own disappointment. Magellan and most of his crew became convinced that their long search was finally over when they sailed into an enormous estuary formed by the raging waters of the Paraná, Paraguay, Uruguay and a number of other smaller rivers which converge at that very spot to empty into the Atlantic. Magellan ordered the captain of the *Santiago*, João Serrão, who was a relative of Magellan's good friend Francisco Serrão, to investigate this possible passage while he continued to probe southward with the rest of the ships. After only two days of sailing along this arm of the sea, Captain Serrão rejoined the fleet with the disappointing news that the gulf he explored merely led to a freshwater river, a sure sign that this was not the passage they sought.

Captain Serrão and his crew had sailed into the Rio de la Plata, a region first explored by a Portuguese expedition led by both Gonzalo Coelho and Amerigo Vespucci in 1502. Both of these men knew they had trespassed onto the Spanish side of the demarcation line as evidenced by the fact that neither explorer bothered to lay claim to their spectacular discovery. Fourteen years later, Juan Díaz de Solís, who had replaced Vespucci as Spain's pilot major, led his own expedition in search of the elusive southwest passage to the Indies, and by closely following the path of his predecessor he managed to arrive at nearly the same spot. After navigating a brief stretch of the Uruguay River, Solís and eight other sailors rowed ashore to officially claim this land for Spain. Shortly after they made landfall a wandering party of Charrua warriors emerged suddenly from the jungle and, without any provocation from the Spaniards or hesitation on their own part, fell upon the sailors with a savage fury. The brutal attack occurred in full view of those still on board the ships, but the sailors could only look on helplessly as their comrades were butchered to pieces and, as if this was not terrifying enough, they were forced to watch in horror as the victorious Charrua began to gnaw away at the flesh and bones of their victims. With their commander now dead the Spanish sailors quickly retreated from the Uruguay River and immediately set a course for home. One member of the Spanish shore party, Francisco del Puerto, was spared by the Charrua warriors and spent the next decade as their prisoner until he was rescued by Sebastian Cabot, the son of the explorer John Cabot, who sailed under the colors of the Spanish flag on that particular expedition. Cabot's mission was to sail directly to the Indies for the express purpose of promoting commercial ties between Spain and the Orient, but he was diverted from this course by natives' tales of vast amounts of silver and gold that supposedly flowed from the region he dubbed the Rio de la Plata.

With the fast approach of winter in the southern hemisphere and a rising level of discontent brewing amongst the members of his crew, a frustrated Magellan turned his attention toward locating a suitable site where the fleet could safely wait out the change in seasons. On the last day of March 1520 he finally located such a spot at San Julian, a harbor situated along the coast of Patagonia and not too far from the strait that had continued to elude him up to this point. When Magellan informed the crew of his change in plans a number of sailors began to grumble about the captain's decision, claiming they would rather return home or risk continuing forward than have to spend the entire winter at San Julian. When several of the more vocal crew members persisted in their complaints the captain-general settled the issue by having them placed under arrest. With order finally restored, the rest of the crew, with the exception of the Spanish captains, complied with Magellan's orders to go ashore for the celebration of Palm Sunday Mass and to begin the construction of temporary shelters.

The Spanish captains, Luis Mendoza, Gaspar de Quesada, and the deposed captain Juan de Cartagena, had all been secretly plotting a takeover for some time, and now they saw an opportune moment to put their mutinous scheme in motion. It was a relatively simple plan: take control of the fleet, kill Magellan, and then sail back to Spain. On the night following Mass, Quesada and some thirty of his rebellious sailors rowed quietly toward the *San Antonio*, and once alongside they were helped on deck by another mutineer already on board, Geronimo Gurra. Busting into the cabin of Álvaro de Mesquita, a Portuguese relative of Magellan who had recently been selected by the captain-general to replace the Spaniard Antonio de Coca as the captain of the *San Antonio*, they awakened the officer from his sleep and then proceeded to clap him in irons. Back on deck, Quesada announced to the still groggy, but entirely surrounded, crew that he had assumed full command of the *San Antonio* and they could either choose to remain free men by joining his band of sailors or spend the rest of the voyage chained below deck alongside their deposed captain. Juan de Lloriaga, the ship's master-at-arms, ignored the demands made by Gaspar de Quesada and bellowed out a distress call in the general direction of the rest of the fleet. An enraged Quesada plunged his sword deep into the chest of Lloriaga but the wounded officer continued to cry out the alarm. It would take five more penetrating thrusts of Quesada's sword to silence forever the voice of the loyal Lloriaga. With the *San Antonio* now securely in Quesada's hands, several captured sailors chose to join the rebellion; but a great many decided to remain devoted to Mesquita and Magellan and therefore, just as promised, were chained in irons and thrown below deck.

Magellan awoke at the break of dawn only to learn of the unexpected capture of three of his ships during the night and the disconcerting news that the mutinous Spanish captains now meant to take control of both his ship and the *Santiago*. During that fateful night, Luis Mendoza of the *Victoria*, Gaspar de Quesada of the *San Antonio*, and Juan de Cartagena as the self-appointed captain of the *Concepción* had strategically maneuvered their vessels in a manner that appeared to form an insurmountable blockade that barred any possible means of escape for the two Portuguese captains. News of the night's dramatic turn of events reached Magellan with the arrival of a small boat that had been rowed over by six of Quesada's sailors. The rebel faction presented Magellan with a letter from their captain, which called for the captain-general's immediate and unconditional surrender. Stalling for time, Magellan sent these men back to Quesada with a note stating that he would be willing to discuss the matter with him aboard the *Trinidad*. Fearing that their former commander was laying a trap, Quesada had the six sailors return with a letter declining his offer to meet face to face and restating his previous demand for the unconditional surrender of both the *Trinidad* and the *Santiago*.

While Quesada's men were steadily rowing toward the *Trinidad*, Magellan huddled with two of his most trusted officers, brother-in-law Duarte Barbosa and master-at-arms Gonzalo Gómez de Espinosa, and together they came up with a daring scheme, one which they hoped would counter the momentum and direction of this mutiny. Luckily for the crew of the *Trinidad*, the rebel's skiff pulled up along the side of their boat which was blocked from the view of those on board the *San Antonio*. Quesada's six messengers were pulled aboard the boat and immediately taken prisoner by the crew of the *Trinidad*. Espinosa and five other loyal sailors took their place on the craft carrying with them a message from Magellan along with some very well concealed weapons. Knowing that his men would be recognized as impostors before they ever reached the San Antonio, Magellan instructed them to row instead towards the *Victoria* to deliver his ultimatum to Captain Mendoza. Following in the shadows of Espinosa's craft was a long boat from the *Trinidad* being rowed ever so stealthily by Duarte Barbosa and fifteen other well armed sailors.

As they came near Mendoza's ship Gonzalo Espinosa held Magellan's letter high above his head and continued to wave it from side to side until he managed to catch the attention of the crew aboard the *Victoria*. While Mendoza and his men were distracted by the unexpected arrival of messengers alongside their ship, Barbosa and his men strategically positioned themselves on the other side of the *Victoria*. Once on deck, Espinosa handed the note over to Mendoza, who evidently found Magellan's reply quite amusing. As the Spanish captain burst into an uncontrollable fit of laughter Espinosa grabbed hold of him, pulled out his concealed dagger and plunged it hard and deep into Mendoza's throat. Even before the startled crew of the *Victoria* had time to react to the brutal assassination of their captain, Barbosa and his men were already aboard the vessel with their swords and firearms in hand. Caught off guard the mutineers immediately laid down their weapons and surrendered the ship to Espinosa and Barbosa.

Now that he had regained the advantage Magellan turned the tables on the mutineers by positioning his three ships in a manner that barred the escape of the *Concepción* and the *San Antonio* from the harbor. In the middle of the night a desperate Gaspar de Quesada decided he would try to break through Magellan's blockade. Once the *San Antonio* was within range of the *Trinidad*, Quesada issued the order to open fire, but none of the crew would obey his command. At that same moment, Magellan issued the same order, only his command was followed without question. After letting loose a volley of gunfire Magellan's sailors boarded the *San Antonio* and without encountering any resistance from its crew were able to quickly seize Quesada and place him in chains. The rebellion was quelled for good when on the following morning, just shortly after sunrise, Juan de Cartagena, realizing the utter hopelessness of his situation, surrendered the *Concepción* to Ferdinand Magellan.

It was Magellan's wish to mete out justice as swiftly as possible. He was also determined to administer a punishment that would be as brutal and painful as he believed the situation deserved. On the 4th of April a trial was held on land and the first defendant called to face the judgment of Magellan was the slain Luis Mendoza. After a reading of all the charges, the captain-general found the lifeless bloody body of Mendoza guilty of treason and ordered that his corpse be hanged and then drawn and quartered. The four quarters of his butchered body were to dangle from crudely constructed gibbets so that all could gaze upon the punishment doled out for the heinous crime of treason.

Gaspar de Quesada was the next mutineer summoned to face the ire of Ferdinand Magellan. Quickly found guilty of both treason and the calculated cold-blooded murder of Juan de Lloriaga, Quesada received the same sentence as the one pronounced just moments earlier against the corpse of Luis Mendoza. But Magellan had a difficult time finding anyone willing to act as Quesada's executioner. A traitor's death was a gruesome sentence to witness. In accordance with the custom of the time, the victim was first hung by the neck, but in a manner designed to prolong his suffering by strangulation. This meant that the condemned person was still alive when the executioner sliced open his belly and began to slowly draw the intestines from his writhing body. The final brutal act was known as quartering: a process whereby the traitor, regardless of whether he was still alive or already dead, had his arms and legs severed from his torso. When no one stepped forward to execute the imposed sentence, Magellan turned to Luis de Molina, Quesada's personal secretary, and offered him a full pardon if he would perform the task. Molina was quick to refuse the offer but when Magellan countered that he could spare Quesada much pain and suffering with a swift beheading from his sword, he paused to reconsider the proposal and to consult with the convicted Quesada. He begged his old friend to spare him the indignity and terrible pain of a traitor's death, and Molina felt compelled to grant the Spanish captain his last request. Once Quesada was beheaded his lifeless body was quartered and each limb was hoisted onto a separate pole.

Juan de Cartagena was also found guilty of treason but, because of his many prominent connections at court, was spared from the same grisly sentence that had just been imposed upon his fellow conspirators. As punishment for his role in the mutiny, Magellan decreed that Cartagena was to be marooned on the coast along with Padre Pedro Sánchez de Reina, a treacherous priest who had actively participated in the insurrection. Their fate—other than their eventual demise—remains a mystery. As for the forty-plus sailors and officers who had sided with the insurgent Spanish captains they were all found guilty of treason. Magellan purposely delayed pronouncement of their sentence so that they might wallow in thoughts of despair and fear before he finally decided to grant them a conditional pardon for their crimes. Included among those pardoned for their participation in the plot to overthrow Magellan was the pilot of the *Concepción*, Juan Sebastián de Elcano, one of the few men who lived long enough to complete the voyage around the earth. Forever grateful for his forgiveness, the crew remained faithful to Magellan until the very end.

Managing to put the recent insurrection behind them, Magellan and his crew returned to the difficult tasks at hand. They took to repairing their weather-worn ships and, in anticipation of the coming winter, hunted for food. Their favorite quarry turned out to be the bountiful but flightless penguins, whom the explorers referred to as black geese. While Magellan and most of the sailors stayed behind at Port San Julian, João Serrão and the crew of the *Santiago* continued to explore southward along the coast in search of the ever elusive passage. After more than a fortnight of battling storms and bone-chilling gale force winds, which were severe enough to restrict the distance of their travel to but a mere fifty miles, they were able to find sanctuary at the mouth of a river that the captain christened the Santa Cruz. The *Santiago* remained at this location for a full week before finally attempting a return to the sea. However, just as they sailed out of the estuary the Spanish vessel was slammed by winds powerful enough to drive the ship back into the shallow waters of the river. The sheer force of the waves ripped the rudder out from under the ship while above deck the howling winds blew away the boat's mast. Serrão and his crew strained with all their might to steer the ship toward a nearby sandbar and once there the men were able to abandon ship just moments before she broke apart from the impact of the unrelenting waves crashing against her hull. The storm's fury claimed the life of one sailor who drowned after he was knocked off deck by a wave that crashed into the side of the *Santiago*.

While the survivors were all thankful for having been spared from the terrible wrath of the sea the sailors soon realized that they were suddenly exposed to new and perhaps even greater perils. They found themselves stranded during the dead of winter, on the wrong side of the wide Santa Cruz River, with barely any provisions. Realizing that their only chance for survival was to somehow get word of their desperate plight to Magellan, Serrão and his crew constructed a crude raft made of wood salvaged from the strewn wreckage of the *Santiago*. Two volunteers guided the craft across the river, and once on the other side they marched north, in the general direction of Port San Julian. It took them eleven days to find their comrades and by that time the two wanderers were so starved and exhausted they were but a few steps away from death. Magellan immediately dispatched a rescue party and within a few weeks Serrão and his men were reunited with the rest of the crew.

During their stay at Port San Julian the Spanish explorers had a chance encounter that was to become the basis of a legend that would persist for many years thereafter. Sometime around the early part of June a number of curious, but friendly, natives strode into their camp and commenced trading with Magellan's sailors. What set these Indians apart from those encountered on any previous Spanish expedition in the New World was their tremendous height. The Arawaks and the Caribs were generally smaller than the average European, a height advantage that merely added to the Spaniards' air of superiority. But the Tehuelche Indians who inhabited the land known as Patagonia were from different stock and to the amazement of Magellan and his men they stood much taller than they. In his recollection of their very first encounter with these natives Antonio Pigafetta recorded that, "One day suddenly we saw a naked man of giant stature on the shore of the harbor, dancing, singing, and throwing dust on his head. When the giant was in the Captain General's and our presence, he marveled greatly, and made signs with one finger raised upward, believing that we had come from the sky. He was so tall that we reached only to his waist, and he was well proportioned."

Along with their towering stature these natives were endowed with enormous feet, a sight that inspired the awe-struck Spaniards to name these giant people Patagonians, the Spanish term for "big-footed people." Magellan managed to sever the friendly relations that had begun to blossom between both parties when he took two "Patagonian giants" as prisoners. It was his plan to bring them back to Spain as proof that what they had seen was actually true. Planning to take even more prisoners, Magellan sent João Lopes Carvalho and a small band of sailors to raid a nearby Patagonian village. The natives, however, fought back with such tenacity that the Spaniards were forced to retreat back to their camp with little to show for their effort except for the loss of one of their own. Neither of the two captured Patagonians would survive the long and arduous voyage that still lay ahead for Magellan and his band of explorers.

MAGELLAN'S STRAIT

On August 24, 1520, the marooned Juan de Cartagena and Padre Pedro Sánchez de Reina watched from ashore as Magellan's ships sailed from Port San Julian without them. The four ships coasted southward until they came upon the Santa Cruz River, a point where Magellan decided they would wait out the few remaining weeks of winter. On the 18th of October the fleet promptly weighed anchor and resumed their search for the strait to the "Other Sea." Three days later the fleet rounded the Cape of the Virgins and Magellan was rewarded with his first sight of the passage that would one day bear his name. Agreeing with Magellan's conclusion that this probably was the gateway to the Sea of the South, the pilot of the *San Antonio*, Esteban Gómez, recommended that they mark the location on their charts, but instead of attempting to steer through the ominous looking passage he proposed that the fleet should turn about and sail directly to the Moluccas by the known eastward path. Naturally, Magellan scoffed at Gómez's preposterous proposal.

The four ships sailed slowly along this winding course and when they reached what appeared to be a promising passageway Magellan sent the *San Antonio* on ahead to investigate while the rest of the fleet continued on its current course. A mutiny broke out on board the *San Antonio* when it became painfully clear that they had come upon another dead end. This time the rebellion was led by Esteban Gómez, the same sailor who had recently suggested that they should abandon this quest and who had also harbored a deep resentment toward Magellan ever since the captain-general overlooked him for the vacant post of captain aboard the *San Antonio*. Placing himself at the helm, Gómez had Magellan's appointed captain clapped in irons and then ordered the crew of fifty men aboard to reverse course and sail on a heading that was to eventually bring them back home to Spain.

When the *San Antonio* failed to return with news of its findings Magellan sailed back to the spot where they had parted company and then spent the next three weeks scouring the entire stretch of the strait in hopes of finding his lost vessel. Besides a genuine concern for the safety of the missing crew the primary reason for such a lengthy and exhaustive search was that the *San Antonio*, being the largest of the ships, carried a disproportionately large amount of their essential provisions. When his search failed to turn up any trace of the *San Antonio*, Magellan concluded that somehow and somewhere the ship had sunk to a watery grave, taking along with her everyone and everything on board.

The three remaining ships resumed their voyage, continuing to probe every nook and cranny of this water route, in the faint hope of finding the outlet that would lead them to the "Sea of the South." As they passed through the strait the sailors noticed an ominous sight emanating from the not so distant southern horizon. Over the period of several nights the fearful sailors had observed numerous fires burning off in the distance, a spectacle that caused many to conclude that they had sailed so far south that they were now in close proximity to the outer regions of Satan's cursed kingdom of

Hell. What they had actually seen was nothing more than the bonfires of the natives who lived at the extreme southern tip of South America. The Portuguese named this ominous location Tierra de los Fuegos, or Land of the Fires, and to this day the region is still referred to as Tierra del Fuego.

After having come upon yet another river that emptied into the strait, Magellan anchored his ship and went ashore to see if he could get a better fix on their present position. Following a page from the annals of Balboa's epic journey, Magellan climbed to the top of a nearby hill and as he peered out to the west he caught a glimpse of the blue Sea of the South. Ecstatic over the sight of what lay just ahead the captain-general rushed back to the ship to announce his discovery to the weary crew. Rejuvenated by these glad tidings, the crew rushed into action the moment Magellan issued the order to set sail.

On the 28th of November, after more than a month of navigating the winding 334 mile long channel that connects the two great oceans of the world, Magellan's ships finally sailed onto the waters of the Southern Sea. After having waged a long and wearisome battle against unusually strong currents, rapidly rising tides, fearsome williwaws—extremely strong gusts of wind that appear without warning and pack enough force to suddenly flip a vessel upside down—and their own growing sense of doubt many of the crew, including Magellan, wept tears of joy when they emerged from the waterway that emptied them onto the other side of the world. Their joyous celebration was accompanied by a spontaneous outbreak of song and dance as well as the random firing of their weapons. Marveling at how tranquil these waters appeared Magellan renamed this vast body of water El Mar Pacífico, or peaceful sea. As for the waterway he had just navigated the captain-general christened it the Strait of All Saints, but future cartographers and historians took to labeling it the Strait of Magellan—a fitting tribute to the man who had succeeded at bridging the waters of the Atlantic and Pacific oceans.

THIRTEEN

When the World Became Whole

The Sea of the South

TESTING THE LIMITS OF ENDURANCE

Before attempting a crossing of the newly named El Mar Pacífico, Ferdinand Magellan and his men made sure that they stocked the *Trinidad*, *Concepción*, and the *Victoria* with as much fish, fowl, and game as they could possibly catch and store. In an effort to escape the bitterly cold conditions that still hovered over this part of the southern hemisphere the explorers steered northward along the coast of present-day Chile, a stretch of land long known to the natives as Tchili—their term for snow. On the 22nd of December, after having sailed nearly 1,000 miles towards the north, Magellan and his sailors left the comforting sight of the South American coastline and veered westward into the vast unknown.

Unfortunately for these brave explorers, the route that Magellan had charted and strictly adhered to lay well beyond the sight of the many Pacific islands that could have served as way stations to support their basic needs. Day in and day out all that the men could see in every direction was a seemingly endless body of water. Adverse winds and contrary currents all contributed in part to the prolonged suffering that Magellan and his crew were forced to endure. The wretched condition of their badly weather-worn vessels made an already desperate situation all the more precarious. Even before they entered the Pacific Ocean their ships had already been ravaged by the usual effects associated with such an exceedingly long voyage, and once out in the open sea the vessels began to leak so badly that the pumps had to be manned constantly in order to keep the boats afloat.

Magellan's motley crew soon found themselves with a great deal more to grumble about. Their supply of edible food and drinkable water dwindled with each passing day. What little fresh food that remained aboard ship quickly rotted from prolonged exposure to the intense and unrelenting heat of the tropics. Once those perishable stores had vanished the sailors were then fed a diet of heavily salted meat and fish accompanied by tasteless dried biscuits. But over time even these standard forms of preservation broke down and turned to a disgusting slimy goo, or as Pigafetta recorded: "We were three months and twenty days without getting any kind of fresh food. We ate biscuit which was biscuit no longer but a powder full of worms." Even their fresh water had turned foul in both taste and smell, so much so that they could only beat its taste by holding their noses as they drank. With no islands in sight to provide them with desperately needed relief, many of the men begged the captain-general to abandon his quest and return to the known shores of South America. But they had long passed the dreaded point of no return; to turn back now meant certain death from starvation while continuing forward they still could cling to the faint hope of finding relief at the Spice Islands.

It was not until January 24, 1521, that the crew finally found something to rejoice about. For on that day the ships dropped anchor at the tiny island of Puka Puka, which they called St. Paul's, and once ashore they proceeded to stock up on what little nourishment this small isle had to offer—mostly bird eggs and shellfish. On February 4th they sighted Vostok Island but its terribly strong currents and treacherously rocky coastline prevented any possibility of their making a landfall at this island. The warm water surrounding Vostok Island was an inviting home to a great number of large sharks, a sight which prompted the sailors to christen this little rock in the sea the Isle of Sharks.

In addition to their lack of food and fresh water, the crew had to contend with the multitude of rats who boldly competed for both victuals and space aboard the ships. Since misery loves company, lice and fleas joined in and nearly ate the sailors alive. Magellan's ships had become an ideal breeding ground for disease, and for many, death soon became a welcome relief from such an agonizing ordeal. When the food finally ran out the starved sailors scrambled to eat sawdust or fought one another over the privilege to gnaw on the tasteless leather of the yardarms. Rats became a much sought after delicacy, and those who still had the strength to capture the elusive little rodents often turned a tidy profit by selling a share of their catch to the weaker sailors. But in short order, the fleet's company of rats were hunted into extinction.

The near unbearable stench of sickness and death aboard the three ships grew greater with each passing day. Weeks at sea with no fresh vegetables or fruit had given rise to the dreaded disease known as scurvy. For the afflicted sailors the first noticeable sign that they had been stricken with this mysterious malady was a painful swelling of their gums; shortly thereafter the rot spread rapidly, eventually rendering their gums entirely black with decay. At this stage the men could only watch in helpless horror as their teeth, which now had little to cling to, began falling from their infected mouths. Weakened by both hunger and disease many sailors lapsed into a coma—a sleep from which there was no awaking. Nineteen of Magellan's men were given a burial at sea during this grueling leg of the journey.

DISASTER IN THE PHILIPPINES

On March 6, 1521, after nearly three months of continuous sailing since their departure from the shores of South America, Ferdinand Magellan and his exhausted crew came upon the island of Guam, the largest and southernmost island of the Marianas chain. The Spanish explorers found the natives of this land to be quite friendly and extremely willing to share what little they possessed. But by the same token, these generous Polynesians expected the Spaniards to reciprocate in kind. Boarding the Spanish vessels in overwhelming numbers the curious natives generously helped themselves to just about any item they could carry back to their own boats, even taking the valuable longboat that was tied to the *Trinidad*, which they attached to a canoe and hurriedly towed back to their village. Infuriated by these blatant acts of thievery, Magellan took forty armed sailors ashore to lead an assault against the nearby native village. The vastly superior weapons of the Spaniards sent the frightened villagers scurrying for the safety of the jungle, but not before seven determined natives died in a desperate but futile attempt to defend their turf. In addition to reclaiming most of their stolen property, including their precious longboat, Magellan's men managed to confiscate a healthy haul of rice, coconuts, pigs, chickens, vegetables, fruits, and fresh water. Before returning to their ships, the captain-general ordered his men to set fire to the many huts that formed the village as well as the numerous canoes that were docked at the water's edge. Saying good riddance to the island Magellan referred to as the Isla de los Ladrones (Island of Thieves) he then resumed his search for the Spice Islands.

On the 16th of March, after nearly a week of relatively smooth sailing,

Magellan's ships reached the shores of Homonhon, one of the many small islands that are part of the archipelago known as the Philippines. Since many of his men were still suffering from the terrible effects of their prolonged voyage across the ocean, Magellan had his men erect a number of tents to serve as makeshift hospitals for the deathly ill. While enjoying a day of rest at this seemingly uninhabited island they were surprised by the sudden appearance of a small band of Filipino hunters. Fortunately for the Spaniards, Magellan's Malayan slave, Henrique, understood enough of the Tagalog tongue to serve as an interpreter. Noticing the wretched condition of these Spanish sailors the islanders took pity on them by leaving a generous portion of the fresh coconuts and fish they had brought with them. The Filipino men promised that they would return shortly with even more food. Grateful for their unsolicited acts of kindness, the sailors handed over some of their mirrors and caps to these friendly natives.

True to their word, the Filipinos returned seven days later in two canoes. Besides bringing more food and drink for the starving sailors they also brought along their tribal chief and several members of his royal entourage. While a sampling of the Filipino cuisine was certainly a welcome sight to the still recovering crew, the sailors found it extremely difficult to take their eyes off the many golden ornaments that adorned the bodies of the chief and the many members of his inner circle. They inquired as to where they might find more of the glittering material used in the design of their earrings and bracelets, and the natives told them there was much gold to be found to the south, just across the Gulf of Leyte. Eight days of rest combined with generous portions of fresh food certainly restored the crew's health, but it was the enticing prospect of finding gold which helped rekindle their spirit of adventure. Magellan knew, by virtue of his northerly position, that he was not yet in the immediate vicinity of the Spice Islands; even though the rest of his officers advised him to get back on course for the Moluccas, he could not, however, resist the temptation to explore the remote possibility that he may have stumbled upon an even greater find.

On March 28th, following a leisurely three day voyage across the Surigao Strait, Magellan's ships landed at the island of Limasawa. It was here that they were greeted by Rajah Colambu, the ruler of a relatively small island inhabited by an apparently poor and primitive people. But all was not as it appeared. In celebration of their arrival the rajah hosted a gastronomical feast for Magellan and his officers at the beach where they had just landed. They dined on generous portions of rice, fish, and roasted pig and enjoyed the sweet intoxicating effects of the natives' palm wine, all of which were served to them on plates and in cups made of pure gold. With the help of Henrique, the explorers were able to ascertain that abundant quantities of gold, silk, porcelain, and a vast array of spices could be found along the mainland of Mindanao. They were also told that once there they would find Filipino merchants carrying on trade with merchants from many other lands, particularly those hailing from the land of China. Chinese merchants had been making the trek across the waters of the South China Sea to dock at the islands of the Philippines as far back as the 10th century, if not before. During their magnificent feast, Magellan did his best to impress Rajah Colambu and his loyal subjects with an orchestrated show of Spanish might. He treated them to a deafening display of gunfire, which both frightened and astonished the natives, and then, to further emphasize the fact that their primitive weapons were no match against the strength of his soldiers, Magellan had one of his men dress up in a full suit of armor to demonstrate how it made his sailor impervious to the dagger thrusts of three different men. After the celebration was over many of Magellan's men retired for a night of exotic pleasures in the comforting arms of the village's beautiful Filipino women.

Rajah Colambu offered to personally guide Magellan and his men to the capital city of Cebu, where he would provide them with an introduction to the *datu* (the native term for their almighty ruler), Rajah Humabon. The *Trinidad*, *Victoria*, and *Concepción* all reached the harbor of Cebu on the 7th of April at which point the commander punctuated their arrival by letting loose a barrage of cannon fire that, just as Magellan had intended, struck fear into the hearts of Cebu's many citizens. Once ashore, Magellan was met by Rajah Humabon, a short and corpulent ruler whom he found, at first, to be less inviting and far more demanding than Rajah Colambu had been. Humabon made it clear that it was mandatory for any ship that docked in his harbor to pay a tribute to the *datu*, the payment customarily being in gold. Humabon became greatly angered when Magellan refused to honor this demand, and a tense situation would surely have turned deadly had it not been for the timely intervention of a visiting merchant from Siam. He warned the rajah to be cautious in his dealings with these men who stood before him, for they were from the same lands as those who had shown such ruthless determination in the bloody and devastating campaigns that resulted in the capture of the heavily armed ports at Calicut and Malacca. Now that he saw the Spaniards in a different light, Humabon wisely chose to extend the hand of friendship to them. Almost at once the explorers got down to the business of trading their wares for the gold of Cebu: beads, mirrors, bells, and caps were bartered for the golden nuggets that flowed naturally from the hills of this land.

Magellan and his men were appalled by many of the pagan practices of the Filipino people and as Christian soldiers in the service of Spain they

were morally and legally obligated to use whatever means they deemed necessary to turn such heathens into true believers of their God. In keeping
with their religious rites, the Christian explorers held a large and open Mass
along the beach. Also in attendance at this service were both rajahs and
their considerable entourages. The breaking of the bread, the partaking of
wine from the sacramental cup, and the solemn pomp of their religious
ceremony were a truly enlightening experience for Rajah Humabon, who,
following the conclusion of the service, asked if he might be worthy enough
to receive a Christian baptism. His request was gladly granted. Father Pedro
Valderrama administered the sacrament of baptism to Rajah Humabon,
and the converted *datu* was christened "Don Charles"—in honor of the
young Charles I of Spain. Rajah Colambu then lined up to receive his formal initiation into the Christian community and he was closely followed
by the rest of the local chiefs. When Rajah Humabon's wife Queen Juana,
whom Antonio Pigafetta described as "...young and beautiful, covered with
a white and black cloth. She had very red lips and nails, and wore on her
head a large hat made of palm leaves," asked if she too could be blessed, a
grateful Magellan presented her with a small wooden statue of the baby
Jesus, which is still on display at the Convent of Santo Niño in the city of
Cebu. According to Pigafetta's account, nearly eight hundred natives were
baptized on that day.

While a great number of Filipinos lined up to be baptized as Christians, few of them were converts in the truest sense. Most of them still faithfully clung to their old religious beliefs and ceremonies. When Magellan
learned that one of the rajah's relatives had been stricken with an unknown
illness that had left him bedridden, he saw an opportunity to demonstrate
to the citizens of Cebu that the God of the Christians was more powerful
than all of their gods combined. While offering to cure this member of the
royal family Magellan also made sure to extract a pledge from the royal
household that they would immediately dispose of all their pagan idols if
he was successful in curing this man of whatever it was that ailed him.
Magellan had one of his priests baptize the patient and then he proceeded
to force feed the sickly man a diet of milk of almonds, a specially prepared
drink known as mandolata. To the amazement of everyone present, and
very probably Magellan too, the man recovered from his sickness and within
a few days was up and walking around. News of Magellan's miracle spread
rapidly throughout Cebu and within a short period of time most of her
citizens rushed out to become baptized, but not before they removed and
destroyed the graven images that they had worshiped previously. By week's
end, practically the entire population of Cebu had been converted to Christianity.

On April 26, 1521, Rajah Humabon was visited by a lesser chief named Zzula from the neighboring island of Mactan. Though a ruler himself, Zzula, like Colambu, was a loyal subject of Humabon's. Now he came to Cebu with news of a powerful rival Mactan chief, named Lapulapu, who sought to establish an independent kingdom that was subject to no one but Lapulapu. Don Charles appealed to Magellan to join forces with him "to fight and burn the houses of Mactan to make the king of Mactan kiss the hands of the King of Cebu." Seeing in this request of the *datu* yet another opportunity to secure the loyalty of the Filipino people, Magellan willingly agreed to become Humabon's ally.

Most of Magellan's officers and sailors disagreed with his decision to get involved in what they believed was nothing more than a tribal dispute. Several crew members tried to persuade him to leave this land at once in order that they might get back on track for their original destination—the Moluccas. But Magellan was a man of his word and there was nothing his men could possibly say or do that would make him break his promise to the rajah of Cebu. Despite all their complaints and misgivings these brave sailors were not about to abandon the very man who had guided them half-way around the world. During the midnight hour of April 26th the three Spanish ships were escorted from the harbor of Cebu by a fleet of sixty large native vessels manned by a massive force of Cebuano warriors and the mighty rajah of Cebu. Humabon was eager to witness what Magellan assured him would be a swift and thorough defeat of the rebel forces led by the insolent tribal chief named Lapulapu.

Once they had reached the nearby island of Mactan the captain-general sent a messenger ashore to let Lapulapu know that a peaceful resolution was still possible, provided that he was willing to swear allegiance to both the rajah of Cebu and the king of Spain. But Lapulapu, who was not intimidated by the bold threats issued by these white men, replied that he had no intention of serving any other master and if they wished to do battle then they should commence to doing so at once or leave his island forever. When the emissary returned with the chief's unrepentant reply, Magellan turned to his crew and asked for volunteers to join him in battle. Fifty-nine men responded to the captain-general's call to arms by raising their muskets and swords and piling into three of the fleet's longboats. Eager to join in the fray, the warriors from Cebu began preparing to wage war with the rebellious islanders, but Magellan, in a vain attempt to impress his new allies, boasted that his men alone could easily take control of the island and that the rajah's forces should remain behind to watch and savor the glorious victory that he was about to hand to them.

On the 27th of April, just about three hours before the break of dawn,

Magellan and his comrades began rowing toward the beach of Mactan. It was an ill-conceived plan from the very beginning. Within two hundred yards of the shore their boats became wedged in the coral reefs and rocks that had become exposed during the peak of ebb tide, thereby forcing the would-be conquerors to get out and slosh through the remaining stretch of shallow water leading to the shore. It was at this point that the captain-general made a fateful decision that would ultimately affect the final outcome of the Battle of Mactan. Fearing that the salt water would corrode their metal armor Magellan ordered his men to remove their leg armor and leave it in the boats. Eleven men stayed behind with the longboats while Magellan and the forty-eight other sailors waded toward the shore. Once they reached the beach they found themselves confronted by several hundred Mactani warriors who believed they could scare Magellan and his men away with a simple show of force. While a barrage of musket balls from Magellan's men failed to fell any of the enemy, the noise and smoke from their weapons was frightening enough to send the natives scurrying from the shore. Now that he had established a beachhead the captain-general chose to employ the same tactic he had used at the island of Guam to strike terror into the hearts of the native population—he would set fire to their entire village. Two men were sent ahead to begin torching the thatched huts, but they only succeeded in igniting the ire of the natives who, once they saw what these two were up to, surrounded and swiftly executed both of them. Stirred to a frenzied state, Lapulapu and his warriors charged toward the beach to confront the European invaders.

Magellan and his men soon heard the shrill screams and pounding feet of the fast approaching warriors and they hurriedly loaded their weapons in anticipation of the impending attack. However, the brave sailors were not prepared for the sight of so many warriors, a number estimated at close to fifteen hundred by Antonio Pigafetta. Letting loose with what they prayed would be a suppressing round of fire the Spaniards succeeded in mowing down a great many of the charging Mactanis, but Lapulapu's warriors refused to yield any ground. Hurdling over the bodies of their fallen comrades the natives swooped down upon the Spaniards before they had an opportunity to reload their weapons. Lunging at them with bamboo spears, machetes, and sheer determination the natives pushed Magellan's small armed force back to the water's edge. The natives pelted the Spaniards with all sorts of projectiles, and when several of their fellow sailors fell dead in the water just moments after having been struck by the enemies' missiles the Spaniards were unexpectedly confronted with one of their gravest fears: poisoned arrows and darts were part of the Mactanis' deadly arsenal. Most of Magellan's men had donned their armor breastplates before the battle but the

Mactanis quickly learned that the enemy did have an Achilles heel. Aiming for the limbs, primarily the legs, the Mactanis quickly gained the advantage over their adversaries and the battle was soon on the verge of becoming a full scale massacre.

The Spanish explorers and the estimated one thousand Cebuano warriors who had remained behind with the fleet watched in helpless disbelief and horror at the tragic events that were quickly unfolding before their very eyes. Magellan and his men fought valiantly but with their ranks thinning rapidly the captain-general saw no choice but to order his crew to retreat to the safety of their nearby longboats. While most of the wounded and battle weary soldiers waded back into the ocean Magellan and a handful of men, including Pigafetta and Henrique, stood their ground to cover the withdrawal of their comrades.

In his recollection of Magellan's bravery during the Battle of Mactan, Antonio Pigafetta wrote that "...an Indian threw a bamboo lance in his face, and the captain immediately killed him with his lance, leaving it in his body." Unfortunately for our hero this was the beginning of the end. Suddenly, Magellan felt the sharp sting of a poisoned arrow that had penetrated his armor and as he reached to pull it out a Filipino warrior slashed him across his unprotected left leg with the cutting edge of his sword. As Magellan began to sway from the effects of these blows the Mactanis instantly swarmed around him so as to prevent the other Spaniards from coming to his rescue. The natives mercilessly hacked away at the captain-general with their machetes and in those last remaining painful moments of life Ferdinand Magellan summoned enough inner strength to look up to see if his men were out of harm's way.

Comforted by the knowledge that his sailors, including Pigafetta and Henrique, had escaped, Magellan collapsed face down in the sand while the Mactanis continued to butcher away at his now lifeless body. In memory of his brave leader Pigafetta later recorded that "...they slew our mirror, our light, our comfort, and our guide."

The Long Way Home

A Forced Departure

Nine Spanish sailors, including Ferdinand Magellan and Cristóbal Robelo, the recently promoted captain of the *Victoria*, died that day on the shores of Mactan Island. Perhaps the most serious injury inflicted by Lapu-lapu, who later became a national hero because of his stunning victory over the Spaniards, was the loss of their reputation as mighty warriors. No longer cloaked in an aura of invincibility the Europeans were suddenly exposed as the mere mortals that they truly were. As the initial shock of the captain-general's death began to fade the men started to bicker amongst themselves over who should succeed as the commander of the expedition. Following a heated debate and a divided vote the crew finally agreed upon a joint command led by João Serrão and Duarte Barbosa. The wounded Henrique, who probably grieved more than any man over the death of Magellan, had expected to be granted his freedom now that he no longer had a master, but Barbosa refused to set him free. It was a decision that the newly appointed captain would later regret having made. The joint captains set a course for Cebu where they hoped to nurse their wounds in the comforting arms of the recently converted Don Charles while pondering over their next course of action.

The defeated fleet made it safely back to the harbor of Cebu on May 1st, at which point Duarte Barbosa ordered Henrique ashore with a message addressed to the rajah. To remind the Malayan of his still lowly status as a slave, the captain gave him a swift kick in the rear to send him on his way. After Henrique's meeting with Rajah Humabon, the new captains were invited to come dine with the king of Cebu. Thankful for his gracious hospitality, both Serrão and Barbosa gladly accepted his royal invitation. The joint commanders came ashore with twenty-seven other sailors, including the pilot João Lopez Carvalho and petty officer Gonzalo Gómez de Espinosa. Sitting down to enjoy yet another elaborate Filipino feast, the Spaniards were unaware of the fact that a bitter and resentful Henrique had cooked up a sinister plot with the rajah of Cebu. Both Carvalho and Espinosa became suspicious over the presence of so many armed warriors in attendance at the banquet but neither man was able to convince the others that anything was out of the ordinary. Trusting to their own instincts the pilot and the petty officer managed to slip away from the feast without being noticed and quickly returned to the safety of their ships. Their suspicions were soon confirmed when they heard the sounds of a great commotion emanating from the island.

Shortly after Carvalho and Espinosa had left the great banquet, the rajah unveiled his grand surprise; on his orders the Filipino warriors pounced on their Spanish guests and proceeded to butcher away without the slightest show of mercy. Though startled by the sudden fury of this attack, many of the sailors desperately tried to fend off their attackers but they were quickly overpowered; others tried to escape by running away but they were hunted down and slaughtered the moment they were apprehended. The blood-curdling screams of their comrades rang painfully loud in the ears of those safely aboard the ships and Carvalho tried his best to silence those sounds with a cannon bombardment aimed directly at the center of Cebu. As the smoke began to clear the sailors were able to make out the faint sight of one of their own being dragged out to the docks. Forced to kneel while facing in the direction of his ships, a bound and badly bleeding João Serrão cried out that Barbosa and all the others, except for the traitor Henrique, were dead, and a similar fate surely awaited him, Serrão, unless Carvalho sent ashore a longboat loaded with a cargo of valuable tribute for presentation to the rajah of Cebu. Carvalho ceased firing but his instincts told him that the rajah was merely laying another ambush and therefore decided not to risk any more men in an attempt to barter for the freedom of his good friend and captain. Serrão watched in disbelief and horror as his shipmates ignored his impassioned plea for help and hastily prepared to sail from the harbor. Assuming command of the expedition, João Carvalho ordered the men to raise the anchors, and after one final barrage of cannon fire, the ships sailed off on an undetermined course. As for Serrão, we can only assume that he joined his fallen comrades in the afterlife shortly after being abandoned by his shipmates.

Following the bloody massacre at Cebu the surviving members of the expedition spent the next six months roaming the numerous islands that are a part of the Philippines. With a crew that had been whittled down to less than one hundred and thirty, and with many of these men still weak from illness, there were simply not enough able bodied men to handle the exhaustive rigors required to sail three large vessels. Therefore, when the ships reached the island of Bohol, just to the south of Cebu, Carvalho ordered the least seaworthy boat, which happened to be the *Concepción*, to be stripped of all essential cargo and its crew to be divided between the *Trinidad* and *Victoria*. It is generally assumed that all of the captain-general's logs, charts, and notes were still aboard the vessel when it was put to the torch, and if this is true then Carvalho denied mankind the true record of Magellan's epic voyage. After setting fire to the *Concepción*, the two remaining ships continued on in search of both food and direction. Wandering aimlessly between the many island of the Celebes and Sulu seas, and even touching the coast of Borneo, Carvalho and his crew often resorted to piracy in order to satisfy their basic needs as well as their particular, and sometimes peculiar, whims. Captain Carvalho apparently developed an insatiable fondness for the companionship of the exotic women who inhabited these islands and after several stops he had managed to accumulate for himself a considerable harem of slave girls to satisfy his many sexual needs and desires.

These constant congressional practices consumed the greater portion of Carvalho's time and energy. By the time the wandering explorers reached the coast of Borneo, Carvalho had become so addicted to the company of his women that he even consented to a request from his fellow officers that he relinquish his command; but he only agreed to do so on the condition that he could keep for himself his bevy of beautiful women.

Juan Sebastián de Cano, a Spanish navigator who originally served aboard the *Concepción* and who is also known simply as El Cano, was appointed captain of the *Victoria*, a rank which entitled him to share command of the expedition with Gonzalo Espinosa, the captain of the *Trinidad*. The two commanders continued along the coast of Borneo, reaching as far as the town of Brunei before heading back out to the Sula Sea. While at Brunei the sailors were treated to a rich reception from the wealthy Sultan Bulkiah. Greeted in the harbor by emissaries aboard royal boats lavishly decorated in gold and fully loaded with splendid gifts for the taking, the explorers were cordially invited to visit their island paradise. Once ashore, the officers were escorted to the sultan's palace where they found themselves humbled by the overwhelming amount of wealth on display. The enormous quantities of precious gems, gold, silver and silk put to shame the simple offerings that the Spaniards had brought as tribute for this powerful ruler. Sultan Bulkiah was revered as an earthly god by the people of Brunei, and the Spanish officers were only allowed to view him from behind a screened and curtained adjoining room. All communications with the omnipotent ruler were carried on through royal interpreters and mediators. When they learned that the sultan, who admired the superior vessels of his visitors, was secretly planning to gain control of their ships the Spaniards foiled his plans by slipping out of the harbor unnoticed. Their days of wandering aimlessly finally ended after they managed to capture a local vessel whose navigator knew the way to the Moluccas.

Finally, on November 8, 1521, after having spent more than two grueling years at sea, the expedition finally reached the shores of the fabled Spice Islands. As soon as the two ships dropped anchor in his harbor, El-Mansur, the sultan of Tidore, sent forth dignitaries to offer his official greetings and to invite the foreigners to come visit with him. Hoping to avoid the same mistake they had made previously at Cebu, but realizing that they had little left to offer in the way of tribute or trade, El Cano and Espinosa forcefully persuaded Carvalho to part with the precious women he kept for himself in order that they might have something of value to offer to the sultan. Delighted with this lovely addition to his own sizable harem, El-Mansur presented the Spaniards with a large cargo of cloves. At that time cloves could only be found on the islands of Tidore, Ternate, Bachan Makian, and Moti, which therefore made them one of the rarest and consequently one of the most valuable spices in the world.

Leaving the friendly isle of Tidore, the daring adventurers sailed on to Ternate, the island paradise where Francisco Serrão, Magellan's friend and former comrade, supposedly still resided. Even though they came bearing bad news concerning the fate of their fearless leader, the surviving crew members hoped Serrão would still honor them with the same generous invitation he had extended to Magellan, to come share in the great wealth and magnificent splendor of the Spice islands. But the explorers had to tread lightly at Ternate once they learned that Francisco Serrão had recently been murdered, as had his benefactor, the sultan of Ternate. Both men had been purposely poisoned and now the surviving sons squabbled over who would ultimately reign supreme on the island. Working their charm on the surviving members of the ruling family, El Cano and Espinosa succeeded in bartering their few remaining items of trade for another large and valuable cargo of cloves.

THE TREACHEROUS PATH HOME

With a full load of precious cloves and a great longing for the sight of home, the adventurous sailors began making preparations for their long overdue return to Spain. But danger lurked ahead. Portuguese officials had anxiously followed the progress of Magellan's expedition as best they could and consequently their large fleet, which was stationed in that distant part of the world, had been placed on full alert with instructions to use any and all means available, including deadly force, to keep the Spanish expedition from completing its mission. Cognizant of the fact that they were trespassing in waters infested with Portuguese patrols, the Spaniards decided that their best chance of eluding the enemy would be to sail home by different routes. The *Victoria* would stay the course by sailing westward across the Indian Ocean and on around the continent of Africa until it reached the shores of Spain. At the same time, the *Trinidad* would retrace their previous course across the Pacific in hopes of reaching a Spanish outpost along the coast of Central America before making it return to Spain. Both vessels were set to sail on December 18, 1521, but as soon as they put out to sea the *Trinidad* began taking on water at an alarming rate and the two ships were therefore forced to head for the shores of nearby Tidore.

Having determined that the *Trinidad* was in dire need of extensive repairs before it could possibly chance another voyage across the vast expanse of water that separated them from the Americas, Espinosa, Carvalho and their crew of fifty-two men had little choice but to remain at the island of Tidore to complete the vessel's overhaul while the crew of the Victoria prepared for their solo voyage westward. Three days after the emergency landing, the crew of the *Victoria*—forty-seven anxious sailors under the command of Juan Sebastián de Cano, including Antonio Pigafetta and an additional thirteen Moluccans—said goodbye to their comrades. With their cargo bay full of cloves, they weighed anchor and followed the flow of the seasonal trade winds they hoped would propel them across the enormous breadth of the Indian Ocean. It took the crew of the *Victoria* nearly a month to thread their way through the maze of islands located in that part of the world. The cautious course they followed in order to avoid detection by any Portuguese vessels that might be sailing in those same waters contributed greatly to their prolonged voyage at sea.

Once the Spice Islands were well behind him, El Cano set his ship on a course for the Cape of Good Hope. While his chosen path across the Indian Ocean intentionally steered them clear of the known traditional Portuguese trade routes, it was, unfortunately, a route that took the broadest possible course across this immense body of water. Prior to reaching the Cape of Good Hope they encountered one of those violent storms which, during his earlier historic voyage, had given Bartolomeu Dias cause to christen this ominous promontory the Cape of Storms. The *Victoria* and her crew battled heroically against the relentless rage of the storm, but eventually the combined fury of the wind and sea tore apart the ship's foremast and the sailors had no other choice but to drop anchor at the cape. Stormy weather kept them stranded in nearly that same spot for the better part of nine weeks, but finally, on May 6, 1522, they managed to break free of the cape's powerful hold on them and began a northerly swing away from the shores of West Africa.

Of all the harrowing experiences they had endured on their epic voyage it was this final stretch toward home that certainly aroused the greatest fear in the hearts and minds of the crew sailing aboard the *Victoria*. They were on a course that ran parallel to the heavily trafficked shipping lanes of the Portuguese trade fleets in a badly battered ship that could not possibly outrun the heavy guns of the enemy. To be captured at this point would, at the very least, result in their incarceration, but it was the extreme scenario, an execution at sea, that most feared would occur should they happen to be caught at this point. Compounding these imagined fears was the very real danger of their starving to death long before they ever reached land. After nearly two months' sail from the Cape of Good Hope, the crew of the *Victoria* faced many of the same extreme scenarios it had faced during the previous tragic crossing of the Pacific Ocean. Even though they rationed their provisions as best they could, the food and water eventually ran out and many of the men, especially those who still had not recovered completely from their previous bout with scurvy, grew weaker with each passing day. The prolonged effects of malnutrition, dehydration, and sheer exhaustion combined to bring about the death of an additional twenty-one sailors before land was once again sighted.

The remaining courageous explorers came upon the Cape Verde Islands in July, and even though El Cano and his crew knew this to be a Portuguese controlled port of call their present situation had become so desperate they were willing to risk such a landing. After dropping anchor in the harbor, El Cano sent his healthiest sailors ashore in the longboats to procure both food and water. By using a cover story that the *Victoria* had been separated from its homeward bound Spanish fleet by violent storms they managed to earn the empathy of the Portuguese residents and thus were able to obtain an ample supply of rice and fresh water. The Portuguese colonists even pitched in to help them load their cargo onto their longboats, but after two boatloads had already been sent back to the *Victoria* they learned just what it was that the Spaniards secretly had stored in the hull of their ship. Since cloves could only be found in lands that lay well beyond the other side of Africa the Portuguese realized they had been duped by these cunning Spaniards and in anger they grabbed hold of the next fully loaded boat that was preparing to row back to the ship. Thirteen of the Victoria's crew were detained while the governor of the island sent a message to El Cano demanding that he surrender his vessel and crew at once. Knowing that there was nothing he could do to save his captured comrades, and that his own surrender would certainly condemn the remaining crew to a prison cell and very probably a trip to the gallows, El Cano responded to the governor's request by raising the ship's anchor and sailing swiftly away from the island.

With a remaining crew of only seventeen sailors and just four Moluccans to handle the rigorous chores of sailing the *Victoria*, it took El Cano until September 6, 1522, to finally be able to steer his badly damaged vessel into the docks at Sanlúcar de Barrameda. Continuing on up the Guadalquivir, the *Victoria* and her skeleton crew reached the city of Seville two days later, where news of their arrival was enthusiastically received by the many citizens who had long ago given them up for dead. Fifty-two thousand pounds of cloves were unloaded from the hull of their ship, the sale of which eventually produced enough revenue to cover the entire cost of the expedition but yielded little in the way of profit for its investors and barely any money for those who had risked their lives on this incredible odyssey.

Spain's own King Charles, who had since their departure been elevated to emperor of the Holy Roman Empire, awarded El Cano a royal pension that was to be paid from future proceeds of the profitable spice trade which was sure to emerge as a result of their historic voyage. The appreciative emperor also provided the *Victoria*'s captain with an elaborate coat of arms that was embroidered with a globe and encircled with the inscription *Primus circumdesti me* ("Thou first circumnavigated me"). While there was no family left in Spain to mourn the passing of Ferdinand Magellan—his wife Beatriz Barbosa had died sometime and somehow before the year 1522, as had their young son Rodrigo—Antonio Pigafetta made sure that the rest of the world knew and remembered all of his many great deeds and accomplishments by returning to Italy and, in 1524, turning the extensive notes he kept during the long journey into a book about the Magellan expedition. A number of other survivors, including El Cano, dictated their recollections of the voyage, but it is Pigafetta's rendering which is considered by most historians to be the definitive account of the voyage that finally succeeded in making the world whole.

None were more surprised by the sudden arrival of the *Victoria* and its crew than the surviving mutinous members of the *San Antonio*, the vessel that had deserted the expedition back at the passage later known as the Strait of Magellan. Under the command of Esteban Gómez, who had previously served as the ship's pilot, the *San Antonio* and its crew of mutineers found their way back to Spain in May of 1521. To justify their own rebellious conduct, Gómez and his crew spoke falsely of Magellan's command, spreading malicious lies and gross exaggerations that succeeded in smearing the good name of the captain-general. As for the unfortunate Álvaro de Mesquita, the deposed captain who had been returned home in chains, he was thrown into a dark, dank prison cell, where he surely would have languished until his dying day had it not been for the timely intervention of the crew of the *Victoria*. Grateful for his release from jail, but understandably bitter over the way he had been treated, Mesquita returned to his native Portugal to serve under King Manuel.

As for the fifty-four comrades who stayed behind at the island of Tidore, they spent the better part of three months working at a feverish pace to repair their severely damaged vessel before attempting their planned trek across the Pacific Ocean. The difficult task at hand combined with the sweltering heat ultimately proved too demanding for the likes of João Lopes Carvalho, the pilot who was supposed to guide them home, and he simply dropped dead from sheer exhaustion. Finally, in April of 1522, the repairs were completed and the *Trinidad* set sail for the Spanish colonies located at Panama, and once there, they hoped to transport their valuable cargo of cloves to the other side of the isthmus where they would then be boarded onto another vessel bound for Spain. Unfortunately, they failed to take into account the westerly winds that steadily blow across the Pacific during that time of the year. For several long and difficult weeks the crew heroically fought against unfavorable winds, raging waters, and foul weather, but in the end it was the elements that emerged victorious.

After they had been blown as far north as the island of Japan (Cipangu) the weary crew decided to risk a return to the Moluccas, where hopefully they could rest and regroup before embarking on another attempt across the Pacific Ocean. However, Espinosa and his crew soon discovered that their ship had sustained damage that was significant enough to hinder her performance at sea. As they drifted ever so slowly southward the crew was once again forced to confront the all too familiar horrors of hunger, thirst, and the unwelcome return of the much dreaded scurvy. The already weakened sailors perished at an alarming rate, and by the time their ship reached the Moluccas there were but nineteen men still clinging, though barely, to life itself. But upon their return to the Spice Islands the Spaniards discovered that their terrible ordeal was far from over. Waiting to greet them was a Portuguese fleet that had recently been dispatched to the Spice Islands to secure a trade accord that would further tighten Portugal's control over the lucrative spice trade. After being imprisoned aboard one of the Portuguese vessels the surviving explorers found themselves being constantly ferried from one island dungeon to another. A more permanent confinement awaited them in India where they were subjected to routine beatings and various other forms of torture. Disease and inhumane treatment eventually claimed the lives of fifteen men before their captors showed any sign of mercy. After having spent more than two years in prison, Espinosa and three other survivors were released and permitted to return to Spain where a grateful king rewarded them with a modest pension.

Spanish authorities sought to capitalize on their newly discovered way to the Spice Islands in 1525 by dispatching another fleet to follow the route forged by Magellan and El Cano. Seven ships set sail under the command of García Jofre de Loaisa, and serving as second in command of the expedition was El Cano. As his annual pension was dependent upon the development of profitable trade relations with the Spice Islands, it was certainly in El Cano's best interest to sign on for yet another expedition. Besides, there was no one better qualified to guide this expedition than the pilot-captain who had already sailed there and back.

Even though the Spaniards did their best to prepare for the absolute worst, El Cano still found himself having to relive many of the painful and horrifying experiences that had plagued the Magellan expedition. Even before they reached the edge of the Pacific Ocean the commanders were faced with the loss of three vessels—two by desertion and another due to the terrible ravages of the sea. For those who made it through the long and difficult passage there were still several thousands of miles of ocean to cross before the Moluccas would ever come into view. Just as before, there was not enough food and water to sustain the whole crew for a voyage of such magnitude. Malnutrition and disease claimed the lives of most of the crew including the two commanding officers, García Jofre de Loaisa and El Cano. Only one ship with but a few survivors aboard ever made it to the island of Tidore. In that same year, Charles V, Holy Roman emperor and king of Spain, commissioned Sebastian Cabot, son of the explorer John Cabot, to lead three ships on a similar course to the Orient, although the small group did not sail until later. Cabot never reached the Strait of Magellan. He was sidetracked from his mission by tales of great wealth said to be located somewhere along the Rio de la Plata. Cabot would spend the next three years searching in vain for riches which never materialized before he finally gave up on his fanciful quest and returned to Spain empty-handed.

Spain and Portugal would continue to contest each other's claims to ownership of the Spice Islands as well as the archipelago later named in honor of the Spanish king Philip II, the son of Emperor Charles V. The issue was finally settled once and for all with the signing of the Treaty of Sargossa in 1529. While Spain sold her claims to the precious Spice Islands for the princely sum of 350,000 ducats, she managed, however, to maintain title to the many islands of the Philippines, a possession that was to become one of the crown jewels of the vast Spanish Empire. The right of passage through the Strait of Magellan was of little concern once Spain discovered that it was more advantageous and less risky to simply transport trade between the Far East and Europe across the divide of Central America. While Juan Sebastián del Cano was honored for being the first to circumnavigate the earth, a strong case can be, and has been, made that the true credit belongs to Ferdinand Magellan, an assumption based on the furthest eastern point he supposedly reached while in the service of Portugal and with the farthest western point he reached while in the service of Spain. It seems only fair, when taking into account all the trials and tribulations this man endured and suffered during his quest, to give Ferdinand Magellan the glory for this great achievement. To do so certainly makes for a fitting conclusion to this story of the age of the European explorers—the men who went to the ends of the earth.

Bibliography

Barraclough, Geoffrey, editor. *HarperCollins Atlas of World History.* Ann Arbor, Michigan: Borders Press, 1999.

Berthon, Simon and Andrew Robinson. *The Shape of the World: The Mapping and Discovery of the Earth.* Chicago: Rand McNally, 1991.

Boorstin, Daniel J. *The Discoverers.* New York: Vintage Books, 1985.

Bricker, Charles. *Landmarks of Mapmaking: An Illustrated History of Maps and Mapmakers.* New York: Dorset Press, 1989.

Camusso, Lorenzo. *The Voyages of Columbus 1492–1504.* New York: Dorset Press, 1991.

Daniel, Hawthorne. *Ferdinand Magellan.* Garden City, N.Y.: Doubleday & Company, 1964.

Day, Avanelle, and Lillie Stuckey. *The Spice Cookbook.* New York: David White Company, 1964.

DeSanti, Louis. *Columbus and the New World: Hero of the Millennium.* McLean, Va.: Millennium Publishing Company, 1990.

Descola, Jean. *The Conquistadors.* New York: Viking Press, 1957.

Durant, Will. *The Renaissance.* New York: Simon and Schuster, 1953.

Encyclopædia Britannica. 23 vols. Chicago: Encyclopædia Britannica, Inc., 1972.

Garrison, Omar V. *Balboa: Conquistador.* New York: Lyle Stuart, 1971.

Hale, John R. *The Age of Exploration.* New York: Time-Life Books, 1966.

Hart, Henry H. *Marco Polo: The Venetian Adventurer.* Norman: University of Oklahoma Press, 1967.

Humble, Richard. *The Explorers: The Seafarers.* Alexandria, Va.: Time-Life Books, 1978.

Landstrom, Bjorn. *Columbus.* New York: Macmillan Company, 1966.

Mandeville, John. *The Travels of Sir John Mandeville,* transl. by C.W.R.D. Moseley. London: Penguin, 1983.

Marx, Robert F., and Jenifer Marx. *The Search for Sunken Treasure.* Toronto: Key Porter Books, 1993.

Morison, Samuel Eliot. *The Admiral of the Ocean Sea: A Life of Christopher Columbus*. New York: Little, Brown and Company, 1942.

_____. *The European Discovery of America: The Southern Voyages 1492–1616*. New York: Oxford University Press, 1974.

Parry, J.H. *The European Reconnaissance*. New York: Walker and Company, 1968.

Prestage, Edgar. *The Portuguese Pioneers*. London: Adam & Charles Black, 1933.

Stefoff, Rebecca. *Vasco da Gama and the Portuguese Explorers*. New York: Chelsea House Publishers, 1993.

Thornton, John. *Africa and Africans in the Making of the Atlantic World, 1400–1680*. New York: Cambridge University Press, 1992.

Wright, Louis B. *Gold, Glory and the Gospel*. New York: H. Wolff, 1970.

Index

Abreu, Antônio de 212, 213
Abyssinia 14, 16, 66, 70, 215
Adahu, African chieftain 53, 54
Aden 69, 209, 215
Afonso V, king of Portugal 52, 59, 61, 62, 63, 64, 67, 77, 78
Aguado, Juan 132, 133
Albuquerque, Afonso 204, 205, 206, 207, 208, 209, 210, 211, 212, 213, 214, 215, 216
Alenquer, Pedro de 137
Alexander the Great 43
Almeida, Francisco de 205, 206, 207, 208, 244
Almeida, Lourenço 207
Amboina 212, 213
Amsterdam 203
Antillia (Seven Cities) 37, 40, 75, 79, 83, 101, 113, 136, 160
Antipodes 48
Antwerp 152, 153
Arana, Diego de 109
Arawak tribe 108, 121, 122, 189, 222, 225, 256
Argon Khan 22, 24
Arias Dávila, Pedro see Pedrarias
Aristotle 29, 43, 166
Atlantis 75, 158
Azores 40, 41, 47, 59, 111, 112, 147, 163

Bachan 270
Bahama Islands 103, 107, 113, 115, 179, 225

Balboa, Vasco Núñez de 226, 230, 231, 232, 233, 234, 235, 236, 238, 239, 240, 241, 248, 258
Baldia, Afonso 49, 50
Bali 212
Banda 212, 213
Barbosa, Beatriz 244, 274
Barbosa, Diogo 244
Barbosa, Duarte 244, 247, 249, 252, 253, 268, 269
Barcelona 32, 67, 113, 114
Bardi 32
Bastidas, Rodrigo de 226, 230
Behaim, Martin 59, 244
Bimini 222
Bishop Hugh 13, 15
Bobadilla, Francisco de 170, 171, 172, 185, 187, 188, 190
Bombay 207
Borneo 212, 214, 269, 270
Bristol 157, 158, 159, 160, 161
Buil, Bernardo 119

Cabot, John: first voyage 156, 157, 158, 159; second voyage 160, 161, 163, 165, 251
Cabot, Sebastian 157, 158, 161, 251, 276
Caonabo 123
Cabral, Gonzalo 40
Cabral, Pedro 138, 148, 149, 150, 151, 152, 153, 155, 180, 181, 184, 185, 187, 203, 205

Cádiz 120, 125, 177, 179, 186, 221
Cairo 68, 69, 135
Calicut 10, 68, 69, 142, 143, 144, 145, 151, 153, 154, 155, 210, 211
Cananor 152, 153, 206
Canary Islands 40, 41, 77, 78, 101, 112, 116, 120, 166, 169, 177, 189, 248, 249
Cano, Juan see Elcano
Cantino, Alberto 183, 185
Canton 219
Cão, Diogo 64, 78, 86, 87, 185
Caonabo 127, 130, 131, 133, 176
Cape Bojador 49, 50, 52, 54
Cape Breton 159
Cape of Good Hope (Cape of Storms) 88, 89, 137, 139, 147, 150, 187, 204, 205, 208, 272
Cape Verde 54, 56, 59
Cape Verde Islands 81, 116, 117, 138, 140, 149, 166, 180, 273
Carib tribe 108, 121, 122, 126, 130, 179, 189, 222, 223, 225, 227, 229, 231, 256
Cartagena, Juan 247, 248, 249, 251, 252, 254, 256
Carvalho, João Lopes 256, 268, 269, 270, 274
Castro, Fernando de 40, 41
Cathay 16, 23, 26, 27, 47, 77, 98, 100, 101, 103, 105, 107, 113, 115, 126, 128, 133, 159, 160, 177, 179, 187, 219, 223
Cebu 263, 264, 265, 268, 269
Ceram 212
Ceuta 33, 34, 35, 36, 37, 50, 51, 53, 55, 218
Ceylon 24, 207
Champagne 30
Charlemagne 7
Charles I, king of Spain and emperor of the Holy Roman Empire 244, 264, 274, 276
Charles VIII, king of France 91
Charrua tribe 251
Chaul 207
Cibao 125, 127, 131
Ciguare 226
Cipangu 26, 47, 75, 77, 78, 100, 101, 105, 106, 107, 109, 110, 113, 115, 126, 160, 223, 275
Coca, Antonio de 249, 252
Cocachin, Mongol Princess 22, 23, 24

Cochin 152, 153, 155, 206, 207, 208, 210, 216
Coelho, Gonzalo 180, 181, 249, 250
Coelho, Nicolau 137
Coimbra, João de 137
Colambu 262, 263, 264
Columbus, Bartolomeo 73, 89, 128, 132, 133, 158, 168, 169, 171, 172, 173, 186, 188, 193, 195, 197
Columbus, Diego (brother) 120, 127, 128, 129, 130, 132, 168, 169, 171, 172, 186, 198
Columbus, Diego (son) 73, 80, 166, 198, 202, 221, 222
Columbus, Christopher 27; early years at Genoa and Portugal 71, 72, 73, 74, 75, 77, 78, 79, 156, 157, 158; final voyage 185, 186, 187, 188, 189, 190, 191, 192, 193, 194, 195, 196, 197, 198, 199, 202, 220, 222, 223; first voyage 98, 99, 100, 101, 102, 103, 104, 105, 106, 107, 108, 109, 110, 111, 112, 113, 114, 115, 139, 148, 159, 175, 176, 236, 247; resident of Spain 80, 81, 82, 85, 89, 90, 91, 92; second voyage 118, 119, 120, 122, 124, 125, 127, 128, 129, 130, 131, 132, 133, 134, 136, 224; third voyage 165, 166, 167, 168, 169, 170, 171, 172, 177, 178, 226, 227
Columbus, Fernando 188, 197, 202
Comogre 233, 234, 236
Constantinople 5, 14, 17, 24, 43, 57, 58, 59, 72, 77
Cordova 81, 93
Coronado, Francisco 237
Corte-Real, Gaspar 163, 164, 165
Corte-Real, João Vaz 162, 163
Corte-Real, Miguel 163, 164, 165
Cortés, Hernán 241
Cosa, Juan de la 177, 226, 227
Costa Rica 192, 223, 226, 241
Covilha, Pedro de 67, 69, 70, 86, 135, 137, 138, 140, 143
Crusades 8, 9, 11, 14
Cuba 106, 107, 108, 113, 128, 191, 194, 220, 222, 230
Cubagua 223, 225
Cunha, Tristão da 204, 205

Da Gama see Gama
Darién 232, 233, 234, 235, 237

De Soto, Hernando *see* Soto
Dias, Bartolomeu 68, 69, 86, 87, 88,
   89, 135, 136, 137, 138, 140, 149, 150,
   185, 272
Dias, Dennis 54, 88
Díaz, Bernal 237
Diu 207, 208
Duarte, prince of Portugal 34, 50, 52, 59

Eannes, Gil 49, 54
Elcano, Juan Sebastián de (El Cano)
   255, 270, 271, 272, 273, 274, 275,
   276
Elmina, fortress of 66, 74, 138
Enciso, Martín Fernández de 230, 231,
   232, 233, 234, 235, 237, 238
Eratosthenes 43
Ericsson, Leif 75, 162
Erik the Red 161
Escobar, Pedro de 137
Escobedo, Rodrigo de 100, 103, 123
Esdras 75, 167
Espinosa, Gonzalo Gómez de 249, 252,
   253, 268, 270, 271, 275
Esquivel 222

Faleiro, Rui 244, 245, 246, 247, 248
Ferdinand, king of Spain 66, 67, 81,
   82, 84, 85, 89, 90, 91, 93, 94, 95, 96,
   97, 98, 100, 106, 111, 112, 113, 114, 115,
   116, 117, 118, 125, 126, 132, 133, 136,
   148, 166, 170, 178, 179, 186, 187, 188,
   192, 198, 203, 233, 234, 235, 236,
   239, 240, 244
Fernandes, Álvaro 56
Fernandes, João 55, 56
Fernando, prince of Portugal 50, 51, 52
Fez 52, 67
Fieschi, Bartolomeo 195, 198
Flanders 73
Florence 11, 32, 67, 77, 174, 175
Flores 212
Fonseca, Juan de 118, 119, 176, 235,
   244, 245
Fugger 32, 205, 246

Gama, Estevão da 136, 137, 142
Gama, Paolo da 137, 143, 147
Gama, Vasco da 27; final journey 216;
   first voyage 137, 138, 139, 140, 141,
   142, 143, 144, 145, 146, 147, 148, 149,

150, 151, 158, 184, 185, 186, 187, 203,
   205, 206, 208; second voyage 153,
   154, 155, 165, 188, 189, 190, 191
Genoa 11, 12, 24, 25, 30, 32, 58, 71, 72,
   73, 78, 89, 98, 114, 156, 195, 204
Ghenghis Khan 16, 17
Goa 10, 69, 206, 210, 211, 214, 215, 216
Gold Coast 52, 61, 63, 66
Gomes, Diogo 59
Gomes, Fernão 62, 63
Gómez, Esteban 257, 274
Gonçalves, Antão 52, 53, 54, 55, 62
Gorbalan, Gines de 125
Granada 82, 83, 84, 85, 89, 90, 186,
   205, 238
Greenland 161, 162, 163
Guam 261, 266
Guancanagari 108, 109
Guaraní tribe 250
Guarionex 169, 190
Guatiiguana (caciqe) 130
Guitérrez, Pedro 109, 123
Gulf of Aden 11, 68
Gulf of Oman 11, 204
Gulf of Persia 68, 69, 204
Gutenberg, Johannes 26, 199

Hanseatic League 30
Harana, Beatriz Enriques de 202
Havana 222
Henrique 212, 262, 267, 268, 269
Henry VII, king of England 89, 158,
   160
Henry the Navigator 33, 34, 35, 36, 37,
   38, 39, 40, 44, 45, 46, 48, 49, 50, 51,
   52, 53, 54, 55, 56; death 59–60, 61,
   70, 78, 137, 218
Herjolfsson, Bjarni 161, 162
Herodutos 44
Hipparachus 43, 45
Hispania: conquest by Moors 6, 44
Hispaniola (Española) 107, 108, 109,
   110, 113, 115, 122, 129, 131, 133, 166,
   170, 171, 172, 179, 187, 189, 191, 195,
   196, 220, 222, 224, 226, 227, 229,
   231, 234
Holy Roman Empire: establishment 7, 8
Honduras 241
Hormuz 20, 204, 205, 215
Hottentot tribe 139, 208
Humabon 263, 264, 265, 268

Iceland 75, 161
Imago Mundi 75, 86
Inquisition, Spanish 84, 94, 95
Inter caetera 116–117, 118, 130
Isabela (colony) 125, 127, 128, 130, 131, 168, 169
Isabella, queen of Spain 66, 67, 81, 82, 84, 85, 89, 90, 91, 93, 94, 95, 96, 97, 98, 99, 100, 106, 111, 112, 113, 114, 115, 116, 117, 118, 125, 126, 132, 133, 136, 148, 166, 170, 178, 179, 186, 187, 188, 192, 197, 203, 221, 223, 238

Jamaica 191, 195, 196, 220, 230
Java 212
Jerusalem 8, 9, 27
Jesus Christ 7, 12, 14, 19, 20, 32, 64, 71, 96, 192
Jews: moneylenders 32; religious persecution 92, 93, 94, 95, 96, 97, 100
John I, king of Portugal 33, 34, 35, 36, 50, 52
John II, king of Portugal 62, 63, 64, 66, 67, 69, 70, 78, 79, 85, 86, 88, 89, 91, 96, 101, 112, 113, 116, 135, 136, 137, 205
John III, king of Portugal 216
Juana, queen of Cebu 264
Judas Iscariot 47, 74, 234

Kilwa 154, 205, 206
Kublai Khan 16, 17, 19, 20, 22, 23, 24, 25, 70, 106, 187

Labrador 159, 160, 162, 163
Lagos 35, 41, 54, 71, 73
Lapulapu 265, 266, 268
León, Ponce de *see* Ponce de León
Lisbon 34, 50, 64, 73, 85, 86, 112, 113, 138, 147, 149, 153, 164, 180, 182, 183, 185, 203, 204, 205, 242, 243, 244
Lloriaga, Juan de 252, 254
Loaisa, Garcia Joffre de 275, 276
Lombards 32
Lombok 212
London 73
Lucayan tribe 105, 225

Mactan 265, 266
Madeira 38, 39, 40, 41, 56, 79
Magellan, Ferdinand: clash with King

John 242, 243, 244; final voyage 259, 260, 261, 262, 263, 264, 265, 266, 267, 274, 275, 276; voyage across the Atlantic 245, 246, 247, 248, 249, 250, 251, 252, 253, 254, 255, 256, 257, 258; voyage to the East Indies 205, 206, 208, 209, 210, 211, 212, 213
Majid, Ahmad Ibn 142, 145, 146
Makian 270
Malacca 209, 210, 211, 212, 213, 214, 215, 217
Malindi 69, 141, 142, 143, 146, 219
Mandeville, John 13, 27, 107, 222
Mangi 26, 77, 103, 107, 113, 126
Manuel, the Fortunate 61, 96, 97, 137, 145, 147, 148, 149, 152, 153, 154, 163, 164, 165, 180, 187, 203, 204, 205, 207, 208, 216, 219, 242, 243, 274
Marchena, Antonio de 80, 90, 91
Margarit, Pedro 127
Margarita 223, 225
Mecca 15, 69, 154, 156, 211
Medici 32, 174, 175, 179, 199
Méndez, Diego 195, 196, 197, 198
Mendoza, Luis de 247, 248, 249, 251, 252, 253, 254
Mesquita, Álvaro de 252, 274
Mohammed 6
Mohammed II 57, 58
Molina, Luis de 254
Moluccas (Spice Islands) 208, 212, 213, 217, 242, 244, 245, 246, 248, 257, 265, 270, 272, 275, 276
Mombasa 69, 141, 142, 147, 206, 209, 219
Mongols 7, 16, 17, 22, 26
Monomotapa 219
Moors 6, 7, 33, 34, 35, 44, 51, 55, 83, 84, 89, 90, 92, 95, 97, 171, 203, 238, 242
Mossel Bay 87, 139
Moti 270
Mozambique 69, 140, 141, 147, 209
Musa, Mansa 15

Narváez, Panfilo 222, 230
Navidad (fort) 109, 110, 123, 124, 125, 126, 127, 129
Nestorians 13, 14, 15, 17, 21
Newfoundland 159, 161, 162, 163, 164, 165
Nicaragua 223, 241

Nicuesa, Diego 227, 229, 232, 233, 235, 238
Nova Scotia 159, 162
Nubians 70
Nunes, Goncalo 137
Núñez de Balboa, Vasco *see* Balboa

Ojeda, Alonso de 120, 125, 127, 130, 131, 171, 176, 177, 178, 222, 226, 227, 229, 230, 231
Ormuz 69, 209
Ottoman Empire 26, 58, 72, 77
Ovando, Nicolás de 187, 188, 189, 190, 195, 196, 197, 221, 226, 227

padrão 64, 140, 149
Paiva, Alfonso de 67, 69, 86, 135
Palos 80, 98, 99, 113, 114
Panama 223, 226, 232, 235, 241
Panciaco 233, 234, 236
Patagonia 251, 256
Pearlonso, Nino 222
Pedrarias 235, 238, 239, 240, 241
Pedro, prince of Portugal 34, 48, 50, 52
Pereira, Nuno vaz 206, 208
Perestrello, Bartholomew 38, 73
Perestrello, Felipa 73, 202
Pérez, Juan 90, 91, 98
Persian Gulf 11, 20, 24
Philippines 212, 213, 261, 263, 269, 276
Pigafetta, Antonio 247, 250, 256, 260, 266, 267, 272, 274
Pinzón, Francisco 99, 100
Pinzón, Martín 99, 100, 102, 103, 107, 110, 113–114
Pinzón, Vicente 99, 100, 103, 110, 113, 150, 177, 187
Pires, Tomé 219
Pisa 11
Pizarro, Francisco 229, 231, 232, 235, 236, 238, 240, 241
Plato 75
Pliny the Elder 47
Polo, Marco 16, 19, 20, 21, 23, 24, 25, 26, 27, 48, 70, 77, 105, 107, 114, 128, 159, 187
Polo, Matteo 17, 19, 20, 21, 23, 24
Polo, Niccolo 17, 19, 20, 21, 22, 23, 24
Ponce de León, Juan 120, 222
Póo, Fernando 62

Pope Alexander VI (Rodrigo Borgia) 116, 117, 118
Porras, Francisco 195, 197
Prester John 12, 13, 14, 15, 16, 21, 25, 27, 37, 59, 64, 65, 66, 67, 69, 70, 75, 86, 135, 141
Ptolemy 40, 43, 44, 75, 77, 82, 177, 201
Puerto Rico 122, 220, 222
Pythagora 43

Quesada, Gaspar de 247, 248, 251, 252, 253, 254
Quibian 193
Quilon 155

Reina, Pedro Sánchez de 254, 256
Rio de Janeiro 181, 249, 250
Rio de la Plata 250, 251, 276
Robelo, Cristóbal 249, 267
Roldán, Francisco 168, 169, 170, 171, 190
Roman Catholic Church 6, 31, 32, 48, 84, 116
Roman Empire: cause and effects of collapse 5
Rustichello of Pisa 25

Sagres 37, 41, 45, 46, 71
Saint Brendan 40, 74, 75, 157
Saint Elmo 48
St. Helena Bay 139
Saint James 35, 83
Sala-ben-Sala, governor of Ceuta 35
salt, African trade in 63
San Sebastián 229, 230, 231
Santángel, Luis de 90, 91, 98
Santo Domingo 168, 169, 171, 173, 188, 190, 194, 195, 197, 220, 223, 227, 229, 230, 232, 233
Segovia, Sánchez de 100
Senegal 37
Sequeira, Diogo Lopes de 209, 210, 211
Serrão, Francisco 205, 209, 210, 211, 212, 213, 242, 245, 250, 271
Serrão, João 248, 250, 255, 256, 268, 269
Seville 93, 130, 175, 182, 183, 188, 197, 221, 244, 248
Sierra Leone 56, 62, 138
Silk Road 10, 16

Slave Trade: native African 54, 55, 56,
    64, 65, 66; native American 121, 132,
    164, 179, 223, 224
Soarez, Lope 216
Socotra 204, 206
Sofala 69, 205, 209, 219
Solís, Juan 182, 250, 251
Soto, Hernando de 237
Spice Trade 9, 11, 12, 23, 25, 28, 30, 36,
    37, 47, 68, 113, 138, 140, 141, 142, 151,
    152, 153, 155, 158, 172, 217
Strabo 43
Strait of Gibraltar 6, 12, 33, 44, 50, 73,
    83
Sumatra 23, 24, 212, 214
Sumbawa 212

Taino tribe 105, 126, 127, 225
Talavera, Bernardino de 229, 230
Talavera, Hernando de (commission)
    82, 85, 90
Tangier 50, 51, 52
Tehuelche tribe 256
Teixeira, Tristão 38
Teobaldo of Piacenza 19
Ternate 213, 242, 270, 271
Terreros, Pedro de 190
Tidore 270, 271, 274
Tierra del Fuego 258
Timbuktu 15, 36, 53, 63, 219
Toledo, treaty of 112

Tordesillas, treaty of 117, 129, 136, 138,
    149, 244
Torquemada, Tomas de 94, 95
Torres, Antonio 125, 126, 129, 130, 132,
    190
Torres, Luis de 100, 106, 107
Toscanelli, Paolo 75, 77, 78, 79
Triano, Rodrigo de 102, 103, 115
Trinidad 167, 177
Tristán, Diego 193
Tristão, Nuno 52, 53, 54, 56, 57, 65

Valderrama, Pedro 264
Velázquez, Diego 222
Venezuela 177, 178, 223
Venice 11, 12, 19, 22, 23, 24, 30, 32, 48,
    58, 71, 156
Veragua 226
Vespucci, Amerigo: credited as the dis-
    coverer of a New World 199, 201,
    202, 220; early years 174, 175; first
    voyage 176, 177, 178, 179, 227; pilot
    major of Spain 182, 183, 198; second
    voyage 180, 181, 249, 250
Vikings 7, 162
Vinland 75, 158, 162

Waldseemüller, Martin 15, 201, 202

Xeres, Rodrigo de 106, 107

Zarco, João 38, 56